The Years of the Life of Samuel Lane, 1718–1806

1754.

A Moderate Winter, Remarkable for an Uncommon cold Day, cuming up Suddenly the 22 of Jan. in which many People out a fishing, & otherwise expos'd perished. — a fruitful Summer. — pretty Sickly.

38. Deaths in Town.

1755.

A Moderate Winter (which is ye 3rd Successively) a Midling Crop of Hay — a light crop of Corn, being green. A troublesome year on account of the War: and Remarkable for Earthquakes in Divers parts of the World. — pretty healthy

15. Deaths in Town.

1756.

a fourth Open Winter Successively; many people Plow'd and fenc'd in the Month of February: and as good Carting as in Summer. — we have a fruitful Summer; and Unfortunate in the War. — Healthy time.

14. Persons Died in Town.

1757.

a hard Winter, much Snow; great Scarcity of Hay. verry Sharp Drought in Summer, which cut Short the fruits of the Earth. — a terrible Sickly time of fevers in this Town, & other places. — Unfortunate in War.

36. Persons Died in Town, & 4 of its Inhabitants Died in the War. This year

1758.

a verry hard Winter, Deep Snows, and the Most difficult passing we have had for 10 years. the latter end of March the Snow being 3 or 4 feet Deep, was hard like Ice; and people Sleded upon it, over fences &c. Hay Scarce. Wet Summer; much grass; but Corn being green, Stank in our Chambers. — a bad hooping Cough among Children. Successful in War this year. — Corn Sold 4 £ a Bushel

30 persons Died in Town.

The Years of the Life of Samuel Lane, 1718–1806

A New Hampshire Man and His World

Jerald E. Brown

Edited and Introduced by
Donna-Belle Garvin

University Press of New England | *Hanover and London*

University Press of New England, Hanover, NH 03755

Printed in the United States of America

5 4 3 2 1

All photography of New Hampshire Historical Society objects is by Bill Finney.

Frontispiece: Five years of notable events, captured succinctly in Samuel Lane's journal. Lane Family Papers, New Hampshire Historical Society.

Decorative borders: The printers' ornaments appearing throughout the book are reproduced from volumes that Samuel Lane owned and that are now in the New Hampshire Historical Society library.

Cover illustrations: FRONT, quilt (detail), made prior to 1840 from printed fabric originally used in a dress worn in the 1790s by Samuel Lane's second wife, Rachel Colcord, or his daughter-in-law Eunice Colcord Lane. New Hampshire Historical Society, gift of Priscilla Lane Moore Tapley. BACK, surveying compass and drafting instruments used by Samuel Lane in 1752 to lay out lots and draw the plan for the new settlement of Holderness. New Hampshire Historical Society.

Library of Congress Cataloging-in-Publication Data
Brown, Jerald E., 1953–
The years of the life of Samuel Lane, 1718–1806 : a New Hampshire man and his world / Jerald E. Brown ; edited and introduced by Donna-Belle Garvin.
p. cm.
Includes bibliographical references (p.) and index.
ISBN 1–58465–051–6 (cl : alk. paper) — ISBN 1–58465–052–4 (pbk. : alk. paper)
1. Lane, Samuel, 1718–1806. 2. Stratham (N.H.)—Biography. 3. Stratham (N.H.)—Social life and customs—18th century. 4. Country life—New Hampshire—Stratham—History—18th century. 5. Shoemakers—New Hampshire—Stratham—Biography. 6. Tanners—New Hampshire—Stratham—Biography. 7. New Hampshire—Social life and customs—18th century. I. Garvin, Donna-Belle. II. Title.
F37 .L363 2000
974.2'6—dc21 99–089809

Contents

Foreword

In the Lane house, barn, and outbuildings in Stratham, New Hampshire, my family was surrounded by belongings of earlier generations: books, furniture, clothes, shoemaking tools among them. Most prized were the Lane family papers. In the fireproof safe lay documents, folded neatly in sixths; annual journal almanacks (or diaries), tied in bundles by decades; record books; receipts. A morocco-bound book contained two digests that our ancestor Samuel Lane made from his almanacks late in life.

The Years of the Life of Samuel Lane is based on the Lane family papers. Some were given to the New Hampshire Historical Society in 1914; the rest were held by the family until recently. Most of the eighteenth-century papers were written by Samuel Lane (1718–1806). Samuel was the first Lane to live in Stratham, New Hampshire. During the Second World War, when my mother, my brother, and I lived on the property that Samuel purchased in 1741, we were the last. My mother sold the property in 1955. She gave the papers to me, and I took them to my house in Maryland.

Family members had received copies of *A Journal for the Years 1739–1803 by Samuel Lane of Stratham, New Hampshire,* after it was published by the New Hampshire Historical Society in Concord in 1937. Editor Charles Lane Hanson had transcribed the two digests and, drawing on additional papers, added a preface and a twenty-two-page essay on Samuel Lane. Unfortunately, he did not always note his sources.

Over the years, I saw this volume cited in books on the eighteenth century. I also received letters from researchers, forwarded from the Stratham Library, asking whether Samuel Lane had an entry about a certain local craftsman or had mentioned making a globe. Once, searching for an answer, I turned up a daybook recording Samuel Lane's shoemaking activities. The left-hand page listed both shoes made and mending done for customers; the right-hand page noted how the debt was paid. Usually, it was by barter—a length of cloth, a load of bark, a half day of plowing. Combined with the original almanack entries, there was a wealth of unpublished eighteenth-century information.

I checked with the staff of the New Hampshire Historical Society. They had the rest of Samuel Lane's daybooks and were interested in seeing my collection. As *A Journal for the Years 1737–1803* was out of print, I wondered whether they would consider publishing a revised edition.

On my next trip to Stratham, I drove over to Concord, and the society's staff and I had a mutual show-and-tell session. They had Lane account books, surveying maps, dowry lists; I had almanacks, wills, house contracts. The combination was a treasure trove. All of us agreed that the Lane papers should be made better known, but the society had no funding or staff available to produce another Samuel Lane book. I decided then to persevere and give whatever help I could.

My eighteenth-century papers were put on loan to the society, to be donated outright when the book was well in hand. A Lane Papers Project fund attracted matching corporate gifts. My uncle, John W. Lane, donated a computer and printer for the project and also made a gift of Samuel Lane's compass, tripod, and measuring chain. Jerald Brown, a doctoral candidate in the History Department of the University of New Hampshire, computerized the original almanacks and did additional research. An editorial committee of well-known New Hampshire historians offered guidance.

One of the hurdles was presenting sixty-five years of journal entries without risking tedium. Jerald Brown, who chose Samuel Lane's world as the subject of his doctoral dissertation, found a solution to this problem. He divided Lane's life into decades, each dominated by his main occupation at the time, and wrote scholarly, annotated essays to describe each aspect of Lane's life's work.

Donna-Belle Garvin, director of research and publications at the New Hampshire Historical Society, has edited Jerald Brown's dissertation to produce the text of this book. Society curator Hilary Anderson helped with illustration research.

I would like to give my most grateful thanks to everyone who participated in the Lane Papers Project, especially to John Frisbee, director of the New Hampshire Historical Society, who kept the Samuel Lane book on track, even while carrying out major building, renovation, and conservation projects.

The reader would understand that best by making a journey to Concord and visiting the society's splendid Museum of New Hampshire History in Eagle Square and its excellent library at 30 Park Street. All collections have been cataloged and conserved to the highest standard. The reunited Lane family papers, spanning three centuries, are now there, along with books, silhouettes, drafting instruments, the globe, and other artifacts. In the words of Samuel Lane, "things look verry forward."

Bethesda, Maryland Priscilla Lane Moore Tapley

Author's Acknowledgments

At the University of New Hampshire, Charles Clark's graduate seminars and his wise counsel concerning research and writing inspired in me a passion for New England history. Steve Cox, former assistant director of programs and publications at the New Hampshire Historical Society, oversaw the early phases of the Lane Papers Project, sharing his knowledge of New Hampshire history and his sense of humor. New Hampshire State Archivist Frank Mevers allowed me free access to the archives and was generous with his time, advice, and friendship. Above all, the hand of Laurel Thatcher Ulrich, a superb teacher, imaginative scholar, and understanding mentor, helped guide my work to its fruition.

I would be terribly remiss not to mention three others who supported me throughout this extended project. Priscilla Tapley, animated by a love of history and a sense of her family's past, had the vision and perseverance that made this book possible. D-B Garvin, enthusiastic even after working nights and weekends, whittled a lengthy dissertation into a readable work. The contributions of all were legion, but any mistakes are my responsibility alone. Finally, I thank Sheila Jackson Brown, whose support, patience, and love have made all the difference.

Upperco, Maryland J.E.B.

Editor's Acknowledgments

Only through the cumulative efforts of generations of Lane descendants has the publication of a book about Samuel Lane—his life, world, and work—proven to be possible today. Together, the Lanes have treasured and preserved—and, more recently, have shared with others—the documents and artifacts that they inherited from their ancestor Samuel Lane. Through their public spirit, generosity, and patience, members of the Lane family today carry on the legacy of their eighteenth-century forebear.

Priscilla Lane Moore Tapley, a professional librarian herself, recognized the importance of keeping the family collection together and of making it available for future research. She not only donated a major collection of Lane manuscript material to the New Hampshire Historical Society but also encouraged and supported its study and publication.

Priscilla Tapley's generous funding for this project was matched by the Norfolk Southern Foundation and supplemented by the Atlas Electric Devices Company of Chicago (of which John W. Lane was chairman of the board). This support enabled the New Hampshire Historical Society to employ the author of this book, Jerald E. Brown, to undertake the project of studying, transcribing, and annotating the almanacks (or diaries) kept by Samuel Lane for more than sixty years.

The Years of the Life of Samuel Lane is a condensed and illustrated version of Jerald Brown's 1994 doctoral dissertation, "'Settling in the World': Family Economy in Colonial New Hampshire through Samuel Lane's Diaries." Among those involved in advising Jerry Brown in his study of the Lane Family Papers, and later in writing his dissertation, were Laurel Thatcher Ulrich (his dissertation adviser), Charles E. Clark, J. William Harris, and W. Jeffrey Bolster, all of the University of New Hampshire; William L. Taylor of Plymouth State College; Frank C. Mevers of the New Hampshire Division of Records Management and Archives; and Donna-Belle Garvin, the editor of this volume.

The Years of the Life of Samuel Lane not only reveals the many facets of Samuel Lane's life and work but also explores his world through pictures, artifacts, and documents. Such a richly illustrated volume is necessarily the product of many groups and individuals. Above all, we are indebted to the University Press of New England for helping to turn the staff's vision for this book into reality. Society curator Hilary Anderson assisted with the illustrations, tracking down elusive images, ordering and coordinating photography, and reviewing captions. Special Collections staff members Sherry Wilding-White and Candace McKinniss willingly scanned countless documents, while Bill Finney photographed all the New Hampshire Historical Society objects pictured in this book. Milli S. Kenney, Ellen Kwan Lewis, and Amy McGonagle helped with editing and proofreading.

Colleagues at institutions around the country assisted with illustration and other research. They are too numerous to mention by name, but we would like to extend our thanks to everyone who helped in any capacity. Most especially, we are grateful to the staff at the New Hampshire Division of Records Managements and Archives. In addition to providing more illustrations than any other outside repository, the State Archives made available its facilities and expertise so that the Society could microfilm the Lane diaries.

All manuscript materials that are illustrated but not otherwise credited are from the Lane Family Papers. Thanks to the generosity of members of the family, these papers are now housed together permanently at the New Hampshire Historical Society.

D-B.G.

Introduction

A New Hampshire Man and His Place in the World

DONNA-BELLE GARVIN

Public Thanks giving Day Morning Nov. 21. 1793. as I was Musing on my Bed being awake as Usual befor Day-light; recollecting the Many Mercies and good things I enjoy for which I ought to be thankfull this Day; Some of which I have Noted after rising as follows. viz.
The Life & health of my Self & family, and also of so many of my Children, grand Children, & great grandchildren; also of my other Relations and friends & Neighbors, for Health peace & plenty amongst us.
for my Bible, and Many other good and Useful Books, Civil & Religious Priviledges, for the ordinances of the gospel; and for my Minister.
for my Land, House and Barn and other Buildings, & that they are preserv'd from fire & other accidents.
for my wearing Cloathes to keep me warm, my Beds & Beding to rest upon
for my Cattle, Sheep & Swine & other Creatures, for my Support.
for my Corn, Wheat, Rye, Grass and Hay; Wool, flax, Syder, Apples, Pumpkins, Potatoes, Cabages, tirnips, Carrots, Beets, peaches and other fruits.
for my Clock & Watch to measure my passing time by Day and by Night
Wood, Water, Butter, Cheese, Milk, Pork, Beefe & fish, &c
for Tea, Sugar, Rum, Wine, Gin, Molasses, peper, Spice & Money for to bye other Necessaries and to pay my Debts & Taxes &c
for my Lether, Lamp oyl & Candles, Husbandry Utensils, & other tools of every Sort.
&c &c &c
Bless the Lord O my Soul and all that is within me, Bless his holy Name. Bless the Lord O my Soul, and forget not all his benefits, who Satisfieth thy mouth with good things &c. psal. 103. 1,2,5.

Samuel Lane[1]

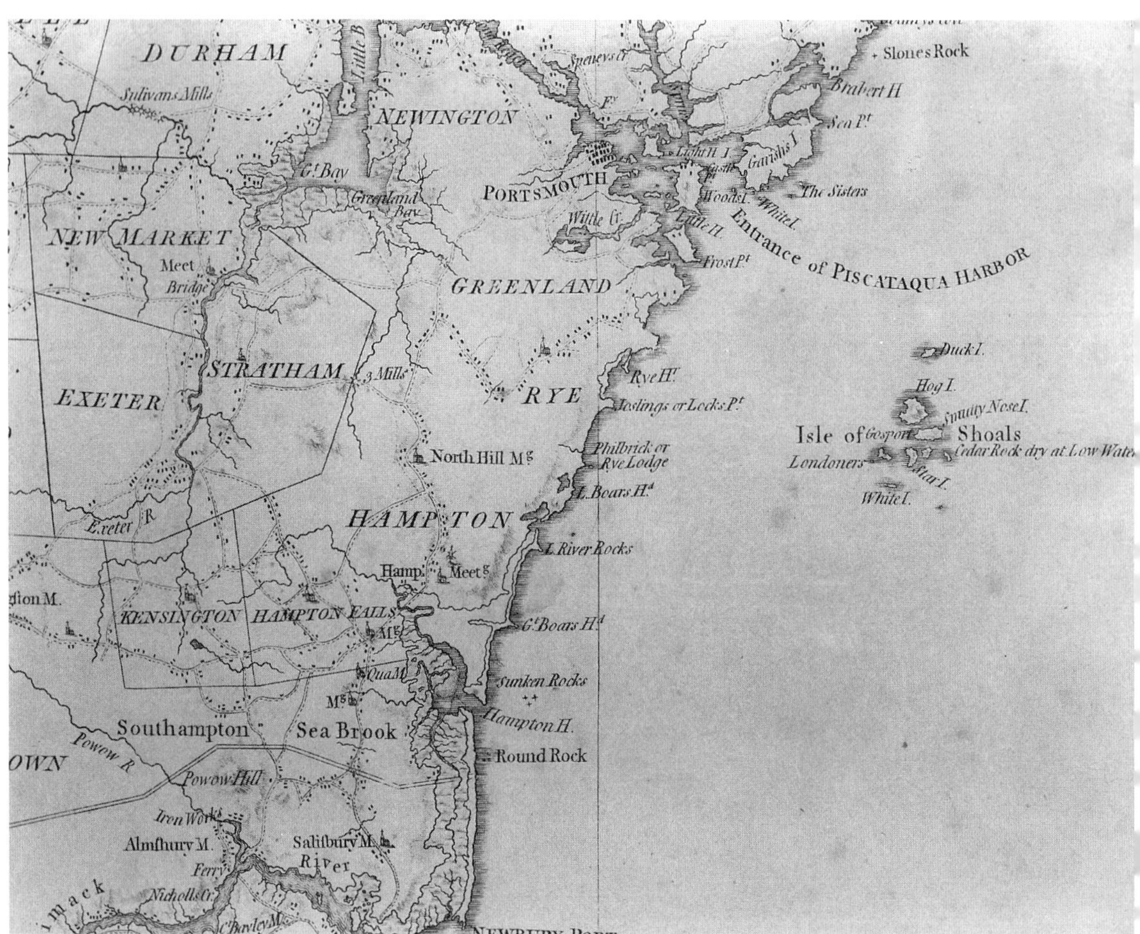

Coastal New Hampshire, a detail from Samuel Holland, *A Topographical Map of the State of New Hampshire*, 1784. *New Hampshire Historical Society.*

Born and raised in Hampton, Samuel Lane moved at the age of twenty-two to nearby Stratham. Except for an occasional trip to Boston or to the Isles of Shoals, he generally conducted business within a region reaching from Portsmouth and Great Bay at the north to the Merrimack River (beyond the Massachusetts border) to the south.

On Thanksgiving morning in 1793, seventy-five-year-old Samuel Lane of Stratham, New Hampshire, expressed thanks for seemingly simple things in life: his family, his farm, his tools, his faith, his livelihood, his production, his sustenance, his health, his existence. The apparent simplicity of Samuel's list belied the social and economic complexity of the Lane family's eighteenth-century world.

Much of what Samuel Lane was grateful for that day, from his leather and land to his livestock and crops, resulted from his own steady labor and that of his family. A tanner and shoemaker by trade, Lane produced leather, a versatile and essential material at that time, from raw animal hides. Trained also as a surveyor, he plotted a good portion of New Hampshire's developing landscape. As a farmer, he depended heavily on his "creatures," not only as food for his family and animal power for his work but also as a marketable commodity. Nor were Samuel's crops of grains, fruits, and vegetables something he could take for granted, given the changeable climate of New England.

Samuel's trading activities, centered in the nearby city of Portsmouth, brought exotic spices and beverages from around the world to his family's table, as well as sophisticated textiles to adorn their persons and homes. All members of the Lane household, male and female, played critical roles in obtaining the various natural and man-made commodities for which Samuel thanked his creator.

Samuel Lane as an Individual

Stratham's Samuel Lane was remarkably successful at achieving a comfortable and secure life for himself and his family. Samuel, moreover, recorded and attempted to quantify every aspect of his own unique experience. With the exception of one month when ill, he kept a daily diary for more than sixty years. He concluded each diary, which he called his "almanack," with an annual summary and later selectively abstracted information from his diaries to present in a variety of ways. Whether he did this mostly for himself, for his descendants, or for the sake of history is impossible to say.

The Lane diaries, together with approximately fifty years of daybooks (Samuel's daily financial records), survive and form part of the New Hampshire Historical Society library collection.[2] Samuel Lane's daily life, in all its intricacy, is better documented than that of any other individual living in colonial New Hampshire, with the possible exception of either Bedford's Matthew Patten or Keene's Abner Sanger.[3] In addition, the Lane records offer glimpses into the lives of Samuel's immediate and extended family and his large network of acquaintances.

For the most part, Samuel Lane's life and work were inseparable. According to Stratham's Reverend James Miltimore in an 1807 tribute to the recently deceased elder of his church, Samuel was "usefully economical in the distribution of his time. . . . He caught and arrested the flying hours, and marked them down for useful purposes."[4] However, the minister continued, Samuel "did not permit himself to be incessantly occupied, in manual labor." Instead, as Samuel's eulogizer further explained, "while his public and private occupations seemed sufficient to engross his whole time, such was his uncommon diligence & judicious management of every passing moment, that he not only did his proper work & business in season, but found opportunities to devote a considerable portion of time to useful reading."[5]

Gravestone for Deacon William Lane, Hampton, 1802, by Jeremiah Lane. *Courtesy Glenn A. Knoblock.*

Deacon William Lane was one of four younger brothers who followed Samuel Lane into the shoemaking trade. Another brother, Jeremiah, a tailor by training, carved gravestones as a sideline for residents of his own and surrounding communities.

Painted cupboard, attributed to joiner Samuel Lane of Hampton Falls, early 1700s. *Courtesy Yale University Art Gallery, The Mabel Brady Garvan Collection.*

Chests and cupboards by joiner Samuel Lane of Hampton Falls, the shoemaker's uncle, survive in museum collections today. The shoes and boots for which the Lane family became noted, however, do not survive. They wore out with use.

His Family and Household

Born in Hampton, New Hampshire, in 1718, the eldest son of Joshua and Bathsheba Lane, Samuel was part of a large family of craftsmen-farmers. His grandfather, tailor William Lane, moved from Boston to Hampton in the 1680s. Samuel apprenticed with his shoemaker father but taught himself to tan, probably by observing tanners who produced leather for his father. One of Samuel's uncles was a house carpenter and joiner (a finish woodworker). Five of Samuel's brothers also became cordwainers (as shoemakers were then usually called); one became a joiner like their uncle, and another followed their grandfather's profession of tailoring. According to a mid-nineteenth-century family reminiscence, six of the seven brothers "had their Shops adjoining to their Houses. . . . They all had Farms which they carried on in connection with Trades. . . . There were none of them Poor, nor were any of them very Rich."[6] Samuel trained all three of his own sons as shoemakers and tanners; at least one son-in-law apprenticed with him as well.

The family gained a regional reputation for the quality of its leather products. Early shoemakers usually did not mark their work, however, and only a single shoe attributed to a Lane cordwainer is known to survive today.[7] Yet the family name has become associated with other outstanding examples of material culture from the Hampton vicinity. Samuel's brother Jeremiah, the tailor, has recently been identified as the carver of a group of distinctive gravestones found in Hampton Falls, his place of residence, as well as in surrounding towns.[8] And a local variety of painted case furniture has long been linked with Samuel's joiner uncle, another Samuel Lane of Hampton Falls.[9]

Until Samuel the shoemaker moved inland to Stratham in 1741, the Lane family remained in the established coastal community of Hampton. As early as the mid-seventeenth century, according to a contemporary account, the region's "great store of salt marsh did intice . . . people to set downe their habitation there."[10] A visitor to the area in 1660 found Hampton residents "living weell by Corne and Cattle, of which they have great store."[11] By the early 1700s, a "great town" stretched at this location along the main north-south route linking Boston with Maine.[12] Those traveling this highway noted the "fine open country" and extensive meadows, and passersby remarked upon the "abundance of Stacks of salt hay cut."[13] As there was comparatively little upland for pasturing, however, many of the residents were employed in fishing and shipbuilding in addition to farming.[14]

In 1740, Samuel completed his apprenticeship with his father. Soon Samuel became engaged to Mary James, a Hampton girl, and

Haystacks on Hampton Falls and Seabrook Marsh, late 1800s. *New Hampshire Historical Society.*

Hampton and other towns along New Hampshire's short coastline were blessed with extensive tidal marshes, from which farmers harvested salt hay for their livestock. Though Stratham was inland, Samuel Lane owned some marshland on the Squamscott River.

he sought a farm to settle on. Land in Hampton being scarce, the newlyweds moved inland to nearby Stratham. As Samuel prepared to move to Stratham, his parents welcomed their sixteenth child; all but two of them survived childhood.

Both at home in Hampton and in Stratham, Samuel's daily life primarily focused around his family and household. At that time families were generally large. More men than women had come to the New England colonies in the seventeenth century. This unequal distribution of the sexes, together with the ready availability of land, encouraged colonists to marry earlier and have larger families than was then customary in Europe.[15]

Most colonial households spanned several generations and often included members who were not close relatives. In addition to indentured servants and apprentices, the frequent exchange of labor meant that outsiders sometimes lived, worked, and socialized with a farm family for weeks at a time. Families with many children often sent their older sons and daughters to learn new skills while helping neighbors and distant relatives. Schoolteachers and wards of the town often lived with local families.

African American slaves were not as common in rural towns like Hampton and Stratham as in those nearer Portsmouth; each of these smaller communities reported three or four slaves at the time of the 1773 census.[16] Not until the following year was there any evidence of a slave within the Lane household. In 1774, Dinah came to live with the Lanes when her mistress married Samuel. In New England, most slaves lived with their owners, often in the attic of the house.[17]

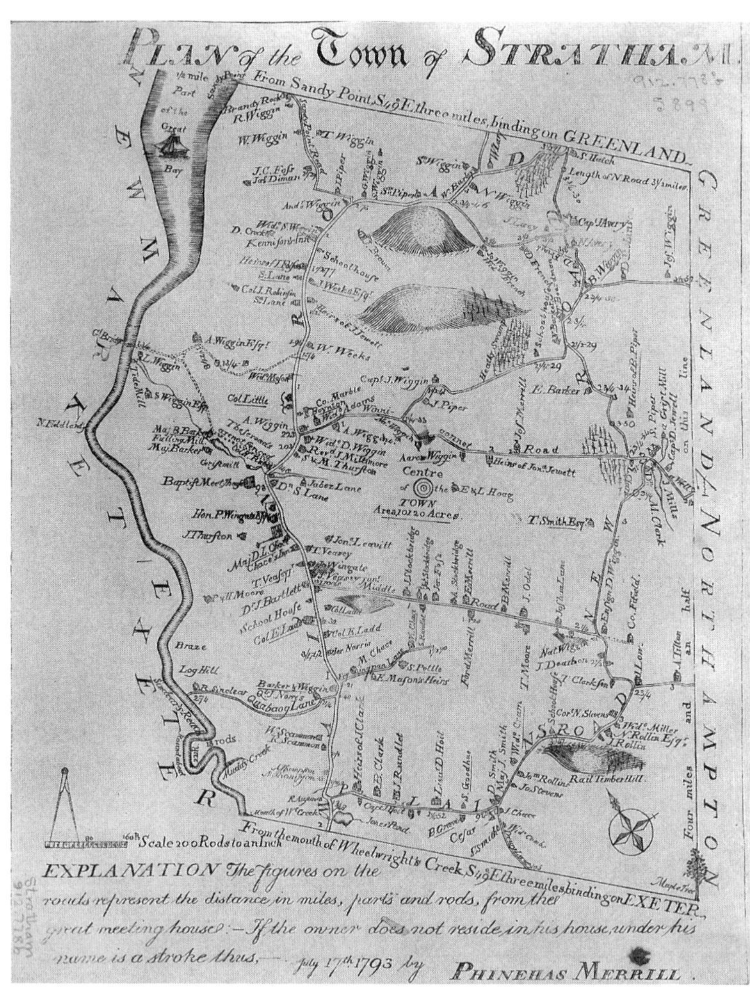

Plan of the Town of Stratham, by Phinehas Merrill, 1793. *New Hampshire Historical Society.*

During the eighteenth century, Stratham developed into a well-populated agricultural community. Samuel Lane's chosen town was situated inland. The Squamscott (or Salt) River, which formed its western boundary with Exeter and Newmarket, however, connected all three towns—via Great Bay and the Piscataqua River—with the world of trade beyond.

His Neighborhood and Town

Samuel and Mary moved to Stratham in 1741. The property on which they constructed their house and tanyard adjoined a mill-pond on Sawmill Brook, where the Wiggin family operated grist- and sawmills. Essentially a frontier settlement at this time, Stratham nearly doubled in population between 1732 and 1775. As the community developed, it provided more and more of the basic services and amenities the Lanes needed. By the 1750s a fulling mill, where homespun cloth could be dyed and pressed, operated just downstream, and before long, a malt mill was added to the town's early industries.[18] The Lanes employed a number of Stratham weavers, tailors, joiners, and blacksmiths to undertake specific projects for them, from erecting the structures they needed on their farm and in their tannery to helping produce the marriage gifts they planned to give their daughters.

Samuel and Mary lived on the main road, just north of where both the meetinghouse and the neighborhood tavern stood, at the community's social, though not its geographical, center. Although most eighteenth-century meetinghouses lacked spires and bells, Stratham and many neighboring towns boasted both from early in the century. According to one area traveler during the 1740s, "In this part of the country one would think there were a great many towns by the number of steeples you see round you, every country meeting having one, which by reason of their slenderness and tapering form appear at a distance pretty high."[19]

The meetinghouse, serving both secular and religious functions, provided a true community center. But townsmen often met in the local tavern to conduct official business because the meetinghouse was unheated and drafty. A tavern near the meetinghouse was, in fact, considered a necessity. In the neighboring town of Greenland in 1734, residents petitioned for Enoch Clark to be granted a license to run a tavern near the meetinghouse, "the want of which we find hurtful on many accounts."[20] In Stratham, Chase's tavern, for decades run consecutively by Thomas, Love, and Dudley Chase, stood next to the meetinghouse.

In Samuel's day, hardly any adult male resident in a small town like Stratham escaped serving as a town official. To keep proper order in its jurisdiction, a town needed not only selectmen, a town clerk, a constable, overseers of the poor, highway surveyors, and assessors but also fence viewers, hogreeves, a pound keeper, corders of

SETTLING the AFFAIRS of the NATION.

Settling the Affairs of the Nation, line etching, London, 1784–1800. *Courtesy, Winterthur Museum.*

In towns like Stratham the local tavern provided a center for business and community affairs. Samuel Lane spent considerable time in the stimulating atmosphere of Chase's nearby tavern. While there for a committee meeting or a deed signing, he would also share a pipe of tobacco or a mug of flip with his neighbors.

"View of the Bridge over the Piscataqua," ink sketch by Robert Gilmor, 1797. *By courtesy of the Trustees of the Boston Public Library.*

Until the bridge known as the Great Arch of the Piscataqua first spanned the northern neck of Great Bay in 1794, most east-west traffic on the way to and from Portsmouth passed to the south of the large tidal estuary through the town of Stratham.

wood, sealers of leather, surveyors of lumber, and a tithingman (to enforce the laws against travel or disturbances on the Sabbath or in the tavern). Samuel assumed more than his share of town responsibilities, filling many of these offices at one time or another. He also served as clerk of the church's building committee, as a deacon, and later, as an elder.

Trained as a land surveyor as well as a leatherworker, Samuel used his drawing, figuring, and writing skills to help his Stratham neighbors in less official ways. Altogether, he logged considerable time at Chase's neighborhood tavern, meeting with committees to conduct town business and with individuals to write their deeds, plot their land, or tend to their probate needs.

Another local landmark not far from the meetinghouse and tavern was the ferry across the Squamscott River, which formed the town's western boundary with Newmarket and Exeter.[21] Until a bridge was finally built in the early 1770s, reliance on a ferry hampered westward travel beyond Stratham. A ferryboat—one that, however, could not carry "Carts and Teams" and could not cross "at Certain Seasons of the year"—was run by Samuel's neighbors, the Wiggins, who, along with the Leavitts, were among the wealthier families in the vicinity.[22]

The village of Stratham developed along a road early known as "the King's Great Highway" and later as the "Country Road."[23] Though narrow by today's standards and undoubtedly impassable during certain seasons of the year, this "highway" was the primary land route between the port of Piscataqua and interior towns from Exeter to Concord.[24] A large tidal estuary to the north of town, known as Great Bay, long served as a barrier to overland transport by other routes, even while it facilitated inland water transport to towns around its shore, as well as along rivers emptying into it.

Because the road through Stratham was so well traveled, a remarkable number of early visitors to the area recorded their impressions of the surrounding countryside. After rating the condition of the road itself as "fine" to "excellent," they collectively described it as passing through a "well-tilled region" set among a "beautiful interchange of small hills and valleys," and "extreamly well Inhabited all the way."[25] As early as 1750, the land was "generally Cleared" and open, as it must have remained in 1800, when a visitor from Massachusetts noted that "the spire & lands of Newmarket enriched the view."[26] The road continued through the adjoining town of Greenland before reaching the seacoast at Portsmouth. In describing the comparable landscape there, travelers noted the presence of numerous cattle "dispersed over fine meadows" and farmers "in easy not affluent circumstances."[27]

The Squamscott, known locally as the Salt River because of its tidal nature, was navigable upstream from Great Bay to the falls at Exeter. Considerable river traffic passed Stratham's ferry to and from the flourishing lumbering and early industrial center at Exeter. Yet it was said of Stratham in 1817, in what was probably somewhat of an exaggeration, that "farming is so exclusively the employment of the town, that, although a navigable river adjoins it, there is not a wharf, vessel or boat belonging to the place."[28] In 1773, a "Great Bridge" replaced the Stratham ferry, despite Exeter's persistent objection that the span would disrupt river traffic. Twenty-seven years had passed since the first petition by local and inland inhabitants seeking such a bridge to facilitate east-west transport.[29]

The Managers of New-market
and Stratham LOTTERY, No. 4, hereby inform the Public, That the Drawing of ſaid Lottery will *certainly* commence on the ſecond Tueſday in March next, at the Houſe uſed for that Purpoſe, near the Spot where the Bridge is building; at which Time thoſe who incline may attend. *Feb.* 7. 1771.

Tickets in the above Lottery,
may be had of the Managers and Printers, if ſpeadly applied for.

Notice of Newmarket and Stratham Bridge Lottery, *New Hampshire Gazette*, February 15, 1771. *New Hampshire Historical Society.*

The opening of a bridge across the Squamscott in 1773 was, from Samuel Lane's perspective, one of the important milestones of his lifetime. Twenty-seven years after a group of area residents had first petitioned the government for such a bridge, a lottery helped raise funds to build it.

By the time of the American Revolution, Stratham boasted many of the features that, a few decades later, Reverend Jeremy Belknap, New Hampshire's first historian, would describe as comprising an ideal community:

"A View of Portsmouth in Piscataqua River," mid-1770s, aquatint, from the *Atlantic Neptune*, 1781 edition. *New Hampshire Historical Society.*

"This town enjoys a fine Air by Standing upon arising ground and command[s] a fine prospect from the Center every way and is Certainly the most agreeably Scituated for Pleasure or Bussiness of most places I have Seen." *Some Cursory Remarks Made by James Birket in His Voyage to North America, 1750–1751.*

Were I to form a picture of happy society, it would be a town consisting of a due mixture of hills, valleys and streams of water: The land well fenced and cultivated; the roads and bridges in good repair; a decent inn for the refreshment of travellers, and for public entertainments: The inhabitants mostly husbandmen; their wives and daughters domestic manufacturers; a suitable proportion of handicraft workmen, and two or three traders; a physician and lawyer, each of whom should have a farm for his support. A clergyman of any denomination, which should be agreeable to the majority, a man of good understanding, of a candid disposition and exemplary morals; not a metaphysical, nor a polemic, but a serious and practical preacher. A school master who should understand his business and teach his pupils to govern themselves.[30]

His Business Community

Even the ideal community at this time, however, made no claim to self-sufficiency. In fact, all the rural towns of the region looked to Portsmouth as a center for trade and commerce. Country people for miles around referred to the seaport as "the Bank," a familiar term deriving from the settlement's early name, "Strawbery Banke."[31] After settling in Stratham and establishing a business of his own, Samuel Lane made increasingly frequent trips to "the Bank" to exchange shoes and agricultural products for crafts and imported goods available only in the larger town.

Merchant, engraving from *The Book of Trades, or Library of the Useful Arts*, White-Hall, Pennsylvania, 1807. *Courtesy, The Winterthur Library: Printed Book and Periodical Collection.*

Samuel Lane was well acquainted with many of the Portsmouth merchants who imported goods from around the world and exported surplus from New Hampshire's forests, fisheries, and farms. Wood and wood products in particular became a specialty of Piscataqua, as the port was commonly known.

Portsmouth benefited greatly from a natural harbor. The port's location a little upstream from the outlet of the Piscataqua River made it readily defensible and, as George Washington noticed in 1789, the depth of water near shore allowed ships to "lay close to the Docks . . . when at the Town."[32] Because of the rapidity of the Piscataqua's current, the harbor almost never froze. Perhaps most important, Great Bay's network of inland rivers gave access to extensive white pine forests. Lumber and wood products of all sorts were important trade commodities, and the port became noted particularly for its pine mast timbers.[33]

"In the five years between 1770 and 1775, over a thousand vessels left Piscataqua for the West Indies, southern Europe, and Africa. These ships carried nearly seventy-four million board feet of sawn pine planks and boards, plus almost forty-two million handsplit shingles and some 98,000 clapboards."[34] Portsmouth merchants provided wood and wood products to the fishing communities of Newfoundland and Nova Scotia as well. Vessels departing for all points of the compass carried large numbers of barrel hoops and staves, cart wheels and axletrees, boats and oars, oxbows and yokes, house frames and window shutters, tables and chairs. Portsmouth became a major shipbuilding center as well.

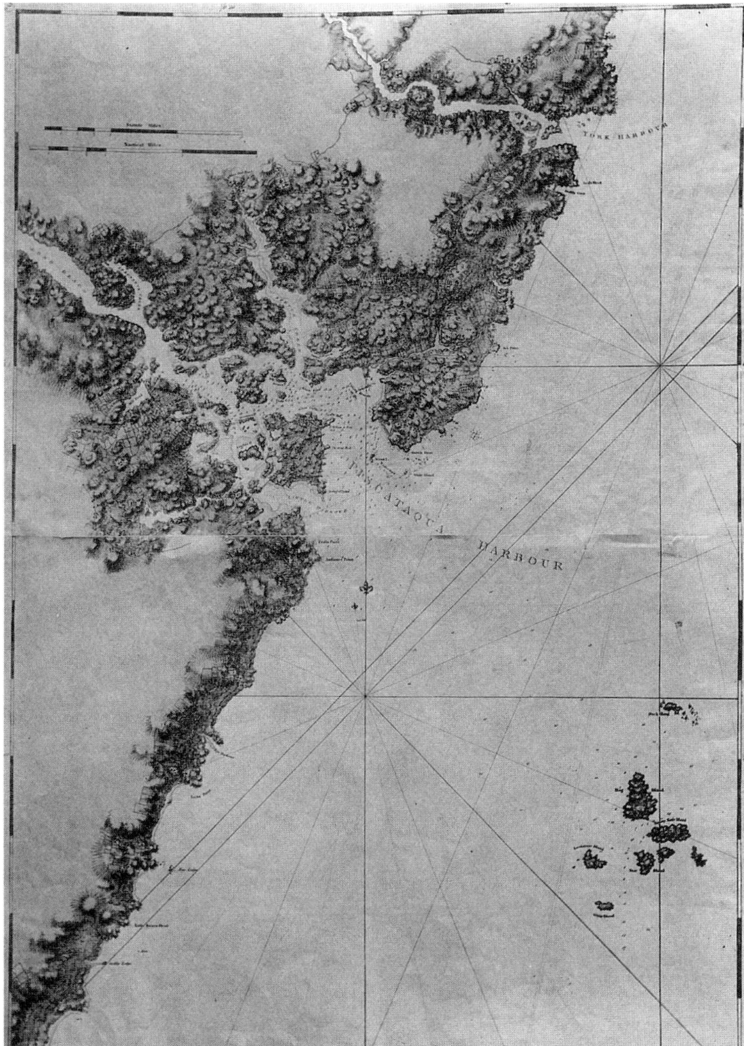

Chart of Piscataqua Harbor, from the *Atlantic Neptune*, 1779. *New Hampshire Historical Society.*

Portsmouth was the region's gateway to the world. The island-studded mouth of the Piscataqua River provided a sheltered harbor for seagoing vessels. A network of inland waterways, which converged near this location, brought a wealth of marketable commodities to the seaport.

As time passed, the seaport's developing rural hinterland began to produce a surplus of agricultural commodities. During the early 1770s departing vessels carried overseas more than five thousand sheep, fifteen hundred oxen, and over six hundred horses (all with "provender" for the voyage), together with unknown quantities of turkeys, geese, and other poultry; large numbers of barrels and tubs of preserved beef; and over ten thousand bunches of onions. Other agricultural commodities were shipped out of the port in smaller quantities, varying according to their bounty in a given season and including potatoes, beeswax, soap, lime, butter, cheese, apples, cider, and peas.[35]

During this era an increasing flow of traffic by both land and water strengthened ties between New Hampshire's developing rural

Long Wharf and vicinity, from "A View of Portsmouth in New Hampshire Taken from the East Shore," mid-1770s, line engraving from the *Atlantic Neptune*, 1778 edition. *New Hampshire Historical Society.*

"As the town Stands partly upon a point that Jetts out into the river it makes very good Conveniencys for Building wharfs and warehouses on each side out of the Stream where Ships of any Burthen may lay & discharge their cargos into the warehouses wth out Expence or trouble." *Some Cursory Remarks Made by James Birket in His Voyage to North America, 1750–1751.*

communities and the world beyond, via the port of Piscataqua, as Portsmouth was then often known. Cargo vessels known as gundalows could be spied from Stratham's shore, plying the Squamscott River, carrying goods from Exeter to Portsmouth. On any given day, farmers driving carts loaded with produce plodded by the Lane house in Stratham on their way to market in Portsmouth. The pace of traffic resembled that of a brisk walk, rarely exceeding five miles an hour. On a regular basis, Samuel joined this parade; sometimes as often as twice a month he set out, driving oxen and carrying lamb quarters, cider, cheese, and shoes toward the Bank. Even in winter, normal amounts of snowfall did little to impede traffic along New Hampshire's roads. Sledding proved one of the most efficient ways to get goods to market. It was the deep mud, produced as the frost worked its way from the ground in the spring, that posed the greatest challenge to traffic on this "highway."[36]

Once in the crowded and busy port, Samuel and his fellow countrymen transacted business with individual merchants and craftsmen. According to an English visitor in 1750, "they have no fixt market but the Country people come to town as it suits them with such of the Commoditys as they have for Sale by which the town is pretty well Supply'd with Beefe, Muton, and other Butchers Meat; they have plenty of large Hoggs and very fat bacon."[37]

Samuel patronized a number of merchants, either at shops adjoining their warehouses on "Long Wharf" or beside the single paved street that "runs along the river bank."[38] He also visited merchants and craftsmen on King and Queen Streets in the center of town, near the Parade and the North Meeting House. As travelers frequently pointed out, the town, comprising about seven hundred dwelling houses, was built almost entirely of wood. Many of the shops Samuel visited were likely rooms within or attached to their owners' residences.

In 1773, Portsmouth boasted 4,372 inhabitants; 160 of them, or 4 percent, were slaves. Samuel made shoes not only for Portsmouth residents of European descent but also for their African servants. In return for all of these sales, he purchased imported items that he and his family needed: tea, coffee, rice, rum, chocolate, spices, nails, awl blades, needles, silk, lace, and indigo.

JUST IMPORTED from LONDON, And TO BE SOLD

By John Noble,

PERUKE MAKER,

At his SHOP near the Swing-Bridge in Portſmouth ;

An Aſſortment of HAIRS, *fit for Working*, viz.

WHITE, black, and brown Horſe Hair ; white Goat Ditto ; Mohair Crowns ; broad and narrow Wigg Ribbon Cawles ; Raw Silk, and fine purple Mountain Thread.------*N. B.* Any Gentlemen may be ſupplied by ſaid *Noble*, with Wiggs of any Faſhion, at the cheapeſt Rates, with Fidelity and Diſpatch.

Advertisement of John Noble, peruke maker, from the *New Hampshire Gazette*, June 10, 1763. *New Hampshire Historical Society.*

Shops of craftsmen and merchants lined King and Queen Streets, which ran parallel to each other near the statehouse. On April 10, 1765, Samuel Lane paid John Noble £28 to make him a wig, which may have incorporated hair imported from London.

A number of specialized craftsmen that small rural communities could not support plied their trades at the Bank. At different times, Samuel bought such items as silver spoons, shoe buckles, a seal, earrings, and sleeve buttons from David Griffeth at the "Sign of the Goldsmith's Arms" in Queen Street; beaver and felt hats from a hatter, Thomas Hatch; and a wig from John Noble, peruke maker.[39] Signs identifying craftsmen's wares lined King and Queen Streets. After 1756, merchants and craftsmen also advertised in local printer Daniel Fowle's weekly *New Hampshire Gazette*, to let "gentlemen in town or country" know that they might be supplied at a particular shop with products "cheaper than they can get in Boston."

Colonial Portsmouth was also the seat of provincial government. For almost half a century, three generations of Wentworths

Portsmouth, from James Grant, *A Plan of Piscataqua Harbor*, watercolor, 1774. *New Hampshire Historical Society.*

Still known to many in the eighteenth century by its earlier name, Strawbery Banke, Portsmouth was the region's leading marketplace and port, as well as the capital of the province. Wharves lined the riverside, and at the center of town (here marked "B"), the statehouse stood near the first (or north) meetinghouse.

appointed by the king governed New Hampshire from the seaport. Official business, along with trade, therefore, brought people from all over the province to the capital. One New Hampshire citizen complained in 1765 (only a few years before the provincial legislature first divided New Hampshire into counties) that "there is but one place in the province at which the courts of justice are held, viz. at Portsmouth, one of the extremities, for which reasons many of the inhabitants often have to travel 150 to 200 miles on very trifling occasions."[40] Until 1760, when the government built its first statehouse, with rooms for the legislature and the courts of justice, officials carried out all such functions in local taverns. Province treasury records include payments to tavern keepers for "house room, firewood, and candles."[41]

New Hampshire's first statehouse, opened 1760; conjectural drawing by William Paarlberg for Adams and Roy, Inc., Historic Structures Report, 1988. *Courtesy William Paarlberg.*

Official business as well as trade brought Samuel Lane on a regular basis to Portsmouth, or as he called it, "the Bank." After 1760, most provincial activity took place at the new statehouse, where the courts and legislature met.

Samuel had many reasons for traveling to the Bank: to trade for himself, his family, and his neighbors; to attend court, sit on juries, register deeds, and transact business with the probate judge; to hear a noted minister preach, witness a hanging, and see a ship launched. When in town on official business, sometimes he ate at a Portsmouth tavern. There were four within sight of the new statehouse: Foss's, Tilton's Marquis of Rockingham, Stoodley's "At the Sign of the King's Arms," and Packer's.

More frequently, Samuel stopped on the way home from the Bank at Enoch Clark's Greenland tavern to enjoy a flip or toddy and refresh his horse with "a treat of oats." Greenland boasted several taverns, standing as it did at a busy crossroads where the north-south route from Boston through Hampton into Maine met the great highway passing between Portsmouth and Exeter.

Samuel's earliest trading ventures, starting while he still lived in Hampton, took him nine miles off the New Hampshire coast to the desolate Isles of Shoals. At midcentury, about fifty or sixty families lived mainly by fishing on the largest of this group of islands. As described at the time—and little changed today—the islands are "an Entire bed of rocks which produces no herbage or Any kind of Corn, grain, or Timber."[42] As a result, island residents depended on trade with the mainland. Samuel, following in his father's footsteps, exchanged shoes and work boots for fish to eat, cod liver oil to work his leather, and whale oil for his lamp—a tin lamp was one of the first items he purchased when living on his own. In later years, instead of going himself to the islands, he routinely met fishermen from the Shoals at the ferry landing on the Squamscott to make similar exchanges of household products, including butter and cheese, for oil.

Samuel's father, Joshua Lane, made a trip to Boston at least once a year and sometimes twice, apparently to trade. Samuel, who seems never to have accompanied his father, started journeying there him-

Mar. 13 & 15. To 2 Days to Court (Exceeding bad passing) Self & Horse 5£ p Day — 10 – 0 – 0
~~13.~~ pd Capt. Foss for mr Bordman & my Dinners 24/ Each & 2 Drams 16/ — 5 – 12. – 0
13 & 15. pd mr Folsom for half a Mug of flip for mr Bordman & my Self 6/ Ditto 6/ — 0 – 12. – 0
Aug 6. To 1 Day to Court (Hay & Harvest time) Self & Horses Journey 5£ — 5 – 0 – 0
pd Capt Foss for Dinner 24/ & Drink 13/ — 1 – 17. – 0
7. To 1 Day to Court Self & Horse 5£ pd Foss for Dinner 24/ & Drink 6/ — 6 – 10 – 0
Sept 16. To 1 Day to Court Self & Horse 5£. pd for Dn Bordmans & my Dinners to Foss 48 — 7 – 8. – 0
17. To 1 Day to Court Self & Horse 5£. pd Stavers for our Dinners 52/ & Foss for Drink 13/ — 8 – 5 – 0
18. To 1 Day to Court Self & Horse 5£. pd Foss for our Dinners 48/ — 7 – 8. – 0
18. paid Capt Foss for 3 Double Bows Punch for ye Jury 7-16-0 — 7 – 16 – 0
pd Mr Parker a Fee 12£ pd Emery Ditto 6 pd for Punch for Emery 13/ — 18 – 13. – 0
2 – 0 – 0

Portion of bill from Samuel Lane to the town of Stratham for "Costs of the Lawsuit Commenced by Wm. Pert & Joshua Rawlings," 1765–1766. *Courtesy New Hampshire Division of Records Management and Archives.*

While at the seaport handling legal matters, Samuel Lane sometimes bought dinners and drinks for himself and others at nearby taverns, notably Zachariah Foss's State House Tavern and John Stavers's Earl of Halifax.

self a few years after settling in Stratham. At first he went every two years, then every three, then not for almost a decade. While on his first trip to Boston in 1745, he bought some books. In 1753 he arranged to purchase a new surveyor's compass from mathematical instrument maker Thomas Greenough.[43] Beginning in the 1740s, he subscribed to a Boston newspaper, which informed him of the products and services available in that metropolis.

In the meantime, Portsmouth's own offerings multiplied rapidly. Around 1756, Daniel Fowle, New Hampshire's first printer, moved from Boston to Portsmouth, where he set up a press and printed a weekly newspaper, occasionally producing books and pamphlets as

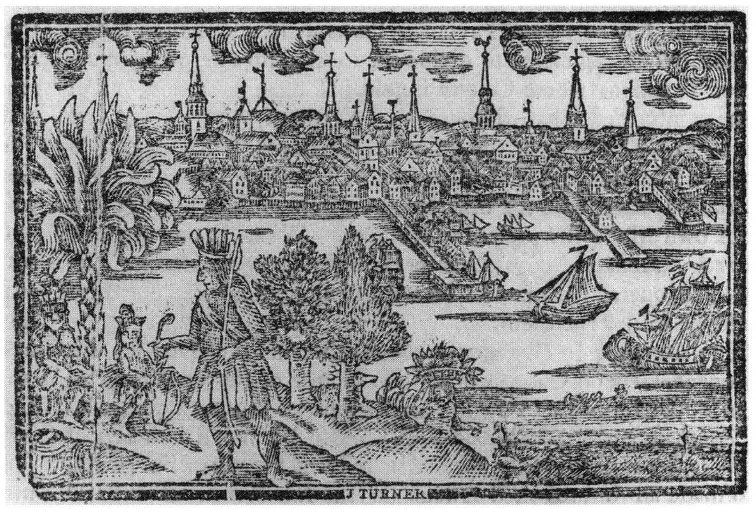

View of Boston, engraving by James Turner, first published in *The American Magazine and Historical Chronicle*, 1743. *New Hampshire Historical Society.*

Every other year, starting in 1745, Samuel Lane followed his father's practice and journeyed to Boston. As the products and trades that Portsmouth could offer him multiplied through the decades, Lane's trips to Boston became less frequent and eventually ceased.

Trade card of Andrew Barclay, Boston bookbinder and seller; engraved by Thomas Johnston, mid-1700s. *Courtesy, American Antiquarian Society.*

On his earliest visits to Boston, Samuel Lane purchased a number of books. By the 1760s, Portsmouth merchants were advertising a wide selection of titles, and Daniel Fowle and William Appleton were printing and binding books there as well.

well. By the mid-1760s at least one bookbinder and seller offered his wares "at the Sign of the Bible and the Crown" on Queen Street.[44] And if Samuel could have waited a few years for a new compass, he might have decided to buy one from William Hart, who by 1757 had established himself as Portsmouth's first mathematical instrument maker.[45]

Samuel's trading area encompassed the northernmost range of towns in Essex County, Massachusetts. He purchased his first clock from David Blasdel of Amesbury, pewter and other items for his daughters' wedding "portions" from Newbury, and cart wheels from a wheelwright in Salisbury. In fact, he transacted more business in Salisbury, Massachusetts, than anywhere other than Stratham or Portsmouth. This was primarily because he took much of the leather he tanned to Stephen Merrill, a currier there, for finishing. It is unclear whether Merrill was the region's leading currier or Samuel continued to patronize a craftsman his father employed. In 1758, at the height of Samuel's tanning business, he made nine trips to Salisbury. Salisbury was "an ancient town," at one time considered a twin to Hampton, but by the 1790s it had outdistanced its northern neighbor in "appearance of life and activity."[46]

Surprisingly, Samuel and his sons traveled more frequently to Salisbury and to Portsmouth than to Exeter, only three miles to the west. During Samuel's earliest years in business, Exeter was largely a lumbering and shipbuilding center. As one traveler observed in 1750, an "abundance of Lumber is brought down to this town by Land carriage and afterwards is rafted down the river to Portsmo[uth]."[47] By the 1770s, Exeter had grown in size and significance to become "the second town in New Hampshire" and had advanced far beyond the rough way of life associated with lumbermen.[48] By then "the gentle Folks" at Exeter had gained a reputation, for which they were known as far away as the Connecticut Valley, for "lov[ing] to live up to the tip top of the Fashion."[49]

One reason that Samuel did not do much trading in Exeter, despite its relative convenience, was an economic one. He recorded more than once in his diary such statistics as "Corn that Comes from over Seas is Sold for 40s . . . out of the Vessel at the Banke & 45s at Exeter."[50]

At the time of the Revolution, New Hampshire's government moved inland to the smaller town of Exeter for safety. An Italian traveler reported in the 1780s: "[T]he public archives were transferred there lest they should fall into the hands of the British; and the General Court of the state still meets in that place."[51] Just before the war, moreover, the legislature had divided New Hampshire into counties for the first time, and courts for Rockingham County, which included Stratham, now convened in Exeter. The sudden

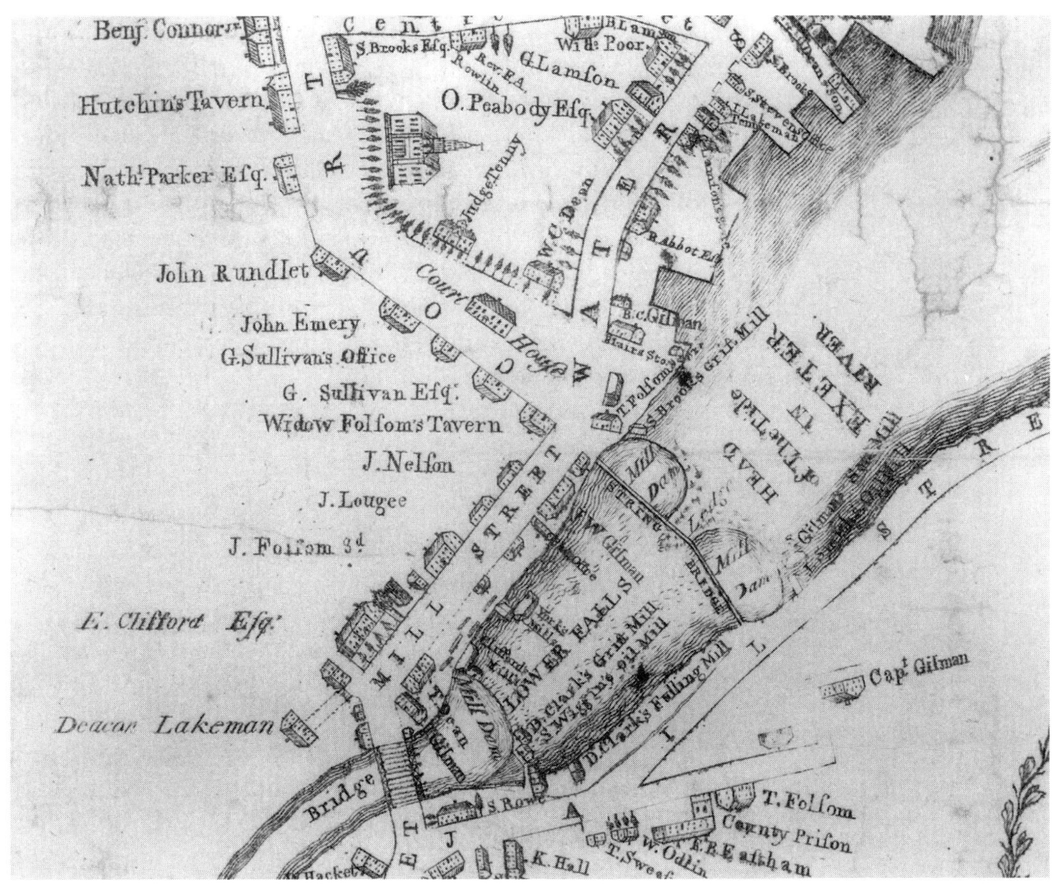

transformation in the position of these two communities fostered rivalry. George Washington noted during his tour of 1789 that "a jealousy subsists between this town [Exeter] and Portsmouth; which, had I known it in time, would have made it necessary to have accepted an invitation to a public dinner [in Exeter as in Portsmouth]."[52]

These developments prompted Samuel to frequent Exeter increasingly through the years. At first, his trips up the Squamscott related to land surveying projects, purchase of shingles and other wood products, and jobs taken to the many mills employing the extensive waterpower there. With the advent of the county system, he also attended court in Exeter, went to committee meetings, recorded deeds, and purchased books at house vendues (auctions). By the 1790s, Exeter had also become noted for the "great quantity of saddlery . . . manufactured [there], more probably than in any other town in New England."[53] Samuel sometimes sold leather and skins to saddlers in the new capital, as well as to other leather workers in the region.

Courthouse and mills from *A Plan of the Compact Part of the Town of Exeter at the Head of the Southerly Branch of Piscataqua River*, by Phinehas Merrill, 1802. *New Hampshire Historical Society.*

In 1773, Exeter became the seat of Rockingham County and, a few years later, of the new state government. Only two-fifths the size of Portsmouth at this time, Exeter was known as a lumbering center and boasted extensive waterpower. After the Revolution, Samuel Lane spent an increasing amount of time in Exeter, attending court and taking work to the mills.

The horizons of Samuel Lane's world extended beyond local trading outlets, however. Samuel and his family regularly returned to Hampton to visit and help relatives living there. Given the instability of the Stratham church during the years of religious revival known as the Great Awakening, the Lanes attended meeting at Hampton and took their children to be baptized there. Samuel's diary reveals as well a large number of visits to relatives of different generations who had moved to towns reaching from Seabrook to Sanbornton. Family visits increased noticeably each time a child was born. The numerous and caring extended family provided each other continuous loyalty and support.

His Province and State

By the late 1740s, Samuel was also undertaking an increasing amount of surveying work in outlying towns. During a burst of land speculation following the end of King George's War in 1748, a group of Exeter people employed him to venture with them into the wilderness northwest of Lake Winnipesaukee to lay out the new town of Holderness.

At the time of Samuel's birth in 1718, New Hampshire's approximately ten thousand residents clustered mostly in seven towns along the seacoast and lining Great Bay (Portsmouth, New Castle, Hampton, Kingston, Exeter, Stratham, and Dover). Between 1720 and 1780, however, colonial governors chartered more than 150 new inland townships. During the same period, residents subdivided older towns to accommodate population growth.

In this era of expansion and development, coastal speculators acquired large quantities of inland territory as an investment rather than for immediate settlement. Much of this speculation eventually was rewarded: following the end of the French and Indian Wars in 1763, settlement advanced rapidly up New Hampshire's fertile river valleys from southern New England. By 1770 the colony boasted a population of sixty thousand, twenty times that of a century earlier. According to a French traveler visiting New Hampshire in 1782, "this country has a very flourishing appearance . . . new houses are being built and new farms being settled every day."[54] Four of Samuel Lane's five daughters participated in this inland migration, settling with their husbands in either Northwood or Sanbornton.

In 1750, Samuel was appointed an assistant to the surveyor of His Majesty's lands in New Hampshire. In this role he became deeply involved with the province's physical development. Yet his focus remained local. Only during the Revolutionary crisis did he participate at the provincial or state level in politics or government.

Just prior to independence he was elected a delegate to the Provincial Congress at Exeter. He did not note any of its proceedings in his diary.

His Nation

It was in daily work and in local matters, rather than on the state or national scene, that Samuel Lane perceived his role. He read and reported with interest and concern news from around the country and the world, yet his own place was on the banks of the Squamscott River. He harbored no personal ambition to hold high office but supported his well-to-do friend and neighbor, Reverend Paine Wingate, who eventually served in the United States Congress.[55]

The sudden disruption brought about by the Revolution undoubtedly posed a serious challenge to Samuel's own sense of identity and to that of his neighbors. Expressing a sense of place and order typical both of his own personality and of his era, Samuel had, in earlier years, always followed his name and the date on the cover of each of his annual almanacks with: "Stratham in New Hampshire in New England in the sixteenth year of the reign of George the Second of Great Britain King." During the 1760s a number of schoolgirls living in Portsmouth displayed similar security as to their position in the world when they embroidered variations on the following popular verse into their needlework samplers:

Sarah Sherburne is my name
England is my nation
Portsmouth is my dwelling place
And Christ is my salvation.[56]

For any of these colonists to have his or her place within the world altered so dramatically required considerable personal adjustment. In the case of Samuel Lane, this process was reflected in a period of indecision as the Revolution loomed. He "lef of[f] drinking T-a" to protest British policy in the wake of the Stamp Act, and continuing that resistance in 1775, he served as delegate to New Hampshire's Provincial Congress. Yet his discomfort with the unknown—a potential break with England—soon became clear. In January 1776 he helped compose a petition from the inhabitants of Stratham to the Committee of Safety at Portsmouth, complaining that the committee's actions looked "too Much like an open Declaration of Independency, which we can by no means Countenance."[57]

In the end, Samuel, together with his sons, signed the Association Test, aligning themselves firmly with the rebellion.[58] Interestingly, "in the state, as a whole, nine tenths of the people gave their signa-

The Battle of Lexington, April 19, 1775, engraving by Amos Doolittle, 1775. *Courtesy, Winterthur Museum.*

The Revolutionary War that enmeshed the nation barely touched Samuel Lane's daily activity. Although he noted with concern the "most Unnatural Civil War Between great Britain and America" begun at Lexington, his life continued to follow its usual routine.

ture, but in Stratham 131 signed, 42 refusing [i.e., fewer than seven-tenths signed], thus making the Tory element stronger here than in almost any other town in New Hampshire."[59]

His Physical World

Samuel's daily physical world, unaltered by the political events of the eighteenth century, continued to pose severe challenges to him, his family, and his neighbors. During times of severe drought, famine was never far away. In 1749, Samuel reported, "Cattle are So poor that they are ready to Stagger as they walk along the road"; in 1752, that "it would make almost the hardest Heart ake to hear the Complaints of Multitudes of people ready to famish for want of food"; in 1753, "especially in the out Towns, . . . Many . . . can Scarcely rise out of [their] chairs without help they are So weak"; and in 1762, "Many people come about beging for a quart of Corn at one House, & a quart at another, & so from House to House."[60] Life in colonial New Hampshire was often difficult, and the struggle for survival was real.

The refreshing thundershowers that Samuel frequently described as bringing welcome relief from hot, dry weather brought their own dangers. Samuel's father, struck and killed by lightning on his own doorstep in 1766, was only one of many people recorded at the time as meeting this fate.[61]

New Hampshire's changeable weather could pose a variety of

problems for families like the Lanes. Sometimes terrible freshets proved destructive. At other times it was hard to get cornmeal ground because the rivers were too low for the mills to operate.[62] A Spanish tourist, visiting Portsmouth in October 1784, exclaimed: "The weather here is so variable that there have been more than thirty-one degrees of change in the thermometer in the course of twenty-four hours. It must be added that the cold is so continuous that for nine months of the year the inhabitants are forced to maintain fires constantly in their homes. With how many disadvantages these poor people struggle! And how many obstacles their indefatigable industry overcomes!"[63] Some winters, though, were surprisingly mild; one year, Samuel reported in February, "the Frogs are out verry thick."[64] Other years he described snow filling the roads "higher than the tops of the fences" and people "oblig'd to Cut down Apple trees to Burn."[65] During the winter of 1747–1748, Samuel recorded twelve feet of snow in Stratham.[66]

Disease was another challenge of Samuel's natural environment. In the 1730s several New Hampshire towns lost between one-third and one-half of their children to a virulent throat infection (probably diphtheria). In Kingston, not a single one of the first forty victims of one epidemic recovered.[67] In Stratham, six children succumbed to the so-called throat distemper in two days in 1742. Beginning when he first moved to Stratham, Samuel recorded all deaths in town in his annual almanack. During the epidemic of 1742 there were so many deaths (mostly children) that he recorded them in a separate pamphlet. Two families in Stratham lost six children each.

Samuel viewed such events as divine will and was resigned to them, as were his neighbors. He was thankful for things great and small alike: after a hard summer in 1762 he was pleased to report, "[W]e have a Vast help this fall by a verry Unusual great Quantity of Acorns & Nuts, by which Much More Pork is fatted this fall, than was fatted by Corn last fall."[68] During better times he could relish

"Uncommon Difficult Measureing by Reason of the Depth of Snow," from "A Plan of the Estate of Benj[a]. Smith of Exeter Dec[ease]d," April 1, 1757. *Courtesy New Hampshire Division of Records Management and Archives.*

Samuel Lane's physical environment was a harsh one, in which weather, disease, and natural catastrophes could sometimes present almost insurmountable challenges.

A Plan of the Estate of Benj[a] Smith of Exeter Decd
measured Apr 1.1757. pr S Lane

NB. I count this Plan not perfect by Reason of the
uncommon Difficult Measureing by Reason
of the Depth of Snow

nature's abundance: "[T]he fruits of the Earth look wonderful forward & flourishing." Samuel saw the seemingly unpredictable world in terms of a divine plan. One October he marveled that "flowers in Gardens put out wonderfully," delighting more particularly because of the season.[69]

His Intellectual and Cultural World

Samuel's fairly extensive library of 307 volumes helped bolster his religious convictions with learning. "His Bible, together with experimental and practical treatises in Theology, were his pleasant and profitable study."[70] Samuel kept a list of all his books, from which we know that he read mostly on religious topics. Yet he was interested in geography, history, and astronomy as well. He also owned practical works on surveying, apprenticeship, farming, and the law. He habitually marked sections in the margins that intrigued him and sometimes copied out particularly meaningful passages.[71]

As his eulogizer, the Reverend James Miltimore, recalled: "He delighted much in reading; and often, as he himself has told me, has quitted his pillow in the night, when others were asleep, trimmed his lamp, and occupied the midnight hours in reading."[72] One of his grandsons recalled that on Sundays "between the forenoon and afternoon service, it was [Samuel's] practice to read a portion of Henry's Commentary on the text of the morning Sermon." During those hours, if anyone in the family "had occasion to speak one to another it was always in a Whisper."[73]

Samuel's intellectual universe was a broad one. Many of his books were doubtless imported from England and written there. He always read the newspaper, subscribing to the *Boston Evening Post* before the *New Hampshire Gazette* began publication in 1756. At some point in his life, Samuel was inspired to make or obtain a globe of the world. This globe, which descended in his family, is believed to be the earliest known American-made globe. It is symbolic, in many ways, of the Lane family's worldwide associations through trade, learning, and politics.

Stratham does not appear to have had its own library until the 1790s, when twenty residents joined to form a social library, a proprietary institution popular at the time.[74] Nor was there much in the way of art or music to brighten Samuel's world. Tavernkeeper Dudley Chase, the third member of this family to run the neighborhood tavern, was remembered as "fond of music" and to have "played the flute with skill."[75] Music, however, was not commonly heard even in church until the very end of the 1700s. The historian of the nearby town of Hampton Falls later explained: "[B]ecause there

An Account of the Books I
own; Number'd as follows.
March 5th 1762. Sam Lane
continued after, as I Purchase them

Mr Janeways token for Children No 1
Dr Mather Concerning Comets — No 2
allens Allarm to ye Unconverted. given Sufe No 3
Bunyans Sighs from Hell given Mary 4
School of good Manners — 5
mortons Spirit of Man Sanctified &c 6
Morril. Preperation for Eternity given Sufey 7
Baxters Call to ye Unconverted given Sufe 8
Dr Mather upon Conversion given Bathsheba 9
Gouge's Young Mans guide given Saml 10
The glorious Daughter — 11
mr Cooper on quenching ye Spirit — 12
Whitefields Journal — 13
Dr Colmans Sermon on ye Union — 14
Ashtons Memorial — 15

"An Account of the Books I own." *Lane Family Papers, New Hampshire Historical Society.*

A list Samuel Lane kept of all 307 volumes he owned offers insights into his intellectual and cultural milieu. The majority of his books dealt with religious topics.

was a scarcity of Psalm books in the early times[,] the deacons read two lines which were then sung by the congregation who got the words in that manner."[76] Samuel long served as one of the deacons in Stratham's church.

In April 1782, however, a group of ten women and twenty men, including two of Samuel's sons, began meeting "for the sole purpose of attaining more knowledge in vocal musick."[77] In August that year, Samuel referred, perhaps somewhat skeptically, to what was probably the first performance of this choir as "the great Singing Lecture."[78] We learn from Samuel's grandson Ebenezer that, far from feeling deprived for not having previously experienced the joy of such music, his grandfather "had considerable difficulty with the new Method of Singing and New tunes . . . introduced into Public Worship. He said it was like speaking in an unknown Tongue to him, he could not understand it. . . . The tunes had many Slurs in them and were much repeated, while one part were using one set of Words, another part a different set and so on, [but] as he was alone in it he gave it up after a while and was peaceable."[79] Ebenezer Lane concluded, "There was more or less difficulty on that subject, among many of the Churches," and the Hampton Falls historian tells us further that "deacons in some instances did not yield without a struggle."

Samuel Lane's terrestrial globe, made of pine; mid-1700s. *New Hampshire Historical Society.*

Though neither the probate court nor the Lane family ever inventoried Samuel Lane's personal possessions, one of his most unusual belongings appears to have been this globe of the earth. Samuel Lane is said to have made this solid wood globe, one of the earliest surviving American-made examples of the form

By the 1790s, Samuel Lane's Stratham most likely had attained the final criteria to qualify, in historian Belknap's view, as an ideal community. In addition to the more basic features mentioned earlier, Stratham supported "a social library, annually increasing, and under good regulation. A club of sensible men, seeking mutual improvement. A decent musical society." As Belknap himself concluded, "Such a situation may be considered as the most favourable to social happiness of any which this world can afford."[80]

No oil portrait survives to record the appearance of Samuel Lane or any member of his immediate family. Only a paper silhouette documenting son Jabez's profile exists, along with several unidentified silhouettes that descended in the Lane family. Until the second quarter of the nineteenth century, only the wealthiest New Hampshire residents could afford to have portraits painted. Artists were itinerants and were only occasionally at work even in the larger communities like Portsmouth and Exeter.

Despite the absence of such an image, however, Samuel Lane's own extensive writings, preserved by his family, not only allow us to re-create the essential features of Lane's personality and existence but also help provide a rich perspective on the features and landmarks of his eighteenth-century world.

The Years of the Life of Samuel Lane is the story of how a young man in rural New Hampshire learned a trade and developed a diversity of skills in order to be able eventually to "settle" first himself and then his family as productive citizens in the far from simple world that surrounded them.

The Years of the Life of Samuel Lane, 1718–1806

Chapter 1

Mastering a Trade

In 1781, Samuel Lane's youngest son, Jabez, was twenty-one years old and working in his father's tanyard. On April 5, a warm spring day with occasional rain, Jabez put ten hides in a vat to soak off the dirt and flesh while his father went to the Exeter court. More than two weeks later, he "work'd" the hides, scraping off the debris, and "put them into the Limes," where they remained for six weeks. In his "Tanyard Journal" under June 2, Jabez wrote,"took hides out of Limes . . . unhair'd & fleshed and laid the Sole Leather 1st Layer." Jabez repeated this cycle throughout the summer until the hides were removed from the tanning pits as leather in the late fall. By 1781 this process had been repeated on the same site for forty years, first by Samuel and later by his sons.[1]

This dimension of Samuel's work, tanning and shoemaking, is most of all a story of his youth and early adulthood. As a child he trained at his father's side to be a shoemaker. In an intriguing turn of events he also acquired tanning skills. These crafts, though the foundation of his prosperity, held little glory or glitter. As Edwin Tunis has written, "When the wind was wrong, nearly every village in early America was within smelling distance of a tanyard."[2] Every town needed a tanner, and leather-related trades were an important adjunct to colonial agriculture.

Samuel took in hides from surrounding farms, bought bark for use as tannin, and employed local men and boys as laborers in his tanyard and shop. In return he produced the leather that became footwear, clothing, aprons, hinges, horsewhips, and a wide variety of other essential items. Portsmouth merchants stocked Lane shoes in their shops to supply the provincial capital's residents. In agricul-

Tanyard, from Denis Diderot, *L'Encyclopédie, ou Dictionnaire Raisonné des Sciences, des Arts, et des Métiers*, 1751–1752. *Courtesy, The Winterthur Library: Printed Book and Periodical Collection.*

Samuel Lane and his three sons all practiced the same basic tanning methods. In the family's "Tanyard Journal" for 1781, Jabez, the youngest son, recorded that they first cleaned hides of stray pieces of flesh and dirt, then soaked them in vats of lime to loosen the hair, and finally, scraped hair and excess limewater from the hides.

tural Stratham, leather working provided Samuel prosperity, social standing, and a future for his family. This degree of success in such a "lowly" trade would have been less likely in urban Portsmouth or Boston.

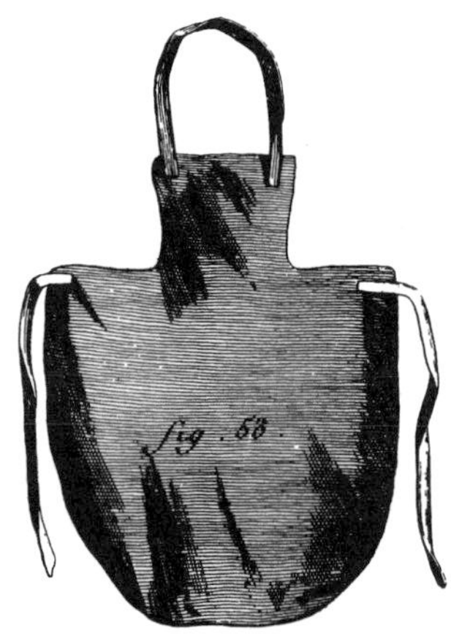

Detail of leather apron, from Denis Diderot, *L'Encyclopédie, ou Dictionnaire Raisonné des Sciences, des Arts, et des Métiers*, 1751–1752. *New Hampshire Historical Society.*

A sturdy, flexible, and versatile material, leather found many uses in eighteenth-century America. Craftsmen like Samuel Lane wore not only leather boots and shoes but also leather aprons.

Childhood and Youth are Vanity

In his late seventies, Samuel Lane prepared a chart summarizing what he considered the main events of his life. At its head he wrote, "The Years of the Life of Samuel Lane, Born at Hampton oct.6.1718. with some things Remarkable Respecting Business & Setling in the World, Births of Children & Grandchildren, Deaths &c as they happened in Each year of his Life."[3] Samuel drew lines lengthwise on an eighteen-by-twenty-four-inch sheet of paper. The amount of empty space he left in the area representing the first eighteen years of his life is striking. From that time on, however, he filled each space with salient events both personal and public.

The chart in fact begins with Samuel's adult life, after he "was Rec[eive]d into the Church at Hampton" in his eighteenth year. Births, marriages, and deaths within his family appear with regularity only after his marriage in 1741. Samuel's chart was a record of the family he headed. For him, what happened before was not a significant part of his own family's accomplishments.

Certainly one unforgettable occurrence during Samuel's childhood was the death of his younger brother, Josiah, when Samuel was ten. Joshua Lane, the boys' father, described in his journal his son's illness, almost certainly throat distemper (i.e., diphtheria):

> on munday my son Josiah was taken ill with a feaver though he was able to sit up a spell every Day untill that Day week and we were in hopes every

Day that he was Rather Better than worse but on munday-following and so untill Saterday was exceeding ill but then seem'd to be better and we in great hopes his distemper was Broke . . . but the night following he seemed to be worse and the next day which was Lords Day he was very ill . . . he continued untill Tuesday night about midnight or Rather past—he fell asleep in Jesus—[4]

The prolonged illness of this five-year-old child, multiplied by the threat of contagion in the household, threw the family into alternating moods of hope and despair. Joshua lamented that his son's "groans were enough to pierce the stoutest heart." However, that episode earned no mention in Samuel's summary of his life. His writings almost totally ignored his childhood.

A citation from Ecclesiastes, "Childhood and Youth are Vanity," is Samuel's only comment on his first four years.[5] Until the late 1700s, as a general rule, society viewed children as unformed adults and childhood as ruled by "inadequacy." Later, "the perception of childhood . . . changed from one of a period of vulnerability and deficiency . . . to that of a vital preparatory stage."[6]

"To School he goes, an active, healthy Lad," from a child's picture book, made for Freelove Wheeler (1752–1831) by William Colwell (1780–1817), Foster, Rhode Island. *Courtesy Rare Book Department, The Free Library of Philadelphia.*

Between the ages of five and ten, Samuel Lane attended school in Hampton. His teachers, Mr. Wingate and Mr. Tuck, presumably taught in town-supported schools.

The Puritan clergyman John Cotton recommended that, after the first seven years of life pass in "lawful recreation," work at a "calling" becomes appropriate.[7] In Plymouth, Massachusetts, after age six or seven, "the young boy appeared as a miniature of his father, and the young girl as a miniature of her mother." Apart from the earliest years of childhood, "there is no sense that each generation required separate spheres of work or recreation."[8]

Samuel's youthful existence ended when "he began to go to School to mr Wingate" at age five. Hampton had been providing schooling for its children "to write and read and cast accountes" since 1649. Though records do not name the teachers during the 1720s, presumably Mr. Wingate taught in the town-supported school.[9] Samuel recorded very little about school, although it is clear his literary and mathematical skills originated there. When Samuel was eight years old, education or the ministry seemed his likely vocation. "I had a Pain in my Knee," he remarked, "which was the Cause of my being Sent to School to Lattin." Mr. Tuck was his "Lattin" teacher.[10]

Samuel may have been a reluctant Latin scholar. He apparently did not choose but rather was "sent" to learn Latin. Two years later, at the age of ten, Samuel recorded, without further explanation or remorse, "I began to Learn to Make Shoes." His shift from Latin to shoemaking meant that Samuel was entering a more familiar world. To him the future lay in continuing his father's work as a cordwainer, producing tangible goods and contributing to the welfare of his family. For the next five years, until he was sixteen, he pursued

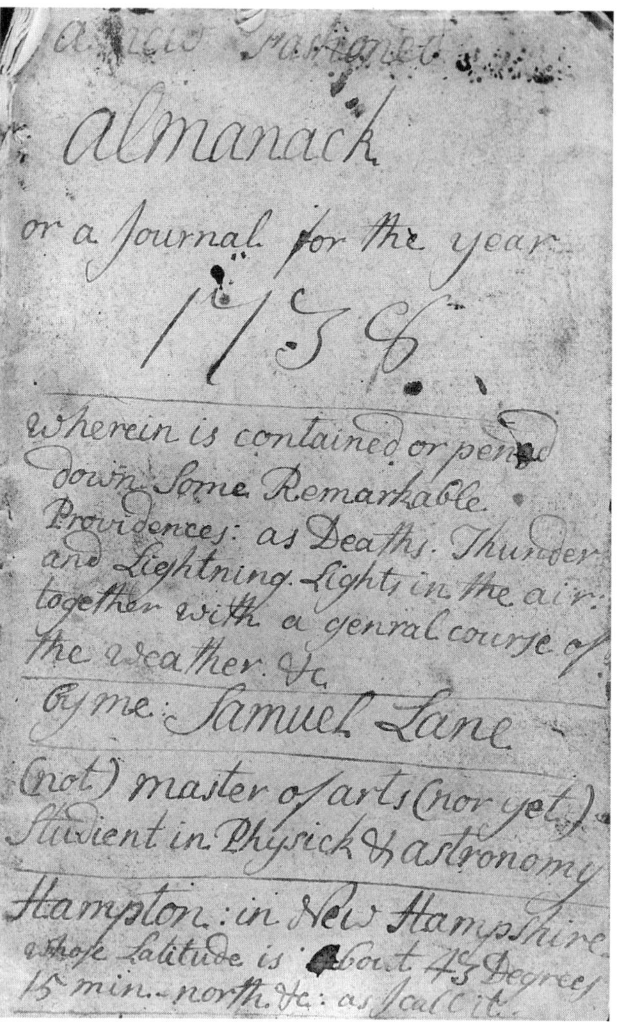
almanack

or a Journal for the year

1738.

Wherein is contained or penned down Some Remarkable Providences: as Deaths. Thunder and Lightning. Lights in the air: together with a genral course of the weather. &c

By me: Samuel Lane

(not) master of arts (nor yet) Studient in Physick & astronomy

Hampton: in New Hampshire whose Latitude is about 43 Degrees 15 min. north. &c: as I call it.

Cover of Samuel Lane's Almanack for the year 1738, "(not) master of arts (nor yet) Studient in Physick & astronomy." *Lane Family Papers, New Hampshire Historical Society.*

Beginning in 1737, Samuel Lane kept diaries, which he called almanacks. In these homemade books he noted the daily weather; births, deaths, and other milestones; visitors and journeys; achievements and notable events.

this calling. "I work'd at the Shoemakers Trade as my Principle Business these years."[11]

How different is the outlook of this rural craftsman from that of the colonial urban elite. Samuel Seabury, the son of an Episcopal minister whose fortunes were in decline, was forced to apprentice to a New York City furniture maker. His thoughts on the way to indentured service were a world away from those of the young Lane. Seabury wrote, "My cousin was going to college an honor for which I felt I would have given the world—and I was going—even then I writhed at the thought—to learn a trade!"[12]

Unlike Samuel Seabury, Samuel Lane apparently never aspired to formal education beyond that offered in Hampton's schools. When nearly through his apprenticeship, he wrote on the cover of his diary: "by me: Samuel Lane (not) Master of Arts (nor yet) Student in Physick & Astronomy." His comment was, if anything, ironic, a passing glance at circumstances that lay beyond his own expectations.

I began to Learn to Make Shoes

To follow his father's calling was Samuel Lane's ordained lot. Joshua Lane's economic circumstances, increasingly strained by a growing family, required that he have help in his shop and around the farm. The shoemaker's universe was a "cohesive world of family and work."[13] Shoemaking was a trade that could be learned at a young age, and Samuel was ready and available early to help provide support. Ten-year-old Samuel could learn his trade alongside his father in the family shop, with minimal capital outlay, sharing many of his father's tools.

Shoemaker at workbench, cutting out leather; engraving from *The Book of Trades, or Library of the Useful Arts*, White-Hall, Pennsylvania, 1807. *Courtesy, The Winterthur Library: Printed Book and Periodical Collection.*

When Samuel Lane was ten, his father began teaching him to make shoes. By the time he entered into formal apprenticeship with his father at the age of sixteen, he had already worked for six years "at the Shoemakers' Trade."

Shoemaking involved four basic steps. First, the shoemaker cut both the upper part of the shoes and the soles out of leather. He then stitched the uppers together, stretched them over a wooden form, or last, and tacked them into place. Finally, he sewed the sole to the uppers, which had assumed the shape of the foot while on the last. A basic shoemaker's kit held eight tools: a knife, awl, needle, pincers, last, hammer, lapstone, and stirrup.[14] An established shop such as Joshua Lane's would have contained a wider variety of tools and devices to produce shoes of quality.[15] Joshua Lane's will mentions a dwelling house, barn, and barkhouse for storage of tanning material.[16] His shoe shop, not listed separately, was quite possibly a room in his house.

Animal skins, the raw material for shoes, were plentiful in rural Hampton. Barreled beef was a staple New England export to the West Indies during this period.[17] Tanners transformed hides from the annual cattle slaughter into leather, which served a wide variety of purposes. The tough but somewhat flexible cattle hides provided shoe soles. The shoe uppers came from softer leathers, made from kid or calf skins, which retained their shape while adapting to the foot's contour.[18] Although the Lanes' own herd provided some hides, most came from neighboring farms. Out of a total of 120 calf skins that Joshua Lane used in 1737, only 5 came from his own animals.[19]

Although a relatively straightforward process, shoemaking nevertheless required mastering the "art and mystery" of a specialized craft, as typically specified in apprenticeship agreements. A great degree of skill was required, and shoes could vary in the quality of their design, leather, and stitching. Of fundamental importance was a proper fit. The long stick and toe-stick were two of the measuring devices used to gauge the length and width of the foot. The measurements were transferred to the last, a wooden form designed

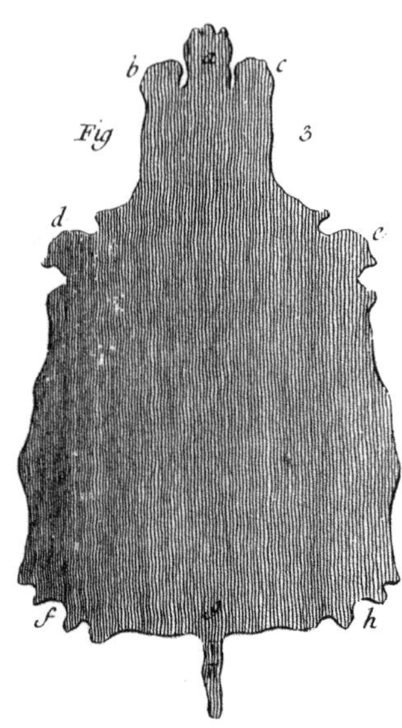

Animal hide, detail from Denis Diderot, *L'Encyclopédie, ou Dictionnaire Raisonné des Sciences, des Arts, et des Métiers*, 1751–1752. *New Hampshire Historical Society.*

Tanners transformed the hides of slaughtered livestock into leather. Of the 120 hides Samuel Lane's father made into shoes in 1737, only a fraction came from his own farm. Saddlers, bookbinders, and leather breeches makers also depended on tanners for the leather they needed in their work.

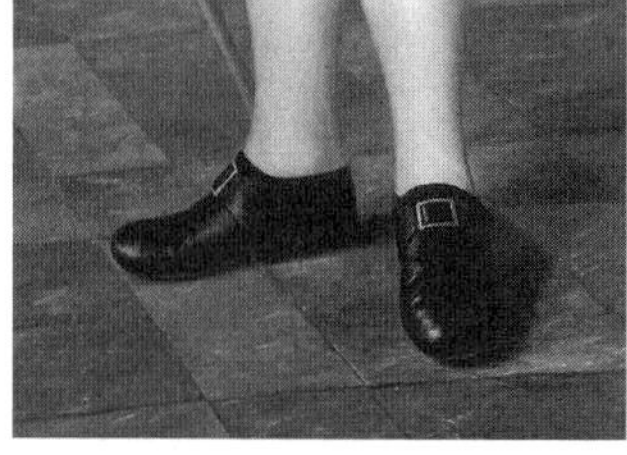

Detail of shoes from portrait of Royal Governor Benning Wentworth by Joseph Blackburn, 1760. *New Hampshire Historical Society.*

Samuel Lane sold sturdy leather shoes to the Wentworths and other wealthy and powerful families living in Portsmouth.

to mirror the foot's shape. Accurate measurements and a good eye were essential in shaping the last, which could be altered either by building up with pieces of leather or by planing down. Customers demanded a good fit: Samuel's accounts show that David McClure brought "a pair of girls Shoes back that did not fitt he had another pair for them."[20]

During the eighteenth century "the order of the day was the straight-lasted shoe." A pair was made from a single last, fashioned to serve both feet.[21] When Samuel made Mr. Moore "2 pair bigness of his right Stout," and "1, a Size Left Stout," he apparently had lasts for both of Mr. Moore's feet, which differed enough so that he referred to them separately. In general, however, the shoes Samuel made were "straight-lasted"; a single last was used to model shoes by the pair. Samuel made eleven pairs of shoes for the Moore household in a single year. The shoes for the men were all measured relative to Moore's lasts. Women's pumps had more general measurements: "a pair Small womens."

In time, Lane shoes gained a reputation on New Hampshire's seacoast. Five of Samuel's brothers followed their father's trade, and the following story about Lane shoes found its way into family lore. The Lanes' work was remembered as "of the most substantial kind. One of them once accused a Trader in Portsmouth of selling many shoes for Lanes shoes, which they did not make; the Trader replied that he did it because his shoes sold so much better, for having their name to them."[22] While the accuracy of this story cannot be confirmed, Samuel clearly made shoes for the households of Portsmouth's political and merchant elite, including Major John Wentworth, Mark Hunking Wentworth, Daniel Peirce, Charles Treadwell, Jacob Sheafe, and Elizabeth Wibird. His shoes sold in the stores of Treadwell, Sheafe, Wibird, Traill, and Marshall, as well as others. In his rural shop, Samuel apparently stayed current with urban fashions so that his shoes were in demand throughout the capital.

The prices Samuel charged offer a clue to the high quality of his shoes. In 1764 a pair of women's shoes sold for £5.10.0 in both Stratham and Portsmouth. Simultaneously, John Dinsmoor in Bedford, New Hampshire, was charging only £2 a pair. Quality certainly accounted for some of this price differential. Samuel's customers were willing to pay almost triple what others in the province were charging.[23]

To produce superior shoes, Samuel experimented with their design. In 1745 he mused, "I think a long quarter[d] Boot is likely to Set best: See when T. Moors is done which is a pritty long quarter." He often noted down processes and ideas gleaned from others, including "Directions for making Lether Bags from Bill Pottle," and the form of a Jock-Top of a Boot

NB. tis between 3 & 4 inches Deep Cut on ye Boot
Lined with Red Stitch'd round where tis pricked
no Garter Strap
the Counter Seam'd on like a gutter Seam

"The form of a Jack Top of a Boot." *Lane Family Papers, New Hampshire Historical Society.*

In learning and practicing the trade of a shoemaker, Lane sometimes made notes on how to put shoes together and how to form long-wearing boots.

"the form of a Jack Top of a Boot."[24] Samuel's education was continuous.

Hampton, first settled in 1638, was a well-established community when Samuel started making shoes there. Little shoemaking was done in the average household, with specialized shoemakers instead providing footwear for the general population.[25] Only rarely did Samuel cut parts for shoes out of leather and sell them unstitched. At this stage of community development, a shoemaker's work was typically "bespoke," that is, undertaken on order from a known buyer.[26]

Rural New Hampshire offered better prospects at this time for cordwainers than did urban centers like Boston. Urban craftsmen held a social rank below that of merchant, clergyman, government official, or attorney.[27] In the colonial hierarchy of trades, shoemakers stood near the bottom, along with tailors and candle makers. In the middle ranks were blacksmiths and joiners, with silversmiths and printers in the top echelons.[28]

Between 1756 and 1775, eight of thirteen Boston shoemakers died without owning homes. "In 1790, shoemakers ranked thirty-eighth among forty-four occupations in mean tax assessments."[29] In the quarter century after 1751, twenty-six of Boston's poor apprentices were indentured to cordwainers. Of those, only six stayed in Boston; the remaining twenty went out to country towns where their futures in general were brighter.[30] In rural New Hampshire, the average cordwainer was middle-class, though some ranked in the bottom third of probated estates by value.[31]

For Samuel, the trade of rural shoemaker held considerable promise of prosperity and community standing. His father, Joshua Lane, was better off financially than his grandfather had been.[32] Joshua Lane held town and church offices in Hampton for many years.[33] Although Joshua's estate was never inventoried, the probate judge,

John Wentworth, set the executor's bond at £10,000. Should that figure approximate the value of his estate, Joshua's household would have fallen somewhere between the upper-middle and prosperous classes of the time.[34]

When the young Samuel Lane decided to make shoemaking his "Principle Business," he did so with the support of family tradition and the expectation of success.

My Service with my Father

When Samuel Lane began a formal five-year apprenticeship with his father at age sixteen, he already knew the basics of shoemaking. Outwardly, his life changed little. His chores around the house and farm continued as he worked at making shoes in his father's shop. Now a full-fledged apprentice, however, he shouldered additional responsibilities that became part of his obligations and training.

The Shoemaker ("De Schoenmaker"), engraving from *Geheel nieuw groot en vermakelijk Prentenboek voor Kinderen*, 1826. *Courtesy, The Winterthur Library: Printed Book and Periodical Collection.*

A shoemaker's apprentice at this time would have learned to stitch shoe parts together while steadying his work between his knees with the help of a stirrup or footstrap. He would also gain experience in measuring a customer's foot and in choosing an appropriate last (or wooden model) from which to mold the shoe.

Children were essential to the prosperity of a rural family. Under the supervision of their parents, daughters helped produce dairy products, garden produce, and cloth, and boys toiled in the shops, fields, and barnyards. Unlike Samuel Seabury, who left his father's home in New York City to learn a trade, farm children could expect to find plenty of work at home. If their number became so great as to be unmanageable under a single roof, sons and daughters entered other households to work.[35]

In 1734, ten children—eight boys and two girls—made up the Lane household. Bathsheba Lane gave birth to another daughter one month after Samuel's service began. There is no mention of Joshua Lane employing an apprentice before Samuel. Until then, with ten young children in the house, an apprentice might have been more burden than help. Beginning with Samuel, however, several of Joshua's sons served him in succession.

There is no evidence of a written indenture, legally initiating the apprenticeship and specifying the obligations of the parties. However, clues to Samuel's duties are found in his diary and daybooks during the years of his service. Judging from these records, Joshua planned an education for his son of which the "art and mysterie" of shoemaking was but a part.

The apprenticeship system ensured the transfer of skills and knowledge between generations. The master-apprentice relationship mirrored that of father and son in the family.[36] A master's moral guidance for the youthful apprentice was perhaps as important in eighteenth-century society as the specific skills passed on. In a world that recognized little qualitative difference between child and adult, apprenticeship "provided safe passage from childhood to adulthood in psychological, social, and economic ways."[37]

AND the ſaid *Solomon Bartlett* for himſelf *and for his heirs* doth hereby Covenant and Promiſe to teach and inſtruct, or cauſe the ſaid Apprentice to be inſtructed in the Art, Trade or Calling of a *Cordwainer* by the beſt way or means that he may or can (if ſaid Apprentice be capable to learn) and to find and provide unto ſaid Apprentice good and ſufficient *meat, drink Clothing Lodging and other necessaries fit and Convenient for Such an apprentice in Sickness & in health also to send said apprentice to School one Month Annually during the said term to be instructed in Reading writing and arithmetic* during the ſaid Term; and at the expiration thereof ſhall give unto the ſaid Apprentice *two Suits of wearing apparel good and new one Suitable for the Lords days and the other for working days also one Yoke of Stout Oxen five years old and one middling Cow for Size five years old*

Portion of a cordwainer's apprenticeship agreement between Daniel Chase of Newbury, Massachusetts, and Solomon Bartlett of Deering, New Hampshire, February 26, 1800. *New Hampshire Historical Society.*

The terms of Samuel Lane's apprenticeship with his father do not survive, but they were doubtless similar to those in this printed indenture of a somewhat later date. The education provided an apprentice generally extended beyond the "art or mystery" of his chosen trade to include reading, writing, and arithmetic.

Indentures often included provisions for instruction in reading, writing, and sometimes ciphering—"the customary elementary education" in colonial America.[38] New Hampshire law required the master of an apprentice to fulfill these basic educational responsibilities.[39] Ensuring the individual's development in a number of areas, the apprenticeship system nurtured a citizen as well as a craftsman.

Samuel had already attended school and was literate when his apprenticeship began. His general education, however, did not stop during his service. At age nineteen, he "went to School to Esqr Palmer to Learn to Cypher and Survey Land."[40] Samuel Palmer was a noted surveyor, and six years after studying with him, young Samuel Lane took the oath to become a surveyor of land. Joshua appears to have provided his son the training needed to follow in his own footsteps. Samuel's diary suggests that his father measured land in addition to farming and shoemaking.[41]

From the master's perspective, labor at shoemaking was no doubt only one of the benefits of indenture. Young Samuel's apprenticeship provided an education in many other areas. His daybooks show that his father trained him in household and business matters that went well beyond basic shoemaking. The role of family continued to remain central, ensuring that a wide range of lessons was passed on from master to apprentice. That he served as apprentice to his father rather than outside the Lane household probably only strengthened the lessons learned.

Shoemaking stood, however, at the core of Samuel's apprenticeship. "The last 5 years of my Service with my Father viz from 16 to 21 years of my age," Samuel remarked in 1739, "I made 1430 pair of Shoes."[42] This means that on average he made 286 pairs per year or 5½ pairs per week. Though his production was small compared with that of his own children later in the century, Samuel's output as an apprentice must have contributed significantly to the welfare of the Lane household.

In addition to shoemaking, Samuel was exposed to the logistical

(43)

The Rule of Fellowship

In the working this Rule there is no difference betwixt it & the Rule of Three, where every mans Stock being added togather the Total must be the first number of the Rule of Three the gains, the Second. and every mans particular Stock the third; The use of this Rule is therefore to give to each Partner, his just and equal Share. Observe then as the whole Stock is to the whole gain So is every mans particular Stock to Each mans particular gain, &c

2 Merchants Company A put in 20£ B put in 40£ and they gained 50£ I Demand each mans part of the gains

If £60 gain 50 — 20 gain — If 60 gain 50 — 40 gain

A. 16-2/3, B. 33-1/3 } Answer — 50-0

3 farmers hired a Shepherd to keep their Sheep £7-10s per annum A Comitted 430 Sheep to his Care, B 357 — D 500 — I Demand how much Each man must pay of this 7-10.

If 1287 — 150 — 430 A. If 1287 — 150 — 357 B. 1287 — 150 — 500.

A 2-10-150/1287, B 2-01-783/1287, D 2-18-354/1287 Answer.

Total 7-10-000

Four Merchants ventured to Sea a Stock of £2465 whereof A put in 700 B 960 & C 207 & D 598 and they gained 2000 but the Tempestuousness of the weather arising they were obliged to Cast overboard as Many goods Amounted to 769 I Demand What Each man must bear of this Loss.

A. 2465 = 769 = 700 — B. 2465 = 769 — 960 — 2465) 769 — 207 — D. 2465 — 769 — 598.

A — 218-930/2465, B — 299-1205/2464, C — 064-1423/2465, D — 186-1372/2464 The Answer.

Total 769-000

The Fractions 1205, 1423, 930, 1372 — 2465) 4930 (2

June 7th 1777.

Calculations from Jabez Lane's student copybook, 1777. *Lane Family Papers, New Hampshire Historical Society.*

During Samuel Lane's apprenticeship he attended school to learn "to cypher and survey." He almost certainly practiced calculations similar to those that his youngest son, Jabez, recorded in his copybook forty years later. Before printed textbooks became common, students copied problems and solutions in a book of their own to which they later could refer.

realities of managing a house and farm and to the importance of record keeping in carrying out those responsibilities. Samuel began a daybook on the first day of 1736, when he was seventeen, and recorded loads of wood brought by Jonathan Towle and Stephen Batchelder. The year's heating season ended with David Smith bringing "a little load," the twenty-third delivery of the winter, on April 3. In March, Samuel's accounts show that Joshua Lane paid for a load of wood taken "to grandfather." Each generation helped support the others. In all, thirty-four loads of firewood entered the household that winter.[43] Samuel was responsible for keeping records of who delivered each load and the number of loads brought to that point. This probably became Samuel's duty because he was most likely to be at home to receive the wood and because it was good training in bookkeeping. Responsibility for price and payment was as yet left to his father.

have Communion with a few
be intimate with one.
Deal justly with all.
Speak evil of none.

A verse from Samuel Lane's 1736 daybook. *Lane Family Papers, New Hampshire Historical Society.*

At the age of eighteen, Samuel Lane copied this inspirational verse, alongside business records he was keeping for his father. The lyric appears to contain his basic philosophy of life.

Samuel also kept a similar "Account of the Corn we Bye." Although the Lane farm produced grain, it was insufficient for household needs. In 1736, Samuel accounted for the purchase of nearly fifty bushels of corn and eight and one-half bushels of barley, oats, and rye. Again, Samuel's task was simply to record the purchase; how and when it was paid for was his father's concern.

"Work hired in the year 1736" was another account Samuel kept. Though incidental to his apprenticeship as a cordwainer, careful record keeping was critical to the overall operation of the household and to his training in business. This account lists people employed to labor in the barnyard and growing acreage of the Lane farm. Samuel, seventeen in 1736, was the only son old enough for heavy field work; his next oldest brother, William, was just thirteen. Five of the fourteen workers listed in the account were Lane relatives. The labor performed reflects the diverse production of this small New Hampshire farm: "harrowing about one acre of corn," "doing flax," "plant[ing] Petaters," "mowing great-meadow & barley," and "mowing oats."

The Lanes' labor requirements also reflected the seasonal rhythm of farm work. In mid-April, with the frost out of the ground and mud season over, laborers helped clean up after the long winter by "carrying out muck." It could take several days to rid a barn of the winter's accumulation. Then came preparation of the fields—plowing, sowing, and harrowing. During June and July tending crops took precedence, whether weeding, harrowing, hilling corn, or mowing the fields. The season culminated in the fall's harvest.

Samuel did not document whether he worked in the fields along with the hired help during the summer season. Lower shoe production that season, however, suggests that his responsibilities may have included work on the farm. When Samuel noted on September 27,

1737, "we finished harvest," the implication is that Samuel, his father, and his younger brothers participated in the work.[44]

The Lanes often utilized local youth to work on their farm, and a lively exchange of labor took place between neighbors. The largest segment of the work force in colonial America was youth, both boys and girls, who worked in family enterprises or went out to work in other households.[45] For farm work in 1736, the Lanes hired thirty-three days of labor; the total was less in 1737, twenty-two and one-half.[46] By then William was fourteen, old enough to help with the field work. By the end of Samuel's apprenticeship, the Lanes probably had enough sons of working age to become suppliers to Hampton's labor market rather than hirers of labor.

Samuel's apprenticeship ended when he was twenty-one and his younger brother, William, destined also to become a cordwainer and tanner, was sixteen. William apparently also apprenticed with his father, for he lived at home during these years. Joshua, now fifteen, was to become a carpenter and cabinetmaker, suggesting that his father preferred to train just one son at a time. Young Joshua went elsewhere to learn his trade.

"Memorandum of the Shoes I made . . . in those 5 years with my Father." *Lane Family Papers, New Hampshire Historical Society.*

Memorandum of the Shoes I made
and the Lether I Tan'd, from the time I was
16 years old, to the time I was 21 years old, or out
my time with my Father, which was oct 6. 1739.
in those 5 years with my Father, I did as follows,
I made 1430. pair of Shoes.
I Tan'd 162. Sides of Sole Lether, and
84 Sides of Uperlether. and
316 Calf Skins, &
14 Kip-Skins. &
209 Sheep Skins. &
16 Dog Skins. &
1 Hog Skin. &
2 Wood Chick Skins: besides other work at farming
as appears by Dayly Journals. S. Lane.

Samuel's brothers Isaiah and Josiah also took up their father's calling. The Lane boys who became shoemakers appear to have served their father in succession, their birthdays being at least five years apart. The exception to this pattern was Ebenezer, who was born in 1733; his later teen years fell during Isaiah's apprenticeship with his father. But by then, Samuel was established and thriving in the trade and ready to accept his younger brother as an apprentice.[47]

In Joshua and Bathsheba Lane's household, family and apprenticeship were inseparable. Whenever possible, sons pursued their father's calling, and their training extended beyond craftsmanship. In Hampton and many other communities like it, crafts were but an extension of the agricultural society. Only if the apprentice emerged from his training fully prepared to serve both the economy and the society could his service be counted successful.[48]

I . . . Learn my Self to Tan

When Samuel Lane entered his apprenticeship in 1734, his father did not have a tanyard. Joshua procured leather by buying hides from neighbors and sending them out to be tanned. Samuel carefully noted the weight of each hide, from whom it was purchased, and the date in his accounts. Fifty-nine of the seventy-nine calfskins they obtained in 1737 were taken to be made into leather by craftsmen who specialized in tanning.[49]

Perhaps as a result of this inconvenience, Samuel recalled about his first year of service, "I began to try to Learn my Self to Tan, with 4 mean Sheepskins." Describing a reversal of the usual apprenticeship relationship, he continued, "My Father Seeing I could make Lether, let me Tan Some for him the next year." As there had been no previous mention of his father's ability to tan, Samuel presumably learned by observing the process when delivering hides to tanners.

On January 14, 1737, Samuel "carried 30 hides to Bradford for Maj^{r} Osgood: weight:1437." On January 26, the Lanes sent twenty-two hides to "mr Clarkson."[50] The next year, Samuel "Taned 27 Sheepskins, 2 Calfskins & 1 Dog Skin." He noted his success with pleasure: "The calfskins being my Fathers, his Currier sent him word to let that Man Tan all his skins next year, that Tan'd Them 2—for they were the best Lether he had; which Encouraged me verry much."[51]

Until his son became interested in leather production, Joshua Lane owned no special tanning equipment. In 1735 and 1736, Samuel tanned "in Tubbs at my Fathers Well."[52] Samuel's initiative in learning tanning appears to have given Joshua enough confidence in his son to invest seriously in this venture. The construction of a fully

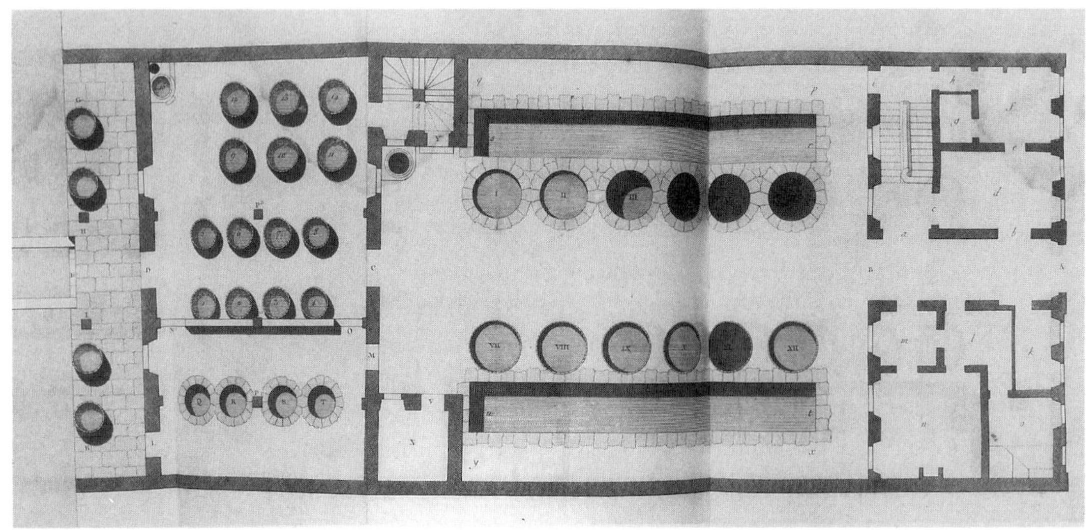

Tanyard, showing tanning pits, from Denis Diderot, *L'Encyclopédie, ou Dictionnaire Raisonné des Sciences, des Arts, et des Métiers*, 1751–1752. *Courtesy, The Winterthur Library: Printed Book and Periodical Collection.*

Tanning involved successively immersing the hides in water, lime, and tanning solution. Samuel appears to have learned the process while observing the tanners to whom he made deliveries for his father. The ideal tanyard pictured here almost certainly boasted more tan pits than the local operations Samuel saw.

equipped tanyard on the Lane farm brought about a sudden increase in tanning output.

The needs of the colonial tanner were modest:

> The rude appointments of a tannery, as generally built before this time [1794], embraced a greater or less number of oblong boxes or hogsheads sunk in the earth near a small stream, and without cover or outlet below, to serve as vats and leeches. A few similar boxes above ground for lime vats and pools, an open shed for a beam house, and a circular trough fifteen feet in diameter, in which the bark was crushed by alternate wooden and stone wheels, turned by two old or blind horses, at the rate of half a cord a day, completed in most cases the arrangements of the tanyard.[53]

Recognizing the limitations of tanning in "Tubbs," Samuel and his father "put down three Tan Pitts: & one Lime Pitt. and one water pitt" in October 1737.[54] Samuel began using these pits the following spring.

The purpose of tanning was to chemically alter the skins by permeating them with tannin, found in oak or hemlock bark, to prevent their deterioration. The work was labor-intensive, dirty, and smelly. The tanner would first place the hides in a pit of water to remove dirt, blood, and loose flesh; Samuel referred to this process as "to put in Soak." Loosening the extraneous material could take anywhere from three to twelve days.

The next step was "liming," or soaking the hides in a mixture of lime and water to loosen the hair from the hide. Then, the tanner would lay the hide over a beam and, using a special knife, scrape off the hair. Soaking in a mixture of tanbark and water came next. At first, Samuel put his hides in "handlers," small vats in which the hides were alternately agitated and taken out to drain. Once the tanyard was built, he would transfer hides from the handlers and lay them flat in pits where he could immerse them in tanning solution. Once completely saturated, the hides were removed and hung up to dry.[55]

Samuel's 1737 daybook offers a glimpse of the work involved in tanning. From March 21 to November 21 he worked twenty-eight days at tanning. In March and April he soaked and limed hides and calfskins and on "June 13 unhaird 39 calfskins or thereabouts." For the rest of June and July he repeatedly "[l]aid away 7 Larg skins, 2nd Layer," "took out 6 calfskins," "[l]aid away 21 Skins 2nd Layer new hogshed." He didn't finish this process until November 21, when he noted, "took out my last calfskins (20) & 1 dogSkin."[56] The work of a tanner, however, was never done. By that same mild November day, the Lanes had already taken in fifty hides to tan the next season.

Joshua Lane's role in this excursion into tanning is unclear. He certainly had some knowledge of the tanning process. It may have been only when his eldest son reached an age to provide the labor

Skins to the Tanners. 1736
to John Leavit — 32
to mr Knowlton — 24
to Caleb Marston — 6
I tand LL for father — 5
I bought LL — 5
not put in — 10
taken in all this year — 79

Skins from the Tanners.
from mr Knowlton — 4
oct. from mr Knowlton — 4
Febr. from mr Knowlton — 13
I all

"Skins to the Tanners . . . Skins from the Tanners." *Lane Family Papers, New Hampshire Historical Society.*

As Joshua Lane did not tan his own leather, his son Samuel became responsible for delivering the untanned hides his father had purchased to local tanners. An important part of his training as an apprentice was learning to keep accurate and useful business records. Joshua delegated to Samuel the task of accounting for skins and hides going and coming.

an account of the hides & Skins I tan in the following years

	hides	calf skins	Kips	Sheep skins	Dog Skins
1734	00	00	00	04	
1735	00	02	00	27	1
1736	01	10	02	33	
1737	10	130	08	55	7
1738.	55.	80	03	38	4
1739.	58	94	1	52	4
			1 hogsk.	2 woodchick	

"An account of the hides & skins I tan in the following years," 1734–1739. *Lane Family Papers, New Hampshire Historical Society.*

As Samuel Lane became proficient in tanning, his production dramatically increased. His father soon decided to invest in the equipment necesssary to expand into this related trade.

needed that he could afford to expand his business into leather production.

Samuel's success at tanning appears to have convinced his father that this aspect of leather work should be taken seriously. In addition to the "Pitts" they constructed in the fall of 1737, they also built a barkhouse in which to store bark for tanning. The following spring they bought a barkstone and hung it in the newly constructed bark mill, grinding their own bark for the first time on April 18, 1738. They also purchased specialized tanning tools, "a Beaming Knife & Bark Shave," from Major Wingate and dug three more tan pits the next fall.[57]

Horse-operated bark mill, from *A New and Complete Dictionary of Arts and Sciences*, London, 1764. *New Hampshire Historical Society.*

In 1738 the Lanes constructed a mill to grind bark from which they could produce tanning solution. "The mill, being a large round wooden trough, with a pretty large stone set on edge in it, and turned round by a horse," ground the bark (preferably oak) into a "coarse powder."

Although Joshua Lane's own account books do not survive as documentation, the addition of tanning to the Lanes' household production certainly enhanced the family's financial position. The value of the tanned hides that went into the shoes Samuel made as an apprentice amounted to 73 percent of the total cost of the shoes. The labor involved was relatively cheap, only 27 percent of the value of the shoes. Taking into account the average price of a calfskin, tanning at home presented the Lanes with the opportunity to more than double their income.

In general, tanning was a more profitable trade than cordwaining. Between 1630 and 1830 there were twice as many shoemakers as tanners in the Piscataqua region. The average value of a tanner's estate, based on inventories taken between 1754 and 1770, was nearly three times greater than that of a comparable cordwainer's holdings.[58]

During his apprenticeship, Samuel became acquainted with the marketplace as well. In addition to recording firewood, grain, and hides that entered the household and shop, he now had a chance to practice the double-entry accounting system by keeping his father's account with Mr. Sibley. Sibley supplied the Lane shop with wooden heels; poplar was the wood of choice for this purpose.[59] Between February and November 1736, Samuel credited Mr. Sibley with 273 pairs of heels at two shillings, sixpence per dozen. That year he recorded, in partial payment for the heels, three pairs of shoes, two

1738
March 14. 1737/8. we haled home our
Barkstone from caleb Marston,
apr 11. hung the Barkstone 1738
apr 12. we finished the Barkmill.

Samuel Lane's description of setting up a barkstone in his father's mill, 1738. *Lane Family Papers, New Hampshire Historical Society.*

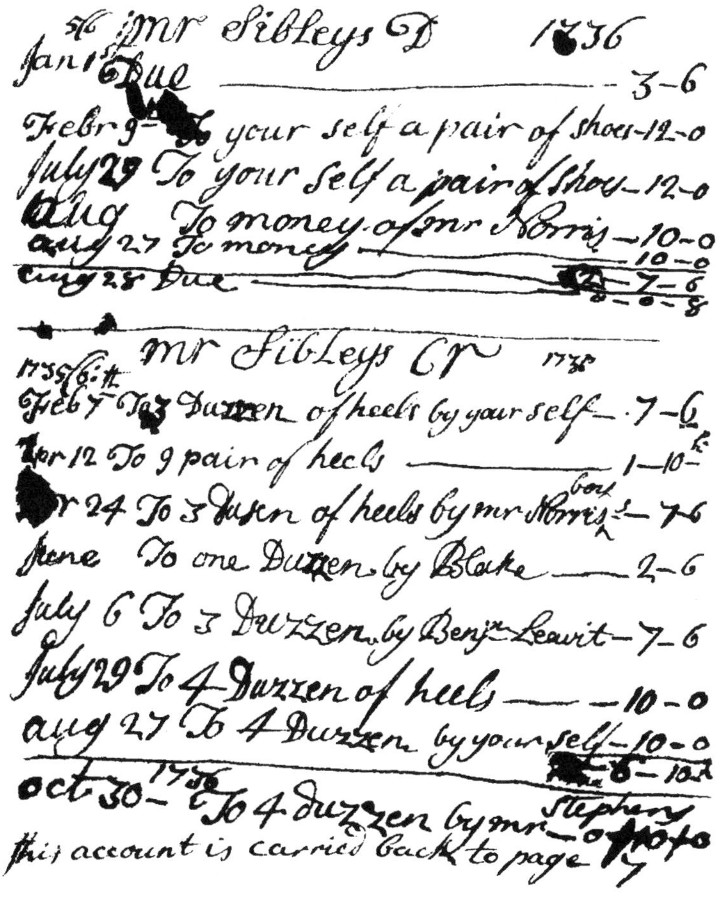

Mr Sibleys Dr 1736
Jan 15 Due — 3-6
Febr 9 To your self a pair of shoes 12-0
July 29 To your Self a pair of Shoes 12-0
Aug To money of mr Norris 10-0
aug 27 To money 10-0
aug 28 Due 7-6

Mr Sibleys Cr 1736
Feb 7 To 3 Duzzen of heels by your self 7-6
Apr 12 To 9 pair of heels 1-10
Apr 24 To 3 Duzen of heels by mr Norris's boy 7-6
June To one Duzzen by Blake 2-6
July 6 To 3 Duzzen by Benjn Leavit 7-6
July 29 To 4 Duzzen of heels 10-0
aug 27 To 4 Duzzen by your self 10-0
oct 30 1736 To 4 duzzen by mr Stephens
this account is carried back to page 7

Samuel Lane's record of the Sibley account, 1737. *Lane Family Papers, New Hampshire Historical Society.*

Samuel Lane trained in double-entry accounting by recording his father's transactions with his wooden heel supplier, Mr. Sibley.

for Sibley and one for Mr. Stephens, who worked for Sibley. The Lanes paid the balance in money.[60]

This single account reflects the complex system of debt, credit, and labor that characterized New Hampshire communities during the eighteenth century. On February 7, 1736, Mr. Sibley delivered three dozen heels and bargained for a pair of shoes, which he picked up two days later. During the spring and summer various people—Mr. Norris's boy Blake, Benjamin Leavit, and Mr. Stephens—all delivered heels for Sibley. Sibley himself brought four dozen to the shop on July 29 and picked up another pair of shoes. In August the Lanes paid Mr. Norris on Sibley's account, which may have been compensation for work Norris's boy had done previously for Sibley. When the Lanes paid £2.7.6 on Sibley's account on August 27, he was there to collect and to deliver four dozen more heels. Mr. Stephens brought four more dozen on October 30, and the Lanes delivered him a pair of shoes ten days later, presumably as payment for service rendered to Sibley.

The Sibley heel account that Samuel kept is illustrative of the maze of debt and credit binding Hampton's citizenry together. Samuel "Reckoned" this account twice during the year and carried it over into 1737, when a similar series of transactions again took place. At a time when accounts might run for years without being balanced, accurate bookkeeping was essential. The accounting system in common use at the time exempted no one. Brothers and sisters and other family members expected each other to pay for services rendered.

oct 15.1737 Horsewhips I have made already is 41
Horsewhips ~~which before this~~ 41
1 Wm Jenkins — oct 15 — 0+6+0
1 Jacob Clifford — Nov 15 — 0+6+0
1 David Marston — Nov 22 — 0+6+0
1 andrew Wiggin before oct — 0+6+0
1 mr Gerrish — Dec 30 — 0+6+6
Thos Dearborn of Chester June 21 + 6+0
1 mr Palmer — 0–6–0
1 Josiah moulton — 0–6–0
1 Ensn Pirkins — 1739 march 23–6–0

Samuel Lane's list of "Horsewhips I have made," 1737. *Lane Family Papers, New Hampshire Historical Society.*

While still an apprentice, Samuel did some work "on his own account." Though limited by obligations to his father, he did enough work on his own to have twenty individuals indebted to him as of December 1, 1736. He traded horsewhips, aprons, buttons, and lace. As apprentice to a shoemaker, he could not trade in shoes but was free to make other types of leather goods for his own, as distinct from his father's, profit. Horsewhips were a popular item at six shillings each. By October 1737, Samuel already had made forty-one whips for customers from Portsmouth, Stratham, Chester, and Hampton.[61]

The individual accounts Samuel developed during his service suggest that his father allowed apprentices a certain amount of time to pursue trade on their own. On plantations in the southern colonies, even slaves could work for pay. Under a labor system known as tasking, slaves were "assigned a certain amount of work for the day or perhaps week, upon the completion of which they were free to use their time as they pleased."[62]

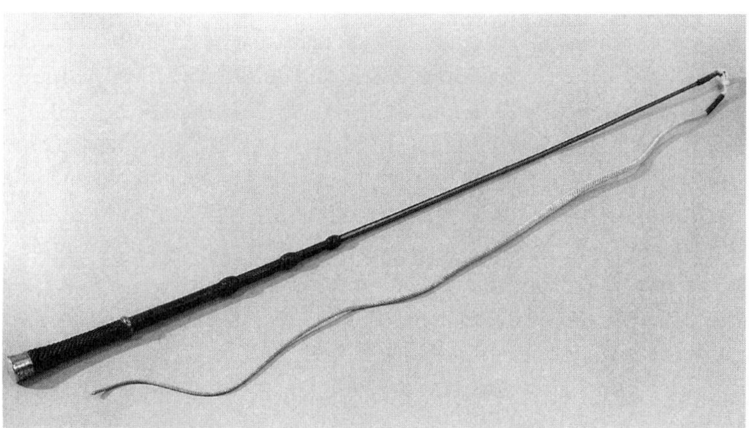

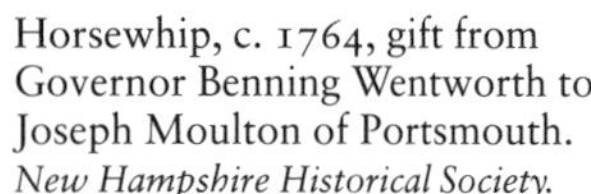

Horsewhip, c. 1764, gift from Governor Benning Wentworth to Joseph Moulton of Portsmouth. *New Hampshire Historical Society.*

While still an apprentice, Samuel Lane produced horsewhips on the side for sale to area residents. By the time he was nineteen years old, he had made forty-one such whips.

The Isles of Shoals, from Samuel Holland's map, 1784.
New Hampshire Historical Society.

The market for Lane products extended to fishermen and their families at the Isles of Shoals, nine miles off the coast at Hampton. Star Island served as the center of the Shoals fishing community.

Samuel traded his own work within the market networks his father had developed. Most of his father's trade was in and around Hampton, although a substantial portion took place at the Isles of Shoals, nine miles off the New Hampshire coast. At the fishing community there, Samuel traded shoes and fishing boots for oil and fish. On the back cover of his daybook for 1736, Samuel reminded himself to settle accounts with some of his customers on the islands: "To Take at the Shoals a fish or two of mr Samll White he had a pair of shoes," and "mr Samll Yettons 4 pair shoes £1-3 if he hes it get a Little parcel of Blu[bber]."[63] His diary indicates a nine-day trip there in October 1738.

"To Take at the Shoals," 1736.
Lane Family Papers, New Hampshire Historical Society.

Samuel Lane kept notes to remind himself of what he should procure on his next journey to the islands.

Oil was a staple of the Lanes' island trade. On a trip from September 30 to October 1, 1737, Joshua Lane "bought a barrel of oyl of D[eaco]n [William] Muchimore price 6+0+0." Over the next two months, fifteen people purchased oil from the barrel in quantities of one quart to two gallons. The Lanes themselves were by far the greatest consumers of oil. They apparently used fish oil to curry and finish leather.[64]

While working closely with his father as an apprentice, Samuel formed relationships that served him in business throughout his life. The fact that, in addition to learning the shoemaker's trade, Samuel learned the trade of a tanner, would have profound impact on his ability to weather the vicissitudes of colonial New Hampshire's economy. When his service ended on his twenty-first birthday, Samuel Lane was prepared to enter not only the world of work, but also—what was an even greater achievement—the world at large.

I was out of my Time

October 6, 1739, was a momentous day in Samuel Lane's life. Having satisfied his obligations to his father and having become skilled in a set of interrelated crafts, he was free to pursue his calling and make his way in the world. The past five years had prepared him for this day. Coming of age was more than a symbolic passage.

The brevity of Samuel's diary entry that day—"I am this Day twenty one years old"—belied its significance. Samuel had never remarked on his birthday in other years. Therefore, his very mention of it at this point marks it as a milestone. The bold writing on the title page of his new daybook expresses both his pride and intent: "Samuel Lane His Book Hampton october 6th 1739. this Day I was 21 years old. a daybook of Debt & credit of all my Tradings & Dealings with all Persons I Deal withall."[65] His trade with "all Persons" was now his own business; he was an independent artisan.

Samuel Lane His Book
Hampton october 6th 1739.
this Day I was 21 years old.
a day book of Debt & credit
of all my Tradings & Dealings with
all Persons I Deal withall.

"Samuel Lane His Book Hampton october 6th 1739. this Day I was 21 years old." *Lane Family Papers, New Hampshire Historical Society.*

On his twenty-first birthday, Samuel Lane marked the taking on of adult responsibilities by setting up his first daybook. In it he began keeping an alphabetical record of all his debts and credits.

This was a busy and exciting time in the Lane household. Thirteen children, including Samuel, called the Hampton farmhouse home; seven of the children were ten years old or younger. Although Samuel had discharged all obligations of his indenture, he continued to live with his parents for the next twenty months. At nineteen, Samuel's oldest sister, Mary, no doubt helped her mother with domestic duties and looked after their younger brothers and sisters. Romance was in the air. Samuel and his sister Mary were courting a sister and brother from the neighboring James family. William, sixteen in June, assumed Samuel's place as apprentice in his father's shop, though Samuel remained nearby to offer aid and advice.

Within this family context, Samuel's relationship with his father had changed, a fact that Samuel acknowledged in several ways. "I work'd in a little Shop I parted off for that use," he wrote, "in one Corner of my fathers Shop."[66] He later wrote of his living arrangements at that time that he felt "[u]neasie in my present Circumstance." In the son's mind at least, one expectation was clear: he should go out on his own as soon as possible and relieve his family of the burden of his support. "My Father had a great Family, and I Knew I was Burthensome to them, tho' I paid for dressing my Victuals, which I provided for my Self after the first year; yet as I wanted to Settle, they also wanted I Should."[67]

Other young men at the time also expressed remorse at remaining dependent on their parents. Samuel Seabury's short-lived apprenticeship with a New York City furniture maker left him in a situation akin to Lane's. Seabury wrote, "There was one circumstance . . . that was a source of annoyance and that was my dependence on my father for boarding and clothes of one of which certainly and perhaps of both I knew he would have been relieved by my continuance at Moneygripe's [an epithet for Seabury's master]."[68]

Samuel, like Seabury, considered himself a burden to his family. In reality he was more likely an asset to the operations of the Lane household. Nevertheless, in his eyes and those of his parents, the time had arrived for him to move on to the next stage of his life.

Joshua Lane did more for Samuel than would have been expected at the end of a typical apprenticeship. It was customary for a master to award an apprentice a bonus upon the fulfillment of his indenture.[69] Called "freedom dues," such bonuses often consisted of a new set of clothes or tools. There is no mention of a clothing provision at any point during Samuel's apprenticeship. Instead of clothing or tools, Joshua gave Samuel "near 20£ old Ten^{r} worth of Lether to begin with he also gave me my Board the first year."[70] This settlement, though modest, fell within Joshua's ability to provide and gave Samuel an immediate opportunity to use his skills toward economic independence.

Shortly after Joshua himself had reached his majority in 1717, his father, William, sold him just over an acre of land in Hampton.[71] This land allowed Joshua to settle in Hampton, establish himself in his trade, and eventually purchase land enough to create a small farm. Although Joshua eventually owned more land in Hampton than his father ever had, none of it passed into Samuel's hands. Since Joshua needed to farm his modest property to support his considerable family, his financial circumstances probably precluded his giving such material support.[72] In addition, Samuel needed property suitable for a tanyard, and Joshua may not have had land to spare fitting that requirement.

Evidence of the change in relationship between father and son appears in Samuel's daybook beginning in 1739. Under "F-^{s} D" ("father's debt"), Samuel listed eight pairs of shoes made on his father's account, the first appearance of shoes in Samuel's records. As an apprentice learned a trade, his work and output in that craft belonged to his master. As soon as Samuel became an independent craftsman, however, Joshua paid him for his work.

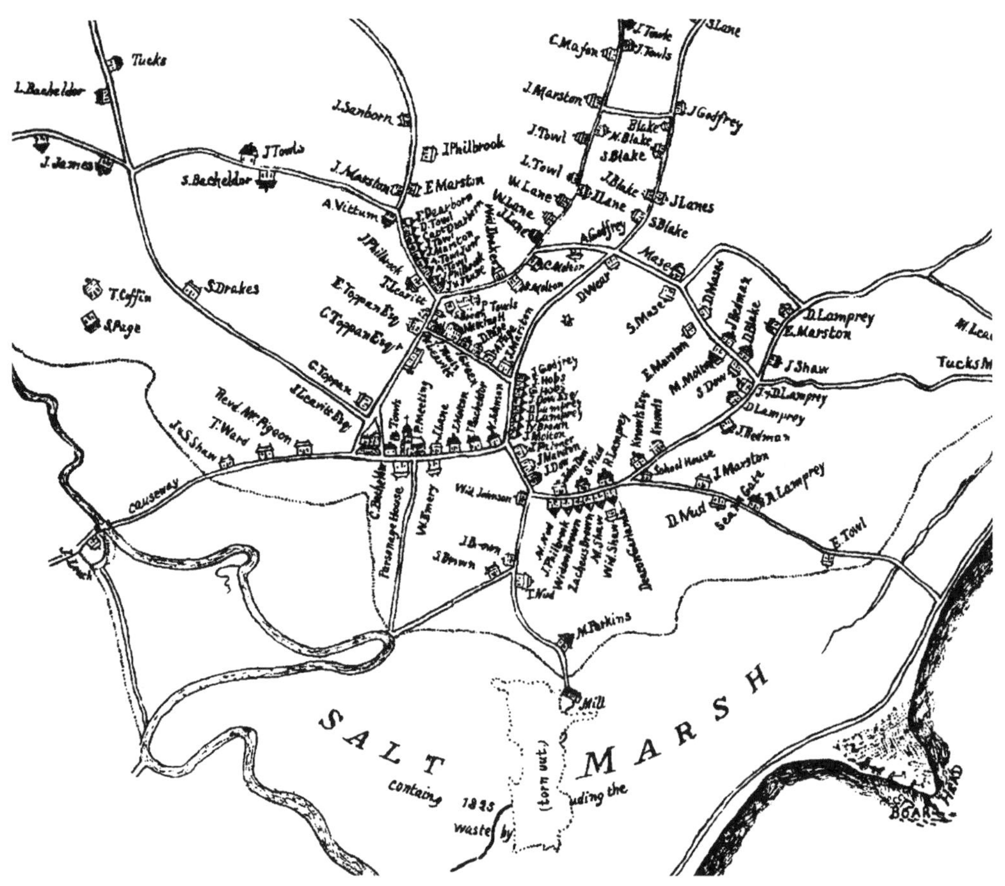

Map of Hampton by Thomas Leavitt, 1806; engraved by James Akin, Newburyport; reproduced in Joseph Dow, *History of Hampton*, 1893. *New Hampshire Historical Society.*

An early traveler described Samuel Lane's hometown as like a flower, with "streets of houses wheeling off the main body thereof." Joshua Lane and his family lived just north of the center, on the main road between Portsmouth and Boston. Both Samuel and his sister married members of the James family, who lived at a country crossroads not far to the west.

The credit side of the ledger, too, reflected changed relations. Credits during 1739 reveal Samuel's fondness for "Syder"; his father paid him with three barrels of the popular drink. Although cider appears to have been part of the upkeep of an apprentice, the board that Samuel's father provided during his first year out no longer included the beverage.[73]

Samuel's first daybook after reaching his majority covered the period from October 1739 until April 1741, while he continued to live with his parents. During his apprenticeship he had carried on his books only two individual accounts, for his father and Mr. Sibley, who provided wooden heels to the shoe shop. Samuel's new daybook recorded exchanges with a large number of people, showing that as an independent artisan, Samuel had advanced from merely making goods to finding markets for them.

Samuel's accounts no doubt underestimate the total volume of his trade. As was often the case, not all transactions were recorded. If goods of equal value were exchanged and no balance remained on the books, Samuel appears to have made no note of the transaction.

By the end of the eighteen months that his first daybook covered, Samuel had provided goods valued at £40.2.3 and received as payment £31.18.7, a balance in his favor of £8.3.8. He accepted diverse payments on his customers' accounts:

Skins, etc.	£ 1-15-00 (5.5%)
Oil	£ 5-15-09 (18.0%)
Money	£12-00-05 (37.6%)
Jars	£ 1-08-09 (4.6%)
Farm Produce	£ 2-10-03 (7.9%)
Fish	£ 1-08-07 (4.6%)
Sundries	£ 6-19-10 (21.8%)
Total	£31-18-07 (100%)

Particularly surprising is the high percentage of payments he received in money. Though cash was then, as now, the preferred form of payment, it was not easy to bargain for in New Hampshire's economy. Samuel's plans for marriage in the not too distant future perhaps made cash payments especially important to him at this time. Setting up a household was a costly endeavor. With no prospect of family land, he would have to buy a homestead. Encouraging payment in cash was the least complicated and risky way of saving for the expenses he anticipated.

"Money being Scarce," the young craftsman wrote, "it was Difficult to get Money for my work." Looking back he recalled his strategy during those years:

> the best Method I could think of was, to make Shoes & Some fishing Boots, for the Shoals; and my practice was when I had got a little Cargo made, to carry them over to the Shoals; and when I could not get money for them, I

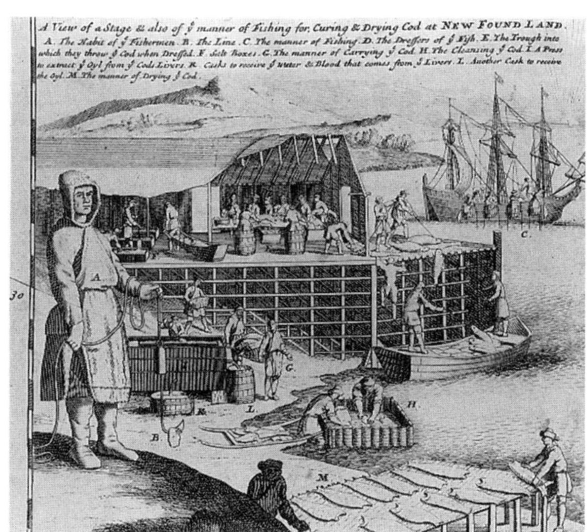

"A View of a Stage & Also of ye manner of Fishing for, Curing & Drying Cod at Newfoundland," from Herman Moll's *The World Described*, London, 1711. *New Hampshire Historical Society.*

In the foreground a typical North Atlantic fisherman wears leather boots and an apron, probably comparable to those Samuel Lane made and sold. Other men nearby spread fish to dry and extract oil from cod livers.

View of Portsmouth from the mouth of the Piscataqua River, 1778; watercolor by Pierre Ozanne. *Courtesy National Museum of Blérancourt, France, PHOTO RM.N.*

Samuel Lane frequently sailed from Piscataqua Harbor to the Isles of Shoals, probably aboard a fishing schooner like the one shown here in the center foreground. At the islands, Lane provided boots and shoes to the fishermen in exchange for fish and whale oil and other commodities.

would Sell them for oyl, Blubber, & Fish &c: I have Draw'd off 2 Barrels of oyl in a fall; & Sold it for Corn; then I would endeavor to turn the Corn into Money; Sometimes get it ground, & hire a Horse, and Carry the Meal to Portsm^{o}, and the Cost of that, Eat up all my gain; only I turned my work into Money.[74]

Many of the people he traded with in his first years were from the Isles of Shoals. Of the seventy-four people listed in his early accounts, about one-third lived on these rocky islands. Samuel went to the Shoals twice the year of his twenty-first birthday and made six trips there the following year. Altogether, in 1739–40 he spent nearly thirty days either at the islands or traveling back and forth.

His four-day trip from November 30 to December 4, 1739, was a typical one. As Hampton had no harbor, Samuel hired Uncle John Nays's horse to take him to Little Harbor in Portsmouth, where he boarded a boat for the Shoals. Upon his arrival that "pretty cool" Monday, he traded with seven individuals. In return for a pair of shoes, Ms. Damral paid him "a Jar 5^{s} money 6^{s} & fish 1^{s}." He delivered five other pairs of shoes to customers that day.

The first of December was another busy trading day; he sold two pairs of shoes and three calfskins, but most of his business that day involved buying. He credited his account with a curried calfskin, five quarts of oil, fourteen pounds of fish, "half a barrel Bluber and 2 DogSkins," and money. In all, he sold £5.8.3 worth of goods and bought £6.8.3. This ratio of his debit to credit was somewhat unusual, for on two other trips for which the accounts exist, he left the islands with a net balance in his favor. On longer stays offshore, he also mended shoes, a service not recorded for this particular trip.[75]

Though Samuel credited much of his early success to Shoals commerce, he also traded a good deal in and around Hampton; in the period following his indenture about half of his seventy-four customers were local. Horsewhips became his specialty. In 1740, Samuel "[s]old many of them by the Dozen at Portsmouth & Elsewhere."[76] Samuel's growing familiarity with Portsmouth markets

A page from Samuel Lane's 1739 daybook. *Lane Family Papers, New Hampshire Historical Society.*

Samuel Lane kept careful track of all his clients' accounts. The "L" page included many of his own relatives, to whom he sold a wide variety of leather products.

Woodcut of a hanging, from *Life and Dying Speech of Elisha Thomas*, 1788. *New Hampshire Historical Society.*

Lane's diary provides a record of unusual happenings in his day. In 1739 a hanging drew Lane to Portsmouth. Almost half a century later, Lane recorded another execution for murder, which attracted crowds to Dover and prompted this broadside.

Hourglass, mid-1700s, originally owned by Mary Towle Philbrick of Hampton. *New Hampshire Historical Society.*

In 1739, Samuel Lane purchased, as one of his first household possessions, an hourglass. Throughout colonial times the majority of families did not own clocks. Instead they relied on hourglasses, sundials, and town bells.

during his apprenticeship established an important long-term outlet for his products.

The extended Lane family also helped Samuel's business; 15 percent of his customers were relatives. Between October 12, 1739, and February 14, 1740, his uncles, Thomas and Samuel, appear in his accounts eleven times as purchasers. They bought shoes, aprons, stirrup leathers, oil, nails, and skins and also had their nephew tan for them. Samuel accepted in return cheese, a seat, "Legs for my compos," and on December 27, 1739, horse hire to "Piscataqua." His diary reveals that December day was when "two women [were] Hanged at the Bank."[77]

Samuel's work in the shop continued much as before, with many of the same customers as during his apprenticeship. He also continued to tan in his father's tanyard, although at a much slower pace. While he proudly proclaimed his newfound independence in entries such as "The first hide I bought after my Time was out," the number of hides Samuel tanned that year represented a significant decrease from his production during his last year of service.[78]

Daybook entries for 1740 tapered off quite dramatically after the winter ended, and it is difficult to gauge the extent of his work that year. Perhaps his circumstances at this time dictated payment on delivery for most goods. In such cases, he would have kept no record of these transactions. His diary reveals no particular reason for an interruption in his work schedule. Clearly, however, he was feeling pressure from other priorities as he planned his future.

About this time, Samuel began to accumulate household goods, to keep his own animals, and to look for a place to live. He exchanged a pair of shoes for "a Tin lamp & hour gl[ass] & thread" in 1739.[79] Even before he finished his apprenticeship, he "Bo't a Calf & hired it kept, and it is now a Cow which is of great Service toward my Support, for milk, Butter & Cheese." By mid-1741, Samuel's livestock included eight sheep and a heifer, in addition to the cow.[80] And finding a place to live was becoming a pressing matter as his courting of Mary James proceeded.

With few clues in the written record, the Lanes' courtship remains understandably a mystery. Born in 1722, Mary was the daughter of local weaver Benjamin James, who served with Joshua Lane on a Hampton Church committee beginning in 1738. It was at this very time that Samuel "began Acquaintance with M-ry J-m-s."[81] The details of the couple's romance are hidden behind the dashes with which he recorded Mary's name. Throughout his life, Samuel followed the convention of replacing vowels with dashes at the slightest hint of a sexual connotation. His barnyard garnered similar respect with such comments as "S-w Pigd [sow pigged, or bred]." Samuel mentioned his wife-to-be nowhere in his diary by her full

The James House (built c. 1720), Hampton, from the *History of Hampton*, 1883. *New Hampshire Historical Society.*

Mary James, who became Samuel Lane's wife the day before Christmas in 1741, grew up in this house. Her father, Benjamin James, was a weaver by trade.

name until after the wedding. At the same time, Jabez James, Mary's older brother, was wooing Samuel's younger sister, Mary. The wedding of that couple, on February 7, 1740, merited but a single comment in Samuel's diary: "Jabez James married."[82]

Given Samuel's own plans to marry, finding a place to live had become a high priority. "I try'd verry hard to purchase a House Lott (for I had Not Money to purchase much Land) I tryed in Several Towns, as Hampton, Northill [North Hampton], Kensington &c but could not obtain a Suitable place for a Tanyard, which caused me much trouble & perplexity."[83] Unfortunately for Samuel, he was seeking land at a time when it was becoming scarce in older established communities, and consequently more expensive. The young man was discouraged, furthermore, from settling where land was available and cheap. At the time, inland towns like Epping and Brentwood, as Samuel once recalled, were "counted too far in the Woods to Settle."[84]

One logical compromise was Stratham, a small town with frontage on the Squamscott River, which emptied into the tidal estuary known as Great Bay: "Sundry times Strongly invited by Mr Coker, Mr Barker, Mr Hill & others (who Traded with my Father) to Settle in Stratham, and Not Suiting my Self any where Else, I went to Stratham on that Account Several times in the months of January & February 1741, to look out a Suitable place; though it was an unsuitable time; for the Snow was verry Deep."[85]

Not until his third trip there did he decide to purchase what he believed would be a suitable lot for his home and business. Mr. Coker, "who was verry kind," Samuel wrote, "[e]ntertained me Sev-

Samuel Lane's house (near center) and neighborhood, from *Plan of the Town of Stratham* by Phinehas Merrill, 1793. *New Hampshire Historical Society.*

When purchasing land in Stratham for his home and business, Samuel Lane deliberately chose a spot near a millpond and brook for his tannery. Tanning required a steady supply of water for washing, rinsing, and soaking the hides.

eral Nights; and went with me to Sundry places to try to procure a House Lott: and on the 19th day of Feb 1741, I Bargained wth Colo Wiggin for a piece of Land on the North Side of his sons Mill Pond Called 2 Acres More or less for 26£, & took a Deed of it & paid him for it, which Exceedingly Rejoiced me, that I had found a spot to Sit down upon; which I tho't would Suit for a House Lott; and a Tanyard by the Mill Pond."[86]

That Samuel should be "strongly invited" to town by a group of Stratham residents is not surprising. Stratham was a growing farming community, and a tannery "was a necessary appendage to every village."[87] With hides available from the slaughter of cattle, abundant bark from forested land, and many streams traversing the township, Stratham possessed the requisite resources for tanning. A nearby tanyard could save a local farmer the burden of carrying hides to a more established coastal settlement for tanning.[88] New Hampshire's growing population found many uses for leather, rang-

Jontʰⁿ Moulton, Esq;

WILL give good Wages for Ten good narrow Ax Men to work for him six Months, to begin their Service on the first Day of April next—Also good Encouragement will be given by said MOULTON, for several Tradesmen, that will set up their Trades in a new Township called Moultonbourough, joining to Winnepisoke Pond, viz. a House Carpenter, a House Joyner, a Black Smith, a Tanner, a Shoe Maker, and a Weaver—Also some good Land and other Encouragements to be given to Settlers, that will settle upon a Tract of Land, called the Addition or third Division of said Township, where the settlement is already begun, and a Plan laid for Twenty Families more, including the Tradesmen, to settle upon said Tract within Twelve Months from the first Day of March next——The Terms and Conditions, and the Plan laid for Settlement may be seen at said Moulton's House at Hampton; and those who incline to take up Land to settle are desired to apply to said Moulton and agree in a short Time.

N B *Hampton, January 1st, 1767.*

Advertisement of Jonathan Moulton of Hampton for a tanner and other tradesmen to settle in Moultonborough, *New Hampshire Gazette*, January 9, 1767. *New Hampshire Historical Society.*

As speculators opened new townships for settlement, they occasionally called for valued craftsmen like tanners to settle in the new town. The presence of such regularly needed craftsmen as blacksmiths and tanners could help in recruiting settlers.

TO BE SOLD at PUBLIC VENDUE, on Wednesday the Tenth of August next, Three o'Clock Afternoon, at the House of Major ----- GREELEY, Innholder in Kingston, about Thirty Two Acres of Land, with a Dwelling-House and Barn thereon, pleasantly situate in said Kingston, on the main Road, leading to Haverhill, with a Brook running thro' it, and every Way suitable for a Trader, Tanner or Husbandman, said place is now in the Ocupation of Mr *Hezekiah Sleeper*, and has been improved for a Number of Years.

N. B. Twas advertised for sale some Time ago, but for Reasons was postpon'd

Advertisement of a farm suitable for a tanner in Kingston, *New Hampshire Gazette,* July 1, 1763. *New Hampshire Historical Society.*

This advertiser calls his readers' attention to how well his property—complete with running water—would accommodate a tannery.

ing from clothing to door hinges. An English observer praised leather's qualities without restraint: "What an aptitude has this single material, in a variety of circumstances; for the relief of our necessities, and supplying conveniences in every state and stage of life!"[89]

A call to practice a trade in a specific community was not uncommon in the eighteenth century. A tanner was an important figure in the transformation of "boundless and unknown Wildernesses . . . into a well-ordered Commonwealth."[90] Attempts to lure craftsmen to settle appeared frequently in newspaper advertisements of the time: "The Trade of a Currier is very much wanted in Middletown, the metropolis of Connecticut." New towns attempted to attract young craftsmen by offering the prospect of accumulating "a pritty Estate in a few Years."[91] In 1741, Stratham held such promise for Samuel.

Settling in Stratham was made easier by the assistance of family acquaintances in the area. Mr. Coker helped the young tanner in his efforts during February to arrange for a house frame. At first,

Samuel's efforts ended in disappointment. On March 2, however, he sealed a bargain with William Moore to build a frame for £30.

Samuel apparently had found ample opportunity to sharpen his bargaining skills during his apprenticeship. His first attempts in February to get a frame for his house failed because he "co'd not obtain to my mind." What made his final agreement with William Moore acceptable is not specified, but the terms must certainly have been advantageous if his dealing for a house foundation is any indication: "I Lett out my Celler to Mr Abr^m Stockbridge to Dig & Stone for 8£ 10s, and he finding it a hard Bargain Desired I wo'd add 30s more to it, which I did, & made it 10£-0s-0d in the whole."[92] While Samuel's sense of value was keen and he bargained accordingly, a sense of fairness appears to have been his overriding principle.

Samuel made nine trips to Stratham that spring to get his lot ready for construction. This was several more than he had anticipated, as catastrophe struck on April 20 while he was there to clear his lot and prepare to dig his cellar: "I . . . Soon Come to Water; and to my great Disappointment, found it wo'd not do to Set a House there."[93] He had spent £26 for a lot on which he could not build. Luckily for him, although at a cost he could ill afford at the time, he was able to purchase two acres on the south side of the millpond adjacent to his first piece. This parcel, acquired in two separate transactions, included a brook for his tanyard and cost a total of £37.

Samuel had been hesitant about purchasing land he had been able to inspect only in February under snow cover. His anxiety proved well founded, and certain comments he made suggest that he considered Colonel Andrew Wiggin's sale of the land villainous. The relationship between Lane and Wiggin, distanced from the outset by differences in their social status, worsened with this land transaction. In later years, Wiggin was the only person, for example, that Samuel ever charged for scraping dung from his hides. Joseph Mason, however, who helped Samuel by selling him the adjacent land, where he finally built his house and tanyard, is ever afterward referred to as "neighbor Mason." Mason was the only Stratham resident Samuel addressed by this familiar title.

Following the resolution of his real estate problems, Samuel's spring proceeded much as before. There is little evidence of shoemaking activity, presumably due to time and effort spent preparing for the move. In March, another sister, Anna, was born, giving Samuel yet another reason to wish to leave his parents' household. In May, he traveled to Stratham several times to measure and buy the second acre of land from Joseph Mason. When Samuel Lane noted on May 28, "I drove my Cow to Stratham to Jno Thirstons where I had Agree'd for my Board," the young leather worker was poised to begin on his own.[94]

I Remov'd my Self . . . to Stratham

On June 11, 1741, Samuel Lane left his native Hampton and went to board in the house of John Thirston at Stratham. His arrangements there were much like those he enjoyed with his parents in Hampton. "I gave mrs Thirston 3s a Week for Dressing my Victuals and I had Milk Butter & Cheese from my own Cow of her Make."[95] Soon after his arrival in town he prepared to raise a house on his newly purchased land. On the fifteenth he went to Portsmouth for supplies, and the next morning work on his house began.

Thomas and William Moore had contracted in March to complete the house frame by June 1. The problem with the site, however, delayed progress for two weeks. The two-story dwelling was to be a modest twenty-eight by twenty-six feet. The Moores promised that "the work Shall be done, workman like and So as the Frame Shall be Judg'd a good Substantial Frame."[96] The raising on June 16 appears to have gone smoothly, for Samuel traveled to Hampton three days later to work in his father's tanyard and spent the night with his parents. Progress slowed after the raising. In July, Samuel contracted to have an eighteen-foot-square cellar dug and a foundation built under the frame by mid-August.

House builder ("Timmerman"), from Jan Luiken, *Spiegel van Het Menselyk Bedryf*, Amsterdam, 1704. *Courtesy, The Winterthur Library: Printed Book and Periodical Collection.*

In preparing to marry Mary James, Samuel Lane built a house in Stratham. He contracted with a number of different craftsmen to dig and stone the foundation, erect the frame, burn bricks, and finish the interior.

In the meantime, Stratham's newest resident did not forget his plans for a tanyard. His barkhouse, raised on July 1, was twenty-six by twenty-four feet, almost as large as his dwelling. Samuel would use this building to store both ground and unground bark, to keep it dry so that the tannin would not leach out prematurely. Without offering explanation, Samuel chose not to cover his bark house until the next year. Most likely, his purchase of land and construction of buildings had stretched his resources to the limit. "I wanted a Tanyard," he later recalled and that fall constructed "a mean Water Pitt with Slabbs." It was not until the following spring, however, that he put down his first two tanning pits.[97]

Because of the initial delay, Samuel had to race to complete his house before cold set in. In July his brick was "Burnt by the Mill-Pond." Twice that year Samuel "burnt clam kill," suggesting that he made his own mortar from sea shells.[98] In August window frames were installed, and in three weeks during September and early October the chimney foundation was laid down and the chimney raised. The roof was shingled and the frame boarded in preparation for clapboarding. On September 22, Samuel recorded, "Brot home our glass & Sep 24. Divided it."[99]

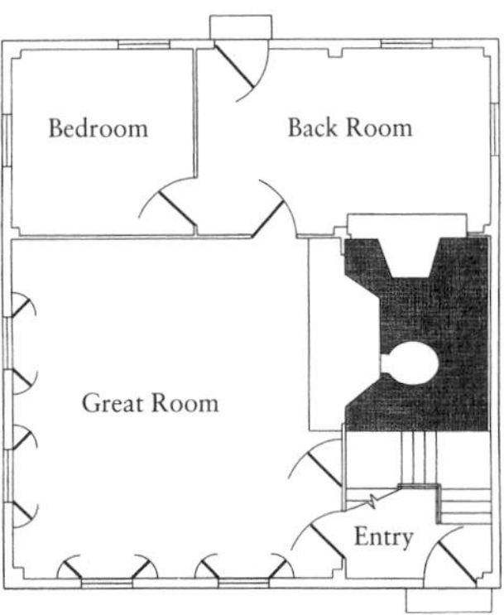

Likely floor plan of Samuel Lane's house in Stratham, based on surviving building contracts. *Courtesy James L. Garvin, New Hampshire Division of Historical Resources.*

Though two stories high, Samuel Lane's house was originally half the size of an average central-chimney dwelling. He added to the house as his family grew. The "great room" had paneled woodwork and window shutters. Contracts specified that the back room be partitioned to provide a small downstairs bedroom.

With the walls in place, work on the interior could begin. "I finished a Room or two in My House as fast as I could, in order to Settle."[100] By then Samuel had a specific deadline to meet. On September 27, 1741, Samuel and Mary's wedding banns were posted.[101] Mary James was to become his wife at the end of December. Samuel hired a joiner, or finish woodworker, to complete the interior of his house. The largest room was eighteen feet square, with two small rooms behind it, one a bedchamber. Samuel's contract with joiner Timothy Jones stipulated that what they called the "great room" be finished with "breast work winscut and mantle-tree-shelfe, & cieling winscut So far as the backroom Door, and make two cubbards according to his [Samuel's] desire. and make 3 four pannel Doores, and case the timbers Doors & window, & make window Shuts & put on washboards: likewise hang the Doores & window Shuts, and fit Sd room all for lath & plastering; and make any Small Shelves that Shall be nescessary in Sd room."[102]

Samuel wanted his house to be more than adequate. The joiner he employed promised to "make good handsome fashionable & Strong window crowns to all the windows in Sd Samuel Lanes house. also a Larg handsome Door crown over the fore Door."[103] By the time of the wedding, three rooms on the first floor were finished. The Lanes, however, would not actually dig a well until the following year. At first, the stream that ran by the house provided their only water.

In December construction stopped temporarily, and Samuel's attention turned to preparations for his marriage. On a "verry pleasent & warm" Sunday in early December, he noted, "I went to the Bank & bought cloth for my wedding cloaths." There is no other mention of travel before he and Mary married, so a local tailor presumably made his suit.[104] On Sunday, December 24, Samuel noted in his diary: "the day of our marriage." Only much later did he more fully document this important event: "I was married at Hampton by the Rev'd Mr. Ward Cotton to Mary James, Daughter of Benjamin James: she was born March 3rd, 1721/2."[105]

It was not until January 6, 1742, nearly two weeks after the wedding, that Samuel brought Mary Lane with her "goods" from Hampton to their new home in Stratham. To his "great Joy & Satisfaction," as he later recounted, he was now "comfortably Setled in my own House; with an Agreable Wife."[106] In all, the year 1741 had brought momentous change to his life: "This year hes been a verry remarkable year with me I have this year (by the help of a kind Providence) bought Land to Settle upon convenient for my buisness; this year I removed from my native Town to another: this year I built me a house to dwell in: this year I rais^{d} my Barkhouse This year I married a wife: & this year I have been comfortably carried

House of joiner Jonathan Low, Portsmouth, built 1743; photographed 1880s. *Courtesy Strawbery Banke Museum; Cumings Library and Archives; Patch Collection.*

The Lane house was practically identical in size to one erected in Portsmouth just two years later. Also built for a craftsman, the Low house stood on a widow's one-third share of a larger lot. The Stratham house probably had a single pitch to the roof rather than the double slope seen here. Its "larg handsome Door crown over the fore Door" likely resembled that on the Low house facade. Shortly before his marriage, Lane recorded "paint[ing] the foreside & East end of my House Red."

through many changes & difficultys and having obtained help from God I am yet a living (though most unworthy) Samuel Lane."[107]

The ensuing winter afforded Samuel ample time to look over his accounts and tally the expenses he had incurred. His four acres of land cost more than twice what he had planned to spend. With no daybook covering this period, any estimate of his total expenses—based entirely on extant contracts—is a conservative one. His building contracts stipulated that at least £75 of the £146 he owed be paid "in Money or passable Bills of credit," which left him, as he entered his new life, with a debt of at least £70.

In fact, wrote Samuel, buying land and building a house "so Exhausted my little Substance, that I was obliged to part with all I Co'd Spare, to pay for it: I Sold a fine heifer Coming in 8, to Timothy Jones for finishing my room for 6£; and Eight Sheep I had wh[ich] I also Sold to John Thirston and all but 1 Cow; which I kept."[108] With his pockets empty, Samuel resorted to borrowing. "I had nothing left to procure my years Pork when I began to keep House: but ran into Debt to D[eaco]n [John] Robinson for half a Hog to live on; which he bro't Jan 20 1742."[109]

During their first few years of marriage, the young couple struggled to economize and pay off their debt. The first winter, Samuel used a room in the house as his shoe shop and hung his hides inside to dry. On December 6 the following year, matters seem to have improved somewhat when Samuel moved into a "New Shop," especially constructed for his work. As he explained further, however, the new shop was where "I and my Wife lived Chiefly this Winter, to

Tall clock by David Blasdel of Amesbury, Massachusetts; owned by Josiah Bartlett of Kingston, c. 1750. *New Hampshire Historical Society.*

For six years after his marriage, Samuel Lane and his family relied on an hourglass for their timekeeping. Like Josiah Bartlett in nearby Kingston, who owned this clock, Lane ordered his first clockworks in 1747 from David Blasdel of Amesbury, Massachusetts. A Stratham joiner made the wooden case for the Lanes' clock movement.

Save Wood."[110] Samuel's shoe shop adjoined the house and shared one of its chimney flues.

The Lanes clearly wanted their home to be respectably finished, but financial constraints forced them to proceed in stages. Exterior trim and clapboarding were not complete for three years, and work on the interior continued for a decade.[111] In 1747, six years after the dwelling was raised, Joseph Hill was plastering the upstairs rooms.[112]

Life in these early years was undoubtedly a struggle, but Mary's presence in the household proved at once a financial asset. As soon as Mary set up housekeeping in Stratham, Samuel no longer needed to pay Mrs. Thirston for "dressing" his food. Mary no doubt would plant a garden and begin herself to process dairy products. As part of her marriage settlement, she brought a heifer and a calf with her to Stratham, though not immediately. As yet, the young Lanes had no barn and little pasture, so they left the bride's livestock in Hampton over the first winter, to save paying their keep. The "goods" Mary brought likely included equipment of various kinds to establish her in household production.

There is no written record of exactly what goods Mary James brought with her to housekeeping. Her father's home in Hampton was a substantial two-story dwelling, but Mary was one of eight children. The only clue to her marriage portion is Samuel's 1783 "Note of Some things left in my House . . . which belong'd to my first Wife."[113] This list, however, contained items brought from Mary's Hampton home at the time of her father's death as well as those that counted as part of her marriage portion.[114] The fact that Mary, at least later in life, owned eight "coverlids"—a large number of bed coverlets for one household at that time—is perhaps not as surprising as it first appears, considering that Mary's father was a weaver by trade.

During their first decade in Stratham, the young couple managed to live in increasing comfort. They purchased furniture from local craftsmen. A variety of textiles from Portsmouth shops—mohair, silk, broadcloth, taffeta, checked linen, and camlet—as well as cloth woven locally, entered the household. From this the Lanes had made "gounds" (dresses), coats, other articles of clothing, table linens, and bed coverings. In addition, stockings, garters, wigs, and hats made their way inland from the Bank. By late summer 1745, Samuel started taking the newspaper.[115] A sure sign that the Lanes were out of debt and in more comfortable circumstances came on August 26, 1747, when David Blasdel, a clockmaker from Amesbury, Massachusetts, brought a clock mechanism to set in a wooden case made by Stratham joiner John Barker. The £26 price of the clock was far more than Samuel had paid for any other household furnishing to date.[116]

Over time, the household's purchases often related to Mary's successive pregnancies. When she first became pregnant in early 1743, Samuel "Bo't Flocks of the Cloathiers & made a Flock Bed this year." Joseph Hill made a "Bedsted" in April, presumably to hold this comfortable mattress stuffed with refuse cotton or wool.[117] After the birth, in 1744, of Mary, the Lanes' first child, they bought a cradle; a month before the birth of Samuel in 1746, Joseph Hill made them a "Trundle Bedsted," as they looked to moving the toddler Mary out of the cradle when the baby was born.

Samuel made little note of such events and never made direct references until the actual day of birth. His seemingly casual entries, such as "My Daughter Mary Born between 3 & 4 o'clock aftern," belied his interest in the health and prosperity of his family. However, Mary's pregnancies usually precipitated changes in the family routine that are discernible despite Samuel's silence. She typically had a difficult time carrying her babies, a condition Samuel almost certainly referred to when he recalled "in 1743, my wife began to be Weakley; and I carried her to Portsm° to Graney Hilton: & went to Dr Sawyer, who helped her verry Much of her weakness."[118]

Mary's first pregnancy probably ended with a miscarriage in 1743, for, during the first two weeks of August that year, a flurry of family visits was sandwiched between trips to Dr. Sawyer. From July 18 to 21, Sister Sanborn stayed with the couple, providing a helping hand, and on August 8, Samuel traveled to Salisbury to see Dr. Sawyer about Mary's condition. Visits from Lucy and Susannah Sanborn and Brother and Sister Row and another trip on Samuel's part to Dr. Sawyer followed in quick succession. A similar pattern of family visits and medical consultations attended Mary's later pregnancies, so it seems likely that her first one ended prematurely.

Mary exhibited similar symptoms again the following spring. Samuel remarked on April 22 that she was ill and, two days later, that his sister Bathsheba had come from Hampton to relieve his wife of some household chores. On May 27, Mary became sick in the meetinghouse; after that, Samuel seems to have taken great pains to provide her with help and ease her burdens. Well before the baby's expected delivery, Samuel hired help to assist his wife around the house. Mary Drake, a cousin from Hampton, worked in Stratham during February 1744, and in June a local girl, Hannah Wiggin, worked there for six days. Mary Drake returned the day infant Mary was born, to help for five days, and other relatives stepped in to assist the new parents. When Mary Drake left, Samuel's mother came for three days; she was succeeded in turn by her daughter Sarah.[119]

The couple relied a good deal on their families' help for the next several years, and a series of visits by Lane and James women al-

"A Little Infant at his Mother's Breast," from a child's picture book, made for Freelove Wheeler (1752–1831) by William Colwell (1780–1817), Foster, Rhode Island. *Courtesy Rare Book Department, The Free Library of Philadelphia.*

The birth of the Lanes' first child, a daughter Mary, in 1744 was accompanied by a flurry of family visits and an increase in hired female help.

ways preceded and followed the birth of each child. The Lanes do not appear to have hired regular help until later in the 1740s; Comfort Cate, for instance, worked six weeks in June and July 1747. After that, a helper in the summer was a common fixture, and increasingly, help came in other seasons; Huldah Davis performed "one quarters Service" in 1751.

The only specific reference to child care came in the wake of Susanna's birth in the summer of 1750, when "wid. Thirston [spent] 3 weeks Nursing at 7/6 p[er] week." Her services in that respect were invaluable to Mary, now responsible for three children, aged two, four, and six, in addition to the newborn baby. No longer needed as a nurse by August and September, widow Thirston was hired for "work" alone and paid only five shillings per week.[120]

Samuel, taking his responsibilities as a father seriously, turned to his work with a new determination.

The Most that ever I Tan[n]ed

The prospect of a family and its consequent expenses encouraged Samuel Lane to work hard to improve his situation. As early as 1742, he wrote, "Having no Creatures to look after this Winter but a Pig; I went to work night and Day, to pay my Debts; and by the last of the Spring I believe I was pritty near out of Debt."[121]

Until Samuel equipped his tanyard for all stages of production, however, tanning took a back seat to shoemaking. With no covered outbuildings during the first winter, he hung up seven tanned hides to dry inside his house. The furious pace with which he made shoes that year consumed much of his own stock, obliging him to buy

Four tanning pits, from Denis Diderot, *L'Encyclopédie, ou Dictionnaire Raisonné des Sciences, des Arts, et des Métiers*, 1751–1752. *Courtesy, The Winterthur Library: Printed Book and Periodical Collection.*

In the mid-1740s four new tanning pits completed the construction of Samuel Lane's own tanyard. Tanners handled hides with special pit tools.

other people's leather. Determined to produce the best footwear possible, Samuel expressed dismay when he had to use undertanned leather because of depleted stock. He began to address this less than desirable situation by constructing tanning pits in May 1742.

After 1740 and 1741, tanning assumed greater importance in Samuel's economic life. Particularly after 1745 his output increased, peaking in 1758, when he noted, "[T]his year I Tan 57 Hides & 140 Calfskins, which is the Most that ever I Taned in a year."[122]

His major undertaking in 1742 was the construction of a shop. One can imagine that Mary Lane soon tired of dodging tanned hides hanging from her ceiling and Samuel making shoes in the bedroom. He had contracted for shop timbers early in 1741, but the frame was not raised until more than a year later. Sixteen feet wide and thirteen in depth, with eight windows, his shop was larger than the typical ten-foot-square shoe shop commonly known as a "ten-footer."[123]

Until 1742, Samuel remained dependent on his father's tannery at Hampton. He took bark "to mr Jewets to grind, and hired his Mill & Horse to grind it, which is Costly." Grinding at another's mill increased the cost of the bark by one-third. In addition, he hired "Justice Leavits oxen to hall Bark from mr Jewets."[124]

The following spring, Samuel built a barkmill in his Stratham tanyard. He proudly noted on June 15, "I ground almost 2 Mills of Bark in my new Mill which is the first that ever I ground in it."[125] Throughout the summer of 1743, Samuel was still boarding and shingling his barkhouse. Once that was finished, the basic elements of his tanyard would be complete. In 1744 and 1747 he constructed four new tanning pits. By the mid-1740s, Samuel had established a working tanyard.

With his business well underway but with debts to pay and family expenses rising, Samuel began to feel the need for help. His own experience certainly made him aware of the value of a good apprentice. However, he hesitated to sponsor one, as he later recalled. "In these years . . . I had no Constant Apprentice . . . but hired Journeymen when I wanted help; to Save my Weakly Wife the trouble of a great family."[126] As time passed, economic necessity forced him to brush aside such concerns, and the Lanes began to have indentured help "come to live."

Notice about death in a tanner's vat, from *New Hampshire Gazette*, September 30, 1774. *New Hampshire Historical Society.*

Tanning as an occupation was not without danger, as this snippet of news from Salem, Massachusetts, suggests.

Salem, September 27.

Laſt Saturday Mr. Eleazer Moſes, jr. of this Town, loſt his Life by falling into a Tanner's Vat.

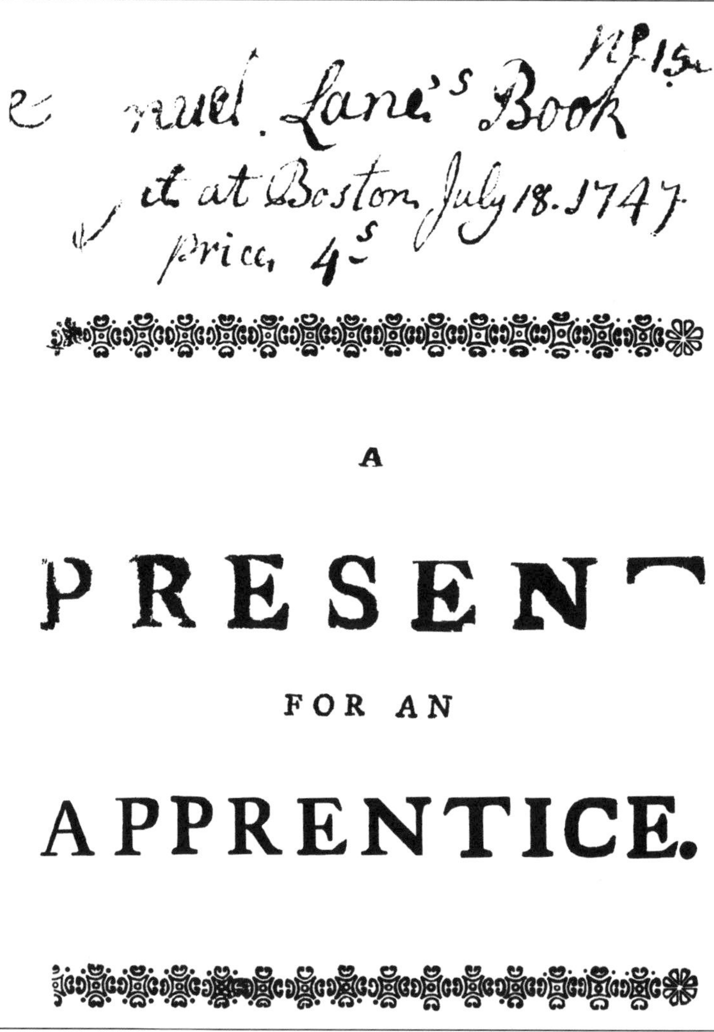

Lane's Book

at Boston July 18. 1747

Price 4s

A

PRESENT

FOR AN

APPRENTICE.

A Present for an Apprentice or, A Sure Guide to Gain Both Esteem and Estate, With Rules of Conduct to His Master, and in the World, London, 1747. *New Hampshire Historical Society.*

When Samuel Lane purchased this volume in Boston in 1747, he may have hoped its advice would help keep his apprentices well behaved.

In keeping with the tradition of taking relatives as apprentices, the first of Samuel's resident helpers, James Critchet and Abraham Perkins, were his cousins. One of James's "two spells" as an apprentice ended in November 1742, when he left the Lane household, and the other began in March 1743 when he "come again."[127] James continued to work for short stints in 1744 and 1745 as well.

Abraham Perkins, another cousin, provided Samuel relatively steady assistance.[128] On April 18, 1743, Samuel "went to Rye for Abraham."[129] This probably coincided with the end of James Critchet's second "spell," which had begun on March 4. It is likely that Abraham's year of service ended sometime in July 1744, for Samuel credited David Huniford, on July 3, "for cutting out two

Jackets & Two pair of Breeches 0+1+6." In another indenture, Samuel stipulated that his apprentice was to have at the end of his term "one Suit of Cloaths Suitable to go to Meeting in; and Another Suit, Suitable for working Days."[130]

While all apprenticeships were mutually beneficial, some proved even more so. In the written agreement between Samuel and Abraham Prescott, the apprentice promised to teach his master "all that I know in all the Rules and Methods of Tanning of Lether and to withold Nothing from him."[131] Just where Abraham acquired tanning skills is not clear. He later appeared in listings as a tanner rather than a cordwainer.[132]

Encouraged by the amount of work indentured help could produce and finding that his household could support another member after all, Samuel endeavored to keep an apprentice on a regular basis. When Abraham left in the fall of 1744, Samuel filled the void with Joseph Jewet and twenty days later with Jonathan Jewet. There is no further mention of these two, so perhaps they were hired only until Samuel's brother Ebenezer could come to live in Stratham in March 1745. Only twelve at the time, Ebenezer was to be Samuel's primary helper for the next six years.[133] By this time, Samuel was traveling more frequently to Portsmouth to sell his leather products and therefore was in greater need than ever before of a trusted helper around home. With Mary Lane tending to young children, he could rest easier knowing that Ebenezer was there to help.

As Ebenezer grew older, he began to travel for Samuel, taking tanned skins to the currier at Salisbury, Massachusetts, accompanying Mary to Hampton, and occasionally going to the Bank. Other Lane brothers from time to time joined them in Stratham. William came frequently, once his apprenticeship with his father ended in June 1744.[134] Even after he married and settled into family life in Hampton, William continued to do outwork for Samuel. In August 1749, for instance, Samuel "carried Shoes to Bill to Make."[135]

Brothers John and Isaiah also traveled from Hampton to help Samuel. John, twenty-one in 1747, spent thirty-one days that year working in Stratham. On April 12, 1750, Samuel "Reck'd with Br Jno Lane. . . . I ow'd him 7-3-0 old Tenor toward making Shoes:

Shoe made by Ebenezer Lane for his daughter Huldah, Hampton, 1759. *New Hampshire Historical Society.*

According to family tradition, Samuel Lane's younger brother and apprentice, Ebenezer, made this shoe for his daughter Huldah. Information written on a scrap of paper preserves the history of the child's shoe. This tiny footwear is the only identifiable example of the Lane family's extensive shoe production.

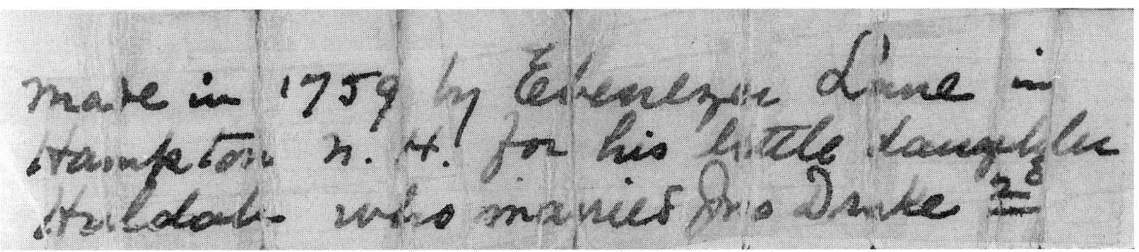

made in 1759 by Ebenezer Lane in
Hampton N. H. for his little daughter
Huldah who married Jno Drake 2d

then I let him have 3 hides weigh'd 121 lb at 18^{d} p[er] lb they come to 9-1-6. and now he owes me: 1-18-6 & the odds between a gallon of oyl & a bushel of Malt."[136]

Ebenezer was the only one of Samuel's brothers who served him as an apprentice, however. Each year Ebenezer lived in Stratham, Samuel clothed him in a new "Jacket & Breeches." Samuel owned Ebenezer's labor and at times exchanged it with his neighbors. On July 22, 1746, Colonel Wiggin benefited from "1 Days work by Eben^{r}."[137]

Samuel's relationships with his apprentices appear to have been cordial, with a single exception. It was important that an indenture specify a trial period, as those bound to serve "seldom had been consulted when they were indentured and many lacked any interest in, or aptitude for, the trade they learned."[138] Jeremiah Avery was to have "Lived with Said Lane Last year upon Tryal in order for an Apprentice; [but] Said Partys not Agreeing to Continue the Lad with Said Lane, Said Avery [the father] took him away from him." The

Runaway ſrom Robert Barber,

the 24th June laſt, a Prentice Boy, named Levi Champman, ſixteen Years of Age, of light Complexion, light Hair, round Shoulders, and goes very ſtooping, and has on one of his Ankles, a bunch made by a cut, carried with him a dark colour'd Clarris Homeſpun Coat, lined with woolen, near the ſame Colour, flower'd Pewter Buttons, a dark coler'd Jacket and Breeches without lining, two woolen Shirts, one cotton and linnen ditto. one pair of blue yarn Stockings. and one new Felt Hat.

And at the ſame Time Run-away, from Benjamin Peaſe, a Prentice Boy, named John Mannary, Shoemaker by Trade, 19 Years of Age, of a very ſmall Stature, his left Eye very ſore, his Hair growing out ; carried away with him a whole ſuit of pepper and ſair color'd Cloaths, a light color'd blue homeſpun Coat, a gray Jacket, a pair Leather Breeches, three Shirts, one pair blue yarn Stockings, one pair new Shoes, and new Felt Hat.

Whoever takes up ſaid Runaways, and conveys them to their ſaid Maſters, ſhall have Four Dollars Reward, and acceſſary Charges. Robert Barber, Benjamin Peaſe.

Newspaper notice for runaway shoemaker's apprentice, *New Hampshire Gazette*, July 19, 1771. *New Hampshire Historical Society.*

Although the indenture signed by a master and apprentice stipulated that a master should not mistreat an apprentice, some found themselves in intolerable situations; others, motivated by adolescent whim, played truant. Only one of Samuel Lane's apprentices is known to have run away. His escape was short-lived—the boy was retrieved the next day.

cause of the dissatisfaction is unclear. Both Lane and Avery felt themselves wronged and sought redress through arbitration.[139] Following this experience with an outsider, it may be no accident that Samuel's next apprentice was a second cousin, Marston Prescott.

Samuel's written indenture with Thomas Hatch, on June 10, 1777, no doubt reflected arrangements typical of such contracts. The agreement bound the apprentice to serve his master "well and faithfully . . . in all Lawful Business, according to his Power Witt and ability and honestly and obediently in all things Shall behave himself toward his Said Master and his family." For his part Samuel was to "teach and Instruct" Thomas "in the Art and Trade of a Tanner, and all Such other Sorts of work and Business as he usually works at, if Said Thomas is Capable thereof." Samuel was to provide Thomas "Suitable Meat Drink Washing and Lodging in Sickness and in health." At the end of his service, Thomas was to receive two suits of clothes.[140]

Woodcut of a pair of runaways, *New Hampshire Gazette*, October 23, 1772. *New Hampshire Historical Society.*

Witnessed by two justices of the peace and registered by the Stratham selectmen, the agreement afforded both parties some measure of protection. Though Thomas had written boldly under his signature, "I hereby Declare my Satisfaction in the above Indenture," he apparently soon developed misgivings. Just five days after everyone had signed the agreement, Samuel wrote in his diary, "Thos ran Away." The following day, however, the Lanes managed to retrieve their new apprentice from Poplin (now Fremont).

Virtually all the years of Samuel's working life, the Lane household boasted an apprentice in residence, often a relative. Following his father's example, however, Samuel employed just one apprentice at a time. Local men and boys, who came on a daily basis or worked by the piece, provided Samuel's other leading source of labor. In Stratham and the surrounding towns, both skilled and unskilled laborers stood ready to help the master craftsman and his apprentice increase their shop's output. One of the regular laborers was Samuel Cate, whose work first appears on record in 1745. Cate made twenty-three pairs of shoes in June and July of that year, working in Samuel's shop and using leather supplied by him.[141]

Samuel probably had an arrangement with Cate similar to that with Daniel Mason, who signed the following agreement on September 26, 1751:

> Reciev'd this Day of Samuel Lane thirty Nine Pounds of Sole Lether at 8^{s} old Tenor p[er] lb price of the whole is £:15:12:0 for which I do promise to pay him as follows viz the one half thereof within two months from the Date hereof in Hides at 16 pence p[er] lb old Tenor. and the other half thereof in Making Shoes at 12^{s} p[er] pair for Shoes & Single channel'd

Pumps and 20^{s} p[er] pair for Double Channel'd Pumps & to make them in the best Manner & to mend what rips for Nothing; & to do them on Demand.[142]

The departure of Ebenezer in June, coupled with the arrival in August of a new apprentice to train, may have prompted Samuel's agreement with Mason. Contract work by individual shoemakers like Cate and Mason, far from threatening competition, allowed Lane to increase the output of his shop as demand necessitated, without taking more than a single apprentice.

Local trade for specific customers provided the bulk of Samuel's business. Most of his accounts in the Stratham area were for individual families and consequently quite small. In January 1745 he wrote in his daybook, "I began to Shoe Daniel Thirstons wife by the year."

Few families needed more than one pair of shoes per person yearly. However, there were exceptions. The various branches of the Wiggin family were major customers and the "W" pages of every daybook are full of transactions with members of that family. Between November 10, 1747, and February 20, 1748, Lieutenant Simon Wiggin purchased sixteen pairs of shoes, for which he traded corn. The lieutenant himself, his wife, his daughter Sarah, and his son Simon received two pairs each; Wiggin's other sons, Henry and Thomas, and daughter Molley each received one pair; Ann Gipson, a housemaid who later worked for the Lanes, received one pair, and another Wiggin maid and girl each received two pairs.[143] Wealthy families like the Wiggins, though, were unusual in Stratham.

Local residents usually compensated Samuel for his work through goods and services they provided themselves. A list Samuel made in 1747, itemizing the type and amount of payment he would accept for his work, demonstrates the flexibility necessary in a rural community. "I think I ought to have according to Rule for Making a pair of Shoes wth other mens Lether ⅔ of a Bushel of Corn or 12 lb of Hide or a calfskin or 12 lb of Beaf or 8 lb of Pork or 1½ Hundred of English Hay brot home or a Days work or ⅓ of a cord of wood or 4^{s}-6^{d} in Money."[144]

In addition to producing "bespoke" work on order for specific customers, Samuel experimented in the retail shoe trade. On March 18, 1752, in a fairly typical transaction, he sold James Moore of Chester "3 pair of mens Double Chanel'd Pumps at 15^{s} p[er] pair & 1 Pair of mens Sh- 13/9 & 1 pair womans Sh 10^{s} all is 3+8+9." Fortunately, Samuel did not have to travel to Chester to participate in this out-of-town trade. In September of that year, he noted that three additional pairs of shoes for Moore were to be "left at Folsoms," a tavern in Exeter, partway between Stratham and Chester.[145]

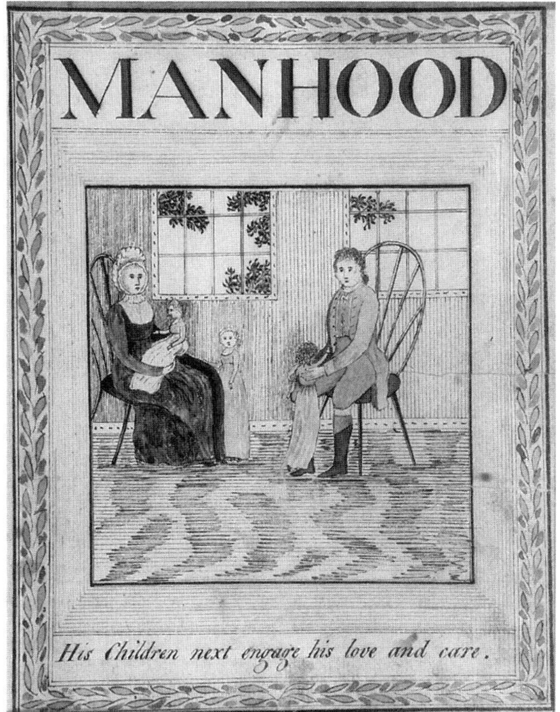
MANHOOD
His Children next engage his love and care.

"His Children next engage his love and care," from child's picture book, done for Freelove Wheeler (1752–1831) by William Colwell (1780–1817), Foster, Rhode Island. *Courtesy Rare Book Department, The Free Library of Philadelphia.*

By 1752, the Lanes had four children and were expecting their fifth. Now well established in Stratham, they began to erect an addition to their house.

An important part of Samuel's retail trade in shoes, however, centered around Portsmouth, and dealings at the Bank appeared increasingly in his accounts. By the end of the 1740s, Samuel traveled to Portsmouth between eight and thirteen times a year, and during the next two decades the frequency of his trips to the seaport nearly doubled. Samuel developed his market for shoes from contacts first made while trading in horsewhips as an apprentice. By 1750 his flourishing shoe business coincided with a new trend toward "ready-made" or "stock" shoes.[146] Despite the high volume of his trade in Portsmouth, however, the majority of his sales were to friends and neighbors in and near Stratham.

By the early 1750s the Lane household had grown considerably. Sarah, born in September 1752, was the fifth child and third daughter. Since 1745 one or another apprentice lived with the family at all times. Providing them with food, drink, and lodging, as promised in their indentures, certainly increased household responsibilities, as did the presence of others living with the family. In 1751, Henry Herring, Stratham's schoolmaster, boarded with the Lanes.[147]

In 1752, doubtless inspired largely by the expected birth of their fifth child, Samuel and Mary decided to enlarge their house. There is little record of the size of the addition. "I think to build my Celler 8 feet Wide 10 Long 11 Deep," he mused but may not have dug a full cellar under the addition.[148] Those dimensions, if in fact the size of the addition, would have added only two rather small rooms to the house. The two-story addition had a bedchamber on the second floor with a garret above and may have included a new or expanded kitchen.

With a growing family of young children, as well as "a Puppie-Dog" which Samuel bought from Mr. Pottle in 1744, there was no lack of household work. Female domestic servants, therefore, found a place at the Lane homestead from time to time. Much of their work was of a general nature, such as the "washing & Scouring" that Huldah Davis did for two days in February 1754. Judith Glanvil's responsibilities in 1750 included "making Gownds 1/6 & cutting 2 pr Jacket & britches 1/3 & one Day washing 1/6 & Making my Britches 1/6, before Making part of Eben^r Jacked 1/3." Another time she spent "2 Days Sowing & making Buttons, & 1 Day Husking."[149]

After a decade of marriage, Samuel and Mary Lane had firmly established their family in Stratham. Samuel's leather work enabled them to acquire land; to build a house, tanyard, and outbuildings; and to furnish their home comfortably. Apprentices and servants were ready and available to assist the family in its daily work. Samuel could now pursue other aspects of his career while Mary focused on the needs of her growing family. The Lanes prospered in rural Stratham. Samuel at age thirty-five was already better off than his father.[150] When, on October 24, 1752, Samuel Lane wrote, "I Set out for Holderness," he was prepared to face a new challenge.

Chapter 2

Shaping Community

While Samuel Lane was establishing himself in the trades of shoemaker and tanner, he also was entering upon a life of service to his community. As a young man, he learned to survey land. With his more general schooling, this provided a combination of skills that he could use not only to measure a parcel of land, but also to divide it among heirs, make a return before the probate judge, and prepare a deed to transfer ownership.

Soon after settling in Stratham, Samuel began assisting his neighbors by plotting land; writing bonds, leases, and deeds; attending to probate matters; and advising on legal and financial questions. Samuel's ability to handle a range of tasks made him the logical person for his neighbors to approach for help in dealing with the complexities of their world. Through this work, Samuel shaped his community and surroundings, both literally in his role as a surveyor and figuratively as a trusted local leader.

The exchange of real estate was of critical importance by the mid-eighteenth century. New townships were developing rapidly and considerable property was changing hands as New Hampshire's population expanded. Samuel's work as a surveyor for the proprietors of new townships, especially for the hotly contested land of Bow, gave him a considerable degree of influence beyond the borders of Stratham. Many important people in New Hampshire government had an interest in the western townships and in Bow in particular. His work for the Bow Proprietors introduced Samuel to men in positions of political power and connected him with the authorities centered in Portsmouth.

Preserved among Samuel's papers is a list of "a Number of Gentlemen of Character that were in Public offices in church and State, in the Province and State of New Hamp^{r} and its Vicinity; of whom I have had some knowledge in their Day; who are now gone the way of all the Earth."[1] The 143 names Samuel recorded included governors, ministers, judges, and other prominent men. That he could draw up such a list is evidence of this rural craftsman's entry into networks of social distinction and political power. Samuel Lane's success in provincial society was only a reflection, however, of the authority he had come to command among his Stratham neighbors.

A portion of Samuel Lane's list of "Gentlemen of Character . . . in Public offices . . . of whom I have had some knowledge in their Day." *Lane Family Papers, New Hampshire Historical Society.*

As Samuel Lane attempted to serve his neighborhood and town in ever-increasing ways, his circle of contacts widened. Eventually, he was acquainted with many New Hampshire leaders of his day. Late in life, Samuel Lane made a list of the dignitaries he had known.

I . . . Learn to Cypher and Survey

In 1736, while still apprenticed as a shoemaker, Samuel Lane began to go "to School to Esqr Palmer to Learn to Cypher and Survey Land." A Hampton surveyor, Samuel Palmer was also "an eminent

A memorandum of a Number of Gentlemen of Character that were in Public offices in Church and State in the Province and State of New Hamp^{r} and its Vicinity; of whom I have had some knowledge in their Day; who are now gone the way of all the Earth —— S. Lane

Lieu^{t} Govr Jno Wentworth
Govr Burnet.
Govr Belcher
Lieu^{t} Govr Dunbar.
Govr Benning Wentworth
Govr Bartlet.

President Weare
President Sullivan

Ministers.
Theo^{s} Cotton
Dr Sewal } Boston
mr Cooper
Dr Elliot
mr Cushing } Salsb
mr Parsons
mr Gookin
mr Gookin Ju^{r}
mr Wingate
mr Tuck
mr Emerson
mr Fitch
mr Shurtleff

mr Jno Cotton
mr Josiah Cotton
mr Ward Cotton
mr Page
mr Saml Webster
mr Whittemore
mr Ben-Parker
mr Tuck Epsom
mr March
mr Lovel
mr Fletcher
mr Edwards
mr Sterns
mr Morril
mr Parsons Rye

Dr Tucker
mr Thayer
mr Elvins
mr Worcester
mr Tappan Kingst^{n}
mr True
mr Brown Portsm
mr Stevens Bosc^{n}
mr Pike
mr Hugh Adams
mr Davidson
mr Nat^{l} Rogers
Dr Appleton

John Phillips of Exeter, oil portrait by Joseph Steward, 1794–1796. *Commissioned by the Trustees of Dartmouth College, Hanover, New Hampshire. Courtesy Hood Museum of Art, Dartmouth College, Hanover, New Hampshire.*

The founder of Phillips Exeter Academy is one of those on the list of men Samuel Lane was proud to have known. While the two were probably associated in more official ways, it is possible that John Phillips relied on Samuel Lane to measure his foot and fit his shoes as well.

teacher of Surveying and Navigation."[2] In preparing himself for this line of work, Samuel Lane was apparently again following his father's lead. While measuring some land in 1754, he noted, "Father also Mesur[d] for [Anthony] Pevy & Theo. Rundlet."[3] Samuel's exposure to mathematics at the town school and his facility in "cast[ing] accountes" helped qualify him for this work.

With real estate so clearly a foundation of colonial wealth, surveying was becoming "an art that all mankind . . . cannot live peaceably without."[4] Moreover, changes in the English land system during the previous century, particularly enclosure and the "great rebuilding" of rural England, necessitated more accurate methods of land measurement and piqued a broad interest in surveying throughout the English world.[5] Across the ocean in New England, the pressure of a growing population was increasing land values, forcing settlement further inland, and making accurate surveys a high priority.

Tangible evidence of the critical nature of surveying in the colonies appeared with the publication in 1688 of *Geodaesia; or The*

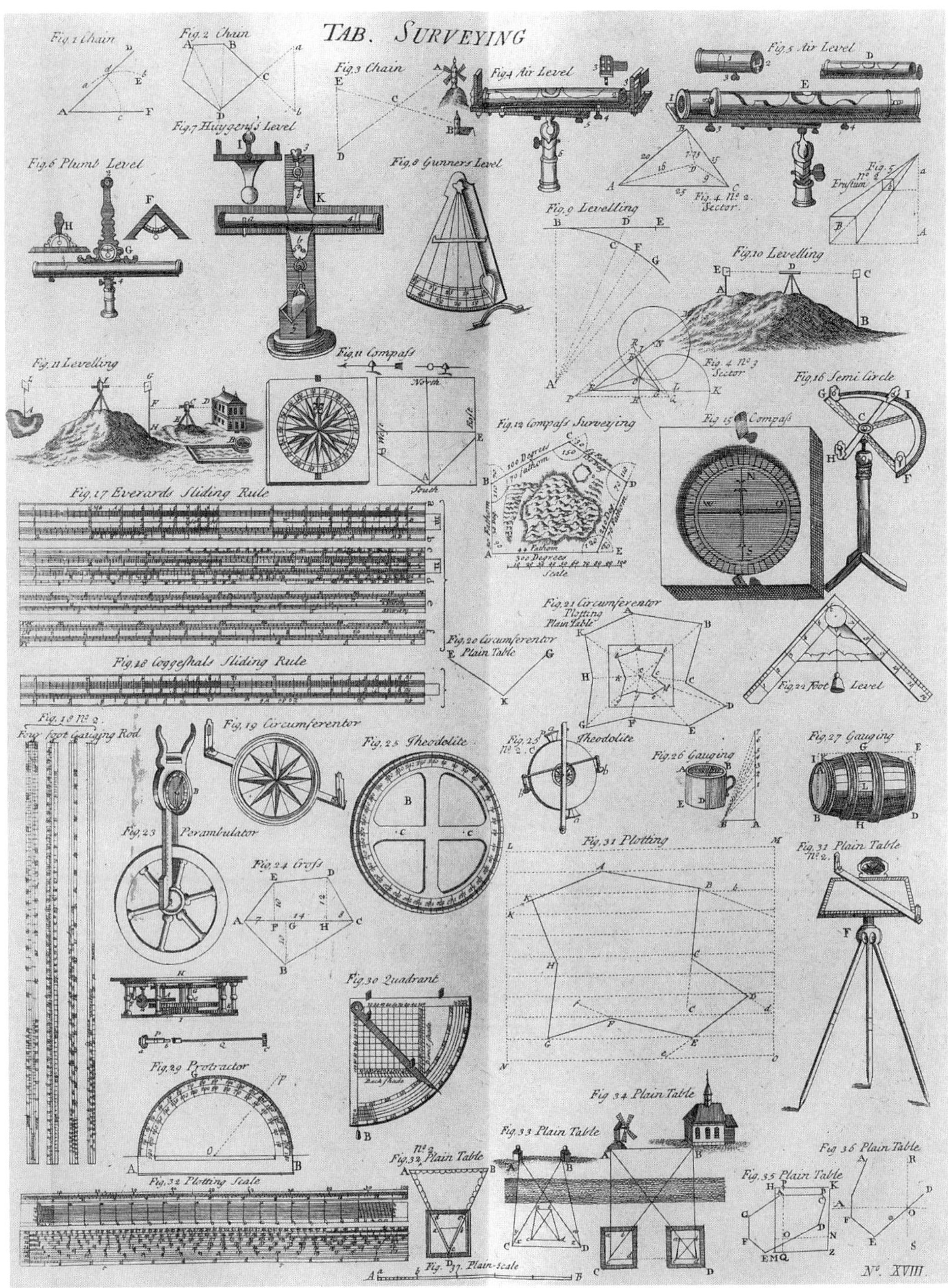

Surveying, from E. Chambers, *Cyclopaedia; or, An Universal Dictionary of Arts and Sciences*, London, 1738. *Courtesy, The Winterthur Library: Printed Book and Periodical Collection.*

While apprenticed as a shoemaker, Samuel Lane undertook to study the "art and mystery" of surveying as well. This occupation, of critical importance in the European settlement of North America, involved a wide range of field and desk work.

Art of Surveying and Measuring Land Made Easie by John Love. Based on the author's experiences in North Carolina and Jamaica, "this was the first work directed specifically to young American surveyors."[6] With little or no prior knowledge of the American "wilderness" on which to base accurate plans, a surveyor's judgment and skill alone often provided the only guarantee of accuracy. The demand for skilled surveyors increased over the eighteenth century.

Striking parallels between Love's printed directions and Samuel's surviving plans suggest that Palmer likely taught Samuel according to Love's methods. Unlike his predecessors, Love offered practical advice on how to measure in the field. More significantly, *Geodaesia* was the first text "to consider the surveying of land in America where the conditions under which the field work was conducted differed from those in England."[7] Samuel owned his own copy of this influential text; acquired May 25, 1745, it is number 40 on a list he kept of his growing library.[8]

Samuel Lane's compass, made by Joseph Halsy, Boston, 1747. *New Hampshire Historical Society.*

To obtain precise surveying tools, Samuel Lane looked to the mathematical instrument makers of Boston. Two of the three compasses he owned were made by Joseph Halsy and Thomas Greenough of that city. Samuel Lane replaced his Halsy compass in 1754, after it had been damaged and a blacksmith had attempted an apparently unsuccessful repair.

Surveying a plot of land involved taking measurements in the field, plotting those measurements on paper, and finding or casting up the area.[9] Measuring angles and distances in the field presented the greatest risk of error to the surveyor. Love's recommended instrument for measuring angles in wooded areas, as well as for large tracts such as were found commonly in America, was the circumferentor, or compass.[10] This instrument had a vernier and a sighting bar with which to measure angles relative to a magnetized needle. With few known points of reference on the ground in unsettled areas, magnetic north provided the only control.

Samuel purchased his surveying equipment from mathematical instrument makers in Boston. A surviving compass, inscribed with Samuel's initials and the date 1747, represents the craftmanship of Joseph Halsy. It apparently replaced one Samuel noted as having lost in January 1746 while "measuring Parsons[s] land."[11] The wooden Halsy compass has a colored compass card measuring 180 degrees from north in either direction, wooden sights, and a three-legged stand.[12]

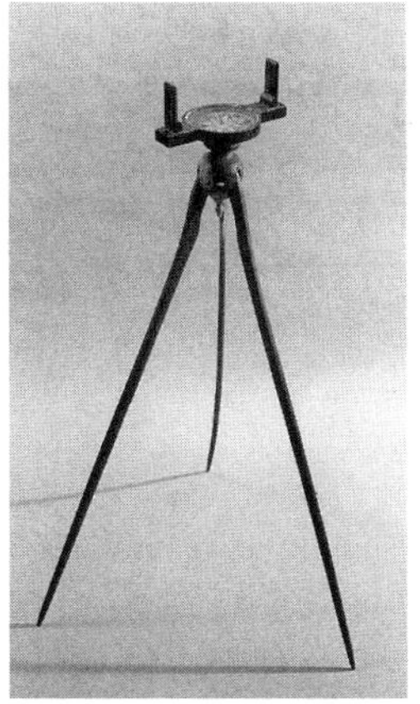

Lane's Halsy compass, mounted on his tripod. *New Hampshire Historical Society.*

Surveyors typically employed tripods to level and steady their compasses. In 1739 joiner Samuel Lane of Hampton Falls made what his nephew and namesake termed "legs for my compos."

Boston in the eighteenth century boasted several instrument makers. Stephen Greenleaf of Queen Street advertised in 1745 that he made and mended "all Sorts of Mathematical Instruments, as Theodolites, Spirit Levels, Semi Circles, Circumferences, and Protractors, Horizontal and Equinoctial Sun Dials, Azimuth and Amplitude Compasses, Eliptical and triangular Compasses and all sorts of common Compasses, drawing Pens and Partagarions, Pensil Cases, and Parallel Rulers, Squares and Bevils, . . . with sundry other articles too tedious to mention."[13]

When Samuel's Halsy compass was damaged accidentally in 1749, Stratham blacksmith Nathan Hoag mended it.[14] Perhaps as a result of this mishap, Samuel looked for a replacement but "was for a long time troubled about getting a Compass to suit him." Finally, he purchased a new one from Thomas Greenough, also a Boston maker. Samuel's grandson Ebenezer recalled that his grandfather once read him a letter stating that his new compass "was as good . . . as could be made in New-England." The degrees of its vernier were cut "very accurately" in brass, and Samuel's name and the date, 1754, were inscribed on the instrument.[15]

Samuel presumably visited Greenough's shop on his four-day trip to Boston in September 1753. The following September he began to send shoes to Greenough; on September 1 he debited the instrument maker's account with "3 pair of Pumps Sent by Mr Coker." Greenough sent word that the price of a compass was £12.10.00. Samuel delivered shoes via Coker two more times, and finally, on October 24, took ownership of the compass, which he used for the rest of his career.[16]

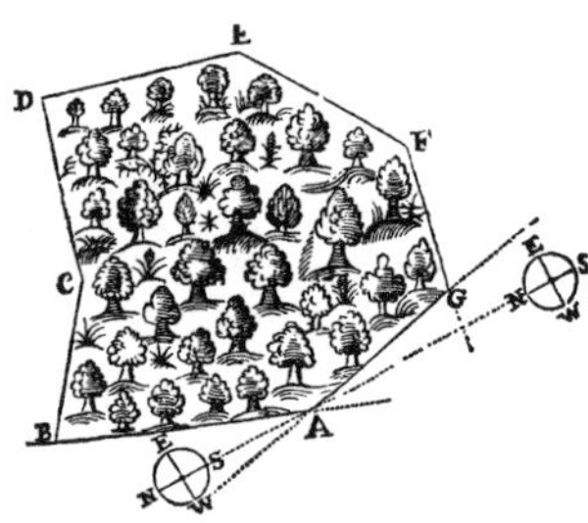

"How to take the Plot of a large Field or Wood, by measuring round the same, and taking Observations at every Angle thereof by the Semicircle," from John Love, *Geodaesia; or, The Art of Surveying and Measuring of Land Made Easy*, London, 7th ed., 1760. *New Hampshire Historical Society.*

Samuel Lane apparently learned surveying according to the methods of John Love. In 1745 he purchased a copy of the English surveyor's influential book. Love, as a result of his own surveying experience in America, published timely advice on how to measure land that, unlike European land, was still largely forested.

In *Geodaesia*, Love offered several methods for determining the angles of a tract. He contended that the most accurate method was measuring from a point within the parcel to each corner, a method feasible only if the land was clear in all directions. New England surveyors had fewer opportunities to employ this method than did Europeans. Cleared areas, existing mainly in settled communities, represented a small proportion of the land measured during the eighteenth century.

Most surveys instead required taking the measurements of the angle from each corner. Love described this procedure as taking "the plot of a large field or wood, by measuring round the same, and taking observations at every angle thereof by the semicircle."[17] This method was not without its problems in the American context, as it required a clear line of sight around the lot's perimeter. However, as boundaries needed to be noted and marked in any event, clearing along the perimeter lines made more sense than clearing lines of sight from a central point.

While in the field, a surveyor not only recorded angles but also measured distances—from the central point to each corner in the first case and around the perimeter in the second. An iron measuring device known as a Gunter's chain was expressly designed for this purpose. The chain consisted of one hundred 7.92-inch links, making the total length of a chain 66 feet. The chain had a handle at each end, to make it easier for two men to pull it straight, and often contained swivel links to prevent kinks from forming. The surveyor compensated for "swag" or sag in the chain by deliberately inflating his measurements. A surveyor's reputation was built on such judgments. Over irregular terrain, as much as one chain per mile might be added as compensation for swag.[18]

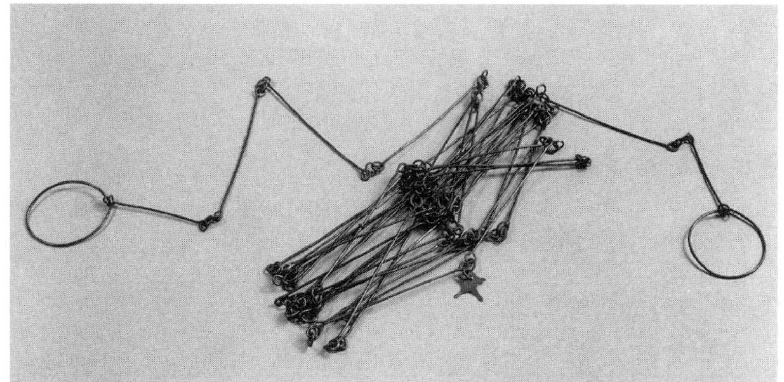

Surveyor's chain owned and used by Samuel Lane. *New Hampshire Historical Society.*

Each link of a surveyor's chain was 7.92 inches long. Helpers known as chainmen, holding handles at each end, stretched the so-called Gunter's chain across the distance to be measured. The surveyor had to compensate in his calculations for the heavy chain's unavoidable sag.

Coordination of the chainmen was the surveyor's responsibility. There were thirty men in the Massachusetts group that surveyed Penacook in 1723; for a surveying trip to Bow in 1748, Samuel hired eight chainmen.[19] In describing the art of surveying, Love cautioned, "Take care that they who carry the chain deviate not from a strait line; which you may do by standing at your instrument, and looking through the sights." Love's seemingly straightforward advice, however, may not have been easy to follow with a large group in a wooded area.[20]

The length of the Gunter's chain was a disadvantage in dense undergrowth, as the links caught in brambles, making it difficult to pull horizontal. Love noted that the chain was too long for use in some terrain, "especially in America," and advised surveyors to use a half or quarter chain instead.[21] Surveyors sometimes found to their dismay that less cumbersome substitutes for the chain, such as hemp rope, which was less apt to become entangled in the undergrowth, proved unacceptable. The hemp shrank and stretched as weather conditions changed, jeopardizing the accuracy of the measurements.[22]

Chains, moreover, were liable to become damaged during the course of a survey. Pulling them tightly through thick undergrowth sometimes caused links to open. Samuel noted in 1750 that his chain had been "cut off," probably from being hacked with an ax as chainmen cleared the undergrowth.[23] Over the years, he recorded buying at least two chains. The one he purchased from John Coker in 1752 probably came from Boston; by 1760, Samuel had enough confidence in a local smith, Nathan Hoag, to commission him to make a new chain. Hoag also mended Samuel's chain whenever required.[24]

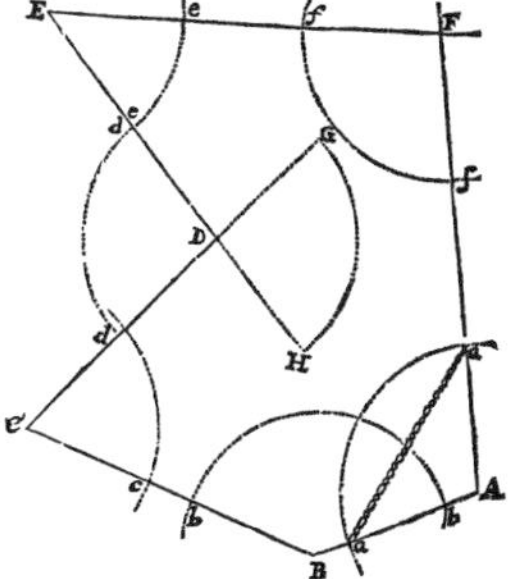

"How by the Chain only to survey a Field by going round the same," from Love's *Art of Surveying. New Hampshire Historical Society.*

A surveyor had to be skilled in the principles of mathematics. Samuel Lane's teacher, Hampton surveyor Samuel Palmer, taught his students both ciphering and surveying.

The units of measure Samuel employed were standard: angle measure in degrees and linear measure in rods.[25] One rod was a quarter chain, or 16½ feet. Samuel's plots and worksheets always note mea-

A TABLE of SQUARE MEASURE.

	Inch.	Links.	Feet.	Yards.	Pace.	Perch.	Chain	Acre	Mile	
Inch	1									
Links	62.726	1								
Feet	144	2.295	1							
Yards	1296	20.755	9	1						
Pace	3600	57.381	25	2.778	1					
Perch	39204	625	272.25	30.25	10.89	1				
Chain	627264	10000	4356	484	174.24	16	1			
Acre	6272640	100000	43560	4840	1742.4	160	10	1		
Mile	4014489600	64000000	27878400	3097600	1115136	102400	6400	646	1	Mile.

"A Table of Square Measure," from Love's *Art of Surveying*. *New Hampshire Historical Society.*

To a surveyor, a chain is a unit of measure, comparable to the ones in more general use. A chain contains four rods (called perches in this table). Ten square chains equal an acre.

surements in rods or fractions thereof. The rod and chain are also units of square measure: 1 acre equals 160 square rods or 10 square chains.[26]

Before Samuel's time, New England surveyors had relied on the eight principal compass points, without attempting more precise degree measure. Landscape features marked boundaries on early surveys, which were rarely drawn to scale.[27] Continued subdivision of the land, as well as alterations accompanying changes in its use, demanded more accurate surveys of the type Samuel produced.

According to Love, a surveyor should "always have in readiness in the field a little book, in which fairly to insert your angles and lines"; Samuel did just that. In a "Pokitbook" that he carried in the field from 1742 to 1749, he headed each page with a description of the parcel being measured: "Land Joseph Hoit bought of Daniel Foulsom Measur^{d} Jan 6.1746/7. p[er] S.Lane."[28] He then described the lot boundaries, through a rather cryptic series of angles and distances, as well as any distinguishing features of the parcel that he felt were worth noting. Lane was clearly following Love's recommended procedure. Love's work played an important role in standardizing practice in his profession; he once pointed out himself that "there are scarce two surveyors in England, that have exactly the same method for their field notes."[29]

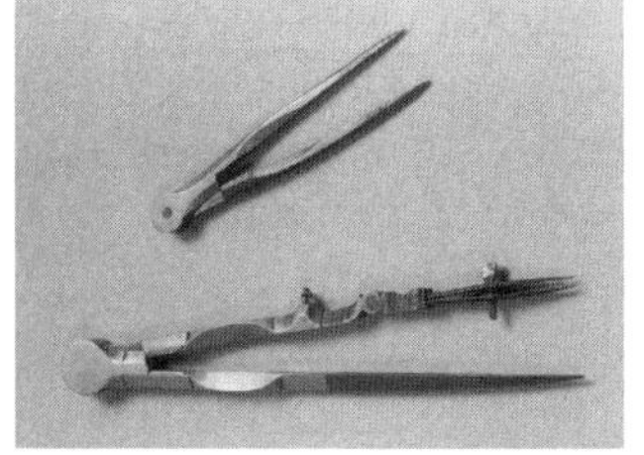

Samuel Lane's brass dividers. *New Hampshire Historical Society.*

After measuring the property, using heavy chain and compass, Samuel Lane next worked with fine imported drafting instruments to plot the land on paper.

On January 6, 1747, Samuel measured a twenty-five acre tract straddling the boundary between Exeter and Stratham, which Daniel Foulsom was selling to Joseph Hoit.[30] Aside from any wooded or overgrown portions to contend with, the "verry cold freezing weather," Samuel noted, made the job difficult. The land to be surveyed, moreover, had been buried two days earlier under "a cold Driving Storm of Snow verry Deep."[31]

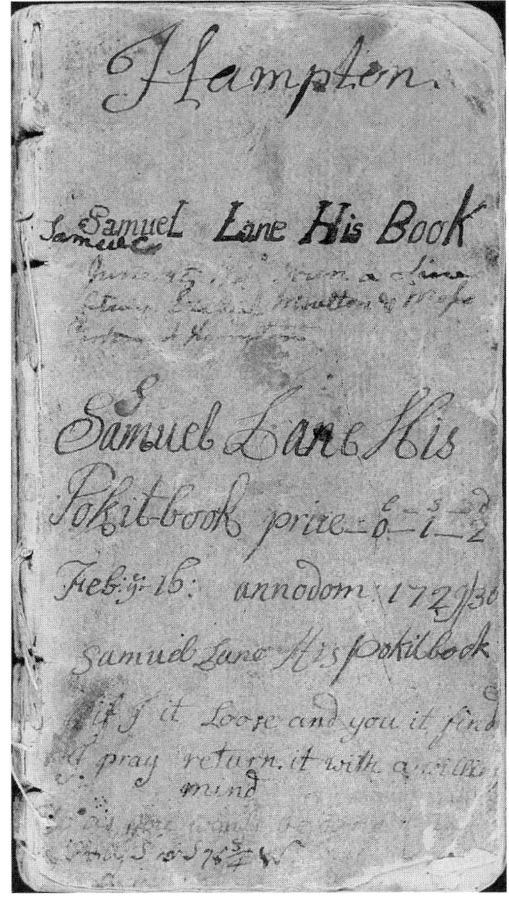

Hampton

Samuel Lane His Book

Samuel Lane His
Pokitbook price – 0 – 1 – 2
Feb ye 16: annodom 1729/30
Samuel Lane His pokitbook
if I it Loose and you it find
I pray return it with a willing
mind

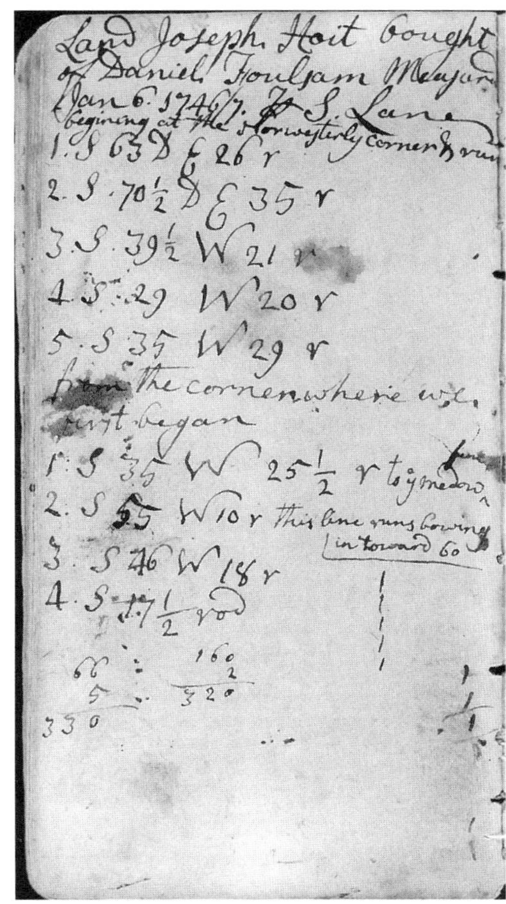

Land Joseph Hoit bought
of Daniel Foulsam Measured
Jan 6. 1746/7. by S. Lane
begining at the Norwesterly corner & run
1. S 63 D E 26 r
2. S 70½ D E 35 r
3. S 39½ W 21 r
4. S 29 W 20 r
5. S 35 W 29 r
from the corner where we
first began
1. S 35 W 25½ r to ye medow
2. S 55 W 10 r this line runs bowing in toward 60
3. S 46 W 18 r

(*left*) Cover of Samuel Lane's pocketbook (or field book). *Courtesy New Hampshire Division of Records Management and Archives.*

Following John Love's specific recommendation, Samuel Lane kept a special book that he carried with him on surveys in which to record his field notes.

Field notes from Lane's pocketbook for measuring parcel sold by Daniel Foulsom to Joseph Hoit, 1747. *Courtesy New Hampshire Division of Records Management and Archives.*

Working in deep snow on a cold January day, Samuel Lane measured land for Joseph Hoit. According to his usual practice, he recorded in his pocketbook the compass bearings in degrees ("D") at each corner of the property, followed by the distance in rods ("r") to the next corner.

After a frigid spell in the field, noting and taking measurements, Samuel surely welcomed the indoor task of plotting and calculating the lot's area. Unlike Bedford diarist Matthew Patten, also a surveyor, Samuel rarely noted exactly when he completed the desk work associated with each surveying assignment. To calculate area, it was first necessary to draw an accurate plan. Samuel oriented his plans to the north, according to the compass bearings taken in the field, and drew them to scale; the Hoit-Foulsom plan had a scale of fifteen rods to the inch.

Samuel's plan for this survey shows the lot bounded by dotted lines. While in the field, he had recorded measurements at eight of the eleven corners, beginning at the northwest. He obtained angle measurements by sighting along the compass from north to south. His first field note, "S 63D E 26r," indicates that the first section of the northern boundary lay sixty-three degrees east of south and ran for twenty-six rods. He proceeded around the easterly side of the land, taking measurements at each of the five corners, then returned to his starting point; he then went around the westerly boundary measuring from its four vertices.

The puzzling aspect of Samuel's field notes, in this case, is that his measurements do not close completely around the lot. There is no description of the southern boundary in the notes, yet it does appear on the final plan. Without those measurements, how did he arrive at the length of the final two sides? The deed for the property provides the answer to this mystery. Daniel Foulsom had agreed to sell Hoit twenty-five acres, which was to be divided from his "home Place" and which lay north of the land Foulsom would retain. The deed specified that the lot was "to Begin at the Northerly End of the

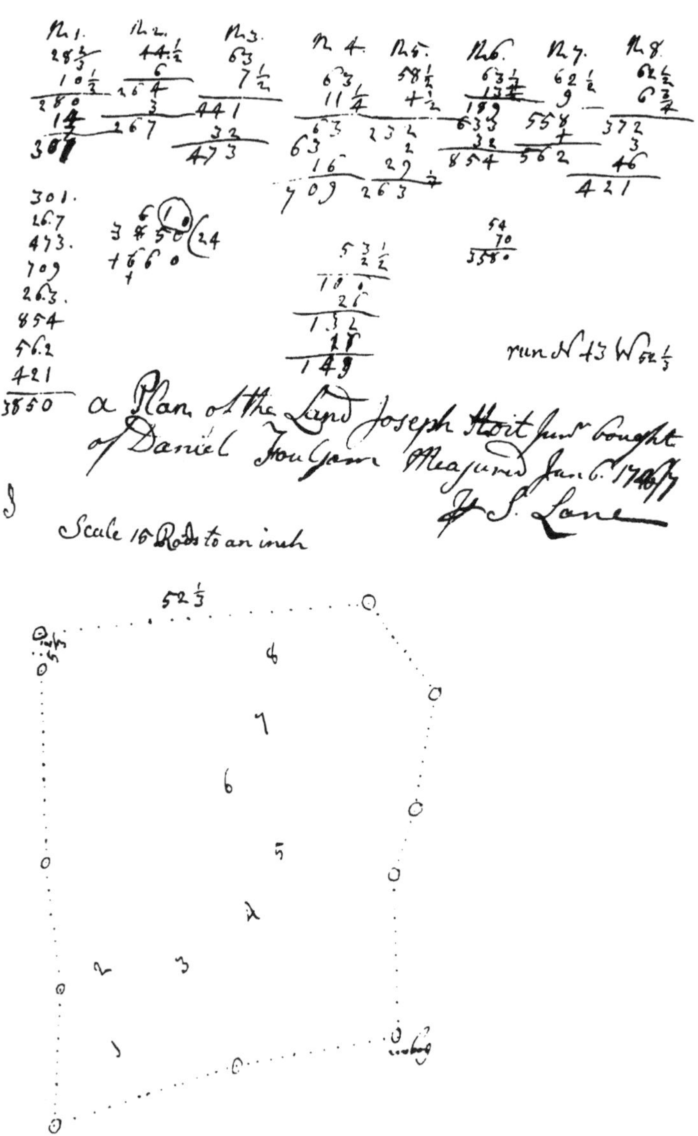

Hoit-Foulsom survey, January 6, 1747. *Courtesy New Hampshire Division of Records Management and Archives.*

Using the angles and distances he had recorded in his field book, Samuel Lane was able to calculate accurately, in the warmth of his home, the acreage being sold, as well as to draw a plan of the lot to scale.

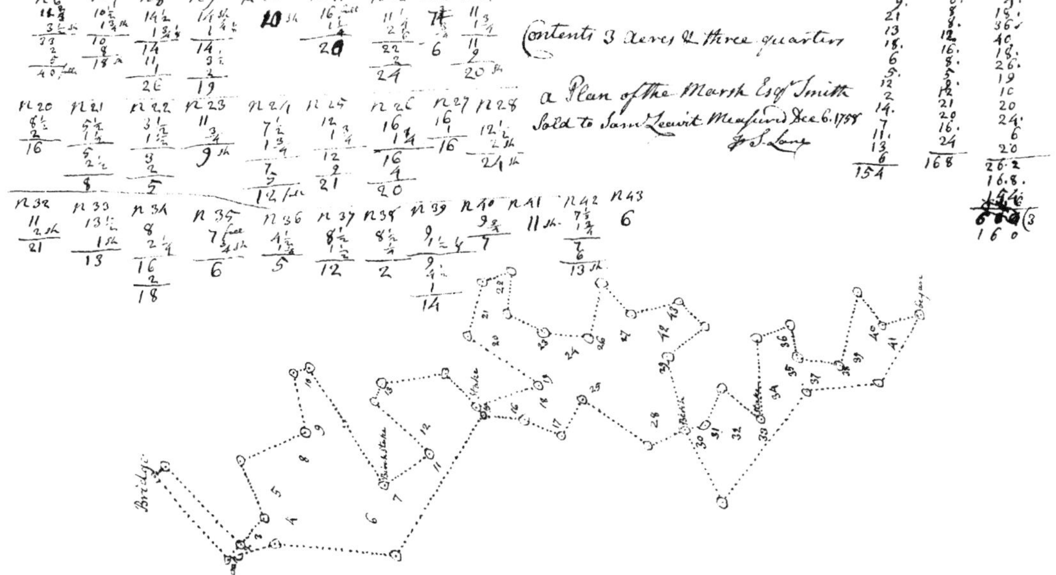

"A Plan of the Marsh Esqr. Smith Sold to Saml Leavit Measured Dec. 6. 1758" by Samuel Lane. *Courtesy New Hampshire Division of Records Management and Archives.*

Samuel Lane devoted much time to laying out the fields, roads, and townships of inland New Hampshire. This survey of a marsh suggests just how complex and painstaking surveying could be.

home Place where I Now Live and So to Extend Southerly into the Lott Carrying the whole Breadth Thereof untill the full Measure of Twenty five acres be Fully Compleated."[32] With the north, west, and east boundaries already established by abutting properties, only the southern boundary remained to be determined. Samuel surveyed what he estimated to be about twenty-five acres, then ran the eastern boundary in the same southerly direction until the piece comprised twenty-five acres. He needed no angle measurements for those corners, only distances, so that he could calculate the area necessary to fill out the lot.

The eight numbers that appear on the plan, inside the dotted boundary line, represent the triangles into which Samuel divided this irregularly shaped parcel to "cast up" the area. Each circled corner represents the vertex of one or more triangles. English surveying texts typically used this method, though Love also demonstrated how trapezoids, circles, and regular polygons could be used as well to compute area.[33] Triangle "No. 1" in Samuel's plan had a base of 20⅔ and an altitude of 28⅔ rods. Using a formula (area equals one-half base times altitude), he arrived at an area of 301 square rods for triangle 1. His computations for eight triangles appear at the top of the sheet. Those eight triangles contain sides he measured in the field and total 3,850 square rods, or just over 24 acres. His calculation, near the center of the second row, shows him juggling the southern boundary to arrive at the last 150 rods to make 25 acres. With an accurate plan drawn to scale, there was no need to return to the field to check his measurements. From the relative warmth of his home, he could determine the southern boundary's bearing and distance, which he then noted on the plan (at the right): "run N 43 w 52⅓."

Whether Samuel was surveying relatively small, cleared seacoast lots such as Foulsom's, or laying out townships in the forests of the eastern frontier as a "Surveyor of Land," his surveys qualified as legal documents, and were the only descriptions available to provincial authorities.[34] Clear land titles and accurate surveys were critical to the orderly development of the province, especially in the vast unsettled interior regions. With good reason indeed, John Love considered a surveyor like Samuel one of society's peacekeepers. Coincidentally, Samuel Lane was honing other skills of a legal nature that complemented surveying and strengthened his service to his community.

Made Hoags & Bordmans writing

The lessons Samuel Lane began at age five in Hampton's school were no abstract exercises but the foundation for an entire aspect of his life's work. Combined with the more specialized ciphering and surveying skills he acquired from Samuel Palmer, his schooling provided a practical basis for contributions quite distinct from his primary business of leatherwork.

Samuel became, in fact, the rural counterpart of Mr. Brown Tymms of Newbury Street, Boston, who in 1718 advertised his bookkeeping services: "keeps Merchants & Shopkeepers Books, also writes Bills, Bonds, Leases, Licences, . . . &c. for any Person that may have Occasion, at reasonable Rates."[35] Life in rural New Hampshire presented Samuel with few opportunities to keep accounts for commercial establishments. However, his own accounts show that he frequently wrote deeds, leases, bonds, and advertisements, on behalf of fellow townspeople.

In his youth, Samuel was already writing for his less literate Hampton neighbors. His 1737 daybook contains a draft of the following advertisement: "Lost between Dr Sargents house in Hamp^{tn} and John Jannens^{s} house in Rye a Saddle with the housen & malepilion: If any person hath taken up the S^{d} Saddle & furniture or can give any inteligence of the same to s^{d} John Jannens Senr they shall be well satisfied Jan 28 1737/8."[36] As New Hampshire did not have its own newspaper until 1756, such an advertisement must have been either placed in a Boston newspaper or posted locally, probably in the local tavern.

Not long after Samuel moved to Stratham, his new neighbors there began to recognize his writing skills and to exploit his ability.

Ebenezer Love

Takes this Method to inform his Friends and the Country in general, that he drafts all kinds of Inftruments, viz. Bills, Bonds, Indentures, all kinds of *Conveyancing*, and other Writings, at his Houfe in Portfmouth. He likewife takes Care of Tradefmens and others Books, Accompts, &c. or will wait on any Gentleman at their Houfe at feafonable Hours on *very reafonable Terms*, and with the greateft Care, Secrecy, Fidelity and Difpatch.

Advertisement of Ebenezer Love, *New Hampshire Gazette*, July 20, 1770. *New Hampshire Historical Society.*

Like Portsmouth's Ebenezer Love, Samuel Lane performed many of the services of a bookkeeper. As far as is known, he never advertised his writing and figuring skills but did this type of work primarily for his neighbors, who knew of his abilities.

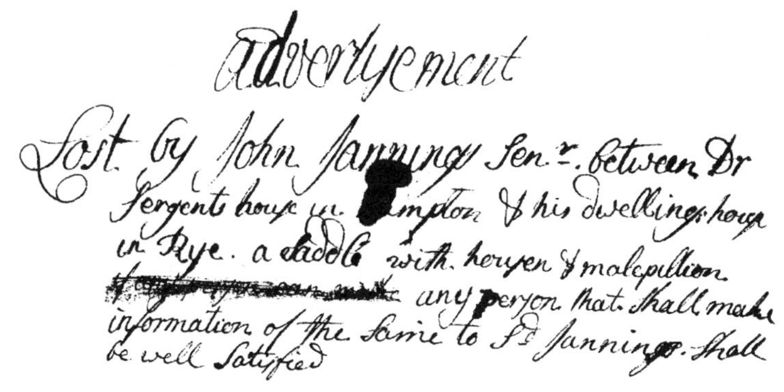

Advertyement
Lost by John Jannings Sen.r Between Dr
Sergents house in [illegible]mpton & his dwelling house
in Rye. a Saddle with houzen & malepillion
[illegible] any person that Shall make
information of the Same to Sd Jannings. Shall
be well Satisfied

Advertisement for a lost saddle, from Samuel Lane's 1737 daybook. *Lane Family Papers, New Hampshire Historical Society.*

Samuel Lane was still an apprentice when he drafted this advertisement for a Rye resident who had lost his saddle.

The amount of "writing" work Samuel undertook increased over the next decades.[37] His daybooks, however, document neither all the writing nor all the surveying he did. Perhaps he maintained separate accounts for this work that have been lost. Sometimes the exact nature of the work Samuel performed is not specified, as when on May 30, 1743, he charged John Barker "for writing." However, over time, Samuel began to detail such entries more specifically.

As Stratham residents gained confidence in Samuel's abilities, the tasks they assigned him increased in difficulty. From simple deeds and bonds, he soon was drafting counter-bonds and double deeds. The first mention in his daybooks of drafting a will is May 5, 1753. A year later his involvement in probate matters had expanded "To writing a Bond & Measuring & Prizing Jms Leavits Estate . . . also writing 4 Adver^{ts} 16^{s}/."[38] Probate activity had few bounds; Samuel even acted as undertaker at times, "going to the Bank for funeral things" and nailing shut a coffin.[39]

Strictly defined, "bookkeeping," as noted in the Boston advertisement shown above, was not a major component of Samuel's work, although in 1776 he did prepare an "Alphabett" as an index for Thomas Moore's account book.

Samuel sometimes acted as a banker. In 1755 he wrote a deed from John Veasey to John Stockbridge and the following day went to Hampton on behalf of Stockbridge "to hire Money," presumably funds to pay for the land. In June 1761, Samuel spent a day in Portsmouth procuring a marriage license for his neighbor, Joseph Mason. The license cost six pounds, and Samuel's expenses added another. The variety of this type of work was endless. Samuel made forty-eight copies of an unspecified document for Nathan Hoag at threepence each in February 1756 and copied more for Hoag the following year.[40]

Samuel's work involved him with lawyers, an elite group in provincial New Hampshire.[41] Samuel Pevy paid him six pounds to

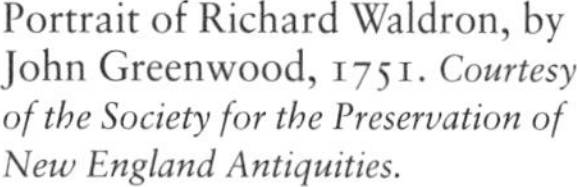

Portrait of Richard Waldron, by John Greenwood, 1751. *Courtesy of the Society for the Preservation of New England Antiquities.*

Samuel Lane helped neighbors with probate and other legal matters. Before long, he was well known in Portsmouth courts. Among the lawyers and judges on Lane's list of "men of character" he had known was Richard Waldron, who appears here with the books and documents of his profession.

go to the Bank to pay lawyer Wyseman Clagett; Lane's diary noted his going to "pay Pevys Debt."[42] He began an account in 1755 with the register of deeds, Daniel Peirce. Between March and June in 1756, Samuel gave Peirce seven deeds to record.[43]

The roughness of signatures on Stratham petitions and deeds suggests that some residents possessed only a signature literacy, or at best a lack of confidence in their writing abilities. Thus, Samuel's skills proved in great demand. Samuel was a justice of the peace for only a brief period in the 1760s so did most such work as a private citizen rather than as a public official.

Samuel's probate work perhaps best illustrates his wide range of expertise. His surveying and trading experience proved invaluable in qualifying him to appraise both personal effects and real estate. As a consequence, Samuel's signature appears often in probate documents relating to residents of Stratham and nearby towns.[44] This work often placed him as well in a position to dispose of unwanted

Ford Merril and Betty Merril
both of Stratham Intend Marriage.
Feb 25. S. Lane J C

Marriage intention of Ford and Betty Merril, written by Samuel Lane. *Courtesy New Hampshire Division of Records Management and Archives.*

Samuel Lane served only briefly in an official capacity as justice of the peace, but his daybooks show that he was constantly writing deeds, wills, and other such documents for Stratham residents.

property, and he sometimes acted as vendue master, or auctioneer, for such sales.

When a New Hampshire resident died without leaving a will, the law prescribed how the estate was to be divided. The widow received one-third of the deceased's personal estate "for ever," as well as a life interest in one-third of all the real property; this was the widow's dower, or thirds. The executor had thirty days to assign the thirds after it was demanded. The "residue" was then equally divided among the children, except for the eldest son, who usually received a double share.[45]

If, on the other hand, a person died testate, the will had to be validated, or proved, and recorded by the judge of probate within thirty days. If the estate qualified as solvent, dividing it could proceed quite quickly. However, if creditors' claims proved numerous, it could take years for an estate to be settled. Even after a widow's thirds were set off, her husband's estate remained unresolved until she too died. John Stockbridge died intestate on February 19, 1782, and soon after, Samuel divided the estate among his widow and children; three years later, Samuel still was working for the estate, distributing the thirds among the children after the widow Stockbridge died.[46]

Samuel's work in probating Satchel Clark's estate demonstrates the delicate role he was sometimes called on to play in such matters. Neighbor Clark died intestate on November 4, 1773, leaving seven heirs: his wife, a son, and five daughters. In early December, a *New Hampshire Gazette* advertisement, placed by Satchel's son John, the recently appointed administrator, asked creditors to bring in their claims on the estate.[47] Beyond that, it seems that John Clark did little else to settle his father's estate during the year following his death.

Clark's delay in dispersing the estate fell hardest on his mother, who was responsible for the care of her three youngest daughters, all minors. One year after her husband's death, Elizabeth Clark found further delay unacceptable and petitioned the court to recognize "the great Difficulties I am Expos'd to in this Cold Season for want of firewood, with Sundry other Damages I Suffer for want of

To the Hon. John Sherburne Esqr. Judge of the Probate of Wills &c for the County of Rockingham.

The Humble Petition of Elisabeth Clark of Stratham in Said County Widow of Satchel Clark late of Sd. Stratham Deceased hereby Signifying to your Honour the great Difficulties I am Exposed to in this Cold Season for want of firewood, with Sundry other Damages I Suffer for want of my Dower being Set off to me out of the Estate of my Said late Husband — Wherefore I hereby Humbly pray your Honour to order the Same to be done which will greatly oblige your Honours humble Petitioner

Witness
John Stockbridg
John Rundlet

her
Elisabeth 2 Clark
mark

Saml. Lane Esqr
John Stockbridge Senr
John Rundlet
Thomas More Junr
John Taylor

I chuse thes thes men
Gen Samuel Lane
John Stokbrige sener
John Rundlet
Cor thomas more Juner
John Stokbrige Juner

Petition of Elisabeth Clark, 1774. Rockingham County Probate Records. *Courtesy New Hampshire Division of Records Management and Archives.*

Some of those whom Samuel Lane drafted documents for were not literate. When Elisabeth Clark petitioned to receive the widow's one-third share of her husband's estate, she signed the document with a mark.

my Dower being Set off to me out of the Estate of my Said late Husband." The petition is written in Samuel's hand and may well have been submitted on his advice. Elizabeth signified her approval by her mark. Her son countered with a petition of his own, requesting that the length of his bond be extended until the following spring. He explained "there are Sundry very large demands agst S^{d} deceased that if the Stock part of the personal Estate should now be Sold they would not fetch So much money as they would in the next Spring."[48]

New Hampshire law stipulated that "the Division of the Houses and Lands . . . be made by Five sufficient Freeholders upon Oath, or any Three of them, to be appointed and Sworn by the Judge for that end."[49] Elizabeth's petition listed Samuel among the five Stratham men she wanted as her committee.[50] As the next step, the probate judge, John Sherburne, named Samuel "Surveyor and Committee Man."

On December 8, 1774, Samuel began his work. That day he measured Clark's land in Stratham, and the next, a wretched day of rain and snow, he spent indoors drawing plans of the land and dividing it. In frigid weather the following week he traveled to Exeter for two days and measured Clark's thirty-three-acre woodlot to make a provision for the widow. Samuel devoted the next two days to "Set of[f] wid Clarks thirds at home." His settlement provided living quarters for her in the "Mansion House," as well as one-third of her husband's personal estate for her use. On December 27, Samuel drew up "the Return of the Land & Buildings belonging to S^d Thirds &c," and the next morning he went to Portsmouth to file his division of the assets with the judge of probate.[51]

Elizabeth Clark was to have use of over twenty-seven acres in Stratham and eleven acres in the Exeter woodlot. As for her rights in her former home, Samuel reported:

> Likewise we have Sett off to Said Widow, the Westerly End of Said House on Said Home place, as far as the Chimney, from bottom to the top thereof: and the Little Celler under the Easterly End of Said House; and Liberty to Bake in the oven, and Draw Water out of the Well: and to pass and repass to and from Said Celler and oven as She Shall have occasion we have also Sett her off the East Barn on Said place; with Liberty of a yard by the Same; and passing and repassing to and from Said House and Barn, with Teems and otherwise, as occasion Shall Require.[52]

Such an arrangement was not unusual at the time.

Elizabeth's son John received "the Kitchen, and the Closet at the Easterly End thereof, in the Mansion House . . . with a Priviledge in the Well," in addition to half the kitchen cellar and one end of the largest barn. The committee also allotted him the fourteen acres on which the house stood. His youngest sister, Hannah, received the shop "for her part of the Buildings," and two married sisters were granted bedrooms in the house as their share, as well as rights to pass and repass through the rest of the house to get to their rooms. John was required to reserve "Liberty for all the other partners in S^d House and Barn of passing and Repassing to and from their Respective parts of the Same, with other Necessary Priviledges about Said House, Barn and Well."[53] He may well have purchased his sisters' shares in the house to untangle this somewhat complex division.

Guaranteed by law, a widow's right of dower represented the minimum support she might receive from her husband's estate. If he had specifically provided for her in a will, she had the option of accepting his provisions or taking her thirds. Samuel wrote many wills that contained specific provisions for the widow, thus helping others avoid the Clark family's uncomfortable situation.

Only after the widow's thirds were set off could the rest of the

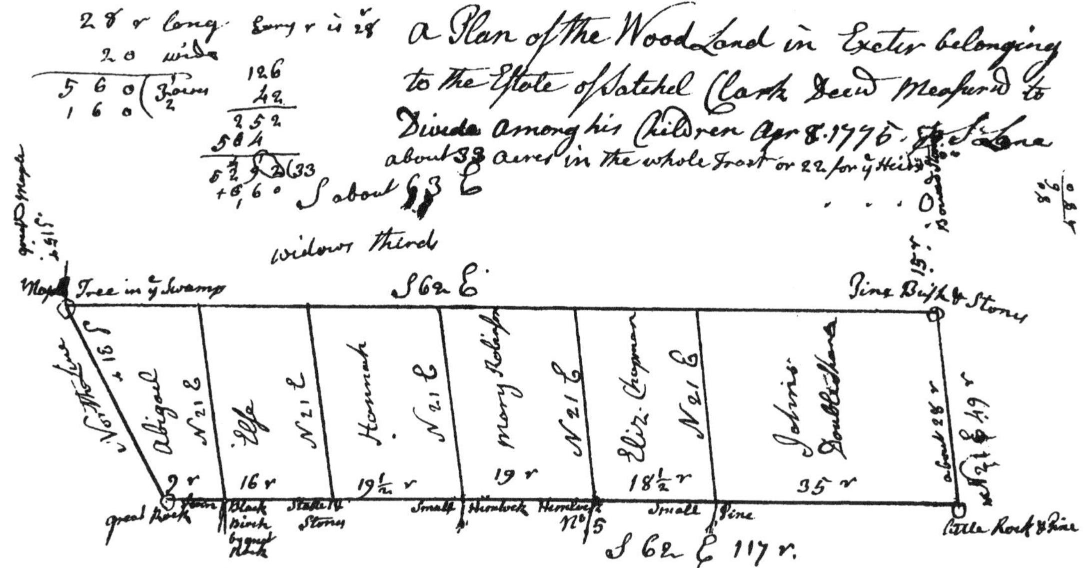

"A Plan of the Wood Land in Exeter, belonging to the Estate of Satchel Clark, Decd., Measured to Divide among his Children," by Samuel Lane, April 8, 1775. Stratham Town Records. *Courtesy New Hampshire Division of Records Management and Archives.*

Because of his multiple talents and resourcefulness, Samuel Lane found himself involved in every aspect of settling an estate, from buying the coffin to dividing the land among the heirs.

estate be divided and distributed among the deceased's children. Samuel did not begin this process for Satchel Clark's estate until the spring of 1775, two years after Clark's death. Samuel spent two days "Measuring & Viewing" Clark's real and personal property in Stratham and another day at Clark's Exeter woodlot, "Dividing the Land there." Samuel had already measured the parcel to set off the widow's dower, so this procedure was simply one of identifying and marking the bounds of each of the six heirs' lots. Two days later, on April 10, 1775, Samuel was "Measuring & Bounding out the Home place into Seven Shares," for eldest son John Clark inherited a double share of his father's estate.

Once Samuel's work in the field was finished, he spent two and one-half days drafting descriptions of each share and writing "a long Return of all the Land and Buildings." Of the five men appointed as a committee to divide the estate, Samuel appears to have done the bulk of the work. On April 13 he went "to Cornet Wiggins by appointment" and waited there for two members of the committee. When they did not appear, he went to Newmarket, presumably to get their signatures on the return he had drafted. Between going to Newmarket and chasing down the other Stratham committeemen, Samuel spent an entire day getting the return signed. The following day, despite cold weather, he went to Portsmouth and presented his findings to the judge of probate.[54]

Less than a week after Samuel wound up the Clark estate, Stratham was abuzz with the news of "the Bloody Battle at Concord." News of the hostilities spread quickly northward; on the day after the battle, Stratham voted to send twenty-five men to Concord. That the townsfolk were nervous is evident in their ready acceptance of reports that British Regulars had burned the towns of Salem and Ipswich. Samuel noted that this "Set people in a terrible fright."[55] Anxiety continued to manifest itself in false reports of British depredations, including the alleged landing of troops at Hampton in May.

This course of events, however disturbing, had little effect on the rhythm of life in Stratham. Samuel was elected a delegate to the Provincial Congress at Exeter. He attended his first session in May, but his life and work changed little otherwise. He appraised the widow Jewet's estate in mid-July and continued regular trips to the Bank to transact business.

Samuel's role in settling estates ranged from surveying land and hearing claims to determining shares and writing deeds. Samuel's combination of surveying and legal skills made him indispensable to his Stratham neighbors, especially since land figured so prominently in eighteenth-century transactions. Certain other parts of the province also boasted an individual like Samuel who combined these several skills.[56] Together, their work was critical to maintaining an orderly and consistent system of property and authority in rural New Hampshire and binding its residents to that system.

Individuals like Samuel made the governmental machinery of New Hampshire work. Stratham's population was largely unschooled in the increasingly sophisticated world where ownership and rights were no longer based on spoken promises but on written documents. Without Samuel's help, many Stratham residents would

Woodcut first appearing as the frontispiece of *The Pleasant and Profitable Companion*, Boston, 1773. *Courtesy, American Antiquarian Society.*

And as it is Customary in all Courts & Societys, to Make Some Generous Grant to any Persons Employed in Such Difficult Intrieguing Business; Therefore Gentlemen, I Rely on your generosity (as The Settlement of the affair has Revolved on you,) to allow me Such a Perquisite as Shall be to The Honour of your Station, to Reward one who Can with a good Conscience Subscribe himself your Careful Laborious Honest Book keeper, as well as Humble Petitioner Saml Lane
Stratham Sept 25·1769.

Portion of a petition from Samuel Lane to Stratham Church leaders, September 25, 1769. Stratham Town Records. *Courtesy New Hampshire Division of Records Management and Archives.*

Samuel Lane once aptly described himself, in a petition relating to town church affairs, as "your Careful Laborious Honest Book keeper."

have been isolated from the very machinery that existed to protect these rights. Furthermore, the dissatisfaction with imperial rule that erupted in 1775 might have surfaced in milder forms at an earlier time had Samuel and others not helped extend the government's ability to serve the public interest.

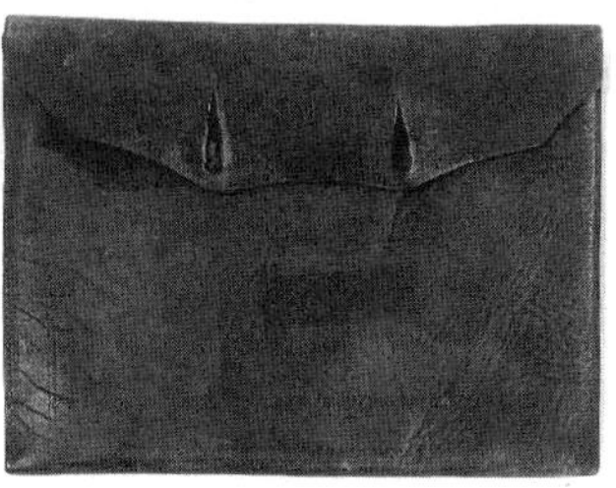

Leather case, marked "Samuel Lanes Paper Case/Stratham Oct 14 1750." *New Hampshire Historical Society.*

Samuel Lane probably made this leather case for carrying documents to and from court in Portsmouth. He also sold printed forms for deeds, bonds, and other agreements and may have carried one of each for ready use.

I Was Chose Tythingman

When evangelist George Whitefield preached at Hampton on October 1, 1740, Samuel Lane was among "some Thousands in the open air" gathered to hear him. Samuel's record of the weather that day, "fresh wind," corroborates the charismatic itinerant's own comment that he preached "not with so much Freedom as usual . . . the wind was almost too high for me." To Whitefield, the impact of his delivery at Hampton proved disappointing, "Some, tho' not many, were affected." It wasn't until Whitefield reached York, Maine, that his words began to rouse his northern New England audience. There, the evangelist "saw the outpourings of the Lord in his Sanctuary."[57]

On the afternoon of October 3, the Rev. Mr. Whitefield was back at Hampton; both the weather and the response to his exhortations contrasted sharply with two days earlier. "Preached to several Thousands of People," he wrote, "with a great deal of Life and Power."[58] Whitefield's short coastal trip brought the revival known as the Great Awakening to northern New England.[59]

Whitefield's journey to New England to raise funds for a Georgia orphanage initiated more than a religious revival. In his wake, the system of communal authority founded on the remnants of the Puritan religion was shaken, and in many places it collapsed. A deeply divided community was a common consequence of the religious revival that Whitefield brought to towns like Stratham. Samuel arrived in town just as "Religeous commotions" were beginning to surface and disrupt the community. The resulting divisions along religious grounds continued in Stratham for nearly thirty years after Whitefield's first New Hampshire sermon.

Town and church were inseparable in colonial New Hampshire; change in one necessitated corresponding change in the other. Towns "were the primary units of political and military organization; they stimulated the founding of religious institutions; they helped promote local economic prosperity; they provided essential social services; and they gave individuals a sense of communal identity."[60]

To carry out such broad responsibilities, the town necessarily drew on locally "recognized pools of leaders."[61] Samuel's success in other areas of work marked him as a potential leader, and Stratham's voters soon called on him to serve the town in various

The Reverend Mr. George Whitefield, mezzotint, London, 1764–1776. *Courtesy, Winterthur Museum.*

On October 1, 1740, Samuel Lane heard the noted English evangelist George Whitefield preach in Hampton. The minister spoke that day outdoors to a large crowd despite high winds. Soon the preacher's charisma had inspired the religious revival that became known as the Great Awakening.

capacities. At different times, he was elected tithingman, pound keeper, town clerk, selectman, auditor, and sealer of leather, as well as deacon (and later elder) of the church. His organizational and writing abilities, his familiarity with provincial officials and procedures, and his evident devotion to the "gospil" made Samuel a person to whom the town would turn often.

By midcentury, church membership no longer was a qualification for holding town office. However, "because churches were a primary meeting place for townsmen in their day-to-day lives, church members were better situated to be active citizens and influential leaders than those outside the churches."[62] Family, wealth, and political connections had less to do with election to town office than willingness and competence.[63] Only ten years after Samuel first arrived in Stratham, the town elected him selectman. He never questioned his role in town affairs, despite attendant hardships. Serving was a duty incumbent on each member of the community.

Playing a leadership role was especially difficult in Stratham during the 1740s and 1750s. A church schism, dividing the town into New Light and Old Light (or revivalist and conservative) factions, affected all town affairs, as well as personal relationships among residents. Samuel maintained communications with those on both sides of the religious debate, and his daybooks list work done for adherents of both views. However, the division itself was very troubling to him, as was the growing secular attitude that eventually followed the decline of the Great Awakening fever.[64] While favoring religious enthusiasm himself, Samuel was no separatist. He supported the old ecclesiastical order while maintaining his own religious fervor.

In March 1744, three years after moving to Stratham, Samuel noted that on "Town Meeting Day. I was chose Tythingman."[65] At that point, Samuel little knew the trouble this position would cause him during the course of the next year. Already, the religious revival sweeping New Hampshire had deeply divided Stratham. A salary dispute had existed for several years between the town and its minister, Henry Rust. When Stratham, at its 1741 town meeting, considered a warrant article "to make an addition to the Revrd m^{r} Rusts Salary as Last year & to give him more if the town sees cause," the town saw no cause and voted no increase.[66] Two years later, the warrant contained more ominous content. Not only were voters asked to consider a salary increase, but the town clerk also noted, "it is Likewise desired by many persons that there might be a commity Chose in Said Town meeting to agree with Sum minister to preach a weekly Lecter." Two weeks later, the meeting approved the article for another minister to serve the town, though this decision was not without opposition. Thirty-two voters registered their dissent, "the two last votes being without Liberty from the Reverend m^{r} Henry Rust and a greavince unto him."[67] Lines between two factions now were drawn.

Several issues were at stake in the church controversy. Perhaps foremost in many minds was the question of Mr. Rust's rights as the settled minister. Rust, ordained in 1718, was Stratham's first minister; his wife, Anna Waldron, was a member of a wealthy and politically connected Portsmouth family. By law, the town had the right to engage more than one minister, although in small towns custom dictated a single clergyman. Rust's loyal parishioners were concerned, furthermore, for the authority he represented. The church was the moral authority and force in the community. To some, division of that authority was tantamount to moral chaos in the community.

The outward manifestations of New Light services, however, may have been what Old Light adherents found most disquieting. The emotional style of the New Light preachers often prompted "bodily effects of conversion—fainting, weeping, shrieking, etc."[68] Samuel first became aware of this novel phenomenon on November 27, 1741, when "People began to cry out, i[n] the Meeting House at the Bank."[69] In Durham, Nicholas Gilman's New Light congregation "made all manner of mouths, turning out their lips . . . as if convulsed, straining their eyeballs and twisting their bodies in all manner of unseemly postures."[70] Those who wished to worship in a more formal manner were at a loss when confronted with the emotional outbursts encouraged by evangelical ministers.

Samuel moved to Stratham just as these controversies were taking shape. As a newcomer, he no doubt felt hesitant to take a strong stand. He was, moreover, of two minds on the issue. All evidence indicates his deep devotion to the church and its teachings. While residing in Hampton, he joined, and perhaps organized, a young men's association with the stated purpose, written in his own hand, "to Glorifie God in the days of our youth: to seek first the kingdom of God and his Righteousness, and to exhort one another dayly."[71]

Samuel clearly supported the religious revival in its early stages. He wrote of "the wonderfull concern on the minds of People of a Spiritual nature in Many places":

> in the latter end of this year [1741] there Seem'd to be an uncommon concern on the Minds of People about their Souls which concern Seem'd to be verry genral almost in every Town in this Province . . . , and I believe I May Say throuout the country about this time. it Seem'd to be genral on all ages & Sexes Black & White, but chiefly on young People. Many in the Meeting-House at once would seem to be Struck down under the preaching of the word crying out what Shall we do to be Saved. also Some Seem'd to be Struck after the Same manner in their own Houses & about their work, & riding the Road & in Divers Manners: Many Seem'd to be under great convictions & in great terrors: Many also Seem'd to be in great transports of Joy. people in genral Seem'd to be verry desirous of hearing the word, & Ministers forward to preach it, and for Some time there was Lecture almost every Day or Night in Many places: & not only publick but private meetings were verry frequent.[72]

However enthusiastic Samuel was at first about the spiritual renewal, he found he could not support the growing animosity between revivalists and the established church. By the beginning of 1743, Samuel, now residing in Stratham, had discovered drawbacks to the wonderful outpouring of spirit that a year earlier he had applauded. His commentary now emphasized the divisions created by the revivals:

> Many People, in some places especially; that a year or two ago, Seem'd greatly concern'd for their Souls, & to have hopeful beginnings; now Seem to run into great extreems on many accounts; especially in exclaiming against Ministers as unconverted, and many will Seperate themselves from their Minister & church, & Set up Seperate Meeting & Meeting-Houses, & get preachers of their own way of thinking, to preach to them. they refuse to come to the Sacrament, or to have their children Baptized by those Ministers they call unconverted. these things and many others cause great Disturbance in Towns, in churches, & in Familys; Ministers & People, Husbands & wives, Parents & children Divided against each other, Judging & condemning oneanother. these Seperate People are cal'd by Many, New-Lights & Scheemers & the like. these & Such like practices cause many people to Stumble at, and be much Set—against what they Some time ago, cal'd a good work.[73]

Samuel had seen enough to set himself apart from the New Lights, but he was no longer an Old Light either. He endorsed the spiritual enthusiasm inspired by the evangelical movement but opposed the division it engendered within congregations.

In 1744, Samuel described Stratham as plagued by "Sad Divisions," resulting from "people Striving to bring in another Man to preach with Mr Rust, which Makes great uneasiness & contention amongst us." The New Light faction had first invited Joseph Adams to preach in December 1742, but his strident attacks on neighboring clergy prompted his arrest for libel. Undeterred by Adams's departure, Stratham's Separates, by 1743 a majority at town meeting, invited a Stratham native, Dudley Leavitt, to preach. Prohibited from using the meetinghouse by the Rev. Mr. Rust, Leavitt preached in Mr. Coker's dwelling, which Samuel reported was "fitted up with the Seats &c for that use."[74]

In the fall of 1744, the Separate faction decided to flex its muscle. "We . . . have agreed with a minister & parpose (God Willing) to carry him into the pulpit in the Meeting house to preach one part of the day." The "agrieved Brethren" then asked Mr. Rust to "forthwith Inform us which part of the Day you will preach." Their warning, "Dont think that we are in Jest," was not idle.[75] On September 30, the Separates carried out their design, which, according to Samuel, resulted in an "unaccountable uproar Made by bringing a man [clearly Leavitt] into the Pulpit to preach half the Day with mr Rust."[76] During the afternoon service, when Rust was "at prayer in the pulpit," Leavitt attacked him, crying out that he "Could as well Joyn with the Devil as with m^{r} Rust in prayer." To ensure that Rust's supporters did not miss the point, he added that he "Could as well

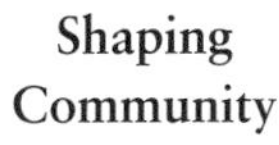

Joyn with the pope in Saying Mass as with . . . Rust in prayer." Dorothy Jewet, a Leavitt supporter, taunted Rust to "Come down" from the pulpit, calling him the "[s]on of the Divel."[77]

Such behavior made the breach between the two factions irrevocable. Rust's ties to the prominent Waldron family doubtless reinforced a complaint his supporters made to the governor. The following Sabbath, the high sheriff, Mr. Packer, removed Leavitt by force from the meetinghouse pulpit. Rust supporters then won a lawsuit against Leavitt, who departed town, only to experience a similar situation in Salem, Massachusetts. Denied access to the meetinghouse there, he was ordained under an apple tree in the fall of 1745.[78]

Samuel's election as tithingman at the 1744 town meeting placed him at the center of this controversy. In New England at this time, the tithingman was responsible for reporting any breaches of the Sabbath laws. Leavitt's entry into the meetinghouse, Samuel later lamented, "was a Damage to Me I being Tything Man that year and obliged to Complain of Such Disorders as was then in Town."[79] In all, he spent thirteen days in Portsmouth at court as a result of

"Town Meeting," line engraving by Elkanah Tisdale, published in John Trumbull, *McFingal*, New York, 1795. *Courtesy Massachusetts Historical Society, Boston.*

The eventual effect of Whitefield's visit was deep division within the church, between so-called New Light and Old Light factions. Just prior to the height of the ensuing controversy, Samuel Lane was elected Stratham's tithingman. As such, he was responsible for keeping order in the meetinghouse. A tithingman, standing to the left of the pulpit, holds the rod of his office, entitling him to enforce discipline as necessary.

this disturbance. The day after Sheriff Packer removed Leavitt, the King's Attorney sent for Samuel, whose testimony before Hunking Wentworth prompted the justice to send the case to Justice George Jaffrey's court. From there it was remanded to the Court of Quarter Sessions, which met for two days in early December. On appeal, it was heard before the Superior Court of Judicature for nine days in March the following year.[80]

Certainly, with an infant daughter in the Lane family and tanning work to be done, time spent in court was a nuisance. However, the need for Samuel to take sides in the dispute may have been, from his own viewpoint, what caused him the greatest "Damage" in the end. Until now, his diary alone held his true feelings on the issue. Following the meetinghouse "uproar," he no longer, however, enjoyed the luxury of remaining silent. Just over a month after that event, Samuel appeared in the town record opposing the machinations of the Separates.[81] He and sixty others signed a petition registering their dissent to outfitting a second meetinghouse for Dudley Leavitt or defending him at the town's cost in the lawsuit. Samuel's previous public silence appears to have been an attempt to refrain from taking sides in hope of conciliation and consensus. After the affair with Leavitt, Samuel could no longer countenance separatism. Despite his initial inclination toward the religious zeal evinced by the New Lights, he finally cast his lot with Stratham's Old Lights.

Leavitt's departure was but a temporary setback for the Separates. As Samuel noted, "by far the Major Part of the people Saperate from mr Rust." During the summer of 1745, they worshipped at the Separate meeting in Exeter. In the fall, however, Joseph Adams reappeared in the makeshift meetinghouse at John Coker's. Further sparring matches ensued, as the Separate faction sought to have Adams ordained. Samuel continued to register his dissent at town meetings, even though the majority voted to settle Adams.

Adams, however, had so offended New Hampshire's clergy by his personal attacks that a church council of neighboring ministers could not be gathered to perform the ceremony. The Separates finally got two New Light ministers from distant parishes to attend; and despite vocal opposition from seacoast clergy, on March 20, 1747, "Mr Adams was ordained over the Separates in this Town: which was done before Ens. Veazeys House."[82] Thus, the New Lights finally had their way, although the General Assembly exempted Rust followers from the support of Adams's ministry.

Stratham did not host two ministers for long. The Rev. Mr. Rust suffered an injury in July 1748 and died the following year. After Rust's death the town accepted Adams as its sole minister, yet bitterness lingered. At Rust's funeral "the Separatists, being the Major Part of the Town . . . refus'd the Rev. Pall-Bearers the (tho' univer-

A *Saml Lane*

L E T T E R

FROM

Two Neighbouring Associations of Ministers in the *Country*,

TO THE

Associated Ministers of *Boſton* and *Charleſtown*, relating to the

Admiſſion of Mr. *Whitefield* into their Pulpits.

WITH

An APPENDIX, containing the *Advice* and *Reſolution* of a *third* Aſſociation, relating to the ſaid Gentleman.

BOSTON:
Printed by Rogers and Fowle, for S. Eliot in Cornhill.
1745.

Samuel Lane's own copy of *Letter from Two Neighbouring Associations of Ministers in the Country, to the Associated Ministers of Boston and Charlestown, Relating to the Admission of Mr. Whitefield into their Pulpits*, Boston, 1745. *Lane Family Papers, New Hampshire Historical Society.*

By the time this pamphlet was published in 1745 and acquired by Samuel Lane, the advice it contained was already too late to prevent church discord in Stratham.

sally customary) Liberty of the Pulpit." A church convention refused, however, to install Adams because of his past attacks on Rust and on neighboring clergy. Technically, the Stratham church now had no minister, and its administration of the sacrament was illicit.[83]

Years passed before both factions agreed, on August 21, 1755: "That a Joynt Council of Neighboring Ministers and Churches may be Call'd . . . to Determine wither the Conduct of Those Brethren that withdrew from the Rev'd Mr Rusts Ministry was Justifiable . . . [as well as] what Shall be Necessary to be done Relating to the Rev'd Mr Joseph Adams^{s} past Conduct in this place; in order to his being a Regular Minister over this whole Town, and our having Communion with the Neighboring Churches."[84]

On January 28, 1756, the three members of the council—Ward Cotton from Hampton, Nathaniel Gookin from Newmarket, and Samuel Langdon from Portsmouth—exhorted both sides to set aside past differences. Mr. Adams, his supporters, and the Old Light party each offered confessions, and a "Paper of Union" was composed, bearing Samuel's among the twenty-one signatures that included both Old Light and New.

Once the heat of the revival cooled, fatigue resulting from more than a decade of strife appears to have led to a series of attempts at reconciliation on the part of Stratham residents. At each attempt, however, compromise was forestalled by either the minister or the ecclesiastical council. Samuel, in his role as both town official and church member, undoubtedly tried to bring the parties together. Personally, he had no trouble following the theology of Joseph Adams and indeed actively supported his ministry, becoming a deacon of the church less than a decade after Adams's ordination.

Samuel's search for middle ground even during the ferment of the Great Awakening helps to account for his repeated election to positions of authority in Stratham. Town government in the eighteenth century depended on consensus building. Residents saw achievement of "a peaceable Kingdom" as their community's goal.[85] Samuel Lane's lamentations about discord in town are understandably searching and agonizing. He desired peace among his neighbors, and they learned to turn to him for help in finding it.

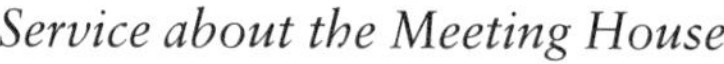

Service about the Meeting House

Sketch of the Stratham meetinghouse, which stood from 1768 to 1837; based on descriptions of the building by older Stratham residents in the late 1800s; published in the *Granite Monthly*, 1899. *New Hampshire Historical Society.*

In March 1767, Samuel Lane joined a committee to "Draw a Plan & Build a New Meeting House" for the town of Stratham. After "having taken pains to View Several Meeting Houses of Different Dementions," committee members selected as their primary model the meetinghouse in adjacent Greenland.

In the late 1760s, Samuel Lane accepted a special assignment that involved both town and church—that of overseeing the construction of a new meetinghouse. This was doubtless the single most time-consuming project Samuel ever undertook for his community.

In a move typifying New Hampshire frugality, Stratham, at its 1767 town meeting, voted to "Build a New Meeting House on the Spot where the old one Stands, provided the Same may be Accomplished by Selling the Pews, together with the old Meeting House without a Tax upon the Town."[86] Stratham's population had more than doubled between 1732 and 1776, and the original structure, built in 1716, was far too small.[87] A committee of seven, including Samuel, was chosen to oversee the project.[88]

Since the "Paper of Union" eleven years earlier, the rancor within the church had subsided, although tensions still existed. No doubt some residents remembered that in 1716 the town could not reach consensus on a site for the first meetinghouse and had to ask the provincial government to mediate.[89] That debate still simmered,

Photograph of meetinghouse interior, Sandown, New Hampshire, built 1773–74; from Historic American Buildings Survey, photographed by L. C. Durette, 1936. *Library of Congress.*

Still standing in Sandown is one of only a few eighteenth-century New Hampshire meetinghouses maintaining its original pew arrangement, both on the ground floor and in the gallery above.

and at another 1767 meeting, Samuel's committee asked to amend the vote to set the new house literally "on the Spot where the old one Stands." The new building, "being Considerable larger than the old House Renders it impracticable to be Set wholly on the Spot where the old on[e] Stands," the committee explained, and further, the new structure "must Unavoidably Extend over a Number of Graves in the Burying place." Common sense dictated the solution: to place the new structure "a little forward of the old one."[90] The great lengths to which the committee went to avoid offense points to lack of unanimity on the subject of the new meetinghouse and to lingering bitterness over the controversies of the 1740s.

Differences arose relating to the meetinghouse in other forms as well. Some townspeople apparently criticized what they saw as the committee's extravagance. The committee met at Chase's tavern on May 25, and while there Samuel "pd wid[ow] Chase Expence [for] Several Meetings before . . . (w^{h} I forget how Much)."[91] The cost of wages and expenses for this large committee, as well as what may have been perceived as a somewhat cavalier attitude toward these charges, appears to have troubled some in the town.

Public concerns about the committee and its work surfaced a week later at the sale of the meetinghouse pews. Besides providing the bulk of the construction funds, the sale of pews would determine the seating plan. By Puritan custom, a committee assigned "each person his or her place, according to rank and importance." A second committee seated the first to obviate any "Grumbling at them picking and placing themselves."[92] The auctioning off of pews to the highest bidder, common practice by Samuel's time, was an attempt to find a more impersonal seating procedure that would eliminate much of this "grumbling." Some of those attending the first vendue of pews in Stratham on June 1, however, "Manifested a Considerable Uneasiness." They complained that the pews "Sold at too high a price, Suggesting that the Com^tee^ appointed to Sell them & Build S^d^ House may have an oppertunity of greatly advancing their Estates by Pocketing Larg Sums of Money for their own private Interest over & above a Reasonable allowance for their trouble & Expence in Accomplishing that affair."[93]

Some of the wealthier members of the community had bought more than enough pews to seat their families. Samuel purchased four pews that day, and his fellow deacon and committeeman, Stephen Bordman, bought three. It is not clear, however, whether those who purchased multiple pews were actually preying on the town's poor as implied or simply doing a good deed by supporting the building of the meetinghouse.

Before the next week's sale, the committee, now aware of these complaints, reconsidered its procedures and decided to start anew. Samuel spent two days drawing a gallery plan and preparing for the sale. However, before any pews were sold the second afternoon:

> in order to forward and Encourage the Building Said House; as well as for Cultivating of Peace & Unity Between Said Parties, as well as in the Town . . . [those assembled] Agree'd that for the future, no more than three of Said Committee Shall be in pay at a time when Acting in that Capacity; and

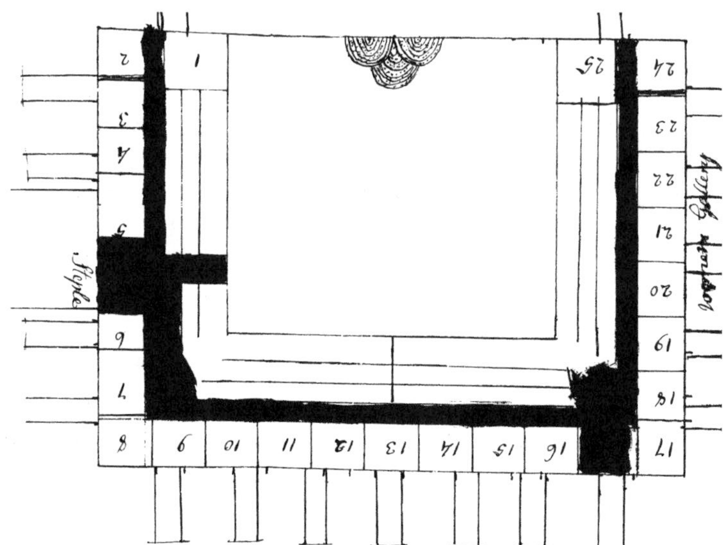

Plan of pews in Stratham's meetinghouse gallery, drawn by Samuel Lane, June 1767. Stratham Town Records. *Courtesy New Hampshire Division of Records Management and Archives.*

As clerk of the building committee, Samuel Lane was responsible for keeping a careful record of its expenditures. Doubtless due to his proficiency in measuring and drafting, the committee entrusted him as well with drawing the floor plans.

Pew No. 1. Knock'd off to Capt. Joseph Hoit for 30-5-0
given up

Pew No. 26 Knock'd off to Esq. Smith for 20-0-0 given up

No. 2. Knock'd off to Cornet Wiggin for 25-0-0 given up

No. 22. Knock'd off to John Folsom for 20-5-0

No. 4. Knock'd off to Lieut. Fifield for 19-15-0 given up

Assignment of pews, "At a Publick Vendue held the 1st Day of June 1767 for the Sale of the Pews in the New Meeting House." Stratham Town Records. *Courtesy New Hampshire Division of Records Management and Archives.*

The pews in an eighteenth-century meetinghouse were private property, transferred from owner to owner by deed, just like land. The building of a meetinghouse was often financed by auctioning the pew space before construction began. In the case of Stratham, the committee found it necessary to auction the pews twice, after complaints of unfairness forced many to give up some of those they had purchased.

that their Wages Shall be three Shillings p[er] Day for Each Man when Acting in that Capacity, they finding themselves Victuals & Drink (Excepting Tavern Expenses which is to [be] Allowed them) also that Each of Said Committee give up the Pews they have already Purchased that there may be a better chance for those that want to Purchase: and that Neither of the Committee Shall Bidd off more than one Pew apiece at above 20£ p[er] Pew.[94]

The sale went on until eleven that evening and continued for two more ten-hour days, until all but a few gallery pews were taken up. Samuel, who had bought three ground-floor pews at the first sale, ended up purchasing only one, though he also bought two less expensive gallery pews. Deacon Bordman bought only one of his three pews back. Samuel, who had initially bid £29 for pew number 25, bought the same pew for £23.13.8 the second day.[95] At the first sale, buyers like Samuel, in their concern with funding the project, apparently neglected to consider possible inequities in the process that disparities in wealth might cause.

Numbered pew door, Sandown meetinghouse, c. 1774; from Historic American Buildings Survey, photographed by L. C. Durette, 1936. *Library of Congress.*

After the pew sales, the meetinghouse committee's next task was to engage a master carpenter. After chosing Samuel as its clerk, the committee decided to hire Nottingham housewright Josiah Clark, and Samuel met with him several days later. He had "a Nip of Punch with Clark" at Folsom's tavern in Greenland while discussing the project. Two days later the committee met with Clark for six hours, and he agreed "that for four Shillings p[er] Day (and be found Victuals Drink & Lodging) I will work for them as a Master Workman in Building the whole of the Frame & Steple of S^{d} House at any time Next Spring or Summer."[96] Later that fall, the committee hired local builder Ephraim Barker to work with Clark.

Barker and Clark began their work on the frame the following spring. After the foundation was built and the sills were in place, final arrangements were made for raising the frame, typically a gala community affair. The committee planned a "Dress Dinner for Raising" and hired Joshua Wingate to prepare the meal. The raising took place in rainy weather on June 15.

Samuel gave no details of the event in his diary. Many accounts exist, however, of rowdiness encouraged by liquor at raisings. A 1738 raising in Northampton, Massachusetts, included expenses for ten gallons of rum and setting broken bones for two men. In Stratham, Joshua Wingate prepared dinners of fish, potatoes, bread, and butter. Twenty gallons of rum, with sugar to accompany it, were available to quench the workers' thirst.[97]

Stratham June 15th 1767 for the Pew No 14. in the Gallery of the New Meeting House Voted to be Built in Said Town Bought this Day of Cornet Thomas Wiggin Stephen Bordman Joseph Hoit Saml Lane Danl Clark Jno Tayler & Simon Wiggin The Committee Appointed to Sell the Same, & Build Sd House I Promise to pay to Said Committee or the Major part of them or Their order Eight Pounds & ten Shillings on Demand in Such Materials as they Shall want for Said House at the Lowest Money prices, or the Money if they Shall Choose it as Witness my hand

John Stockbridge

£ 8-10-0

Promissory note for purchase of gallery pew number 14, June 15, 1767. Stratham Town Records. *Courtesy New Hampshire Division of Records Management and Archives.*

Some who bought Stratham's numbered pews at the auction arranged to pay with building materials that the committee anticipated needing.

Conjectural view of a meetinghouse raising; first published in Charles E. Clark, *The Meetinghouse Tragedy* (Hanover: University Press of New England, 1998); from drawing by John W. Hatch. *Courtesy Maryanna Hatch and Charles E. Clark.*

Samuel Lane helped arrange all details of construction, from contracting with the master workman and obtaining rigging and nails at the Bank to installing the bell. On the day of the raising, workers used pike poles and ropes to erect the first broadside, while the master builder gave orders from above.

The raising did not go entirely smoothly, from Samuel's perspective. In its wake he referred to "old Timber Used & Spoil'd" and to "Damage done to things & trouble runing after them &c &c."[98] The frame must have been well set, however, for Samuel mentioned no damage from an earthquake five days later.

Barker and Clark worked quickly on the finish work over the summer, and on August 12 the committee met to measure and mark out the pews. In December, Samuel drew a plan of the pulpit stairs. By that point, the town may have been holding meetings in the new house. There is no record when that milestone was reached.

As clerk of the building committee, Samuel shouldered the lion's share of responsibility for the details of construction. He ordered and paid for materials and inspected work as it progressed. He also oversaw the budget. The sale of pews raised £18,306 and the sale of the old meetinghouse, £907, for total revenue of £19,213. The committee paid out £15,700 for expenses. The resulting surplus, due back to the pew owners, required Samuel to travel around town settling accounts. In addition, a dispute between the builders and the committee over unspecified work went to arbitration in August 1769. That affair ended in an award to the town of £5.[99]

Pulpit in Sandown meetinghouse, Historic American Buildings Survey, 1936 *Library of Congress.*

It was not until after the frame was raised and the interior almost finished that Samuel Lane drew a plan of the pulpit stairs. While visiting Dover and Greenland meetinghouses, he had measured their pulpits as well as noting their pew arrangements.

As per custom, the committee and its clerk, too, expected and received pay for their service to the community. On March 30, 1770, a little more than three years after he was appointed to the meetinghouse committee, Samuel wrote, "[T]here is now . . . Due to me for what I have already done 1-14-9-1 Lawful Money & nothing to pay it in Except the old pickpoles Cans &c left of Raising." And more work remained.[100]

Samuel previously had written the committee: "As it is Customary in all Courts & Societys, to Make Some Generous Grant to any Persons Employ'd in Such Difficult Fetigueing Business, I Rely on your generosity . . . to Reward one who Can with a good Conscience Subscribe himself your Careful Laborious Honest Book keeper." While this earlier plea had brought remuneration, his later efforts did not. In the end, Samuel concluded his involvement with this project in a manner atypical of his time, "I think not to trouble my Self to keep any further Account about it as to my own time & trouble, but to do it gratis."[101]

Samuel's work on the new meetinghouse was only a small part of his community involvement. He served eight one-year terms as selectman, twenty years as auditor of the selectmen's accounts and pound keeper, two years as assessor, and four years as town clerk and sealer of leather. His dedication to the town was continuous over the course of his lifetime. In addition, from 1765 until 1800, when he was made elder, he was a deacon of the church, keeping its accounts, attending ordinations in other towns, and assisting the minister at the communion table.

From building the meetinghouse to caring for the poor, Samuel was concerned in every aspect of his community's well-being. In 1769, a fairly typical year, Stratham spent 26 percent of its budget for care of the indigent. This was the largest single area of expense for the town. By law, the selectmen were charged with "the Maintenance and Support of the . . . Poor."[102] The town reimbursed individuals for providing such services as "keeping John Morgin one year," "makeing a pare Shoes for W^{d} Avery," and "tea, Sugar molasses for Daniel Davis."[103] Samuel himself provided many goods and services to the poor, including, for example, molasses for widow Philbrook.

To minimize the burden of poor relief on taxpayers, New Hampshire law set certain limits on a community's liability in this regard. To prevent widows from drifting into poverty and becoming wards of the town, for example, a widow's thirds were set off before an estate's creditors could collect. In addition, laws prevented towns from shifting the burden of their poor onto other communities. A 1719 act stated: "If any person or persons come to sojourn, or dwell in any town within this province . . . and be there received, and entertained by the space of three months, not having been warned by the constable . . . every such person shall be reputed to be an inhabitant of such town, or precinct of the same, and the proper charge of the same, in case, through sickness, lameness, or otherwise, they come to stand in need of relief, to be born by such town."[104]

Province of New Hampr } To Samuel Leavit Constable of Stratham in Said Province Greeting.

You are hereby Required in his Majestys Name forthwith on Sight hereof to Warn Hannah Dudley to Depart out of Said Town of Stratham, She not being a Lawfull Inhabitant here; and not to Reside here any Longer, upon Penalty of the Utmost Severity of the Law of Said Province in Such Cases made and provided: And Make Return hereof and of your doings herein to the next Court of Quarter Sessions. Dated at Stratham aforesd Sept 7th 1764

Satchel Clark
Sam Lane } Select Men of Stratham

Authorization for a constable to notify Hannah Dudley to leave town, written by Samuel Lane, September 7, 1764. *Courtesy New Hampshire Division of Records Management and Archives.*

Over time, Samuel Lane served his town in practically every aspect of community business. "Warning out" newcomers to town helped ensure that Stratham taxpayers would not become liable for the support of nonresident poor.

Simply presenting new residents with official notice that they must leave town could absolve the taxpayers, forever, from the burden of their support. Some New Hampshire towns, therefore, served notice to newcomers as a matter of course, to eliminate potential liability.[105] Stratham selectmen regularly directed their constable to warn out visitors who had no evident means of support; in 1771 alone, Samuel wrote warrants to warn five people out of town.[106]

Such action could instigate conflict. Stratham and Exeter disputed widow Mary Florence's place of residence for seven years.[107] Florence had suffered economic hardship during her widowhood, sinking into poverty. She moved to Stratham from Exeter on January 20, 1766, and as she was "Liable to be a Town Charge," just over one month later the Stratham selectmen warned her out and ordered the constable "to Proceed forthwith to apprehend the Body of the Said Mary Florence . . . and Carry her to Exeter and Deliver her to Some of the overseers or Selectmen." Exeter refused to accept the poor woman, who returned to Stratham and lived there at town expense, while Stratham tried to persuade Exeter to meet its responsibility. After spending £7.16.3 keeping Florence in 1769 and having exhausted all avenues but the courts, Stratham sued Exeter in the June 1770 Court of General Quarter Sessions.

In December 1771, Samuel was one of two townsmen voted agents "to prosecute the affair against the town of Exeter."[108] On March 19, 1773, the *New Hampshire Gazette* reported the final verdict: "the Famous Cause between Exeter and Stratham . . . relative to the Maintenance of an antiquated Widow . . . was at length determined in favor of Stratham, and the Bone of Contention sent to Exeter, from which Place, may she in due Time, have a safe, happy, and easy Transition to Heaven, as there has been so much disputing, where her Residence should be on Earth."[109] Litigation was expensive but often was the only recourse left to a town in such cases.

Whenever possible, Stratham followed the example set by overseers of the poor in cities like Boston by apprenticing needy youth in order to defray charges to the town. In 1762, Samuel drafted the following advertisement: "Dorcas Kenison being in a likely way to Recover her health & is now able to Do Some work. Able Persons that [?] to take S^{d} Dorcas for a time on reasonable Terms as Possible to Save Cost to the Town are hereby Publickly Notified that they may have oppurtunity to Agree wth the Select Men upon that affair at Mrs Love Chases on Monday Evening Next at 5 o clock."[110]

Arguments and litigation did not, however, mark most of Samuel's years in office. In a typical year of service as selectman he dealt with such routine matters as assessing the town, setting the tax rate, leasing town lands, and contracting with the meetinghouse sexton, as well as dealing with issues pertaining to the maintenance of the poor. His "writing for the Town" in 1751, for example, included drafting rates, warrants, orders on the constable, an agreement with the schoolmaster, and the town meeting warrant—all valued at seven pounds.[111]

Virtually all Samuel's public service remained within the sphere of the town. Only the Revolutionary War took him beyond Stratham's borders and then just for a short period. He was a member of Stratham's Committee of Correspondence, appointed February 7, 1774, and supported the town's resolve "that the Act of Parliament of Great Brittain, made for the Express purposes of raising a Revenue in America is Unconstitutional and Unjust: and every Person who Attempts to Execute that Act, is an Enemy to this Country."[112] A year later he and Deacon Stephen Bordman were Stratham's delegates to the Fourth Provincial Congress at Exeter. Samuel attended "the Congress" for fifty days, yet never detailed any of the sessions in his diary.[113] For him, what mattered most was local.

Samuel participated in nearly all town activities, with the exception of the militia. As a young man he had served as a drummer in the Hampton troop. However, he later petitioned for and gained a military exemption from Stratham's militia commanders.[114] He stood watch when Indians threatened, but when called to service during the French and Indian Wars, he purchased a substitute, a common practice at the time; on April 26, 1758, he noted, "Training & I pd £50 to Kenison to go in my room."[115]

Even while helping to lead the town as one of Stratham's selectmen, Samuel always remained willing to serve simultaneously in less glamorous roles such as pound keeper and sealer of leather. Duty to the community, not power or monetary gain, motivated Stratham's residents, Samuel among them, to serve their town. Moreover, during the 1750s and 1760s, other New Hampshire towns enlisted his talents as well.

With Exeter People into the woods

Samuel Lane's growing competence as a surveyor coincided with the renewal of provincial land development at the close of King George's War (1744–48). "There is an uncommon Stir among People this Fall after Lands in the Woods," Samuel wrote in 1748.[116] Until the Treaty of Aix-la-Chapelle ended King George's War earlier that year, the French, with the help of their native allies, had attacked English settlements in New England and as far south as New York, effectively stopping new settlement and causing colonists to abandon certain frontier areas.

Stratham, in danger itself for a brief time in 1747, instituted a watch to alarm residents should Indians appear. Samuel watched with his neighbor, Joseph Mason, on April 16, and wrote at the end of the year, "The indians have Done much Damage the Summer Past."[117] Although Stratham escaped attack, settlers farther inland were not so lucky. In the Merrimack Valley, "Woodwell's Garrison was taken April 22 [1746]," according to Concord's Reverend Timothy Walker. "Thomas Cook & als. Killed May y[e] 9. Richard Blanchard scalped June 11. Bishop was captivated June 25. Jon[a] Bradley & als killed Aug:11. Easterbrook killed Nov[r] 10."[118]

The long-awaited conclusion in 1740 of a boundary dispute between Massachusetts and New Hampshire opened up entire new regions to uncontested development. The boundary had been a bone of contention ever since New Hampshire was made a separate province in 1679. Two years earlier, English courts had ruled that the northern border of Massachusetts extended no "further northward along the river Merrimac than three English miles."[119] The charters for Massachusetts and New Hampshire contained contradictory wording and were granted under the mistaken assumption that the Merrimack River ran in an east-west direction over its entire course.

Map showing wilderness north of Lake Winnipesaukee, detail from Col. Joseph Blanchard and Rev. Samuel Langdon, *An Accurate Map of His Majesty's Province of New-Hampshire in New England*, 1761. *New Hampshire Historical Society.*

In the era of expansion that followed settlement of New Hampshire's boundary dispute with Massachusetts in 1740, the work of the surveyor was critical. Between 1748 and 1752, Samuel Lane made at least three trips to lay out the new township of Holderness on the Pemigewasset River, in the unsettled territory between Cusumpy Pond (now Squam Lake) and the White Mountains.

An exploring party from Massachusetts had discovered, as early as 1652, that the Merrimack reached as far north as Lake Winnipesaukee. Massachusetts set its northern boundary marker at the Weirs, and New Hampshire disputed the land claims of its southern neighbor.

New Hampshire attempted several times to gain a favorable settlement of the boundary question but failed even to have the government in England consider the issue. When, during the 1720s and 1730s, Massachusetts granted townships in areas of the Merrimack River Valley that New Hampshire claimed as its own, the issue acquired a new urgency. The province renewed its attempts to bring the question before the royal government. New Hampshire's persistence eventually was rewarded, and His Majesty in council appointed an impartial commission to study the various claims and make a recommendation.[120] The commission met August 1, 1737, in Hampton.

Samuel proclaimed one month later, "this Day the Commitioners Verdict was read." He failed to note, however, that they had come to no definite conclusion respecting the boundary.[121] The commission found that the charters did indeed contain contradictory grants and that therefore only the king could decide which was valid. Much lobbying ensued, in which New Hampshire was aided enormously by its new agent in London, John Thomlinson, who is said to have "completely outgeneraled" the Massachusetts agents.[122]

The final ruling of the king in council, on March 5, 1740, swept aside the issue of contradictory charter grants, attempting to base the decision "on principles of justice and equity."[123] New Hampshire emerged an uncontested victor from this struggle with its neighbor. The newly settled boundary gave New Hampshire even more territory than the province had claimed. Simultaneously, New Hampshire's efforts to obtain an independent and separate governor bore fruit, and Benning Wentworth, son of former Lieutenant-Governor John Wentworth, was appointed the province's first royal governor.

With a boundary decision at last ratifying provincial title to interior lands, with the threat of Indian attack at least temporarily removed, and with a new governor whose royal instructions urged him to promote settlement "on the Frontiers of [the] Province," the foundation was laid for the rapid and wholesale development of New Hampshire's vast interior.[124]

Samuel's involvement with laying out townships began at this time. His prior experience was limited to surveying individual lots. On November 11, 1748, however, he "Agreed with Jer^{h} Veasey to go in the woods." In what was then wilderness, the party was to make a survey of an area east of the Pemigawesset River to accompany a petition to Governor Wentworth for a new township to be named Holderness.

"I went with Exeter people into the woods," Samuel wrote on November 25, 1748, "which is the first time I ever Camp'd in the Woods."[125] On this thirteen-day trip, a group of at least seven men perambulated the proposed township and marked its bounds. Samuel left few notes concerning this excursion beyond remarking on the weather, which was typically changeable: the end of November was "pretty pleasent for the Season of the year," but the first two nights of December were rainy, and then the weather turned cold.

Even with favorable weather, such expeditions held few comforts. On this trip, Samuel carried "1 Cheese 1 Cake 6 Bisket tobacco 2 pipes Blanket compass & Stand Line protractor Dividers Book reading Book coffe Sugar 2 pair Stockins apron."[126] His days were spent running boundary lines and taking notes about the land. In the evening, a campfire provided enough light to make rough sketches from the day's measurements. The party was deep in the wilderness; there were no camps or settlements near. Even fifteen years later, when Matthew Patten surveyed Plymouth, just across the Pemigawasset River from Holderness, the closest lodging, except for a logging camp, was forty-three miles to the south near Concord.[127] The area had been surveyed once before by Ezekial Worthing, who left his initials on a tree.[128]

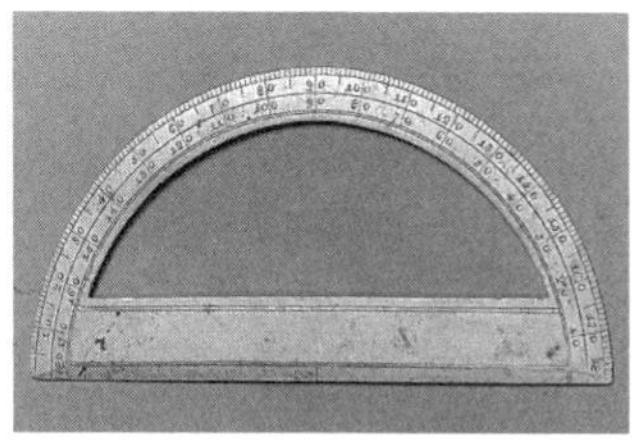

Samuel Lane's brass protractor; engraved on reverse: "Samuel Lane Stratham June 1 1747." *New Hampshire Historical Society.*

Samuel Lane's initial trip to the Holderness area took thirteen days. It was the first time he "ever Camp'd in the Woods." Each night by the campfire he unpacked his protractor and dividers to make rough sketches from the day's measurements.

It is unclear whether Samuel was the surveyor or an assistant on this trip. The group was clearly impressed by his work, however, and on June 13, 1750, accompanied by one of the Holderness proprietors, the young surveyor paid a visit to Governor Wentworth. Two days later, Samuel took the oath as assistant to the surveyor of His Majesty's lands in New Hampshire, assuming the authority for "Surveying & Measuring any of his Majes[ty] Said Lands following Such orders & Directions therein as you Shall from time to time receive from me [the governor] or from the Surveyer."[129] With his new commission in hand and in extremely hot weather, Samuel left for Holderness a second time on June 19.

Following the 1748 trip, Samuel noted nothing in his diary relating to Holderness until preparing for his second trip there in June 1750. The prospective proprietors of Holderness had apparently renewed their determination to obtain a land grant. In mid-July, Samuel presented his survey to Governor Wentworth. It took more than a year from that point for the Governor's Council to consider the petition of "Exeter people" to establish a new town as "surveyed and planned by Sam[l] Lane surveyor." Finally, on October 15, 1751, a charter for Holderness was granted.[130]

Samuel's most extensive work for the now official Holderness Proprietors came the following year. He met with prominent mem-

Portrait of Governor Benning Wentworth, by Joseph Blackburn, 1760. *New Hampshire Historical Society.*

With the Holderness project still underway and possibly because of skills proven there, Royal Governor Benning Wentworth appointed Samuel Lane as assistant to Joseph Blanchard, the "Surveyor of His Majesty's Lands in New Hampshire."

bers of the group several times to discuss laying out lots in the newly created township. In May 1752, Samuel "bargained wth Jno Sheperd to go to Holderness." He may, however, have been hesitant to return "to the woods" during the summer, based on his experience the previous June. Matthew Patten wrote of a trip to the same area, "The reason of my return so quick was the flys was so plenty that I could not work."[131] Samuel's grandson later recalled of at least one such occasion: "After he [Samuel] had been out on one of those Surveying tours for a long time, the Sun and Black Flies, the Moschettoes &c had so altered his countenance, that when he returned home, his Family scarcly knew who he was."[132]

Whatever the reason for delay, Samuel waited until late October —when New Hampshire weather is clear, cool, and bug-free—to travel up the Merrimack River to Holderness to lay out three separate lots for each proprietor. After the third trip there, his involvement with Holderness diminished. He met with key members of the group on several occasions and presented a plan of the lots to the governor, but before Holderness could be settled, hostilities with the French and Indians broke out again. The conditions for settlement unfulfilled, the 1751 charter lapsed, and the area was granted to a different group of speculators in 1761. Samuel's experience with the

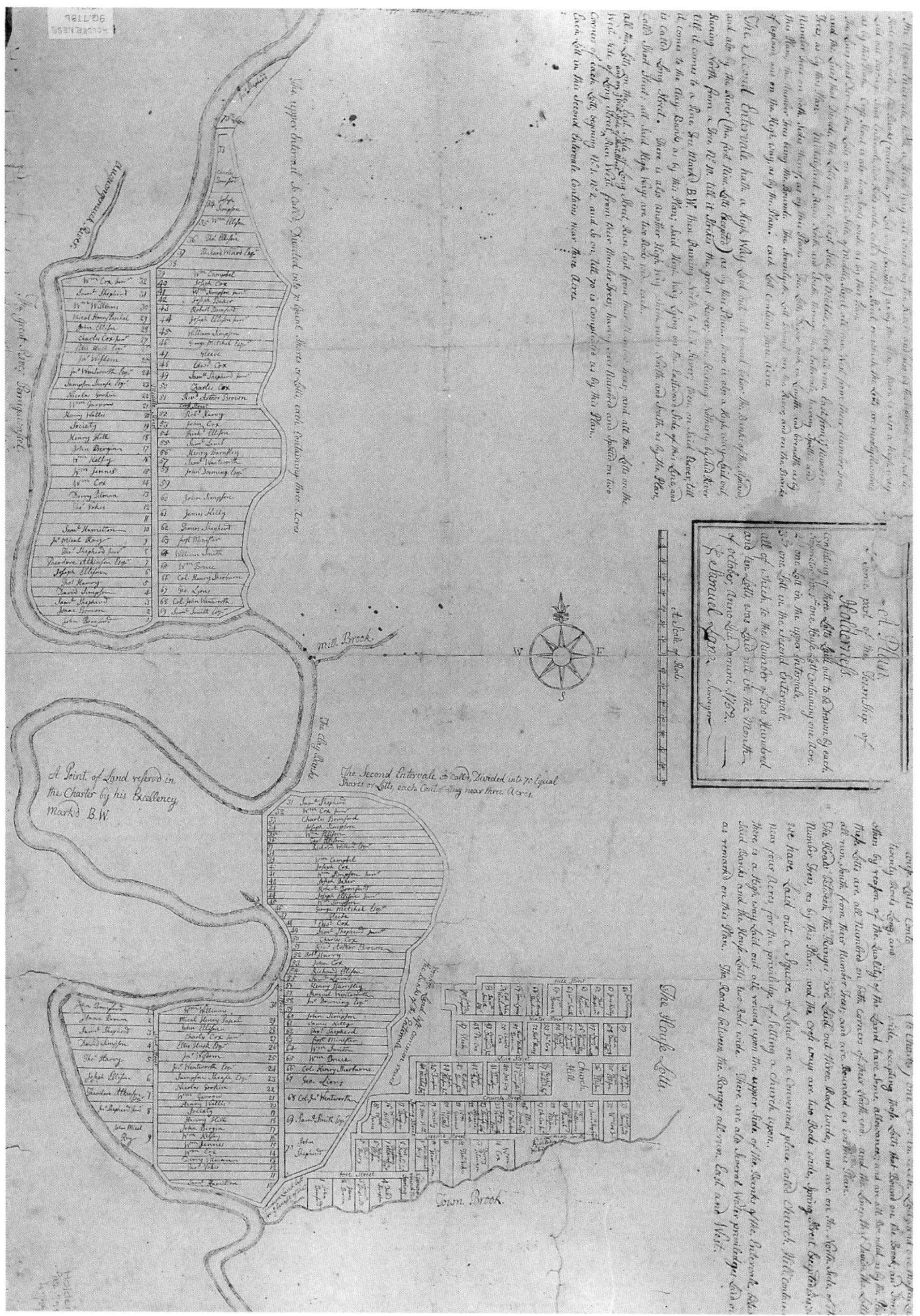

"A Plan of Some part of the Township of Holderness," surveyed and drawn by Samuel Lane, October 1752. *New Hampshire Historical Society.*

About a year after the governor granted Holderness its charter in October 1751, Samuel Lane made a third trip there to survey individual lots for the proprietors. Each shareholder would own a variety of land, including a house lot and farm lots, along two stretches of the fertile floodplain. The following June, Samuel Lane met with the governor to present this plan. As was usual in each new town chartered, Benning Wentworth reserved a prime parcel of land for himself.

Holderness grant was relatively limited. His work for its proprietors foretold, however, what was to become, over the next two decades, a major occupation for Samuel Lane.[133]

Set out to Perambulate Bow Line

Stratham residents took special interest in the township of Bow, fifty miles to the northwest; 91 of Bow's 160 original proprietors were Stratham people. Although few of these landowners planned to leave Stratham to settle in Bow, the prosperity of this distant enterprise affected almost everyone in the older community.[134]

However much New Hampshire's government wanted to fulfill the king's instructions and tame its interior, the salient force driving the province's development was land speculation. Over time, property now in the wilderness would appreciate in value. "Bold speculation was one of the characteristics of the eighteenth century in England and America."[135] Puritan morality, which had eschewed undue personal gain, was giving way to a spirit of risk taking and chance. Gaming and lotteries were becoming popular forms of sport. Massachusetts held its first provincial lottery in 1745; only twelve years earlier, lotteries had been prohibited by the General Court.[136]

Intense land speculation coincided with extended periods of peace. While serving the Crown on military expeditions during the recent wars, colonists had discovered a vast interior available for settlement. War, furthermore, had stimulated the colonial economy; military supply contracts had created surplus capital for investing.[137] Because of British laws that prohibited colonial manufacturing, investment opportunities other than land were limited to fishing, trading, and lumbering. Land, the only resource available in sufficient quantity to absorb America's new capital wealth, soon became the most promising investment of the times.

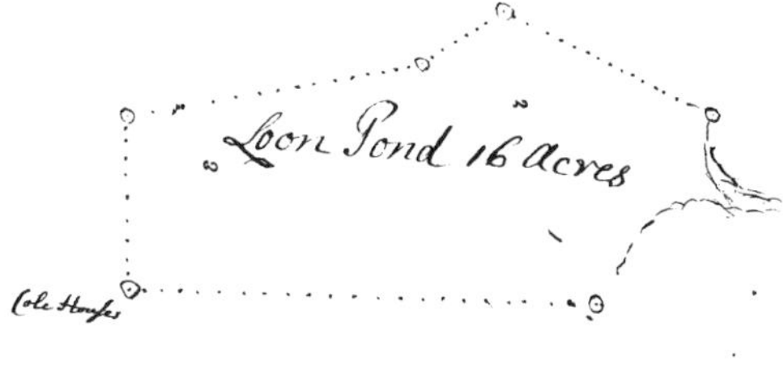

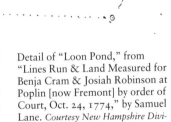

Detail of "Loon Pond," from "Lines Run & Land Measured for Benja Cram & Josiah Robinson at Poplin [now Fremont] by order of Court, Oct. 24, 1774," by Samuel Lane. *Courtesy New Hampshire Division of Records Management and Archives.*

Massachusetts governor Jonathan Belcher advised at least one acquaintance to invest in "uncultivated wilderness lands in this Province," as they are likely to "advance your estate three times faster than money put to interest."[138] Yale president Ezra Stiles noted both the potential gain and the risk of land speculation: "Probably most of the N.H. Rights will become forfeit; perhaps I may clear a few . . . and if my Heirs are careful, they may easily secure them forever."[139]

The proprietors of a new township became owners in common of a tract of land granted by the provincial government.[140] "Proprieties" were first and foremost corporations to facilitate "the profitable distribution of a land grant, and not solely . . . to aid settlement."[141] Their responsibilities were contained in a legislative act of 1719: "[T]he proprietors of the common and undivided lands . . . shall be and hereby are empowered to order, improve, or divide [those lands] in such way and manner as shall be concluded and agreed upon by a major part of such proprietors."[142]

Land speculation and settlement were not unrelated; settled land was far more valuable than undeveloped wilderness. Theodore Atkinson described the dynamics to New Hampshire's London agent, John Thomlinson in 1758: "We Have Generaly tho^{t} it advantagious to give a Certain Quantity of our Own Lotts to Encourage Settlers as for Instance where I have 350 Acres in one Lot I make a Dedd of 50 or 60 acres to Porson he Imediatly Entring & Building a House &c & Putting a family in it which Inhances the Value of the Residue."[143]

In this era of land speculation, "almost any man of whatever station who yearned for a share of frontier territory could somehow find one, either free or at a very small cost."[144] The Massachusetts General Court urged anyone able to pay the £3.5 fee to apply for a share in that province's new western townships. Auctioning off its townships in 1738, Connecticut encouraged any spirited individual to become a proprietor by allowing him three years to pay for his shares. In New Hampshire, land was not as equally available to all: an elite group of the governor's family and close associates received a considerable portion of the land in virtually every township grant. Of those named in Bow's 1727 charter, thirty-three proprietors, or about one-fifth, were intimates, relatives, or political allies of Lieutenant-Governor John Wentworth.[145]

Along with his neighbors, Samuel caught this speculative land fever. He looked to land as a hedge against inflation. Lamenting the high prices and devaluated currency during King George's War, Samuel concluded, "This makes me Desirous of Laying my Money out in Land, which I am trying to purchase but Can't have any oppertunity to bye any that Suits me: and Letting my Money out, it Sinks more than one half in the run of one year: this is Discouraging."[146]

Even before this difficult time, Samuel had begun investing in lands beyond Stratham. In April 1746, he bought one-half of a proprietor's share in Bow from Simon Wiggin, an original proprietor, and in 1751 bought a right in Barnstead from his brother William.[147] For reasons other than speculation, he purchased several tracts in Stratham and Exeter, which he intended to farm and work himself.

Samuel's association with Bow quickly deepened. With many of his Stratham neighbors on the list of original proprietors, it is not surprising that he was called upon to help measure and lay out Bow's common lands. His work for the Bow Proprietors, beginning in 1748, soon involved Samuel in a controversy over land ownership threatening to embroil Bow. In the end, following more than four decades of legal and political battles, Bow set a record as "the subject of more litigation than any other town in the history of this state."[148]

Bow's troubles arose because the boundary between Massachusetts and New Hampshire remained ambiguous until 1740. In 1726, Massachusetts attempted to establish her claim to the region by making a grant of land at Penacook, present-day Concord, New Hampshire, to a group of proprietors from Haverhill, Massachusetts. Later that year, New Hampshire protested this incursion by sending a committee to intercept the Massachusetts surveying party. Ignoring the warning to "withdraw themselves forthwith," the Massachusetts grantees began to settle the area during the winter of 1726–27.[149]

Fearing the loss of valuable lands, Lieutenant Governor Wentworth announced in a 1726 address to the New Hampshire legislature, "The Massachusetts are daily encroaching on us."[150] He countered this invasion with Merrimack Valley townships of his own; in 1727 he chartered Bow, Canterbury, Gilmanton, Chichester, Barnstead, and Epsom. Bow, a grant of eighty-one square miles lying on both sides of the river, was in direct defiance of the Massachusetts settlement at Penacook. The New Hampshire township owed its very existence to the Massachusetts challenge.

Bow's charter resembled that of other New Hampshire grants. To keep their grant, the proprietors had to settle seventy-five families in Bow during the first three years, each in a house on three cleared acres. The charter also required that a meetinghouse "for the Public Worship of GOD" be built within four years. Should hostilities with the Indians resume, the conditions of the charter could be extended.[151] Bow's proprietors slowly laid the groundwork for their settlement. By 1729, they cut a cart path through the forest and laid out enough lots for the first settlers.[152]

In the meantime, Massachusetts made another grant of land south of the Penacook grant to the heirs and survivors of Captain John Lovewell's recent expedition against the Indians. This became the 1728 Suncook grant. While the Massachusetts grantees pursued settlement vigorously, Stratham's efforts to settle Bow paled in comparison. Few attempted to settle Bow even after the disputed areas fell under New Hampshire's jurisdiction. The already established Massachusetts settlements proved a powerful obstacle. Before long, war again intervened, and it was not until peace returned in 1748

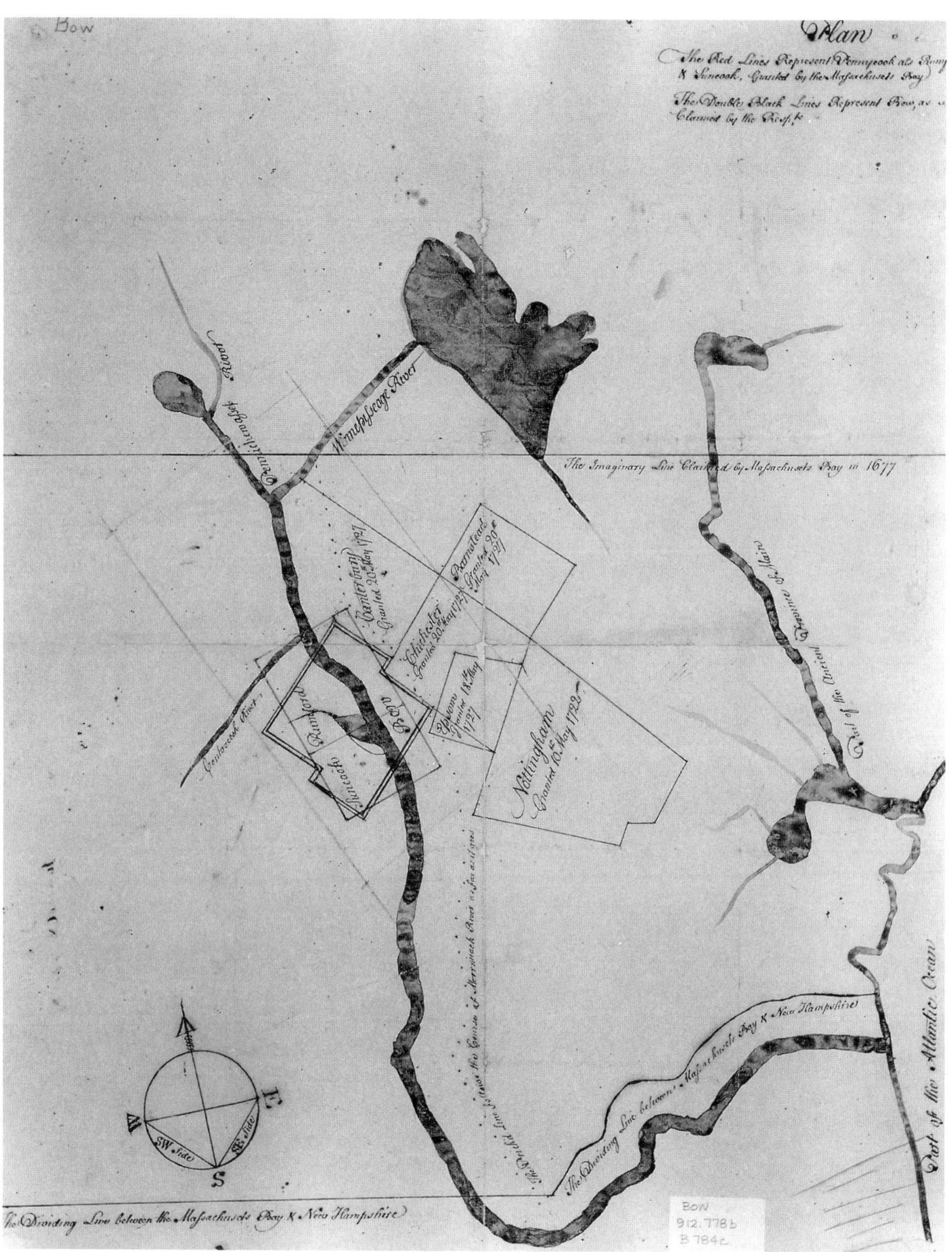

Plan showing overlapping land claims: Rumford and Suncook (granted by Massachusetts) versus Bow (granted by New Hampshire). *New Hampshire Historical Society.*

The conflicting claims of Massachusetts and New Hampshire to lands along the Merrimack led to court battles that lasted for decades. Massachusetts, whose territory extended three miles north of the Merrimack River, claimed as far as Lake Winnipesaukee. Both provinces were eager to establish towns along the rich floodplains near present-day Concord.

that the Bow Proprietors made a strong and concerted effort to exercise rights to their land.

Samuel's interest in Bow had several roots: his half share purchased in 1746, his surveying expertise, and his interest as a member of the Stratham community. Apparently in recognition of Samuel's particular skills, the proprietors, meeting in Stratham on November 11, 1748, elected Jonathan Fifield, Nathaniel Piper, and Samuel Lane to serve as "a Committee to Perambulate the lines around Bow." Piper was an original proprietor, as were two members of Fifield's family; Samuel was a relative newcomer. The committee was to measure and divide "all good land lying on the NE Side of Bow next to Chichester & Canterbury" and to make a return of the division at the next meeting. To accomplish this, the committee had authority to hire a surveyor and four assistants. True to their New England roots, the proprietors stipulated these four men were to "work as cheap as they can."[153]

This was prior to Samuel's 1750 appointment as assistant to New Hampshire's surveyor, Joseph Blanchard, and the committee chose to hire Newmarket surveyor Walter Bryant. Bryant had been the surveyor responsible for marking the boundary between New Hampshire and Maine in the wake of the king's determination, and his name is found on many New Hampshire town plans.[154] Samuel visited him twice before their joint venture to Bow.

Engraving of a surveying party at work, from Dupain de Montesson, *L'art de Lever les Plans*, Paris, 1775. *Courtesy, The Winterthur Library: Printed Book and Periodical Collection.*

Only a week after returning from Holderness, Samuel Lane set out with another surveying party to "perambulate Bow Line." He served as one of four assistants to surveyor Walter Bryant. As it was December, the team worked as quickly as possible to lay out the stipulated lots before winter set in.

On December 15, 1748, one week after Samuel returned home from his first trip to Holderness, he set out with seven others for the Merrimack Valley.[155] The first day's travel took the group to Nottingham, where they lodged with Mr. McClary; the next night they lodged at McCoy's camp in Epsom. Reaching Bow on Saturday, they located the line between Bow and Chichester before going to lodge that evening with Captain Moses Foster near present-day Suncook.[156] The next day being the Sabbath, the group as a whole appears to have had no qualms about attending Suncook meeting, although one might assume it to be enemy territory to agents of the Bow Proprietors.

For a couple of days, rain kept the party close to Captain Foster's, where they laid out lots in the southeast corner of Bow. When the weather cleared and turned pleasant on Wednesday, they began to run the boundary line on the southeast and northeast sides of Bow, camping out two nights. By Friday the party had reached Rumford (as Penacook was then called), where they stayed at Eastman's inn for the night.

The next day, though, one of the party returned to Stratham; the others crossed the river on Eastman's ferry and ran six miles along the northwest border. With no settlements near, they camped that evening, and the next morning four of the six went to meeting at

Rumford; perhaps the prospect of confronting Timothy Walker, minister and leader of the opposition to Bow's claims, was daunting enough to dissuade two from attending.

At this point, the group pressed hard to finish their perambulation; the prolonged winter camping may have inspired them to work faster than they might have otherwise. On both Monday and Tuesday they ran "Near 1 Mile before Sunrise." On their last day of work, Samuel reported that they were nearly stymied in their attempt to return: "we . . . travel'd as fast as we could to the [Merrimack] River; . . . but we could not get over as we expected; and were going toward the pennicook Ferry & found a Float & cut her out of the ice & went over the River & Lodg'd at capt Fosters." The next morning, they left for Stratham in good weather, spending that night in Chester. They returned home on December 29, in "a Storm of Snow 6 or 8 inches Deep & verry cold," after a fifteen-day journey.[157]

Samuel's terse and businesslike notes fail to reveal as fully as he doubtless could the hardships of such a trip. One eighteenth-century Massachusetts surveyor described a similar experience dramatically in rhyme:

Upon our NEEDLE we depend
In ye THICK WOODS our COURSE to know
Then after it ye CHAIN Extend
For we must gain our DISTANCE SO

Over ye HILLS through BRUSHY PLAINS
And HIDIOUS SWAMPS where is no TRACK
Cross RIVERS, BROOKS we with much PAINS
Are forc'd to travel forth & back. . . .

When WEARY STEPS has brought us home
AND NEEDLE, CHAIN have some respite
SCALE and DIVIDERS in use come
To FIT all for next morning light

And though we're CAREFUL in y^e^ same
As HAST & OBSTICLES will yeild
YET after times they will us BLAME
When ROUGH WILD WOODS are made a Field.[158]

Directional compass from a plan of Bow by Samuel Lane. *New Hampshire Historical Society.*

One troubling problem that Bow's lot layers encountered was the existing settlement under the Rumford and Suncook grants. By Wednesday the party was measuring near the east corner of Bow, "which was the place where we intended to begin to Lay out our 2nd Division of Lotts if we could have found Land enough."[159] That there should be a paucity of land in that "wilderness" area is mystifying except that Suncook had laid out lots in the same vicinity and a Plan of the Second Division of Land in the Township of Bow, Laid out in the Month of May Anno Que Domini 1749

℘ Samuel Lane Surveyor: being Employ'd Directed & assisted by Messrs Joseph Rollings, Nath^{el} Piper and David Connor who were chosen a Committee by ye Proprietors of s^{d} Bow to Lay out s^{d} Land.

Legend from map of the Second Division in Bow, by Samuel Lane, May 1749. *New Hampshire Historical Society.*

On his second trip to Bow in May, Samuel Lane succeeded Walter Bryant as the project surveyor. It may have been on this trip that the black flies, which torment all who venture into the north woods in this season, left Samuel's face unrecognizable even to his family.

had begun settling there sometime in the early 1730s. To avoid conflict, the survey party apparently searched out appropriate unsettled areas elsewhere for Bow's second division.

The survey team, after appraising the situation, finally laid out only a few new lots. In April, the proprietors tried once again. This time they "hired Mr Sam^{ll} Lane as a Surveyor and other Necessary assistants to lay out the second division."[160] Samuel succeeded Walter Bryant as the official surveyor for his second trip to Bow; in May the new survey party laid out 150 second division lots. To accomplish this, the committee made the decision to depart from its original instructions and locate the lots in three different areas of the township. Samuel's reference that June to a "Bow Meeting to Draw Lotts &c" suggests that a higher proportion of Bow's undivided common lands, the second division, had passed—in theory at least—into individual ownership.[161]

The conflicting Bow and Suncook grants, however, continued to raise problems with land distribution. Despite the care taken with

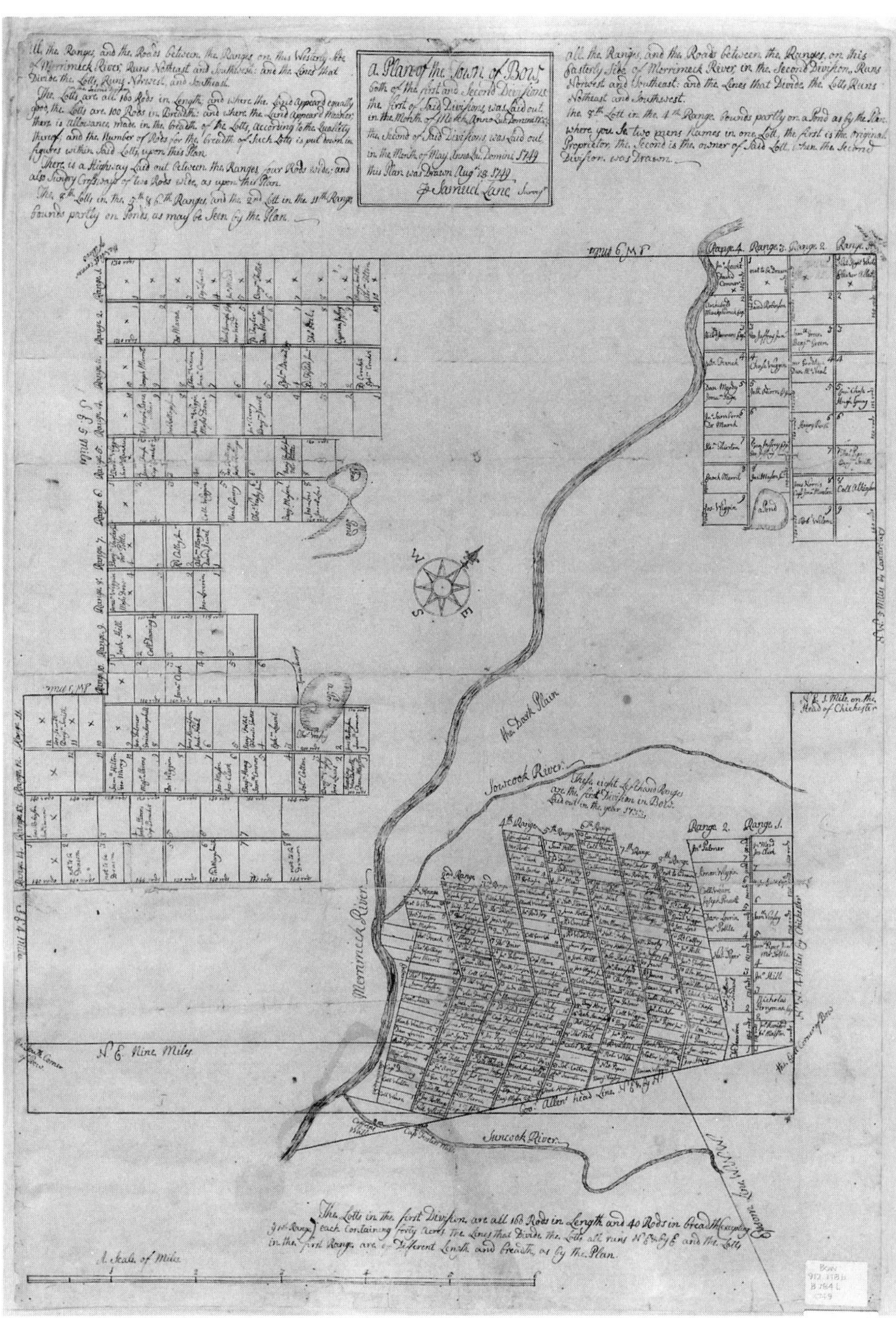

"A Plan of the Town of Bow both of the first and Second Divisions . . . Aug. 28, 1749," by Samuel Lane. *New Hampshire Historical Society.*

Colonial town proprietors developed their townships in sections called divisions, rather than all at once. By 1749, when Samuel Lane traveled to Bow to lay out its second division, he and his assistants had trouble deciding which land to divide in order to avoid conflict with Massachusetts settlers already living there.

the new lots to minimize friction, Bow's first division home lots, laid out in 1733, and eight of the larger second division lots were on land already occupied by the Suncook grantees. Keenly aware of the advantages of possession, Bow's proprietors chose a committee to resolve these conflicts with the Suncook settlers.[162] By virtue of its composition it appears that this committee was chosen more for its ability to awe than to negotiate; its members were all part of the governor's inner circle. The committee had little trouble coming to a "Just & Equitable" agreement with eight Suncook inhabitants who, facing the force of New Hampshire officialdom, decided the best course was to acquiesce to the Bow demands. These Suncook residents each agreed to relinquish "all their Rights to any other lands in Bow afor^{sd} they hold or Claim by or from any Person or Persons within the Massachusetts bay" in return for "forty acres of land at least . . . [to] be allowed to the inhabitants where they have Made Improvments."[163]

With this agreement, Bow began a series of concerted attempts to gain control over or compensation from Massachusetts settlers in the area. Although Samuel was not particularly visible in the public record during this episode, behind the scenes he played an increasingly important role in matters concerning Bow. He helped draw the land divisions that were the basis for this agreement and visited Walter Bryant in Newmarket to "borrow Plans" ten days before the agreement was signed.

Negotiation, although amenable to Suncook, proved unacceptable to Rumford settlers, whose community was well established and who had, in their minister Timothy Walker, a leader willing to stand up to the Bow Proprietors. In describing the Bow perambulation, surveyor Walter Bryant succinctly summarized both the problem and solution: "I . . . found all the Inhabitance to the south of Canterbury & East [of the] Marrimack which are in Rumford to be in Bow."[164] The Bow Proprietors had no intention of forcing Rumford residents from their homes but were determined to receive monetary compensation for their lost land.

Complicating Bow's claim was the king's ruling that the boundary settlement was not to affect private property within the disputed territory. Because of this, the Bow Proprietors were careful to initiate trespass suits against Rumford settlers only if valued for £300 or less, the price above which suits could be appealed to courts in England. This strategy assured Bow that its cases would be heard in the friendly territory of New Hampshire courts.

A 1742 suit between Thomas Brier of Stratham, a Bow grantee, and Andrew McFarland, a recalcitrant Suncook settler, initiated this pattern of litigation.[165] This case appears to have been settled out of court, but the threat of similar legal action may have helped pave the way for Bow's eventual agreement with the eight Suncook settlers. *Brier v. McFarland* demonstrated the Bow Proprietors' determination to exercise their rights through all available means, including the courts.

Rumford inhabitants remained decidedly more determined than Suncook's to fight for the property they had settled and improved. Confronted with Rumford's intractability, the Bow Proprietors renewed their strategy of trespass suits. In 1749 two separate actions of ejectment were pressed against James Mann and John Merrill.[166] Mann, a Suncook inhabitant, may have settled out of court, but Merrill, with the support of Rumford's town assembled, prepared to fight a legal battle with the Bow Proprietors.

The suit against Merrill concerned "Fifty Six acres of land more or Less with the Edifices & Appurtenances" valued at £500. Merrill operated a ferry over the Merrimack, and this suit sought his ferry privilege as well as the fifty-six acres.[167] A jury decided in favor of Merrill in the March 1750 session of the Inferior Court, and the Bow Proprietors immediately appealed to the Superior Court. However, the proprietors failed to pursue their appeal and the case was dropped. With the tract in question valued at £500, a Merrill loss would have allowed him to appeal in England. If Merrill won in England, the case would set a costly legal precedent and perhaps

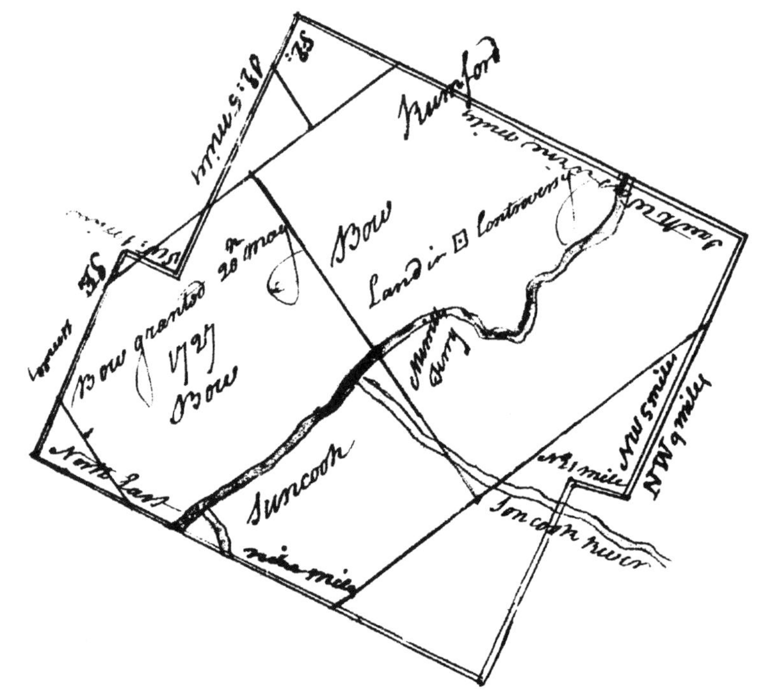

"Land in Controversy" near "Merrill's Ferry," from a map Samuel Lane drew in 1757 for the court (or his personal copy of the same). *New Hampshire Historical Society.*

The king's decision about the provincial boundary in 1740, generally in New Hampshire's favor, was not intended as a threat to existing settlements. Though recognizing the Massachusetts settlers' rights to their land, the Bow Proprietors initiated a series of trespass suits in the hope of gaining some monetary compensation for their lost land. Merrill's Ferry, a desirable site on the Merrimack, was the focus of considerable litigation.

void much of Bow's claim to the lands delineated in its charter. Thus, Bow dropped the appeal but not the cause.

One year and one day after the initial Merrill case, Bow sued again, this time for Merrill's ferry and only eight acres.[168] With that property valued at £300, the Bow Proprietors were assured that this case would remain within the sphere of their influence. Rumford's proprietors, realizing that an adverse decision in any single case would affect all their property claims, voted to, as a group, pay "the Cost of Defending John Merrill." They also chose a committee "to advise and Order Deacon John Merrill how he shall pursue and defend the action."[169]

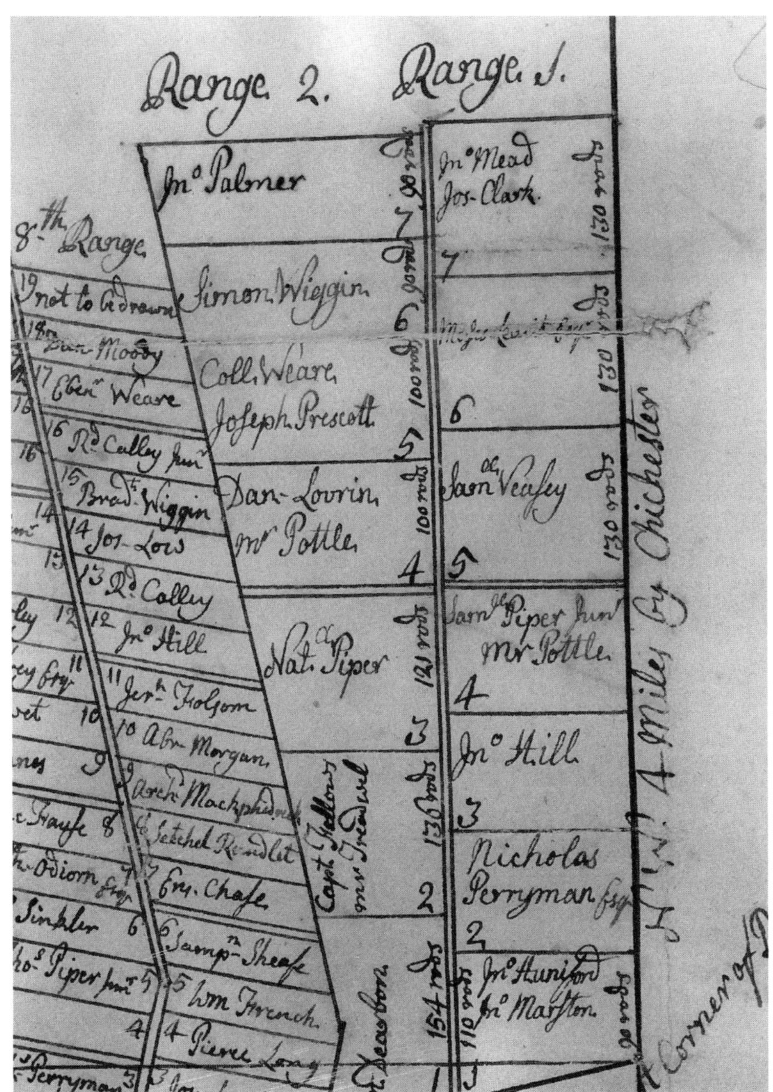

Detail of the Second Division from the "Plan of the Town of Bow," August 28, 1749. *New Hampshire Historical Society.*

New townships at this time were the responsibility of groups of proprietors, who speculated in the future development of a town while typically living elsewhere themselves. Ninety-one of Bow's 160 original proprietors were residents of Stratham. Many of the family names of Samuel Lane's neighbors—Wiggin, Calley, Piper, Pottle, and Huniford—appear on Bow shareholder lists and lot plans.

In a repeat of the previous year's litigation, the Court of Common Pleas decided in favor of Merrill. But Bow's appeal to the Superior Court, where a jury was not involved, was successful, as was a further review. Merrill requested an appeal in England but was denied because of the suit's value.

With their property and improvements at risk, Rumford's four hundred inhabitants instructed the Reverend Timothy Walker and Benjamin Rolfe to petition His Majesty in council for relief. Their grievance, which the Rev. Mr. Walker took to England in autumn 1753, accused Bow of "forcing them [Rumford settlers] out of the valuable improvements they and their predecessors have made at the expense of their blood and treasure," but their real complaint was that "they cannot have a fair, impartial trial, for that the Governor and most of ye Council are proprietors of Bow, and by them not only ye judges are appointed, but also ye officers that empannel ye jury."[170] To the Bow Proprietors' dismay, the king in council agreed to hear the case that October.

The king in council decided in Merrill's favor but only because there was some confusion in the Bow charter over its boundary with Chichester. The two issues on which Rumford hoped the Lords would rule—the validity of Bow's charter, given that the township had not been settled within the stated time, and the clause appearing in the king's boundary decision stipulating that private property was not to be affected—were not addressed in the Merrill decision. Recognizing this as less than an absolute victory for Rumford, the Bow Proprietors continued to press their case.

Chose Proprietors Clerk for Bow

By this time, Samuel Lane's role within the Bow group had changed substantially; he had become proprietors' clerk. As such he found himself in the midst of considerable controversy. Until 1752 his work with the proprietors had revolved around his surveying skills, but that December he began to attend court sessions in the Merrill appeal. In 1753 he followed carefully another case against the Rumford settlers. His involvement would deepen as he joined the group's leadership.

The death of Moses Leavit in February 1754 opened the door to Samuel's advancement. On April 4 the proprietors chose Samuel to replace Leavit as their clerk. Samuel was a logical choice. He was familiar to the proprietors, many of whom were his Stratham neighbors. He also knew the geography of Bow and some of its settlers. Esquire Leavit was a wealthy Stratham landowner and community leader who had sent his son to Harvard. Samuel represented an emerging elite based on talent. A certain status devolved on Samuel as he assumed the Bow clerkship.

"The central figure in any propriety was the clerk."[171] In his new role, Samuel would be expected to keep the proprietors' records, handle correspondence, notify members of meetings, and otherwise represent their interests. Because of the extensive litigation in which Bow was involved, Samuel's responsibilities extended well beyond the norm, however. While most town proprietors met annually, Bow regularly adjourned its meeting, and members gathered, therefore, several times annually. Proprietary business often hinged on the court, whose rulings might come at any time.

With a number of court cases in progress throughout the 1750s, Samuel spent a good deal of time researching background material for these cases in the records. "Meeting at Chases 3 times [in 1755] as comma^{tee} for Searching the Records & Making new Lott papers" and "near half a Day Searching the Book wth Bryant" were typical of the many tasks Samuel performed as clerk for Bow during those litigious years.[172]

Merrill's impending case before the king in council created a flurry of activity. When the decision went against Bow in 1755, Samuel copied "a long Letter from England of 16 pages in octavo, Small hand at 3^{s}/ p[er] Page."[173] In May 1757 he drew "2 Plans of Bow, Epsom Chester Dover, Derry, Exeter, Canterbury, Rumford Notingham & all adjacent Towns, for the Court."[174] "I went to Bank on Bow Case" became a familiar refrain in Samuel's diary.

After the disappointing decision in the Merrill case, the Bow proprietors appear to have developed a renewed interest in compromising with the Suncook and Rumford inhabitants. Mounting legal fees reinforced their desire for settlement. Samuel was directed to make a list of the money raised by Bow "to be appropriated toward Defreying the publick Expenses of Said Proprietors, in Laying out

Province of *New Hampſhire.*

THE Proprietors of BOW are hereby Notified, that their laſt annual Meeting ſtands adjourn'd to Tueſday the ſecond Day of Octo ber next, at Two of the Clock in the Afternoon, at the Houſe of Mrs. *Love Chaſe,* Innholder at Stratham in ſaid Province ; at which Time and Place it is deſired that every Proprietor may be preſent, as Buſineſs of Importance may then be tranſacted. By Order of ſaid Proprietors. *Stratham, Auguſt* 28, 1759.

SAMUEL LANE, Prop'rs Clerk.

Notice in *New Hampshire Gazette* announcing Bow Proprietors' meeting, August 28, 1759. *New Hampshire Historical Society.*

In 1754, as the suit concerning Merrill's Ferry was pending before the king in council, Samuel Lane stepped into a new position of influence: proprietors' clerk for Bow. His tasks suddenly expanded from surveying land to arranging meetings, helping develop court cases, and selling shares.

Chase's (later Emery's) tavern, Stratham; ink sketch by Stan Snow, c. 1950. *New Hampshire Historical Society.*

Chase's tavern witnessed both the rise and the decline of Stratham's era of investment in Bow land. The Bow Proprietors held their annual and committee meetings at Mrs. Love Chase's, and in later years, they conducted tax sales there as Bow land shares decreased in value.

Lands, in fencing and building Houses thereon, and other Necessary Expenses in promoting the publick good of S[d] Township."[175] Although Bow had voted funds in the 1730s to construct a meeting-house and a number of homes for settlers, most of the money they raised through assessments on shares, a total of £5,000, had been spent instead on surveys and legal fees.[176]

The expenses involved in clearing title to the land, in effect, prevented the proprietors from improving their township for settlement. Mounting a legal battle across the ocean in England was an expensive proposition, and colonial money was not accepted as legal tender by the English legal establishment. The Bow Proprietors looked to the provincial government in Portsmouth for help "as the Getting of Sterling money either by way of Bills of Exchange or silver is at Present very Difficult if to be obtained from Private Persons." They asked for a loan of £100 (sterling).[177]

Heavy expenses, with little financial return, resulted in a good deal of tax delinquency. In 1756, Bow held the first of a series of "Sales . . . for the payment of taxes due." At Chase's tavern in

Stratham on March 23, seven lots were sold and three days later, five more.[178] Samuel attended both days, unsuccessfully bidding on four half-rights. In November 1758, Samuel acted as vendue master and in two days auctioned off eighteen half-rights. He received fees for his work: selling (sixpence per pound), attending as clerk, writing advertisements, making copies of the sales, writing deeds, and recording sales.[179]

The tax sales marked Samuel's first personal foray into substantial Bow land speculation. He tested the waters at the March 1756 vendue, bidding on four rights; he was close to the high bid on each. The experience of losing made him bolder the next time, and in July he bought six half-rights out of the twenty sold. These purchases were entirely speculative; he resold them almost immediately.[180] At the 1758 sale he found himself in an ethically ambiguous position as both prospective buyer and vendue master. Those present, understanding his predicament, jointly determined "that the Vendue Master Should have Liberty to Bidd as another Man." This time, Samuel bought eight rights, held onto a portion of them rather than selling them, and began to establish himself as a substantial proprietor.[181]

Samuel indulged in one more speculative burst, buying four common rights at a sale in 1774. However, by that point, the prospect of high returns from such investments had dimmed, and the imperial crisis focused attention elsewhere. By then as well, Samuel's priorities were shifting; he wrote of those later purchases: "Note All the above Common Rights, and all the other Land I own in Bow, I have given a Deed of, to my Son Samuel."[182]

The Bow Proprietors now realized that the assessment being charged on shares, much of which went toward legal fees, was creating hardship for many proprietors. This doubtless contributed further to the group's desire to settle the costly Suncook and Rumford disputes. At the same time, however, Bow continued to oppose the granting of town privileges to either group. In 1750, they protested Rumford's request for town status, arguing its "great Infringement on Land belonging & within the Charter of s^{d} Town of Bow."[183]

In the case of Suncook, always more prone to compromise than Rumford, an agreement was finally worked out. Bow, in hopes of "Saving the great Expense which inevitably attends Contention," proposed voiding its own first division, which overlapped the lots laid out by Suncook, and laying out instead equivalent lots in unoccupied parts of the township.[184] On October 12, 1759, a committee of Israel Gilman, Walter Bryant, and Samuel Lane urged the province to grant Suncook's petition to become a separate parish.[185] The incorporation of the settled part of Suncook as Pembroke, together with the laying out of equivalent lots elsewhere for the Bow proprietors, effectively ended the conflict between the two groups.

Samuel played a role in all negotiations. In the fall, he made two trips to Bow; in September, he spent six days there "Setling Lines &c;" three weeks later, he returned for one week, "Laying out Amendment Lotts." On a very cold first of November, he "wrote Suncook Deeds at my House & Chases." Samuel finally concluded the Suncook affair on November 20, when he settled his account with the committee. He spent a total of fifteen days finalizing this important agreement.[186]

That peace was soon shattered by a new spate of lawsuits with Rumford. Since the king's decision in favor of John Merrill in 1755 the Bow Proprietors seemed more determined than ever to exact compensation for their Rumford claims. In 1755, Bow, casting aside its previous strategy to keep suits within the provincial judicial system, pressed a £1,000 suit against four Concord residents: Benjamin Rolfe, Daniel Carter, Timothy Simons, and John Evans. After its successful compromise with Suncook, Bow looked to a final victory to end the prolonged and expensive legal battles. The Bow Proprietors now openly challenged Rumford to appeal to the Crown.[187]

The case against the four Concord residents was heard in September 1760. The amount of time Samuel alone spent preparing this case suggests that Bow intended thereby to secure title once and for all. Even on the day in May when his son Jabez was born, Samuel spent time looking "over the Records wth Esqr Bryent to prepare for Court."[188] Two days after a favorable verdict was attained in the Rolfe case he made "a large Planing Paper to go to England," presumably for the appeal, and took it to the Bank the following day. His diary and daybooks note more time that fall consulting with Walter Bryant and attending court.

The Reverend Timothy Walker went to England to present Rumford's case in person before the king in council. Bow's communication with English authorities was considerably less direct; Daniel Peirce, the proprietors' attorney in Portsmouth, as usual, sent instructions to Francis Ayers, their agent in England. In preparing to do so on October 22, 1761, Pierce wrote in desperation to Samuel, "Mr Bryent promis'd me that he would call upon You last Saturday . . . for a Copy of the Vote appointing Mess^{r} March Rindge & my Self Agents for the Proprietors of Bow which Copy is not Seen nor heard of I therefore desire you Send me a Copy of Said Vote." There was an urgency to Peirce's request: "If there should be a Westerly Wind tomorrow we must have it by twelve o'Clock or one at farthest or we shall miss this Ship and if we should we had as good miss all the rest." The next day, the wind favored the voyage, and Samuel hastened to deliver the copy himself, despite "a Driving Storm of

Rain & terrible high wind." The eleven-mile trip to Portsmouth took an anguishing four hours that day.[189]

Bow's efforts were fruitless; the royal decision favored the Rumford claim of actual settlement and improvement. Ayers informed Peirce of the outcome and urged him that "if there are any Lands in this Town as Laid out by us which have not been improv[d] they The Prop[rs] of Bow Should take Possession of them, for those are clearly & absolutely their own."[190] Ayers's optimism was not shared across the ocean in Portsmouth and Stratham, and virtually no further effort was made by Bow to improve or settle the area. Enthusiasm for further litigation waned with the loss of this case.

Buoyed by its victory in England, Rumford renewed efforts to incorporate as a town. Now the provincial government supported this move. The continual arguments arising from the controversy had inhibited collection of the provincial tax, at a time of rising expenses due to the French and Indian War. The bickering had allowed each group to blame the other for its inability to meet its tax liability. This gave the provincial government impetus to settle the conflict once and for all. Rumford was incorporated as a town in 1765 and renamed Concord in expectation of future peace with its contentious neighbor. A mere shadow of its former eighty-one-square-mile self, Bow also soon incorporated, holding the first town meeting within its bounds in March 1767.

The Bow Proprietors continued to exist as a corporate entity, for considerable undistributed land within the new boundaries remained under their control. Nor did Bow abandon altogether its claim on Rumford's lands, and the proprietors' persistence finally yielded some results. In July 1771 the Bow group agreed to drop all claims against Concord, in return for a £10 payment for each one-hundred-acre lot within the former Bow limits. Payments were not concluded until 1787.[191]

Samuel continued as proprietors' clerk until 1783, but by then the functions of the propriety had lost much of their former meaning. On April 1, 1779, the Bow Proprietors voted Walter Bryent "all the Money Debts Dues Bills & Bonds &c in any Persons hands . . . Excepting all the Money & Notes in the hands of Samuel Lane Esq[r] of Stratham."[192] By this action, the group essentially transferred fiscal responsibility to Bryant and Lane. However, the relationship between the two was somewhat strained. Samuel added to a copy of the above vote: "and yet [Bryant] Notwithstanding has Since privately taken the Money Due by one of Said Notes [a note held by Samuel]; and refuses to Deliver it up."[193]

While Bow remained Samuel's primary speculative interest until the corporation's demise in the 1780s, he simultaneously invested in other townships. He held a right in Barnstead for over forty years

Reverse of "A Plan of the Estate of Benjamin Smith," by Samuel Lane, 1757. *Courtesy New Hampshire Division of Records Management and Archives.*

Samuel Lane's repeated lettering of the name "Bow" on a piece of paper suggests the extent to which the affairs of the township dominated the life and thoughts of its proprietors' clerk.

before giving it to his son Joshua. His involvement in Leavitstown (later Effingham), a proprietary body centered in North Hampton, was more extensive. He bought one whole right and one half-right in 1769 at tax sales, although he allowed the half-right to be sold for taxes. For the next ten years, Samuel held various offices in the town and the propriety, as well as serving on several committees.[194]

Myriad opportunities for land investment surrounded everyone in New Hampshire. Yet Samuel's commitment to other townships never matched his interest in Bow. Why Samuel stayed the course with the Bow Proprietors can only be explained by its link to his community. Investments promising high returns existed in other New Hampshire townships, as well as in commercial ventures. For Stratham residents, the Bow endeavor was as much a community as a speculative enterprise. Many of Samuel's Stratham neighbors had financial stakes in Bow's success, and it was to their joint advantage that it prosper.

In his role as proprietors' clerk, Samuel Lane drew on his many skills as surveyor, bookkeeper, scribe, and legal advisor to further his community's efforts. Through his work on behalf of Bow, Samuel demonstrated a high degree of competence in these areas, not only to his Stratham neighbors but also to the elite Portsmouth-based segment of the proprietorship. His Bow connections most certainly strengthened Samuel's chances of success both at home and in the commercial world of the provincial capital.

Chapter 3

Exchanging Commodities

Whenever Samuel Lane traveled the eleven miles from his home to Portsmouth, he encountered one or more of the lawyers, judges, merchants, and ministers he knew at the Bank. His status as one who moved within the circle of such "Gentlemen of Character" was a function, however, of service to his community, not of wealth or family connections. He and his children would never be as well-off as Stratham's Wiggins and Leavitts. Yet Samuel found his personal estate slowly accumulating, largely as a result of his forays into the world of trade and investments.

Farming alone could provide a family a certain measure of comfort and economic security, but rarely was that prosperity enough to improve substantially the fortunes of sons and daughters within the lifetime of their parents. By turning his tanning and shoemaking skills into credit with Portsmouth merchants, Samuel enabled his family to acquire useful goods from around the world. He also served as a middleman, helping distribute imported goods from Portsmouth shops to his rural neighbors.

The Lanes enjoyed a family-based economy, in which all members contributed their share to building the household's resources. Men and women, boys and girls all had their own roles to play whether in the production of cloth or shoes, dairy products or agricultural crops. Like others, the Lanes turned to a variety of enterprises to boost their income.

Textile and other household productions, far from promoting self-sufficiency and isolating the Lanes from trade, effectively increased the family's purchasing power in seaport markets. A complex web of relationships, based on needs and on credit, linked

The South West Prospect of the Seat of Colonel George Boyd at Portsmouth, New Hampshire, New England, 1774. Courtesy, *The Phillips Exeter Academy, Exeter, New Hampshire (Gift of Thomas W. Lamont, Class of 1888.)*

One of the main roads that country people traveled in order to market their goods at the Bank passed by the mansion house of George Boyd, at the outlet of the seaport's North Mill Pond. A merchant and shipbuilder, Boyd was among the influential Portsmouth residents whom Samuel Lane knew.

Stratham households to each other, to Portsmouth, and to the world beyond. Samuel's participation in the marketplace drew him increasingly into a commercial environment with a developing capitalistic mentality. Yet for Samuel Lane and others like him, acquiring property and consumer goods was not a goal in itself. Such material possessions were important in ensuring that the next generation would be able to lead equally productive lives.

I went to the Bank

On a blustery day in May 1759, Samuel's business took him to Portsmouth. His activity that day illustrates the importance of the marketplace to his well-being, if not his livelihood. Samuel chose that day, Thursday, May 5, to reckon his accounts; in each store he visited he worked with the shopkeeper to tally up his credits and debits. At one of his favorite spots for trading, Charles Treadwell's store, he "Ballanc'd all acco^{ts}" with the merchant's son, Nathaniel, and "Pass'd Rec[eip]^{ts}." He then proceeded to purchase several items there; besides buying taffeta, silk, a handkerchief, and other textiles, he bought paper, rum, and biscuit. Samuel had nothing to sell the Treadwells that day. On his next two visits though, he would take them veal, butter, cheese, and shoes.[1]

In settling with Jacob Sheafe, Samuel found himself £8.0.3 in the black. He left the Sheafe shop with two pounds of coffee and a primer. He next delivered a pair of large shoes for John Marshall's

Cotton printing from woodblocks; engraving from John Barrow, *A Supplement to the New and Universal Dictionary of Arts and Sciences*, London, 1754. *Courtesy, The Winterthur Library: Printed Book and Periodical Collection.*

Textiles were among the many goods produced in Europe on a larger scale and in a more sophisticated manner than in the colonies. The Lanes, through their own craft, home, and farm productions, gradually developed the means of obtaining imports they needed from around the world. Their oldest daughter, Mary, wore a printed cotton gown at her 1762 wedding.

black servant and then balanced his account at the shop of Elizabeth Wibird. At Wibird's, he purchased four more pounds of coffee. He also transacted business with printer Daniel Fowle; there, Samuel added to his £8.17.0 debt by purchasing two pamphlets and advertising an adjournment of a Bow Proprietors' meeting in the *New Hampshire Gazette*. The number of items on Samuel's agenda that day apparently precluded his tarrying at Enoch Clark's Greenland tavern on his way home, where he usually relaxed with conversation and a toddy and rewarded his horse with a meal of oats.[2]

Samuel's dealings on May 5 reveal the nature of his trade with the merchants and storekeepers of the colonial capital. It is clear that Samuel traded agricultural produce and shoes from his Stratham farm and shop for goods imported from Europe and the West Indies. Portuguese wine, Far Eastern tea, and West Indian rum made their way to Samuel's table, in part because of the butter and cheese his family produced in their dairy and the homespun linen his wife and daughters painstakingly wove.

Besides exchanging goods to meet his own family's needs, Samuel served as a middleman between his neighbors and Portsmouth merchants. Samuel's trade at the Bank was extensive but not nearly so complex as his exchanges in and around Stratham. Transactions with neighbors rarely included cash; instead, payments typically involved labor, raw materials, and agricultural products.

To some extent the Lanes traded merchantable goods directly out of their house in Stratham. Samuel acted as a retail merchant, selling local and imported products such as pottery, cloth, and rum from

Dry goods merchant Elijah Boardman, New Milford, Connecticut, by Ralph Earl, 1789. *Courtesy The Metropolitan Museum of Art, Bequest of Susan W. Tyler, 1979. (1979.395). All rights reserved, The Metropolitan Museum of Art.*

American merchants offered their customers a wide range of imported fabrics. At a time when currency was scarce and fluctuated widely in its value, purchases often required the extension of credit. A merchant kept ledgers in which to record his customers' debits and credits.

his own supplies. The Lane family probably never operated a "store" in a formal sense. Instead, they likely carried just a small inventory that occupied little, if any, specific space in their house. One typical country merchant in 1756 stocked items ranging from necessities to luxuries such as "Calaminico, Cyprus, Hatt band Crape, Black Silk, fans, Stript Caps, Buttons, Ribbon, Gartering, Neck Laces, Ivery Combs and Cartridge paper."[3] Although goods like these frequently entered Samuel's household, they were resold on an irregular basis. He seems to have supplied only a few products routinely.

Jacob Sheafe of Portsm.o Esq.r to Sam Lane Dtr

Apr 26. 1777. To mending your Shoes — — — 0 - 1 - 0
May 17. To a quarter of Veal to y.r Dau.r Mash 12 lb @ 3d — 0 - 3 - 0
July 4. To your Maids Pps 7/ July 21. To y.r Dau.r Ditto 7/ — 0 - 14 - 0
Sept 12. To a quarter of Lamb 8½ lb — — — 0 - 2 - 1
Oct 14. To 7 Barrels of Syder by my Son Joshua @ 20/ P Barrel — 7 - 0 - 0
23. To y.r Black girls Shoes made on a Mans last — 0 - 8 - 0
Dec 16. To your Self & mrs Sheafe Each a good pair of Shoes — 0 - 18 - 0
Apr 1. 1778. To y.r girls Shoes not quite so big as womens — 0 - 6 - 0
Sept 15. To y.r maids Sh. 6 Dol.s Sept 28 Dau.rs Cloth pps 6 Dol.s — 0 - 12 - 0
Oct 15. Madams Cloth Pps 6 Dol. Dau.rs Pps 6 Dol. & mendg y.r own 3 Dol. — 10 - 4 - 1
Nov 6. To y.r girls Shoes 9 Dol.s — — 0 - 5 - 2
1779. To mrs Sheafe mend 4/ Apr 13. To y.r maids Shoes Larg 16 Dol.s — 10 - 9 - 3
May 1. To y.r girls Shoes 10 Dol.s May 19. mrs Sheafe mend ½ Dol — 0 - 5 - 0

June 14. 1779. Ballanced this Acco.t as Equal as we could by Setting one Thing against another

Debit account, Jacob Sheafe to Samuel Lane, 1777–1779. *Lane Family Papers, New Hampshire Historical Society.*

Every now and then, Samuel Lane settled accounts with the merchants he regularly dealt with. If one party owed more than the other, they would mutually agree to an additional exchange of items to balance the account. In this case, as appears on the opposite side of the ledger, Samuel Lane received ten gallons of West Indian molasses and over five hundred imported clapboard nails.

Samuel's first deliberate attempt at retail sales may date from February 17, 1744, when he purchased a considerable quantity of earthenware, more than his small family could use. Clearly intended for resale, this stock soon started to appear as debits in Samuel's accounts with his neighbors. A separate list Samuel kept of "Earthen ware Sold 1744" records nine men and eight women buying forty-two items, including tea, chamber, and butter pots, bowls, mugs, basins, pitchers, and pipkins.[4]

In 1748, Samuel handled the comparable resale of a "Barrel of Bisket" he acquired from Mr. Coker.[5] Oil, however, was the main item distributed on a regular basis from the Lane shop. One of the staples of Samuel's trade with the Isles of Shoals, oil was a product he used routinely. In later years, he obtained his oil from Portsmouth. In all periods, oil sales out of the Lane house were frequent.

Samuel undoubtedly used a certain amount of oil in the course of his work with leather. According to Jeremy Belknap, "besides the fleshy parts of the cod, its liver is preserved in casks, and boiled down to oyl, which is used by curriers of leather."[6] As Samuel took most of his leather for finishing to craftsmen who specialized in currying, it seems likely that much of the oil that Samuel used and sold was whale oil rather than cod liver oil.

Whale oil, known at the time as "train oil," was a valued trade commodity. It was boiled from the blubber of whales and used for lighting but also in various trades, including soap manufacture. Whaling was a more important activity in colonial times than heretofore recognized. In the five years for which the Port of Piscataqua's customs records survive, 1770 to 1775, almost 40,000

Daniel Fowle's print shop; photographed c. 1860. *Courtesy Strawbery Banke Museum; Cumings Library and Archives; Patch Collection.*

Samuel Lane also settled accounts on a regular basis with tradesmen like Daniel Fowle, New Hampshire's first printer. Fowle's shop was one of the few Samuel Lane visited that survived long enough to be photographed. Shortly after 1800 a series of fires reduced much of the port's largely wooden business center to ashes.

Detail of men filling oil barrel in Newfoundland, from Herman Moll's *The World Described*, London, 1711. *New Hampshire Historical Society.*

Oil obtained from codfish and whales was a trade commodity of considerable value in the eighteenth century. Samuel Lane bought oil by the barrel, not only for his own use for leather work and lighting but also for resale to his neighbors.

gallons of surplus whale oil, plus nearly 100,000 pounds of spermaceti candles left Piscataqua bound for the West Indies alone.[7] In 1752 a single vessel carried two hundred barrels of oil to Great Britain.[8] Samuel himself confirmed in writing that the large quantity of oil being shipped to the West Indies was indeed "lamp oyl."[9]

In 1760, Mary Lane appears to have participated in the oil trade on her own account. "My wife bo't a Barrel of oyl of m^r^ Shapley price 60£ old Ten^r^," Samuel noted on October 16, 1760.[10] The record the Lanes kept of oil "Draw'^d^ off" is in Samuel's hand but makes a clear distinction between his "own Store" and the oil purchased by Mary. On October 29 he filled "My 2 Jars in the Chamber & 1 in the Shop" from Mary's barrel. In all, he kept track of sales of eight and three-quarters gallons from Mary's supply that fall and winter, 29 percent of her purchase. In addition, Samuel sold oil to five additional buyers "out of my own Store."

Mary's trade in oil that year appears to have been an aberration. The following year, Samuel, not Mary, bought a barrel. It is not clear why Mary bought the barrel in 1760, although it may have been her acquaintance with Mr. Shapley of Portsmouth that led to the exchange. Samuel usually purchased his oil from a Shoals resident named Tuckerman.

In 1763, Samuel's purchase from Mr. Tuckerman was fraught with problems. Tuckerman "Ask'^d^ 65£ but [there] being Much bluber in the bottom he abated 5£." When Samuel got the barrel home he discovered it was not full, a fact he corroborated by having James Hill measure it. Tuckerman quickly made amends by promising Samuel six quarts of oil to make up the difference.[11] Oil was clearly a valued commodity at this time.

As the Lanes discovered, trading in oil could be fairly profitable. In 1760 they sold oil for £3.10.0 per gallon, which yielded a profit of £45 on Mary's thirty-gallon barrel. The following year a barrel cost the same price, £60, but they charged almost 15 percent more, increasing their profit by £15.

Except for oil, the Lanes' sales of merchantable goods were irregular. Neighbors purchased indigo, pins, textiles, sugar, molasses, rum, and other such products from the Lane inventory but on a relatively small scale. In rural towns like Stratham, retail business often was not a full-time activity. The trade of a country merchant often began with acts of neighborliness.[12] Initial exchanges may have been tokens of friendship rather than strictly business transactions. Even so, in keeping with eighteenth-century practice, all such exchanges involved some form of reimbursement.

On the other hand, Samuel continually noted transacting business for his neighbors at the Bank. On April 16, 1755, he bought sugar and rice for Morris Fling. In September he bought a pound of coffee for Daniel Mason. In 1763 he carried Samuel Neal's calf to the Bank and settled Neal's account with Charles Treadwell.[13]

"Bout at the Bank for Neighbor Joseph Mason" is a phrase that appears in Samuel's daybook with great regularity. After selling Samuel land for his house in 1741, Mason became a close friend. He lived on an abutting farm. His family exchanged goods and labor with the Lanes on a routine basis. Little money changed hands in the course of these transactions, with Mason balancing his account in work and agricultural produce. In April 1754, Samuel recorded what was probably a fairly typical mutual arrangement,"N[r] [Neighbor] Mason plow'd & Harrow'd for me better th[a]n half a Day and the Same Day I went to the Bank for him. I Set one against the other."[14]

In eighteenth-century Stratham, trading was not just a male activity. Half of the eighteen people Samuel sold earthenware to in 1744 were women, and virtually all paid for their purchases in cash. Only one item, Mrs. Coker's teapot, appeared in a daybook account among her husband's debits. Three of the nine men who bought earthenware debited these purchases to their accounts.[15] Likewise, many of Samuel's transactions with his neighbors the Masons, although in Joseph's name, were in reality exchanges between Samuel and Mrs. Mason.

On January 11, 1757, for instance, Samuel's daybook shows that he purchased the following goods in Portsmouth for his close neighbors:

1 Pint ½ Sweet wine 15/ Nutmegs 4/	0-19-0
¼ oz Mace 8/6 D^{o} Scinamon 8/6	0-17-0
½ # Raisons 7^{s}/ pint oatmeal 3/6	0-10-6
	2- 6-6
Sent 34^{s} money & Sed I ow'd her 3/6	1-17-6
Due to me	9-0[16]

Although the above goods were "bout at Bank for nr. [neighbor] Mason," it is clear that Mrs. Mason placed the order and paid the advance of 34 shillings. The account points to Mrs. Mason as responsible for such purchases and for the household cash. Her husband's trade with Samuel nearly always involved labor or agricultural exchanges; the daybooks never recorded money passing between the two men. Mrs. Mason placed the orders for "merchant" goods. She also had a good command of the Mason's finances, in this case telling Samuel the exact amount of credit she had on his account.

As Samuel purchased and sold goods for the Masons regularly, the obvious question is whether he gained any advantage from this work beyond his neighbors' goodwill. It seems that, in this case anyway, goodwill was sufficient. On that January day, Samuel purchased raisins at 14 shillings per pound; one quart of wine for 20 shillings; one-quarter ounce mace, 8 shillings sixpence; and one-quarter ounce cinnamon, 8 shillings sixpence at the shop of Dr. Rogers. These all equal the prices he charged the Masons back in Stratham. At Treadwell's store, Samuel bought one ounce of nutmegs for 25 shillings and three quarts of oatmeal for 21 shillings.[17] As he did not specify how many nutmegs Mrs. Mason took, there is the possibility that he marked them up, but the likelihood of that is slim. For his labor on Mrs. Mason's behalf this day, Samuel asked no compensation.

In 1745, Samuel kept a separate account for "Ms mason" which listed as her debits "muzlin," pins, and pipes; her credits were money and forty-one eggs.[18] Samuel and Joseph Mason exchanged agricultural labor, draft animals, and equipment virtually at par, but any money balance appears to have been kept under Mrs. Mason's watchful eye.[19] This arrangement ended quite suddenly in May 1759 with the £81.15.9 worth of "Sundrys" Samuel bought for Joseph Mason at Charles Treadwell's shop; they were for Mrs. Mason's funeral.[20]

Interestingly, Samuel often appears hesitant to disagree with his women customers about price. Business agreements with men, on the other hand, he set down in his daybooks without any ambiguity. In noting the above transaction, Samuel simply accepted, though perhaps somewhat reluctantly, what Mrs. Mason "Sed I ow'd her," and in similar negotiations with widow Barker he again simply noted down her reckoning, "She talk'd the price must be 3 Bushels of Corn wh She Call'd 12£." Neighbor Mason's mother seems, even more definitely, to have gained the upper hand; Samuel noted "old Mrs Masons Pps [pumps] Should be 5£ pd 3£."[21] In no instances in his dealings with men were the conditions of the exchange so obviously dictated by the other party.

Samuel's daybooks understate the extent of his trading activity. Goods taken on consignment, for instance, never entered his books. And Samuel usually did manage to turn a profit in his trade at the Bank, his dealings with the Masons being an exception. His trade in oil always yielded a profit. And in 1760 he bought butter from Cuffe Nokes in Stratham for 13 shillings per pound and sold it in Portsmouth to widow Elizabeth Sherbourne at 17 shillings.

Only in 1768, however, when he sold in Stratham more than £93 of goods acquired from Portsmouth merchants, was this type of business financially rewarding. Even then, the sale of merchant goods was less than 5 percent of the Lane household's total revenue, in contrast to the leather-related trades, which brought in 61 percent of their earnings that year.[22]

To be S O L D,

By *Jacob Treadwell*

Very low for CASH,

At his Shop in Portſmouth,

BRoad Cloths,	Gauze,	Ironing Boxes,
Serges,	Velvets,	Flat Irons,
Wiltons,	Cyprus,	Locks & Latches,
Ratteens,	Hat Crape,	Hinges,
Bearſkins,	Black and white	Shovel & Tongs,
Druggets,	Laces,	Andirons,
Kerſeys,	Curtain China,	Bellows,
Halfthicks,	Furniture Check.	Candleſticks,
Pluſh,	Bed Tick,	Compaſſes,
Sagathies,	Checks,	Saws,
Colcheſter Baize,	Cotton Gowns,	Curry Combs,
	Dimities,	Rules & Gimblets,
Flannels,	Gingham,	Braſs Cocks,
Blankets,	Gloves & Mitts,	Hammers,
Shalloons,	Necklaces, and	Files,
Tammies,	Earings,	Frying Pans,
Calamancoes,	Snails,	Tobacco Boxes,
Camblets,	Hatts,	Spurrs,
Hungarians,	Ribbons,	Spectacles,
Grograms,	Ferrits,	Scates,
Stript Camblets,	Knee Garters,	Braſs Ink Pots,
Black and color'd	Stay Cord,	
Crapes,	Threads,	Sheers and Siſſors,
Queen Stuff,	Buttons & Twiſt,	Knitting Needles,
Ruffells,		Thimbles,
Worſted Damaſks,	Needles & Pins,	Buckles,
Flower'd Venetian	Tapes,	Corks,
Linens,	Combs,	Cinnamon,
Sheeting,	Caps,	Cloves,
Chints,	Stockings & Shoes	Mace,
Stript Bengall,	Whips & Garters,	Nutmegs,
Handkerchiefs,	None ſo pretties,	Pepper,
Book & Cambrick	Carpetting,	Starch,
Muſlin,	Leather Breeches,	Indigo,
Napkins,	Lines & Bruſhes,	Logwood,
Diaper,	Brads,	Rozen,
Cambricks,	Wool Cards,	
Lawns,	Pewter,	Rum,
Perſians,	Tea Kettles,	Molaſſes,
Ducapes,	Warming Pans,	Cotton,
Luteſtring,	Shoe Pinchers,	Salt,
Sattin,	Nippers,	Grindſtones,
Alimode,	Aul Blades,	&c &c. &c.
Capuchin Silk,	Knives,	

Advertisement of Jacob Treadwell, *New Hampshire Gazette*, December 29, 1769. *New Hampshire Historical Society.*

Samuel Lane served as a middleman, buying a wide variety of "merchant" goods in Portsmouth for his neighbors' use. Many of the things he "bout at the Bank for neighbor Mason," Lane obtained from a store run by the Treadwell family.

Of the diverse family output of goods and services, Samuel's surviving accounts indicate that tanning and shoemaking consistently produced the greatest revenue. An intensive study of three years—1752, 1760, and 1768—reveals that from 66 to 93 percent of the debits, goods, or services he provided others, involved some form of leatherwork. In and around Stratham, in each of the three years studied, the Lane household derived at least half its income from tanning and shoemaking.

Exchanges of textiles, sugar, molasses, wines, and spirits often appear, however, alongside Samuel's leatherwork sales. Except for the few exceptional items brought to Stratham specifically for resale, these goods were first and foremost intended for the Lanes' own use. That these goods were in demand by his own house was a reflection of a similar demand in the community. The Lanes' trading, like that elsewhere in New England, "was geared to the needs of their households within the context of the local community, rather than to the demands of production for profit in the marketplace."[23]

The Lane household was more prosperous than most in the vicinity and had the ability to supply the community with goods otherwise available only in Portsmouth. As the family's own purchases may have influenced others in the neighborhood, the Lanes likely played a small but critical role in the transfer of culture inland. Possibly, the appointments of the home of Samuel and Mary Lane, a couple of middling status, had a greater influence on the tastes and fashions of Stratham's population than those of the wealthier Wig-

Jacob Sheafe, jun^r

Hereby acquaints his Cuſtomers and others that he has Removed to his Store in Queen-Street, next Door to Captain George King's, and three Doors below his Father's, where he has a ſmall Aſſortment of ENGLISH GOODS (among which are ſome of the neweſt faſhion'd Oval Looking-Glaſſes) Alſo, Weſt-India and New-England RUM per Hogſhead ; Sugar per Barrell ; Philadelphia Flour ; Ship-Bread ; Bar Iron ; and a few Hogſheads of STONE-LIME, to be ſold very low for Caſh.

Advertisement of Jacob Sheafe Jr., *New Hampshire Gazette*, August 26, 1774. *New Hampshire Historical Society.*

Samuel Lane never advertised as a Stratham merchant, nor did he keep a store as such. His accounts suggest that the Lanes offered to their neighbors surplus provisions from their own supplies as need arose. Many country merchants are known to have entered business in a similarly informal way.

Chinese porcelain punch bowl, owned by Paine Wingate of Stratham, 1750–1770. *New Hampshire Historical Society.*

One of Samuel Lane's wealthier neighbors, the Reverend Paine Wingate, originally owned this colorful porcelain bowl. En route from its place of manufacture in Asia, the bowl doubtless passed through the hands of a number of merchants in England and Portsmouth before reaching Stratham.

Engraving of a ship, from currency issued Christmas Day 1734, payable to Hunking Wentworth. *New Hampshire Historical Society.*

Samuel and Mary Lane's longing for goods from afar spurred rather than discouraged their own family's production. The benefits of exchange and trade, not the expectation of self-sufficiency, motivated them.

Weaver, from *The Youth's Picture Book of Trades*, Cooperstown, New York, 1842. *Courtesy, The Winterthur Library: Printed Book and Periodical Collection.*

Until after the middle of the eighteenth century, weaving was primarily a man's occupation. Samuel Lane's father-in-law, Benjamin James, was a weaver by trade in Hampton. In the early 1760s the Lanes hired Samuel Allen, a Stratham weaver, to make three coverlets for their daughter Mary.

gins or Leavitts. The lifestyles of those distinguished families may have seemed less attainable and, consequently, beyond what most in the community could dream of reaching.

Whether motivated by neighborliness or a market economy, Samuel Lane distributed consumer goods from around the world to his rural community. Assisting him in this area were the women of the Lane family who, like other Stratham women, helped increase their household's purchasing power in Portsmouth markets by producing both textiles and dairy products.

Sister Elizabeth Come to Weave

The coming of Samuel Lane's sister Elizabeth to Stratham in May 1770 "to Weave" encouraged an important household activity with far-reaching implications for the Lane family. Spinning and weaving not only provided cloth for household use but also freed up resources otherwise spent purchasing basic textiles, significantly increasing the family's purchasing power.[24]

Textiles were of enormous importance to the colonial household and often comprised a significant proportion of a family's wealth. When, in 1759, Samuel tallied his monetary worth, as he did annually, he did not overlook the value of cloth. "I Judg I have added in the last half year past about 500 old Ten[or], besides much Cloathing in the family."[25] Cloth, both wearing apparel and bed furnishings, was essential for comfort in New England's rugged climate; like shoes, textiles merited a relatively high appraisal value.

Textile production was not simply women's work during colonial times. Until the middle of the eighteenth century, in fact, weaving had been by tradition a man's profession. Mary Lane's father, Benjamin James, was by trade a weaver in Hampton. Weaving appears to have shifted from a largely male to a largely female occupation sometime around 1750.[26]

Regardless of whether men or women undertook the final step of weaving cloth, the Lane experience demonstrates that both played a role in producing fabrics critical for use by the entire household. The Lanes drew gender divisions between the various processes of textile production, rather than between the production of cloth and of other goods. The relegation of cultivating and processing raw material to men and boys and working it into a useful product to women and girls applied as much to textiles as to food.

Work performed by family members does not appear in the Lane accounts. Until his children's marriages, Samuel never credited any labor to them, either in the home or in the shop. This was true for his own labor as well. Still, the production of homespun linen offers brief glimpses of the division of labor between men and women as the entire household joined together toward a single goal.

Linen had a multitude of uses as sheets, pillowcases, bolsters, tablecloths, aprons, shifts, petticoats, gowns, gloves, towels, shirts, and trousers. This versatile fabric appeared in virtually every colonial home.[27] Peter Kalm, a European traveler in North America observed in 1749, "They sow as much hemp and flax here as they want for home consumption."[28] Though Kalm failed to note the usefulness of this domestic production beyond the home, linen was clearly valued as a market commodity as well, one "too readily exchangeable and salable to be kept wholly for farm use."[29]

Linen making was a complicated, labor-intensive process. It took more than a year to produce the finished fabric after the sowing of the flaxseed. The cycle began in the fall, when the flax plot was plowed over or "broken up." In the spring, following another plowing, it was time to sow the seed. Depending on the weather in any given year, Samuel planted his flax between mid-April and mid-May.

The division of cultivating tasks along gender lines varied from household to household. After Martha Ballard's husband planted flax, she and her daughters weeded and harvested the plants.[30] In the Lane household the record suggests that Samuel's sons and possibly apprentices assumed many of the cultivating tasks. On May 1, 1769, Samuel remarked, "in all Joshua Sow'd about 1½ Bu. & ½ peck flax Seed."[31] Presumably, once they were old enough, sons Joshua and Samuel prepared the ground and sowed the seed.

Flax plots were small, as the per-acre yield was high; in Pennsylvania, most plots ranged from one-half to two acres.[32] The land the Lanes devoted to flax probably fell within that range.[33] Samuel generally planted flax in several locations, perhaps because he acquired flax plots with his various purchases of land but also because he apparently practiced crop rotation. In 1777 he recorded sowing more than two bushels of seed in four separate areas: behind the house, by Mason's barn, "over" the pond, and in the low ground.[34] The next year he planted flax in none of those places but returned to them again in succeeding years.

Sowing flaxseed to make linen cloth, from *Illustrations of the Irish Linen Industry in 1783 by William Hincks*. *Courtesy American Textile History Museum, Lowell, Massachusetts.*

The entire Lane household became involved in one way or another with textile production. After plowing or breaking up the ground, Samuel Lane's sons and apprentices planted flaxseed in April or May, broadcasting it like grass seed. More than a year would pass between the planting of seeds and the finishing of fabric.

Broadcast like grass seed, flax germinated quickly; in 1773 the Lanes sowed flax on April 5, and Samuel observed eight days later, "my Flax is come up."[35] The plots required considerable attention, particularly weeding. Samuel made no specific references to weeding flax. Though he did hire others to do general weeding, which may have included flax, most likely his children had the responsibility of tending to this chore.

Weeds were but one threat to the young plants. A hard frost in mid-May 1794 killed the flax that had already come up, and in both 1770 and 1793 "worms," Samuel lamented, "eat flax verry much."[36]

Pulling the flax plant, engraving from G. B. Trecco, *Coltivazione e Governo del Lino Marzuolo*, Vicenza, Italy, 1792. *Courtesy American Textile History Museum, Lowell, Massachusetts.*

When the flax was ready for harvesting, usually in July or August, strong men working for the Lanes grasped the stalks, pulling them out of the ground by the roots. After tying them in bundles, they left them to dry until the seed was readily released.

With favorable weather and a certain amount of luck, the flax would be ripe and ready for harvest in late July or early August, approximately three months after it was sown.

The next step involved carefully pulling the stalks from the ground by their roots, tying them in small bundles, and leaving them to dry from several days to several weeks until the flaxseed could be threshed out. At the Lanes', this was male work. Although Mary Lane and her four daughters were available during the 1760s, the record shows that Samuel Neal pulled flax for part of a day in 1765 and the next year Andrew [Wiggin?] pulled for four days.[37] In Augusta, Maine, by contrast, Martha Ballard and her daughters harvested flax themselves; on August 3, 1787, for instance, Martha recorded in her diary, "I have been pulling flax."[38]

Then, striking the seed pods with a mallet released the seeds. Cleaning the seed could take place any season that labor was avail-

Retting the flax, from *View Taken Near Hillsborough in the County of Downe*, published by William Hincks, London, 1783. *Courtesy American Textile History Museum, Lowell, Massachusetts.*

The workers then soaked the flax stalks in a stream or pond and spread them in a field to rot. The disagreeable odor this apparently caused may have rivaled that emanating from Samuel Lane's tanyard.

able. Samuel called this step "fanning flaxseed." After the lighter pod chaff was blown away, the seed was ready to store for planting the next year's crop. Trade in flaxseed for the production of linseed oil developed over time.

Once the seed was separated, the stalks required soaking in water for up to a week. Next came retting, or laying the stalks out on the ground for the outer stalk to rot, a process Samuel called "spreading." It could take three to four weeks before the outer stalk pulled away readily from the fibers within. Then, in September or October, the chore of collecting the flax and laying it away to dry began. The Lanes harvested 122 bundles of flax in 1766; 15 bundles that had been "spread" out behind the barn were stored on the barn scaffold that winter, along with 35 bundles from the "great knowl." The rest of the flax they stored either in the calves' pen and or in the bark-house.[39]

Though much had been accomplished, the flax was still a long way from becoming linen thread. Samuel typically hired male help to undertake the labor of braking, swingling, and flaxing, all tasks necessary to transform the flax into fiber ready to spin. The men's first task was to crush the outer stalk, using an implement known as a flax brake, to separate the inner fiber. Next, scraping the fibers with a wooden swingling knife helped remove any tough outer stalk remaining. Dressing the flax, or, as Samuel called it, "flaxing," encompassed this entire process of separating the fiber from the stalk. "Flaxing" was a hard and dirty job, but a skillful workman could dress forty pounds of fiber per day.[40] Samuel typically hired helpers

Scutching, or swingling, flax, from *The Common Method of Beetling, Scutching and Hackling the Flax*, by William Hincks, London, 1783. *Courtesy American Textile History Museum, Lowell, Massachusetts.*

Samuel Lane's records show that he hired male helpers to wield the wooden swingle, or scutching knife, in an effort to remove the remaining pieces of the stalk and to free the long fibers of flax.

to carry out these processes between October and the following spring. During March 1772, Joseph Mason was credited for "Breaking & Swingling 132¼ flax @ 4^s old Ten^r."[41] Over the winter of 1763–64, Samuel Pevy flaxed for two days in October and for three days the following March.[42]

Hackling, or hetcheling, the flax, from *The Common Method of Beetling, Scutching and Hackling the Flax*, by William Hincks, London, 1783. *Courtesy American Textile History Museum, Lowell, Massachusetts.*

Drawing flax through a series of toothed combs helped separate the longer fibers suitable for fine linens from the shorter ones called tow, used to produce coarser fabric. The absence in Samuel Lane's daybooks of remuneration for hackling suggests that the women of the family undertook this painstaking work.

Once dressed, the flax passed into the women's hands for further processing. Just as the Lane sons' work about the homestead and farm never entered the daybook accounts, neither did linen making by their daughters. Work performed by a household member was not accounted for in this way and is "invisible" in the written record.

"Dressed and twisted together in bunches" by now, the fibers still remained in rough form, and required combing, or hatcheling.[43] The Lanes held the fibers at one end and drew them through a toothed comb known as a hatchel; the same process was repeated while holding the fibers by the other end. The short and broken pieces combed out, called tow, served for coarser fabrics and twine. About one-quarter of the flax actually survived as intact fibers capable of being spun into linen yarn. Another quarter or more became tow, while the rest qualified only as refuse.[44]

Before starting to grow his own, Samuel had paid a premium for combed flax from his neighbors. Simon Wiggin's combed flax commanded 4 shillings more per pound in November 1757 than Widow Wiggin's uncombed flax the same month. The range of prices the Lanes paid for flax, even when in similar stages of production, suggest that the quality of flax varied. In December 1757, two pounds of Samuel Pevy's flax cost Samuel £2; the next month flax from the same source, described as "mean & meanly comb'd," cost 25 percent less.[45] Samuel never mentioned the activity of combing flax. Presumably, Mary and the girls did this; Martha Ballard combed flax two days in October 1789.[46]

Finally, the flax was ready to spin into yarn. Mary James certainly learned to spin before she married. When first living in Stratham, she may not have owned the small spinning or foot wheel on which linen thread was spun. Before three years passed, however, the young couple purchased such a wheel from William Gaut, though it is not clear who at this time processed the flax the Lanes bought to spin.[47] With the purchase of this foot wheel in 1744, Mary had the ability to make yarn from flax taken in.

Within a year of acquiring their flax wheel and with the house beginning to fill with children, the Lanes began to hire women and girls from outside the household to help spin for them. During the summer of 1747, Comfort Cate spent six weeks at the Lanes spinning. Her work corresponds with the "Woolen Webb 103 Skains" produced that year, suggesting that the family owned a woolen wheel as well. Samuel first began keeping sheep in 1746.[48] The next year he sheared six sheep, and his daybook itemized the many steps involved in woolen cloth production:

Woolen Webb 103 Skains	old Tenor
about 34 lb of wool at 14ˢ p[er] lb	23-16-0
Spining at 18ᵈ p[er] Skain	7-14-6
Weaving 32 yds & ½ & ½ ¼ at 2-6 p[er] yd	4- 1-8
fulling Dying & pressing 22 yds	7- 3-0
carrying to the weavers & fetching home	2-10-0
getting it Spun & Dress'ᵈ & greese	3- 0-0
	48- 5-2[49]

The Lanes continued to hire spinners, paying them sometimes by the skein and sometimes by the week. Beck Seavey spun "33 Skains Woosted @4s" in October 1762.[50] In 1754, Huldah Davis worked "2 weeks & 1 Skain over.[51] The previous year, Samuel's sister Bathsheba spent February in Stratham, spinning and perhaps helping care for the children. In a little more than one month she spun 108 skeins, including 36 linen, 42½ woolen, and an unspecified number of cotton. She received £2.16.6 per week for her work.[52] The lack of correspondence between the amounts Samuel recorded as spun and as woven into cloth suggests that family members were actively spinning as well.

Until 1761, when Samuel first grew flax, he apparently bought whatever linen fiber the family needed. His first notes about flax cultivation coincide with his leasing out a farm in return for half its yield. In 1761, Samuel's share from this farm included three bushels of flaxseed and twenty-two pounds of flax.[53] Flax cultivation, moreover, was being generally promoted in America at this time. Samuel would almost certainly have read in the Portsmouth newspaper that spring that Jonathan Moulton, of his own hometown of Hampton, was offering to pay to "take off [his] neighbors' hands" any surplus flax or seed they could produce. Moulton believed strongly that "the Raising of flax deserves more Regard, than has been generally had to it, in this Part of the Province."[54]

Samuel's new venture could be attributed as well to the changing needs of his family, most particularly his daughters. When they first undertook raising flax, the Lane family numbered eight children, ranging from infants to teenagers. A family of ten would have required a considerable amount of fabric for bedding, towels, and clothing. A Pennsylvania family at this time utilized between ten and twenty pounds of combed flax per person annually.[55]

Furthermore, Samuel's oldest child, Mary, was seventeen in 1761 and betrothed to John Crocket. Linen making was presumably a skill the Lanes wished their daughter to carry to her new household

Woman spinning; engraving from *The Cabinet of Useful Arts and Manufactures; Designed for the Perusal of Young Persons*, New York, 1827. *New Hampshire Historical Society.*

When the Lanes purchased their first flax wheel in 1744, Mary Lane did not do all the spinning herself. Nor did Samuel Lane grow his own flax until 1761. In the first twenty years of their marriage, the couple often purchased linen fabric at the Bank, and bought locally both combed and uncombed flax, which they hired women to spin.

Loom, used in Deering, New Hampshire, mid-eighteenth century. *New Hampshire Historical Society. Photograph courtesy American Textile History Museum, Lowell, Massachusetts.*

The Lanes bought their first loom when their oldest daughter, Mary, was seventeen and about to wed. As was the case with spinning, the Lanes hired weavers from outside the household to produce work on their loom. The Lane daughters learned to weave only after their mother's death in 1769. Their lessons coincided with the gradual shift of weaving from a male to a female occupation, beginning in the mid-eighteenth century.

along with finished linen goods. Accordingly, not only did they begin to plant their own flax that year, but they also purchased their first loom. For five days in April, John Barker and a helper built the Lanes a loom.[56] At the same time, a local blacksmith fashioned loom irons and a spindle for one of the wheels.[57] With this investment in equipment, the Lanes now were able to produce linen cloth entirely within their own household.

Mary Lane almost certainly knew how to weave when she married Samuel; her father was a weaver. In 1761, with her youngest son, Jabez, an infant, Mary likely required assistance both with spinning and weaving. Betty Hix worked twelve weeks that year "at finishing the webb." Similarly, in 1763, Unis [Eunice] Kelly wove two webs of cloth containing twenty-six yards. She was paid 6 shillings per yard; Lydia Nokes earned 12 shillings per yard for weaving ticking that same year.[58] Then, for the next couple of years there is little or no mention of weavers from outside the household.

The weaving hired from 1761 through 1763 most likely represented a learning curve by Mary and her daughters. Mary probably had not woven for the first twenty years of her married life, so having an accomplished weaver like Unis Kelly or Betty Hix weave on her own loom would have helped in refreshing her memory, as well as in acquainting her daughters with the process. After a period of demonstration and learning, Mary would then have felt confident enough to proceed on her own with a minimum of outside help.

John Crocket and Mary Lane were Married, oct. 26th 1762.

Mary Lane the Wife of Samuel Lane Died Jan.ry 30th 1769
Aged 46 years 10 Months & 16 Days: having Lived
together in the Marriage State 27 years & 26 Days.

From Lane family record in Stratham Town Records. *Courtesy New Hampshire Division of Records Management and Archives.*

But, in 1767, Mary's health began to deteriorate. Bearing eight children had taken its toll on her already weak constitution. In April and May, "her Sickness" was serious enough to run up an £18.11.0 doctor's bill. The following year, despite the care of Doctor Rust, who tended Mary "in her last Sickness," she died on January 30, 1769, not quite forty-seven years old. "An irrepairable loss to me & my Children," Samuel mourned. Consoled by his faith, however, he acknowledged her death as, "A Holy and Righteous Providence indeed."[59]

During the final two years of Mary's life, the Lanes paid others to do increasing amounts of weaving for them. In late 1766 the widow Sarah Jenness began to weave a good deal for the Lanes, replacing output lost as a result of Mary's declining health. Samuel credited Mrs. Jenness with weaving 188½ yards of cloth in 1768.[60]

Simultaneously, the Lanes' textile purchases in Portsmouth also reflect family happenings and circumstances. Extensive purchases in 1759, 1761, and 1762 represent not only low productivity from the new loom as the women of the family honed their weaving skills but also the impending marriage of daughter Mary to John Crocket. Filling Mary's marriage portion called for the purchase of significant amounts of fabric. A sharp decline in store-bought cloth after 1762 is attributable to the wedding's having taken place and to increased output from the family loom.

In the aftermath of the Stamp Act crisis, the growing troubles with England, too, may have contributed to a dramatic decline in the Lanes' purchases from Portsmouth shops. Colonial boycotts of British goods were a form of protest against British tax policy. Thus, homespun was acquiring new status and patriotic appeal. A lull in imperial controversy coincided in 1771 with a spurt of buying in connection with Susanna's 1772 wedding.

During the first ten years of their marriage, Samuel and Mary purchased few imported fabrics. Prior to the late 1750s, Samuel mostly brought home linen and handkerchiefs from the Bank. He made thirty-three separate purchases of linen during the decade of the 1750s and twenty-two over the next ten years. From 1767 to 1773, however, only three such linen purchases appear on the

The extent and nature of the Lanes' cloth production, as well as their purchase of imported textiles, relates closely to family happenings—whether birth, marriage, sickness, or death. A flurry of purchases at the Bank, as well as local weaving commissions, surrounded each daughter's marriage.

CASH
Given for FLAX-SEED, by
WILLIAM and JOSEPH WHIPPLE, at their Store on Spring Hill, where also is wanted a Quantity of Check'd Wollen and other Cloths, of the Manufacture of the Country.

Advertisement of Portsmouth merchants William and Joseph Whipple, *New Hampshire Gazette*, September 7, 1764. *New Hampshire Historical Society.*

By no means limited to family use, the textiles produced in New Hampshire households found ready markets in the city. No record survives of the Lanes selling linens in Portsmouth, but even so, their savings from not having to buy flax or linen cloth themselves expanded their ability to purchase goods from elsewhere.

books. Clearly, sources of supply closer to home provided more economical substitutes. Linen woven on the Lanes' own loom probably cost 6 shillings per yard; in Portsmouth's shops, linen cost between 25 and 40 shillings.

The savings from the Lanes' own increased production, moreover, allowed them to acquire new and fashionable goods. The Lane family was growing, and with daughters reaching the age of marriage, the purchase of imported fabrics became a matter of course. By the 1760s the family was purchasing materials they rarely, if ever, had bought before. Chintz, shalloon, tammy, lawn, and serge are but a few of the many fabrics that regularly appeared in Samuel's daybooks at this time.

After recovering somewhat from the trauma of their mother's death, the Lane girls attempted to prepare themselves to make up for the loss of her textile output. It was more than a year after her death, however, before Samuel observed "my Daughters Learned to Weave" and "Sister Elizabeth come to Weave."[61] Samuel's sister remained in Stratham for two weeks, teaching nineteen-year-old Suse (Susanna), seventeen-year-old Sarah, and fifteen-year-old Martha to weave. It was too early for Bathsheba, just thirteen that month, to learn this skill. The older daughters still at home had been too

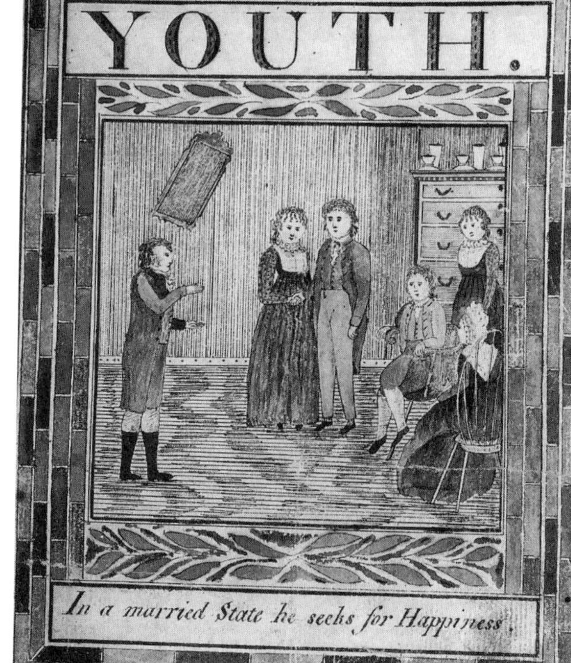

"In a married State he seeks for Happiness," from a child's picture book, made for Freelove Wheeler (1752–1831) by William Colwell (1780–1817), Foster, Rhode Island. *Courtesy Rare Book Department, The Free Library of Philadelphia.*

With the impending marriage of each of his children, Samuel Lane faced the responsibility, as head of the family, to equip his offspring with the fundamental possessions that would ensure successful farms and homes of their own. While he provided his sons with farms, his daughters required instead a full range of domestic tools and furnishings to help set up and run their households.

young to learn from Mary before her sickness, so they now learned from their aunt. The weaving Sarah Jenness had kept up on a regular basis began to taper off about this time. With one daughter after another learning to weave, the Lanes apparently no longer needed their neighbors' help.

Samuel was always proud of his family's textile production. Two years after Mary's death he remarked, "my Daurs [Daughters] Spun 30 Skain."[62] A quarter of a century later he happily observed that his granddaughter Patty, on her tenth birthday, "Spun 4 Skains good Cotton yarn."[63]

Rather than isolating the family from Portsmouth trade, the Lanes' textile production actually allowed them to participate more fully in the transatlantic economy. Domestic products, even when not exchanged directly in Portsmouth shops, freed resources with which the family could purchase goods manufactured elsewhere. Eventually, many of the items Samuel Lane bought from Portsmouth merchants made their way into the marriage portions that he presented each daughter as she came of age, in the hope of ensuring her a comfortable and productive future.

The things I give to my Daughter

Samuel Lane helped supply his home and neighborhood with goods from throughout the British Empire and beyond. Yet his goals clearly extended beyond his individual satisfaction and comfort. The goods he purchased in Portsmouth were intended for more than simple consumption. Certain types of items—textiles, furnishings, and books—he bought both for his family's use and as repositories for his accumulating wealth. In a volatile colonial economy wracked by trade disruptions, war, and inflation, such objects served as relatively safe investments that maintained their value and served as a means for passing wealth on to succeeding generations.

Samuel began the long process of "setling [his family] in the world" with the marriage of his oldest daughter, Mary, in 1762. John Crocket's intentions had become apparent in November 1759, when Samuel noted, in his usual cryptic style on such occasions, "Jn° C——t come 1st t-ime . . . Seeking."[64] He was asking for permission to seek Mary's hand in marriage. Each time a daughter made her intention of marrying known, Samuel's trade with Portsmouth merchants dramatically increased, reflecting his and Mary's desire to equip their daughters with the goods and tools they would need to establish flourishing and productive households of their own.

The Lane daughters' marriage portions were a material manifestation of Mary and Samuel's own way of life, as well as of the hopes

An Account of the things I give to my Daughter
Mary Crocket toward her Portion. Dec 8th 1762. Saml Lane

To one boughten Bed-Tick Bolster & Pillows Containing
9 yds at 65/ & 3½ yards @ 55/ pr yard. all £:38-17-6 [illegible]
and about 42 lb of Choice feathers put therein @ 45/ pr lb } 133-0-0
To 24 yards of China for Curtains at 50/ pr yd £ 60. Ditto £6
Curtain triming 40 yds @ 5/ £:10 Buckram £ 6
Head Cloth £6 Curtain Rings 40/ making &c about 5£ } 095-0-0
To 2 Under Beds — 024-0-0
To Shalloon for a Bed-Quilt 27 £ Lining & Quilting £ 14 Wool [illegible] 065-0-0

To a Homespun Ticken & Bolster & Pillows about £ 35
To about 38 lb of feathers in the Same, Some of them mixed £ 76 } 111-0-0
To one yarn Coverlid £:35. & one Wool & Tow Ditto £:25 — 055-0-0
To 2 Bed Blankets £ 30. one Rag Coverlid £ 12. — 042-0-0
To 4 pair of Sheets £ 85. Bolster Cases, Pillow Cases Napkins, Table Cloths, & Towels, £ 47 } 132-0-0
To a Looking Glass £ 18 — 018-0-0
To 2 Platters or Dishes 6¼ lb @ 32/ pr lb. 10£: —
and Pewter Platters or Dishes 9 lb @ 30/ £:13-10-0 —
To 1 Dozen of Pewter Plates £: 18-10-0 & half Dozen Ditto 8-10-0 } 070-10-0
To Quart Bason [illegible] & 4 Poringers £ 6. Spoons £ 4 —
a quart Pott £ [illegible] and Pint £ 3. [illegible]
To a Brass Skillet and Bail & legs — £: 9-10-0 —
To a Brass Kettle £: 37. Warming-Pan 17-10-0 Skimer 70/ } 068-10-0
To Iron Pott & Bail 7-12-0 Iron Kettle & Bail 5-5-0
frying-pan £ 8-10-0 fire Peal & tongs £: 14. Flesh fork 35/
To Handirons 18 lb @ 20/ pr lb £: 18. Toasting Iron £: 4.
Box Iron £: 6. Heaters £: 5 Iron Skillet 40/ Trammel & hooks 60/ } 075-0-0
To Curtain Rods 5 £. Candle Sticks 50/ — 07-10-0
To a Chest with a Draw & Lock £: 14 —
To a Case of Draws Brasses & Locks £: 66 —
To 6 Black Chairs @ 90/ Each 27 £ —
To 4. Ditto @ 40/ Each £ 8. & 6 Red Chairs £ 15 —
one Great Chair 6 £: one low Chair 50/ — 248-5-0
To one Ovel Table 20 £: one Small Ditto £: 7. —
To one Square Ditto £ 8. two Bedsteads £: 14 Cords £ 6: —
To one foot Wheel £ 16. one Wooling Ditto & Spindle £ 9. —
To a Churn 90/ a Wash Tub 5 £: two Pails 4 £ —
2 Trays £ 4. 1 Bowles 25/ Dishes & plates £ 6. Salt Morter £ 6.
To 3 Punch Bowles 5-10-0 6. Blue & white Plates £ 7.
2 Black & yellow Platters 40/ [illegible] / 2 plates 12/
Mugs 20/ [illegible] Pott &c 40/
Earthen Pans 25/ 2 Glass Bottles 30/
Tea Pott & Tea Dishes 2-5-0 & 2 Wine Glasses 20/
Kenister 12/ Tunel & other Small tin Ware, Coffe pott &c 51/ } 027-5-0
Case of Knives 7-10-0 Cards £: 4 Sisers 15/ — 012-5-0
Sieve 35/ Salt Celler 13/ Knife Basket 25/ — 003-13-0
Pillion & Cloth & feathers £ 25 — 025-0-0
1 Cow 80 £ — 080-0-0
Pictures — 005-0-0
Total about £: 1298-0-0
25 1775. To 2 Sheep 18 £ — 18-0-
1 [illegible] 1776. To a Baking pan 50/ & 1 Pewter plate 30/ —
1776. To 1 Silver Tea Spoon [illegible] Dec 26. 1776. To a Spider 3 £ } — 10-0-0
[illegible] 1777. I Bot a great Pot. 52 lb Cost 81 £ [illegible] Money then was — 81-0-0
1784 half Dozen Black & yellow cups plates &c 40/ — 2-0-0
[illegible] 10. 1785. To a [illegible] Bason 4-8-0 & 2 poringers 2-10-0 — 6-18-0
[illegible] 19. 1787. To a Tin [illegible] [illegible]
[illegible] Mary's Weding Gownd was Cheney Cost 60 £ Since then I
gave her a Stuff gownd to make that good or a Silk one.

"An Account of the things I give to my Daughter Mary Crocket toward her Portion Dec. 8th 1762," by Samuel Lane. *Lane Family Papers, New Hampshire Historical Society.*

Gifts of so-called bridal portions from parents to daughters were fairly common in colonial times. What is perhaps unique in the case of Samuel Lane is that he kept a list of exactly what he gave to each of his five daughters and that these lists survive today.

that they, as parents, harbored for their children's future. Samuel kept a list of what he, as head of the household, gave to each of his five daughters: "An Account of the things I give to my Daughter [daughter's name] toward her Portion."[65] Mary and Samuel wanted their children to benefit from their success and good fortune at the start of their own married lives, when such material possessions would prove most useful. Samuel would leave little to them when he died.

The five lists are virtually identical in the types of items included. Two beds, bedding, and accompanying furnishings head each list. In 1762 the textiles making up Mary Crocket's best bed, including bed ticking, pillows, and curtains, were worth £139.17.6. The forty-two pounds of "Choice feathers" in the best bed alone were worth £94.10.0. In preparing for daughter Mary's wedding, Samuel bought textiles worth £147 from the Portsmouth shop of Charles Treadwell, including "one boughten Bed-Tick Bolster & Pillows," "China," trimming and "Buckram" for curtains, and "Shalloon for quilt."[66]

In 1761, Jacob Treadwell advertised as "Just IMPORTED from LONDON . . . Superfine scarlet, black, blue and cloth colour'd broad cloths; middling ditto; serges; kerseys; bearskins; whitneys; half thicks; bays; thicksetts; fustians; black paduasoys; taffity's; chints damask; callamancoes; tammy's; worsted damasks; shalloons," and many more.[67] Even on the frontier in Kentucky during the 1790s, stores sold forty-two different types of cloth.[68]

Samuel employed several local people to produce items for Mary's portion from both imported fabric and locally spun fibers. Moll Haley made the shalloon quilt, and Daniel Allen's wife wove fifteen yards of blanketing. Lydia Nokes wove thirteen and one-half yards of ticking, while Sergeant Samuel Allen, a professional weaver, made three coverlets. The Lanes hired at least forty-three skeins of

East Chamber of the Peter Cushing House, Hingham, Massachusetts, by Ella Emory, 1878. *Courtesy of the Society for the Preservation of New England Antiquties.*

Beds and bedding headed each daughter's list and, largely because of the imported textiles included, were worth as much as or more than all the other items combined. One of the two beds Samuel Lane gave each daughter, described as the "best bed," boasted a full set of bed hangings, including curtains, head cloth, valances, and quilt.

Bed valance, part of a set of hangings from the Coffin House, Dover, mid-eighteenth century. *New Hampshire Historical Society.*

Unlike the printed cotton hangings in the Cushing House, the Lane girls' "best beds" featured a woolen fabric called china, or cheney, also imported from Britain and characterized by its watered figure. Like a comparable set from Dover, Mary Lane's hangings appear to have had a valance stiffened with buckram and decorated with applied trim.

yarn spun and over seventy-one yards of cloth woven between 1760 and 1762. Much of this work in the years just prior to Mary's wedding almost certainly made its way into her portion.

In Samuel's list of daughter Mary's "things," he valued her beds and related furnishings at £657, or just over one-half the total value of her portion. Most of that value rested in textiles and feathers. The younger Lane daughters, those who married after 1776, received the same amount of bedding, but its value in relation to their entire "portion" had declined. By then, restrictions on imported material due to the war, the girls' own production on the family

Portrait of Mrs. Reuben Humphreys, East Granby, Connecticut, probably 1790s. *Courtesy The Connecticut Historical Society, Hartford, Connecticut.*

One of the next most valuable items on each of the girls' lists was a looking glass, which cost at least £18. Altogether, these marriage portions represented Samuel and Mary Lane's hopes for their children's and grandchildren's future security and social position.

Silver spoon, marked on reverse "D. Griffeth" and engraved "GWL June 28th 1760." *New Hampshire Historical Society.*

loom, and gifts "out of the House" (those not purchased especially for this purpose) combined to lower both the actual cost of the bedding and its value relative to the entire share.[69]

The proportionately high value of the best bed in each inventory may have reflected as well Samuel's sense of the importance of the future generations to a family. The bed had significance "as the place of conjugal union, and of procreation and childbirth," especially for Samuel and Mary, whose own experience placed family at the forefront of their lives. On the practical level also, the bed ensured comfort and warmth in an age when observations like "Sauce froze" show that housing was not always a sufficient defense against the cold.[70]

Pewter platter, by Richard Going, Bristol, England, 1715–1765; owned by the Reverend Samuel McClintock of Greenland. *New Hampshire Historical Society.*

Following textiles on each girl's list is a looking glass, valued at £18 in Mary's case, and then a fairly extensive supply of cooking and tableware made of pewter, brass, and iron. The table service probably came mostly from Portsmouth shops; the dozen pewter plates in Mary's portion came from Charles Treadwell's shop and other "puter" from either Newbury or Enoch Clark's Greenland tavern.[71] Samuel purchased iron skillets, pots, and kettles in Portsmouth, but local blacksmith Nathan Hoag made the andirons, tongs, and toasting irons at his forge. A list of furniture followed, headed by chests of drawers; the value of such case pieces stemmed largely from their function as a repository for textiles. Only chairs, tables, and bedsteads are listed in addition to the chests.

Cast-iron kettle, inscribed: "This I give to my daughter Lydia J. Clap 1801, R. Cady." *Courtesy Old Sturbridge Village (B14070). Photo by Henry E. Peach.*

Samuel Lane also furnished each daughter with a pair of large pewter platters, some of which he may have purchased in Greenland; a "great iron pot" (Mary's weighed sixty pounds); and a single silver teaspoon, probably one of those that Lane recorded purchasing from Portsmouth goldsmith David Griffeth.

The latter part of each daughter's portion reflects some of the household responsibilities that Samuel and Mary believed their daughters would fulfill. Each portion contained a flax and wool wheel, a spindle, cards for combing wool, and "sisers." The lessons learned at their mother's and aunt's sides were to be continued. Very likely each girl had already accumulated her own sewing kit, knitting needles, and the utensils necessary to work with flax and wool yarn, so these items do not appear in the lists. Samuel provided two daughters with their own sheep as well, to get them started in wool production.

Other equipment listed related to dairy work. Mary's 1762 portion lists a butter churn and two milk pails. By the time of Sarah's 1783 wedding her dairying equipment included two milk trays as well. Each daughter also received a cow, just as Mary James had on her marriage to Samuel in 1742.

Although the records are scanty, it appears that family production of milk, cheese, and butter increased simultaneously with textile production during the 1760s. In 1748, Samuel was buying milk from others, as much as thirty-five quarts in February and March alone.[72] During the 1750s, he occasionally sold surplus butter and cheese. Samuel's daybooks point to a rather dramatic change around 1760. On April 3 that year he bought a butter churn from Jacob Low and, within two months began to record the sale of cheese in the Portsmouth shops of Charles Treadwell and Jacob Sheafe. While Samuel noted no dairy sales at all in 1759, he marketed 54¾ pounds of cheese and 11 pounds of butter before the end of the next year.[73]

By contrast, in 1761, Samuel bought one hundred pounds of cheese and nearly twenty-four pounds of butter. Mary and her girls had not stopped churning though. There was "a most Distressing Drought as ever was known," Samuel observed in September, "which Continued till the 19th of Augst and Entirely Cut of[f] our hope of almost all the fruits of the Earth." That fall he explained their irregular dairy output: "People begin to make Butter which has been Exceeding Scarce."[74] In 1762 production picked up. While Samuel bought four pounds of cheese and less than one pound of

STRAINING AND SKIMMING.

Women performing dairy work, "Straining and Skimming," from *The Progress of the Dairy: Descriptive of the Making of Butter and Cheese for the Information of Youth*, New York, 1819. *Courtesy Princeton University Library. Sinclair Hamilton Collection. Visual Materials Division. Department of Rare Books and Special Collections. Princeton University Library.*

Samuel Lane's gifts to his daughters also included a cow for each of them, plus basic dairy equipment: wooden milk pails, a butter churn, and, in one case, milk trays as well. Women appear to have held primary responsibility for dairy work in colonial times. The Lane women often made enough butter and cheese to sell the surplus at the Bank.

butter that year, he sold almost ten pounds more of butter than he purchased.[75]

Although the drought had disrupted the trend, Samuel's sales of dairy goods in Portsmouth generally increased from £15.14.6 to more than £68 from 1760 to 1765. Stratham butter and cheese appeared in the larders of Messrs. Treadwell and Sheafe, widow Sherburne, and Major John Wentworth. By 1782, the year before Samuel's youngest daughter left home, dairy production warranted its own page in his daybook: "Butter & Cheese Made & Sold in 1782"; in that year, sales peaked at 101¼ pounds of butter and 334¼ pounds of cheese.[76]

By the next year, however, the loss of Sarah's labor as a result of her marriage to Matt Thompson, affected Samuel's dairy production noticeably; output dropped to 82¾ pounds of butter and 177 pounds of cheese.[77] Dairy work was clearly the responsibility of the women, and by this time marketing butter and cheese had become an important part of the Lanes' business.[78] Samuel and Mary helped to ensure that their daughters would be able to carry on this profitable production in their new households by giving them each a butter churn, together with other dairy equipment, as part of their portions.

Displaying remarkable consistency over more than two decades, the Lane daughters' marriage portions clearly symbolize Samuel and Mary's concept of a woman's role in family work. As parents, they would provide their sons a completely different form of legacy, though comparable in some ways. The parents' donations to both sons and daughters reflect a society in which male and female had clearly defined roles. All contributed their share to the household and often cooperated in decision making.

Samuel, for example, appears to have done most of the buying at the Bank, whether for the Lane home or the marriage portions. His occasional trips to Portsmouth to return textiles, however, imply that, although Samuel made initial purchases, Mary had a say, if not the final word, in the selection.[79]

The expectations the Lanes had for their daughters are hinted at in their portions and in the items donated at other times as well. In the fall of 1783, Samuel went to Kensington and ordered six clocks from Jeremiah Fellows Jr. for his five daughters and son Joshua.[80] The clock that Samuel had bought in 1747 for his own home almost certainly descended to Jabez.[81] As it is unlikely that young Samuel was left out, presumably his father provided him a clock as well, perhaps one owned originally by a grandparent.

Also distributed separately from the marriage portions were Samuel's books. Samuel placed such value on his books, several of which he purchased in Boston, that he kept a numbered list of the

No 87

This Book I give my 3 Sons, to go round amongst them once a year; and Each may Demand it in the following Months, viz:
Samuel, in Jan. Febr, march & April.
Joshua, in May June July & August.
Jabez, in Sept. oct. Nov. & Dec. — or other wise as they shall agree:
with Liberty to my Daughters to Read, as often as they Request it of their Brethren in reason.
They are all Desired to Regard it as a very Instructive Book, & improve it accordingly, as well as use it carefully. — S Lane

Inscription by Samuel Lane in *The Confession of Faith*, Glasgow, 1763. *New Hampshire Historical Society.*

The fact that the Lane daughters' portions did not include books does not mean that they were illiterate. Samuel Lane paid for his girls to attend private school and shared his books with both sons and daughters. He made careful arrangements for one volume, of which he thought highly, to circulate among his children after his death.

volumes he owned and to whom he gave each. Samuel recorded giving his daughter Mary Crocket five books "when she Mov'd from me."[82] Each daughter in succession received a similar gift. Many of the books that Samuel gave his daughters were religious in nature, which is not surprising, as it reflects the content of much of his library. Just why books were not included in the portions is unclear; it may be because Samuel's books went to both sons and daughters. Because books transcended gender distinctions, perhaps they did not belong in the marriage portions.

The gift of books suggests that the Lanes expected their daughters, like their sons, to be literate and educated members of society. They paid to send each daughter in turn "to School to Mad^m Rust."[83] The widow of Stratham minister Henry Rust kept a private school, primarily, though not exclusively, for young women. As time passed, it appears that Samuel appreciated increasingly the value of schooling to his girls. Mary, the eldest daughter, seems to have received the least education. Each of her sisters, in a virtually unbroken trend, received more schooling than her immediate elder sister.[84] The growing emphasis Samuel and Mary placed on education for their daughters indicates that they had begun to abandon the general notion that a woman's education should be limited to her preparation for marriage.[85]

Samuel's apparent acknowledgment of the importance of having literate daughters had its roots in emerging educational trends. Education was evolving at this time from an involuntary transfer of culture to an activity that was "deliberate, self-conscious, and explicit."[86] The education of the Lane girls reflected the sentiments of Abigail Adams, who believed that "if we mean to have heroes, statesmen and philosophers, we should have learned women."[87]

The formal education Samuel and Mary provided their daughters was but another legacy that, along with the household goods, represented an investment in the survival and prosperity of their family. The Lane brides were prepared to go to their marriages not only with a portion of their family's material wealth but also with skills and knowledge of their own. In addition, Samuel found a way to share, well before his death, another of his assets with his children: the money he had out "at use."

Due to me by Bond & Note

In their daily business transactions, Samuel Lane and his contemporaries faced a challenging variety of currencies, fluctuating widely in value. With respect to the money supply, it was either feast or famine. During a time of inflation, associated as usual with war, Samuel observed in 1748, "Paper Money Sunk so much in its Vallue, that makes it Exceeding Difficult Trading one Among another."[88] In 1765, two years after the Peace of Paris, however, Samuel noted currency problems of an entirely different nature: "Money is verry Scarce & Cattle have fell in the price near half within two years."[89]

In times like these, Portsmouth merchants advertised goods for sale "at the Cheapest rate for Cash."[90] Samuel also offered discounts to encourage cash payment. On July 8, 1745, he sold Ann Gipson "2 Tea pots if she pays money 9^{d} other pay 1-3." This particular buyer did not take full advantage of the opportunity Samuel offered, paying at least partially for the goods she bought that day "in Spining."[91]

As of 1742, New Hampshire's paper currency had depreciated so badly that the government issued a new currency in an attempt to stabilize finances. "New tenor" currency was four times the value of "old tenor;" one pound "new tenor" equaled four pounds "old

New Tenor bill of credit (paper currency), showing the reverse, which provided the equivalent in Old Tenor; engraved by Thomas Johnston, Boston, 1742. *New Hampshire Historical Society.*

In an attempt to improve an unstable financial situation, the New Hampshire government issued a new paper currency in 1742. "New Tenor" was four times the value of the depreciated "Old Tenor" (£8 "Old Tenor" equaled £2, or 40 shillings, "New Tenor"). The new currency did not replace the old, so Samuel Lane kept accounts both ways, depending on his customers' wishes.

tenor." The old currency remained in circulation simultaneously with the new, complicating bookkeeping.

From 1743 to 1754, Samuel headed his accounts each year, "A Day-Book of Debt & Credit for this year according to New Tenor." New Tenor, however, was only grudgingly accepted, and Samuel appears to have acceded to customers' wishes about which currency to use in their accounts. "Old Tenor was the only money of account" in Portsmouth, whereas virtually all his Stratham accounts were posted in New Tenor.[92] In 1754 a woman's pumps cost 11 shillings threepence New Tenor in Stratham, while Portsmouth's Charles Treadwell, buying shoes in quantity, paid 40 shillings a pair, Old Tenor. In 1755, Samuel reverted in his own books to the Old Tenor system, following the Portsmouth merchants' lead. "Although I have kept my Accounts for Several years past in New Tenor I propose this year to keep them in old Ten^{r} because People generally do So &c."[93]

Before long, however, the province adopted still another currency, known as "Lawful Money"; Samuel's 1766 daybook reflects this change, effective the previous year.[94] Certain of his clients resisted Lawful Money just as they had New Tenor. Even after the introduction of Lawful Money, Samuel still reckoned Charles Treadwell's considerable account Old Tenor, while simultaneously posting shoes on Jacob Sheafe's account in Lawful Money.[95]

The state of the currency was necessarily of constant concern to Samuel. Trade, however, continued to flow by other means. Clearly, under such conditions, credit was indispensable in facilitating exchange. Without credit, trade would have been limited to transactions involving cash or the direct exchange of goods, effectively bringing the economy to a standstill.

The majority of exchanges between Samuel and his customers involved what has been called "bookkeeping barter," in other words, exchanges of goods themselves measured in terms of monetary values.[96] In the three years studied, cash never comprised more than 8 percent of payments made to Samuel.[97] Thomas Hancock, a Boston merchant, also rarely settled accounts in cash, "Some traders could apparently carry on long and elaborate series of dealings without any money whatsoever changing hands."[98] Purchasers essentially covered their debts by whatever exchange could be mutually agreed to by both parties.

Though collection of money was a general problem for the colonial merchant, Samuel experienced relatively few problems collecting his due. He never went to the extreme of suing for payment, although New Hampshire courts heard their share of nonpayment suits. The length of time for which tradesmen extended credit varied. For the most part, Samuel balanced his accounts with Ports-

COINS.	Weights. oz.	dwt.	Gr.	Value Old Tenor £ s d	Lawfull Money. s
Guinea	0 .	5 .	9	10 . 10 . —	28/—
Half D°.		2 .	16½	5 . 5 . —	14/—
Moidore		6 .	22½	13 . 10 . —	36/—
Half D°.		3 .	11	6 . 15 . —	18/—
Dubloon or 4 Pistole Piece		17 .	8	33 . —	88/—
Half D°.		8 .	16	16 . 10 . —	44/—
Pistole		4 .	8	8 . 5 . —	22/—
Half D°.		2 .	4	4 . 2 . 6	11/—
Double Joannes or £3.12/ Sterl. Piece		18 .	10	36 . —	96/—
Single Joannes or 36/ Sterl. Piece		9 .	5	18 . —	48/—
Half D°.		4 .	14½	9 . —	24/—
Quarter D°.		2 .	7¼	4 . 10 . —	12/—

ENGRAV'D Printed & Sold by NAT. HURD.

Silver Coins	Weights. oz.	dwt.	Gr.	Value £ s d
Eng. Crown	0 .	19 .	8½	2 . 10 . —
Half Ditto		9 .	16¼	1 . 5 . —
Dollar		17 .	12	2 . 5 . —
Half Ditto		8 .	18	1 . 2 . 6
Quarter D°.		4 .	9	. 11 . 3

NB 24 Grains is one penny w.t 20 Penny w.t one Ounce.

oz. dwt. Gr.	GOLD p.r oz.	SILVER p.r oz.
1 . 0 . 0	£38 . 0 . 0	2 . 10 . 0
. 10 . 0	19 . —	1 . 5 . —
. 5 . 0	9 . 10 . —	12 . 6
. 2 . 0	3 . 16 . —	5 .
. 1 . 0	1 . 18 . —	2 . 6
0 . 12	19 . —	1 . 3
0 . 6	9 . 6	0 . 7½
0 . 3	4 . 9	0 . 3¾
0 . 1	1 . 7	0 . 1¼

Table of coins, weights, and value in Old Tenor and Lawful Money; engraved by Nathaniel Hurd, Boston, c. 1765. *Courtesy, American Antiquarian Society.*

In the 1760s a third standard for currency, known as "Lawful Money," appeared in Samuel Lane's accounts. He now was prepared to reckon accounts three ways, according to client expectations. The great variety of coins in circulation at the time further complicated financial matters.

mouth merchants yearly. His neighbors balanced their accounts with Samuel periodically. At this time, some payment, however small, usually was offered to maintain Samuel's confidence in the business arrangement. It was not unusual for balances to run for several years before final settlement.

In 1755, Samuel must have felt uneasy about amounts owed him, for he made a list "of Some Small old Debts Due to S. Lane." Fifteen names followed, along with a description of the debit and the date it was incurred. In such a small community, a reminder, however, was usually all that was needed to restore both credit and goodwill.

Some merchants made a common practice of "making book accounts over into credit instruments, either notes or bonds."[99] In so doing, they assumed the role of bankers as well as traders. Samuel rarely employed this practice; out of twenty-four notes due him on New Years Day, 1760, only one was "on acco^{t}."[100] However, his daybooks make clear that in other ways he was increasingly becoming a source of capital for his neighbors, lending substantial amounts of money unrelated to his trades. On January 20, 1757, he began keeping an annual list "of what Money is Due to me by Bond & Note."[101]

By this time, Samuel seems to have become aware of the complexity of his growing assets, as well as the need to keep a better record of them. On January 1, 1758, he calculated, "after all my Debts are pd I Judg I have 2000 Due to me and by me as above, which is mostly at use."[102] Almost every year thereafter he accounted for his increase in wealth. In 1761, he noted, "I Judge I Added in all to my Estate in th[a]t year 2000£."[103]

Samuel, not unlike other New England merchants of the time, sought investment outlets for his household surplus. For some, mills absorbed much of the capital, but the rest went into "a favorite form of investment . . . the ownership of land."[104] At the same time, lending money, through notes and bonds, was becoming "one of the safest and least troublesome ways of investing surplus capital."[105] In the Connecticut River Valley and probably elsewhere as well, "it was especially from the lending of money that the merchant obtained his large holdings."[106]

Some of the promissory notes Samuel accepted from individuals were in payment for real estate he sold them; they were, in essence, a form of mortgage. Only a few of the notes Samuel held began as daybook debits; the remainder presumably represent outright loans to individuals in need of money for one purpose or another. Out of the twenty land sales recorded in Samuel's account book, he accepted notes, in at least partial payment, for seven. Samuel first sold land in July 1756 to William Burley Jr. He had just purchased a Bow half-right from Burley's father at a tax auction and on the same day conveyed it to the son. When Samuel made his list of notes due the following January, the younger Burley was indebted to him by note for £34.

Most such land purchasers retired their debt to Samuel fairly quickly. In 1787, however, an unsettled economic and political climate stirred Samuel to press for payment on several long-standing notes. A postwar depression had stalled business and trade. Samuel suffered, too, from the general currency shortage: "Such a Scarcity of Money, that (I may almost Say) No body pretends to pay any Debts, and Scarcely any trading, Except Bartering." The situation continued a year later, "the Wheels of Business & trade Seem to be all Still."[107]

In Massachusetts, similar economic conditions, combined with high property taxes, excited Shays's Rebellion in the latter part of 1786. In June that year, Stratham had taken action, pressing the legislature to issue paper money. Signs of unrest were apparent throughout the summer. The house of an Exeter magistrate, Samuel Penhallow, was vandalized three times, its windows broken with clubs.[108] On September 20 a mob led by Joseph French of Hampstead, John Cochran of Pembroke, and John McKean of Londonderry, surrounded the Exeter meetinghouse in which the General Court was sitting and demanded action on paper money. Peacefully dispersed the following day by the militia, the mob lacked the intensity and anger of Shays's western Massachusetts rebellion, about to take place that December, and the leaders were released after examination by the legislature.[109]

Samuel later recalled of this distressful time, "People verry Uneasie under Publick Debts & Burdens they complain of, not only in this State, but in Massachusetts, frequent Mobbs are Arising."[110] These worrisome circumstances motivated Samuel to attempt to collect at this time on some of his outstanding notes.

Rather than demanding payment himself, Samuel decided to give the unfulfilled promissory notes to his children with instructions to them for collection. On October 28, 1787, for instance, he gave his son-in-law Joseph Clark "a Note from Peter & Ezekial Gilman [of Pembroke] for 18-18-0 Dated aug 5. 1785. w^{h} with 10 p[er] C[en]^{t} Int[erest] to this Day is 22.17-0 he is to get it & give me one half & his Wife tother half."[111] In all, Samuel turned over eleven notes to his children on similar terms.

Samuel's method of collection served a multiple purpose; he relieved himself of collection burdens, for his children acted as his agents, and he received some of the money due him yet passed the rest on to his children at the same time. Samuel renewed some of the notes just before turning them over to his children, apparently confident that the debtors would fulfill their obligations. Other borrowers he considered poor prospects and urged his children "to get [the money] of[f]" them. On average, it took from four to seven years for the notes to be paid. Samuel received his "half" of one share from his son-in-law on June 24, 1791.[112]

In the case of the Gilmans of Pembroke, from whom Samuel had accepted in 1769 a note in exchange for a Bow half-right, Samuel's son-in-law set out as instructed to collect the more than £20 they now owed, eighteen years later. As money was scarce in 1787, Clark was forced to take a yoke of oxen and a horse as partial payment, haggling over their value and finally allowing only two-thirds of what Ezekial Gilman felt the livestock was worth. By the time resulting legal action was settled in 1793, Samuel's loan to the Gilmans had spanned twenty-four years; in a sense it continued even after that, for Joseph Clark gave his father-in-law his own note for £6.[113]

Most who borrowed Samuel's money, however, made sincere

Stratham June 4th 1796
Borrowed & received of my hon.d Grandfather
Samuel Lane twenty dollars which I
promise to pay on demand
20 Dol. Josh.a Lane, Jr.

Promissory note from Samuel Lane's grandson, Joshua Lane, June 4, 1796. *Lane Family Papers, New Hampshire Historical Society.*

Given the monetary situation, credit became a critical part of colonial life. Even relatives gave each other promissory notes; no one was exempt. In the case of grandson Joshua, who borrowed $70 from Samuel Lane between 1795 and 1797, his grandfather never really intended to collect, having written on the back of each note, "this Note is not to be pd unless I Demand it in my Life time." Once, he added "if my Grand Son Behaves well I never intend to Demand it of him at all."

efforts to honor their debts. Weare Drake, a relation through the Robie family, had purchased a right in Effingham from Samuel in May 1786 for the equivalent of eighty bushels of rye. Although Drake had made several small payments on the note, by 1793 interest had swelled his debt to £19. In February he hastened to respond to an inquiry from Samuel: "I Just Receved your Letter Dated the 25th of jany in which you would Be glad i would Take up my noat." Drake continued, "I am sorry Sir you want it at the present Time." He took pains to explain his delinquency: "I hav happened to improve on Dry Land the Last Season By which the Drouth and frost hath Cutt me Short." He went on to reassure his creditor: "Butt hope providence will so favour me in my Labours that By another Season I Shall Be able to pay all my honnest Debts."[114] Drake made good his promise by 1795, and after that his name no longer appeared on Samuel's list of debtors.

Samuel never sued for unpaid debt and in his later years appears to have passed on the unpleasant task of debt collection to third parties, his sons and sons-in-law. For Samuel and his contemporaries, family, community, and long-standing business relationships created a cultural milieu in which credit extension and debt payment were personal and community obligations.[115]

However, Samuel's outlook began to shift slightly over time. His regular lists of "money Due to me," coinciding with evidence of his increased wealth, clearly demonstrate his awareness of the pecuniary advantage of capital formation. Samuel's use of third parties to collect debts in his later years testifies to a transformation taking place, with business transactions becoming divorced from personal relationships. Such a subtle change in the way in which business was

Dr Price Says, one penny put out at our Saviors Birth, to 5 per Cent Compound Interest, would in the year 1781 have increased to a greater Sum than would be Contained in 200,000,000 of Earths all Solid Gold: but if put out at Simple Interest, it at the Same time would have amounted to no more than Seven Shillings and Sixpence.

A description of "Money at Use," written by Samuel Lane in his copy of Salmon's *Modern Gazetteer*, London, 1762. *New Hampshire Historical Society.*

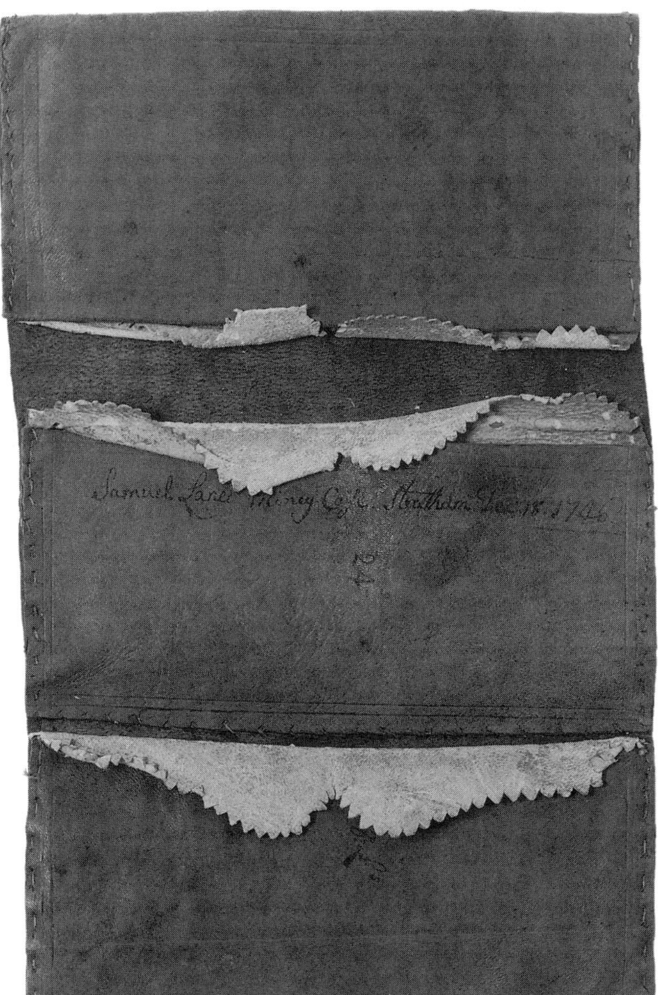

Leather purse, marked: "Samuel Lane Money Case Stratham Dec. 18. 1746." *New Hampshire Historical Society.*

Likely made by Samuel Lane from leather he tanned himself, this pocketbook no doubt once held a bewildering variety of coins and paper currencies.

transacted was to have great impact on members of the next generation. The Lane children would hold assets in business enterprises and bank stock, as well as notes from individuals. Living in a culture somewhat less rooted in personal relationships, Samuel's children already were finding it easier to collect on debts than Samuel would himself, even in cases when trust had been broken by an overdue payment.

Money "at Use" comprised a growing component of Samuel's wealth. He was well aware of and had great respect for the power of compound interest. He even transcribed the words of an authority on the subject into one of his books. "Dr. Price Says," wrote Samuel: "one penny put out at our Saviors Birth, to 5 per Cent Compound Interest, would in the year 1781 have increased to a greater Sum than would be Contained in 200,000,000 of Earths all Solid Gold: but if put out at Simple Interest, it at the Same time would have amounted to no more than Seven Shillings and Six pence."[116]

At first, land was Samuel's investment of choice, but by the early 1770s, collection on notes was routinely adding between £65 and £75 Lawful Money to his estate annually. Samuel's attitude had changed considerably since 1748, when he wrote of money: "Trust it a little while; by the time you get your pay . . . your old Stock with your Labour Added to it, will not procure you Another Stock so good as that you have work'd up."[117]

Samuel was beginning to see investments not only as a means of obtaining greater return for his labor but also as financial opportunities in their own right. By passing on promissory notes to his children, he found he could help build their futures as well. This strategy fit into his grander plan to establish both his sons and daughters in households of their own. Each daugher went to housekeeping prepared to fill an economic, social, and cultural role as wife and mother. Samuel and Mary had designs for their sons too, but "setling" their sons required first the acquisition and cultivation of land. Samuel's plans, if successful, would help ensure both his sons' futures and his own.

Chapter 4

Building Continuity

Above all else, land was the asset around which Samuel Lane's life and that of his family revolved. Sufficient land guaranteed livestock and a leather supply, flax and wool, grain, work, trade, and, most important to Samuel, security. Land conferred on Samuel as well a certain status in his community, not only with ownership but also through the deeds he wrote, boundaries he surveyed, and estates he helped divide for others.

Aware early on of the fluctuating value of money, Samuel translated it into land whenever possible. His financial records offer evidence of the growing importance of land and agriculture to his family. His unfailing daily reports of weather are directly linked to his farming concerns.

The harsh realities of life in northern New England in the eighteenth century meant that individual farms like the Lanes', however versatile in their production, could never be self-sufficient. Necessity forced farmers like Samuel to enter the world of trade. Even in rural areas, "the influence of the market was quite real."[1] Rather than the self-sufficiency of the individual farm, "it was the interdependence of farms that made many of them viable."[2]

Samuel's steady acquisition of land, and his growing success farming it, earned him, after thirty years in Stratham, the unofficial title of Esquire, an honor he unquestionably relished. Samuel, however, did not seek property for its own sake. Instead, his concern for his own and his family's security was ever his principal motivation. Like other farmers of his time throughout the colonies, he appears to have desired "competency," or a comfortable independence, rather than wealth.[3]

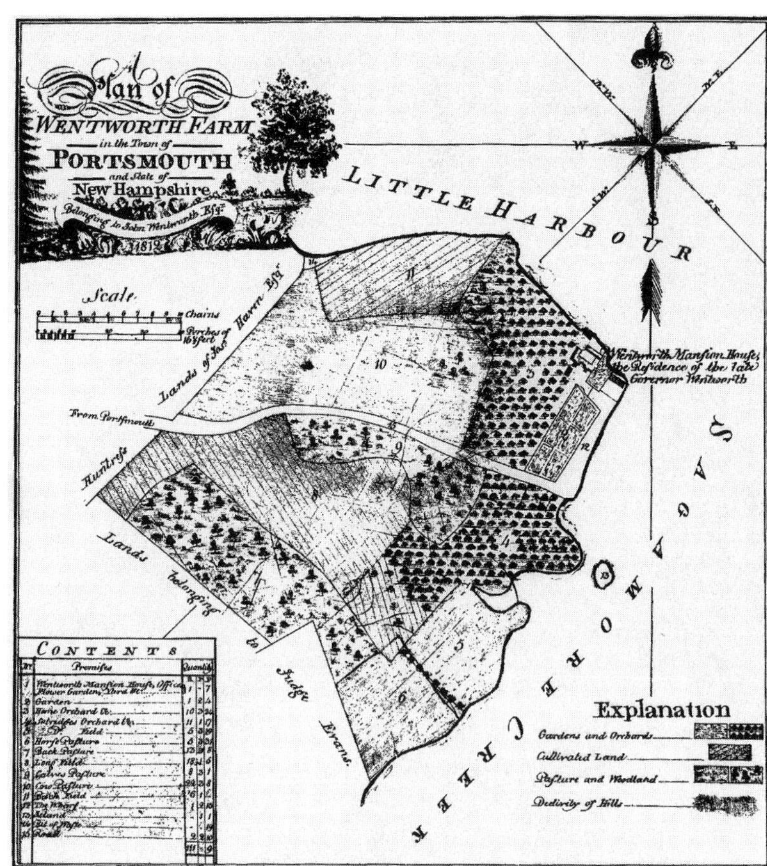

Plan of Wentworth Farm, Little Harbor, Portsmouth, by John G. Hales, 1812. *Courtesy New Hampshire Division of Historical Resources.*

To everyone in the eighteenth century, from the royal governor in Portsmouth to a rural shoemaker, land was a critical asset. To survive in the sometimes harsh and always changeable climate of New Hampshire, a farmer and his family needed to build and diversify their land holdings. It took Samuel Lane thirty-six years to piece together his ninety-six-acre Stratham farm.

Over the course of several decades, moreover, Samuel Lane devoted considerable thought and effort to providing the same security for each member of his family. In his copy of *The Larger and Shorter Catechisms*, Samuel once wrote: "As I desire to do all the good I can to my Children & others while I live; So I desire to do some good with what I Leave behind me when I am gone."[4]

Laying my Money out in Land

In the annual summaries that Samuel Lane wrote at the end of each year, he described 1762 as "the Most Difficult and Most Remarkable year on Many Accounts (I believe) that ever was known in New England." A cycle of climatic extremes reached its zenith that year. A "most hard seveer Cold long Winter" was followed in the spring by a drought for the second consecutive year. "Rich & Poor almost in Genral were all Buyers of Provision; and by the Spring, Many of our good Farmers we[re] almost Destitute of Corn & Meat: So that had not Providence wonderfully Appear'd for us by Sending Provisions from other Countrys, it Seems Many People Must have perished with Hunger."[5] That year, even good husbandry failed to counter New Hampshire's harsh environment, and real danger of famine threatened the region.

While many were suffering the consequences of the drought, the Lane household was reasonably well-off. During that lean year, Samuel did not buy imported corn but instead was able to sell hay; four and one-half bushels of corn; eighty-five pounds of beef, veal, and lamb; and small amounts of other produce to his neighbors.[6] In 1753 and 1754, two relatively fruitful years by contrast, Samuel had found it necessary to purchase fifty-four and one-half bushels of Indian corn and eleven bushels of English grains.[7] After two decades in Stratham, apparently the Lanes were well enough established to weather successfully even severe drought.

Over time, Samuel had developed diversified land holdings, which offered a flexibility critical to a farm family's security. Land conferred a degree of independence from a fickle marketplace and environment. In rural Stratham, work alone could not guarantee such security. The six pages that Samuel bound at the front of his ledger for recording "all the Land that ever I bought (as Near as I can re-

Vignette showing farm scene, engraved by Amos Doolittle, from *A Correct Map of the State of Vermont*, by James Whitelaw, 1796. *Courtesy of Special Collections, University of Vermont Libraries.*

Life on a New Hampshire farm was not always as idyllic as sometimes portrayed. A farmer could labor in the fields all summer only to find his efforts thwarted by drought or hail. He could discover in the fall that, despite the stores he had been attempting to set aside, he did not have enough hay and fodder to keep his livestock through the winter.

member)" emphasize the importance he attached to this fundamental resource.[8]

In his role as head of a household, Samuel purchased land for a variety of reasons, not only to farm but also as an investment for his family's future and a hedge against inflation. Samuel's initial purchase of Stratham land had been guided by the site's potential as a tanyard. The four acres he purchased from Colonel Andrew Wiggin and Joseph Mason in 1741 afforded him the space and resources he needed for tanning but hardly constituted a farm.

Samuel's father, by his own example, had demonstrated to Samuel the need for patience while piecing together a suitable farm. Over thirty-six years, Joshua Lane succeeded in adding 31 acres and 298 rods of land to his original 1-acre Hampton lot.[9]

Samuel began acquiring farmland soon after his marriage. His accounts document his need for land. In 1743, Samuel took hay out of neighbor Mason's meadow and purchased an additional one and one-quarter loads to feed his mare, two cows, and one calf over the winter.[10] That same year, Joseph Mason sold him two and one-half acres of low wet land lying between two branches of the mill brook to the east of his house.[11] Although Samuel called this lot "my swamp," grasses suitable for hay grew abundantly in such marshes or lowlands lying along rivers and streambeds; and lowland meadows produced two to three tons of hay per acre.[12] This particular parcel, however, apparently had been neglected by Mason and was not immediately productive.

Samuel's daybooks mention no immediate work to improve the "swamp," except for a flurry of fencing activity soon after its purchase. As he was busy the next year building a barn and improving his tanyard, he was not able to devote his labor or limited financial resources to improving this lot until the spring of 1745. On a warm June day, he noted, "I Lett my Swamp out to Daniel Thirston to clear."[13] Thirston's contract soon bore fruit. On August 1, Richard Crocket mowed the "swamp," and two days later Moses Thirston hauled hay from it.[14] Although Samuel continued for a while to buy some of his hay, he was on the road to foddering his livestock from his own land.

Establishing a farmstead in Stratham in the mid-eighteenth century posed a definite challenge. The town had been inhabited by Europeans for well over a century. Available open land was becoming scarce, although still somewhat easier to come by than in the older settlement of Hampton. Without sufficient capital to buy an entire farm lot, Samuel had to persuade neighbors to sell him small parcels carved from their own holdings. That was not always an easy task.

Although Samuel now had mowing land, his shortage of pastureland was becoming a problem, requiring him to constantly shift animals in and out of rented lots throughout the summer months:

May 20—put my cows in Ben Leavits pasture & took my horse out & afterwards put my horse in 2 Days with the cows.
June 9 took out my cows & put in my horse
June 17 put my cows in & took my horse out
June 19 took my cows out. June 20 Horse & cows both out.
June 23 & 24 cows were in & June 29 & 30[.][15]

Once Samuel had decided "I wanted to Seek pasturing for my Cretures," Andrew Wiggin seemed the logical person for him to approach.[16] Wiggin, who had sold Samuel his original lot, was the landowner with the largest real estate holdings in the vicinity. During the winter of 1745–46, Samuel approached Colonel Wiggin about the possibility of buying up to ten acres from him. The parcel in question, unused for some time, lay across the road from Wiggin's house. The colonel responded that he needed to look over the land before deciding. Samuel "pray'd him to go as Soon as he could" and even offered him a horse on which to view the land. Wiggin remained noncommittal.

When Samuel resumed his inquiries in the summer of 1746, the cause of Wiggin's indecision was revealed. The colonel gave Samuel permission at this time to stake out the land with his son, Esquire Bradstreet Wiggin. The son, however, seemed reluctant. Samuel finally asked the younger Wiggin, "after Some considerable talk . . . whither he was willing I Should have the Land." Bradstreet's response, though certainly a disappointment, at least clarified the issue: "He told me he could not Say he was willing any Land Should be Sold."

Apparently, there was tension between father and son over this issue.[17] In an older settlement like Stratham, land was at a premium and highly valued by all. Even though Colonel Wiggin owned much property in that locale and was not using this particular parcel, which was overgrown with brush, a member of the next generation opposed the sale. The father may have been at a stage in his life when the land meant less to him, but the son conceived of it as his legacy and was loath to have that diminished. Looking ahead, Bradstreet saw the land as security as he faced the unknown.

In October 1752, nearly six years after these negotiations, Samuel finally purchased from Andrew Wiggin a twenty-two-acre plot that contained the ten acres disputed earlier. As Bradstreet had died just three months earlier, the timing of this sale confirms that the son's opposition had indeed influenced Colonel Wiggin's earlier indecision.

Acquiring enough land to farm in one of New Hampshire's es-

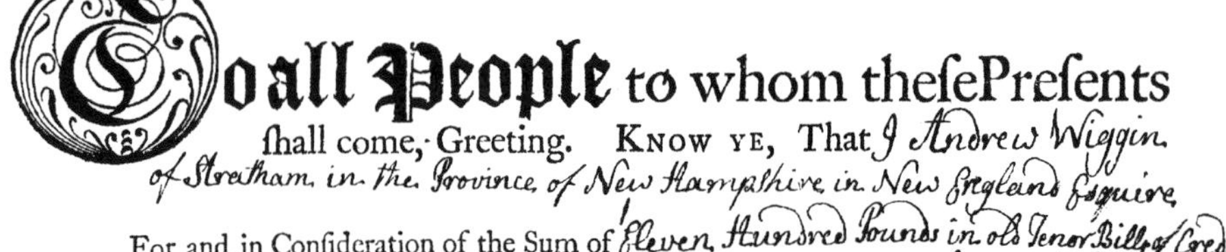
To all People to whom theſe Preſents ſhall come, Greeting. KNOW YE, That I Andrew Wiggin of Stratham in the Province of New Hampshire in New England Esquire

For and in Conſideration of the Sum of Eleven Hundred Pounds in old Tenor Bills of Credit to me in Hand before the enſealing hereof, well and truly paid by Samuel Lane of Stratham aforesaid Tanner — the Receipt whereof I do hereby acknowledge, and my ſelf therewith fully ſatisfied and contented, and thereof, and of every Part and Parcel thereof, do exonerate, acquit and diſcharge him the ſaid Samuel Lane his Heirs, Executors and Adminiſtrators for ever by theſe Preſents: Have given, granted, bargained, ſold, aliened, conveyed and confirmed, and by theſe Preſents, do freely, fully and abſolutely give, grant, bargain, ſell, aliene, convey and confirm, unto him the ſaid Samuel Lane his Heirs and Aſſigns for ever, a Certain parcel of Land Scituate in Said Stratham Containing Twenty two acres, be the Same more or Less, and is Bounded as follows viz. Begining at a Bass Tree, Standing by the North Side of the Brook on which my Mills Stand; and Said Tree is the Southeasterly Corner Bounds of the Town Parsonage Land; and to run from Said Tree Notheast about forty Rods to a Stump Standing in the fence at the Notheasterly Corner of Sd Parsonage Land. and from Said Stump to run East South East, Seventy three Rods and a half, to a Stake & Stones; and from Said Stake and Stones, to run about South thirty five Degrees Westward, Sixty Rods, to a Elm Tree Markd AW. SL. Standing by Said Brook. then runing down Said Brook till it comes to the Tree first Mentioned. —

Portion of deed, from Andrew Wiggin to Samuel Lane, for twenty-two-acre plot, January 9, 1753. *Lane Family Papers, New Hampshire Historical Society.*

Building a farm was difficult in an established community. Samuel Lane succeeded in doing so in Stratham, but it took patience. When he first approached Andrew Wiggin about buying some pastureland he badly needed, his neighbor seemed willing. But with land at a premium, negotiations fell through, due to the reluctance of Wiggin's son. Just three months after the son's untimely death, Wiggin deeded the land in question to Lane.

tablished seacoast communities like Hampton or Stratham was becoming more difficult for each succeeding generation. Samuel's efforts in piecing together the ninety-six acres that eventually comprised the Lane farm took him thirty-six years. In the end his farm contained the whole of neighbor Mason's former fifty-acre farm along with abutting property.

Many in the next generation would find it impossible to acquire land in Stratham to suit their needs. Four out of five of the Lane daughters and their husbands were among those who looked elsewhere for property. Perhaps experiences like that of Samuel's oldest daughter, Mary Crocket, led the others to settle further inland as well.

When Mary Lane married Stratham tanner and cordwainer John Crocket in 1762, they apparently lived on the eight-acre farm that John's father, Ephraim, had sold him. By 1777 the young Crockets' homestead had grown to twenty acres, but that was too small a farm to support their family of six children. The birth of yet another son in April of that year probably forced the couple to reevaluate their existence in Stratham. On November 18, 1778, Samuel accompanied his son-in-law to Northwood, where Crocket signed a deed for fifty-five acres of land with buildings. One of those build-

John and Mary Crocket's house, raised June 1761, Stratham. National Register of Historic Places. *Courtesy New Hampshire Division of Historical Resources.*

After the Lane's eldest daughter, Mary, married John Crocket in 1762, the young couple set up housekeeping in a new house on an eight-acre lot the groom's father had sold him. In 1777, after the birth of their seventh child, the Crockets moved to a fifty-five-acre farm in Northwood. Samuel Lane's four other daughters also moved elsewhere with their husbands, to where land was more readily and cheaply available. (The Crocket house in Stratham later became the Kenniston tavern.)

ings must have been a house, as before long Samuel wrote, "John Crocket & Family Remov'd to Northwood."[18] The fifty-five-acre Northwood farm, moreover, cost only £23 more than the Crockets received from the sale of their twenty acres in Stratham.

Two of Samuel's younger daughters also moved after their weddings to Northwood, and a third settled even further inland in Sanbornton.[19] Their husbands had, even before marriage, been able to buy enough land in these relatively sparsely settled towns to support their families without having to wait for years, and at relatively inexpensive prices when compared to the cost of land in Stratham.[20]

Acquisition of land was only the first of many steps in establishing a productive farm. Land was often wild or overgrown and required improvements. The land Andrew Wiggin finally sold to Samuel, though surrounded by productive acreage, lay unused and neglected. Samuel intended the land to become both pasture and hayfields, and he wasted little time in starting to clear it.

In "an account of the Work I do on the Land I bought of Coll Wiggin," Samuel documented the steps required to ready land for pasture.[21] Tree cutting, log removal, stump pulling, and brush burning took place from December to April. Next to clearing land, fencing was the most labor-intensive task. Throughout January and February, workers hauled materials to the site for a log fence. On March 22, 1753, Samuel and Ben Mason cut stake timber for the fence and the next day hauled it to the land. Almost a month after that they split the stakes and began putting up the fence. The stakes served to hold logs in position.[22]

Fences did not always make good neighbors. The impermanent nature of corner markers frequently led to misunderstanding concerning the exact location of farm lots. Property descriptions relied

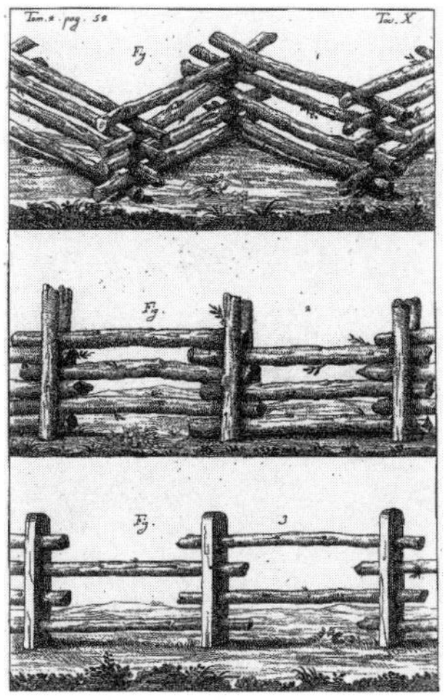

Three types of log fences, from Luigi Castiglioni's *Viaggio: Travels in the United States of North America, 1785–87.* *Courtesy John Carter Brown Library at Brown University.*

After acquiring land, Samuel Lane and his sons set about to fence it. Although stone walls have long characterized the New England landscape, Samuel Lane rarely mentioned building one. Instead, he typically constructed what he called log fences and occasionally a stump fence. Though a traveler sketched those pictured here further south, such fences, even the zigzag type, were not unknown in New England.

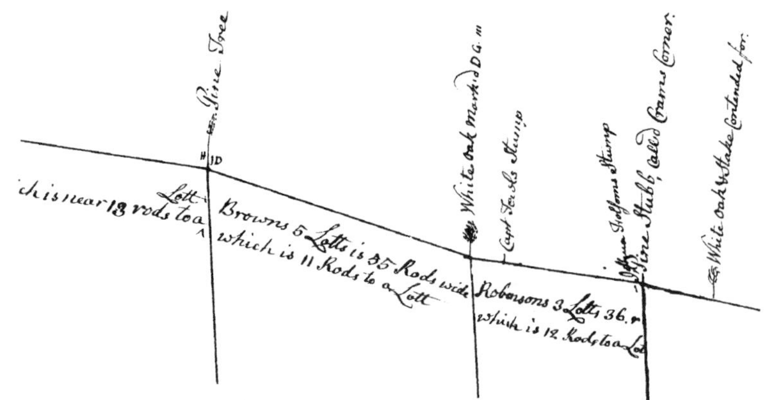

Detail from "A Plan of Land in Dispute between Josiah Robinson & Benjamin Cram, Drawn by order of Court oct 25th 1774 by Saml Lane." *Lane Family Papers, New Hampshire Historical Society.*

Proper placement of fencing and accurate surveying were critical in an agricultural world where land was at a premium. Misunderstanding over such matters could lead to lawsuits, such as one over the location of a fence in Fremont. Samuel Lane, as surveyor for this case, recorded the boundary markers in question.

on stakes, stone piles, and trees to mark the bounds. To eliminate unpleasantness and the expense of litigation, agreements sometimes were drafted to clarify the ambiguities of ownership. Samuel entered into such an agreement with Dudley Leavitt in 1757 after he bought land from Benjamin Hoag, establishing "a full and final Division of fences between Said Lands." After dividing ownership and responsibility for the upkeep of fences, the two further "Agree'd . . . that Notwithstanding the fence between them is Somewhat Crooked; yet it is their full Intent and Meaning that the Line between their Said Lands Shall be a Straight Line."[23]

In 1766, Samuel found himself the center of a controversy over property despite his experience and caution in such matters. He allegedly had overstepped his boundaries, cutting timber and grass on the "mill preveledge" and fencing land he did not own. Rather than suing in a provincial court with all the attendant expense, both parties bound themselves "to the Judgement & final Determination" of a five-member committee of local men. Samuel lost his case on all counts, had to reimburse the complainants for their losses, move his fences, and pay the costs of arbitration.[24]

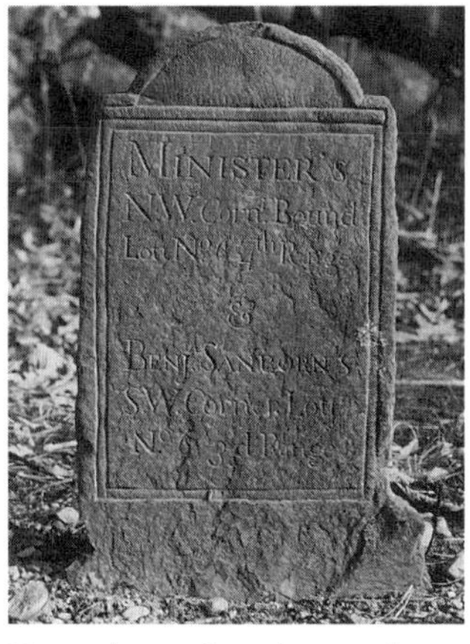

Unusual stone boundary marker in Hampton Falls, carved by Jeremiah Lane, c. 1771. *Courtesy Glenn A. Knoblock.*

If all lot corners were marked as clearly and permanently as the minister's lot in Hampton Falls, much controversy could have been avoided. Samuel Lane's brother Jeremiah, who carved this stone, was a surveyor as well.

Continuing to work on improving the land he bought from Colonel Wiggin, along with a crew of seven others on a cold April day in 1753, Samuel "was hurt by the fall of a tree."[25] Though he was able to travel after two days to Hampton for daughter Sarah's baptism, his injury delayed the fencing work for nearly a month. His crew completed fencing in May, leaving only the construction of bridges over the mill brook to connect Samuel's swamp with the newly improved pasture.

Samuel estimated the cost of the improvements to his land (involving 95½ days human labor, plus 24 days work with a pair of oxen) at £106.8.0 Old Tenor, equal to almost 10 percent of the cost of the land itself.[26] Thus, even for relatively clear land, the costs and trouble of improvement could be substantial.

Province of } To the Revd Mr Joseph Adams Pastur of
New Hampsr } the Church of Crist at Stratham to be Communicated
to the Church &c the Complaint of us the Subscribers
against mr Samuel Lane of this Town of Stratham in
sd Province being In habitants of sd towne vizt that
we apprehend that sd Lane is giuilty of the Breach
of the tenth Commandment much to the Damage of
us as well as Some others which we apprehend we
can upon Due Examination make to Appear by proue
there fore we Think it our Duty to offer to the Same Consideration
of this Church hoping that you would be pleased to take
proper Notice of the Same and that the Matter may be
In quired in Relating to the fact Alledged & That
we may have an opportunety to prove the matter
Complained of which we humbly prey. William Pottle Jr
Jonathan Wiggin
Stratham february 5 ye 1766.

a true Copy as Spell'd & Enterlin'd

Complaint against Samuel Lane by William Pottle Jr., and Jonathan Wiggin, February 5, 1766. Stratham Town Records. *Courtesy New Hampshire Division of Records Management and Archives.*

When the valuable commodity of land was involved, Samuel Lane himself was not safe from embroilment in disputes. In 1766 a pair of Stratham residents accused him of breaking the Tenth Commandment by coveting his neighbor's land. He had apparently fenced land he did not own but willingly moved the fence when requested to do so by a committee established to arbitrate the matter.

Still, after all this work during winter and spring, the new field was rough at best. Since the land had lain fallow for years, weeds, bushes, and trees had crowded out the grass, and whatever grasses remained were of poor quality. Samuel decided to pasture his stock in the new field that summer in preparation for sowing grass seed there the following spring. The animals pastured there in the meantime would contribute their share by browsing to keep down the bushes and weeds. Their manure, according to the science of the day, helped loosen the soil.

The work of land clearing began again in September. Samuel and his apprentice set fire to the remaining brush, the ashes from which would add nutrients to the soil. They then began plowing on November 19. Breaking up land in such neglected condition was extremely hard work for both man and beast. On that day, Samuel's crew consisted of Mr. Mason and two oxen, Andrew Wiggin and two steers, William Pottle's two oxen and plow, Samuel Neal's steers,

Farm scene, Anonymous, *He that by the plough would thrive—Himself must either hold or drive*, 1800, oil on canvas, 35 x 84 in., 1952.1, purchased as the gift of Mrs. Evelyn Roberts. © *Addison Gallery of American Art, Phillips Academy, Andover, Massachusetts. All Rights Reserved.*

Clearing land that was either forested or overgrown after lying fallow for years required extensive labor from both man and beast. "Breaking up" Samuel Lane's new field in 1754 took eight oxen, three men, and a boy. Here one man drives the oxen with a goad while another steers the plow. Other workers burn brush in the distance while the women of the household tend the sheep and cows.

Samuel himself, and his young son, Sam. A total of eight oxen, three men, and a boy, spent half a day plowing. The following two days, five men continued to work the land.[27] Clearing and fencing the field continued the following spring. In July 1754, the first year's labor finally bore fruit; as Samuel reported it, "we Judge I Cut 6 Load of Hay in my New Field."[28]

Over time, Samuel succeeded in expanding his land holdings to create a substantial farmstead. In 1757, Benjamin Hoag sold the Lanes eighteen acres abutting the twenty-two-acre parcel. But the crowning achievement in Samuel's land acquisitions was his purchase of the forty-four-acre Mason farm in 1777. With that addition, he owned nearly one hundred acres on either side of the mill brook. Since Samuel found himself in better financial circumstances as time passed, he was able to offer higher prices for the land he needed. In contrast to £13 per acre for his first Stratham lot, he paid £147 per acre to Nathan Hoag in 1760. Even discounting inflation, Samuel was investing considerably more in his property.

Changing personal circumstances experienced by Samuel's neighbors doubtless played a role in his land purchases as well. Wiggin, Mason, and Hoag all are likely to have felt less need for land as they aged and thus were more willing to part with parcels on the outskirts of their property. When Mason sold his entire farm to Samuel in 1777, he used part of the proceeds to buy another in Epping. Samuel's affection never wavered for neighbor Mason after their first property exchange in 1741. It must have been with mixed feelings that Samuel, together with an apprentice, helped transport Mason's goods to his new home.[29]

Even as Samuel pieced together farmland on his own homestead, he was acquiring properties elsewhere in Stratham with several purposes in mind. In an agreement with John Piper in 1761, Samuel bought nineteen and one-half acres at Great Hill and nearly six acres of salt marsh as well as Piper's two-acre farm. The Great Hill land was both pasture and woodland, and Samuel purchased an additional seven acres there in 1768. These and other such lands offered Samuel versatility: the salt marshes provided hay, and the woodlands produced lumber for sale and for firewood.

Samuel's accounts show a steady increase in income from the sale of forest products, mostly timber and lumber cut from his lands. During the 1760s, when he regularly sold ship timbers to Newmarket shipwright Michael Shute, his revenue from that quarter increased from less than 1 percent to 12 percent of his earnings. In all, Samuel purchased about 306 acres of land in Stratham in addition to several houses and barns.

The Piper farm lay north of Samuel's own house beyond the land of Andrew Wiggin. Its price was substantial, but as a result of twenty years in Stratham, Samuel's various businesses were thriving, and he could well afford the £356 purchase price. With that acquisition, though, Samuel may have reached the limit of his household's ability to farm additional land. With two sons, sixteen and fourteen, an apprentice working in the shop and on the farm, and other responsibilities pressing, particularly his work as clerk for the Bow Proprietors, Samuel had reached the limit of his labor reserves. Until his

Thomas Wiggin's appraisal of twenty oak trees to be purchased by Newmarket shipbuilder Michael Shute from Lane's land on Great Hill in Stratham, January 20, 1767. *Courtesy New Hampshire Division of Records Management and Archives.*

One way that Samuel Lane built his own and his family's future security was by purchasing land with different uses in mind. Oak timber harvested from his woodland on Great Hill was highly esteemed for shipbuilding. Income from the sale of lumber to Newmarket shipbuilder Michael Shute could help offset losses elsewhere.

I the Subscriber being Requested by mess.rs
Michael Shute & Samuel Lane in January 1767 to Set a Vallue
on 20 oak Trees Standing on Sd Lanes Land at
the great Hill in Stratham, which were to be the
Choice & best of all the Trees there, to be paid one
half in Money & the other half in goods.
I hereby Declare it as my opinion (having View'd
Sd Trees Standing & after they were fell) that
Sd twenty Trees are worth one Hundred & Sixty Pounds
old Tenor one half Money and the other half in
goods at the Money price in Portsmouth
Witness my hand.
Stratham Jan 20. 1767. Thomas Wiggin

sons were a bit older, his solution was to lease the newly acquired Piper farm.

John Crocket's brother, Peletiah, leased the farm in 1761, shortly after Samuel bought it. Tenancy served several purposes for all involved. The land was improved and became productive immediately, with no extra effort on Samuel's part. Altogether, the Crockets owned little Stratham property; leasing this farm, therefore, allowed Peletiah to remain near his parents, to begin his own family, and to save money.

According to the tenancy agreement, Samuel was to receive, with some exceptions, half the farm's produce.[30] Crocket was to repair and maintain the fences, deliver half the cider to Samuel's dwelling house, stock the land with two cows and four sheep matching Samuel's stock, and allow Samuel the right to go into Piper's former house to get his half of the English and Indian corn. The productivity of this farm, as recorded by Samuel in "the Incomes of my Farm improv'd to the halves by Pel^{h} Crocket," represented a 9.4% return on its £356.10.0 purchase price. Not only did this tenancy arrangement increase Samuel's farm production, but also his rate of return for this property investment was higher than the typical 6% he was getting for "money at use."

Peletiah Crocket's tenancy lasted only one year, yet his experience confirms that leasing could be an important first step toward farm ownership. The income from working another's property for three to five years could provide enough capital to buy a farm.[31] Spending just one year as Samuel's tenant apparently helped solidify Peletiah's finances. The next year he purchased fifty acres in Gorham, Maine, where he soon moved with his family.[32]

As a rule, landless tenants, though a growing group elsewhere in the colonies, were unusual in Stratham.[33] The capital necessary to stock a leased farm was typically sufficient to buy and settle land in the frontier townships. In 1775, one observer pointed out that tenants were uncommon generally in New England because the lower classes "aim at saving money enough to fix them into a settlement."[34]

The farms and land Samuel purchased that were not contiguous to his own farmstead appear at first glance to have served largely as outlets for his growing capital. In the late 1760s, however, his underlying plans for those lands became clear; he and Mary expected to endow their sons, like their daughters, with "portions." For their sons, though, the Lanes intended to provide farms and land, the wherewithal for them to participate in Stratham's agricultural economy immediately upon marrying and settling down.

Samuel Lane possessed the optimum combination of skills to become a successful landowner. As a surveyor he knew about land and its value, and his writing skills allowed him to produce deeds and agreements to facilitate property transfer. His work as a tanner and shoemaker provided the capital to buy real estate. Yet land itself was not sufficient. As a hedge against bouts of inflation, as a source of food at a time when periodic droughts had "Multitudes . . . beging for a handful of corn," and as a mechanism to inculcate values and a way of life in his children, the family farm was indispensable. Nevertheless, only steady improvements to the land over time would bring the level of productivity, comfort, and security that Samuel yearned to achieve for himself and his family.

Drove my Calves to Leavits Pasture

Between 1754 and 1800, Samuel Lane was elected twenty-seven times to serve as Stratham's pound keeper.[35] In the eighteenth century the pound keeper was responsible for preventing disputes arising from the large numbers of livestock inhabiting any given town. Horses, cattle, and swine often breached the wooden fences designed to enclose them, frequently escaping into cultivated fields. Besides the damage they inflicted on others' property, the animals were in danger of being hurt on the public roads. The owners themselves were "often Loosers by the Damages those Animals sustain."[36] The pound keeper played an important role in an agricultural community like Stratham by helping minimize the damage roving stock might cause, whether to their neighbors' or their owner's property.

Ironically, Samuel could find himself on both sides of the fence, as far as livestock was concerned. In 1756, Samuel charged Nathan Hoag for the labor of rounding up and impounding twenty-three of Hoag's swine. Taking into account the cost of keeping the animals at the pound, it cost Hoag £1.10.8 for failing to control his livestock.[37] In 1763, Samuel's own hogs were the culprits. Under a legal system wherein citizens themselves executed the law, such situations were not unusual.

Registration in Stratham town records of the earmark of Samuel Lane's livestock, 1748. *Courtesy New Hampshire Division of Records Management and Archives.*

Most every family in town owned a number of cows. Samuel Lane purchased his first calf while he was still an apprentice. Marks of ownership were necessary when livestock grazed on common land, or in case a sheep should leap a fence or a cow stray. The pound keeper could recognize Samuel Lane's "creatures" by a crop (shortening) of their left ear and a hole in the right.

Samuel Lane the eare marke of his Creaturs
is a crop of the Left Eare and
a hole in the Right Eare
May the 16 1748

On October 13, Jo Young, one of Stratham's haywards, "Demanded Hog money" from Samuel for allowing his four hogs "to go at Large out of his own Inclosure . . . not yoaked & Ringed according to Law." Samuel appeared before Andrew Wiggin, justice of the peace, on November 8, 1763, to answer Young's complaint. At what Samuel called "Youngs Hog Court" he defended himself by pointing out that the law covered all swine, "excepting they shall be by accident let out of such Inclosure." Esquire Wiggin's decision, given this quandary, was not recorded.[38]

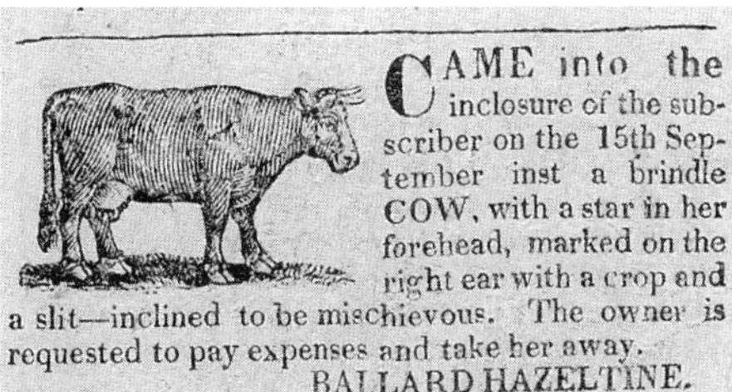
CAME into the inclosure of the subscriber on the 15th September inst a brindle COW, with a star in her forehead, marked on the right ear with a crop and a slit—inclined to be mischievous. The owner is requested to pay expenses and take her away.
BALLARD HAZELTINE.
Concord, Sept. 28, 1821. 32

Advertisement for stray cow, Concord, 1821. *New Hampshire Historical Society.*

The support and regulation of livestock were important considerations for the town of Stratham. As of the 1732 census, livestock comprised 60 percent of the town's total wealth and were worth twice as much as its land.[39] Keeping farm animals, moreover, required significant resources. Throughout New England, farmers everywhere mirrored Samuel's efforts to convert land into pasture and hayfields to support their livestock. Making the countryside suitable for stock raising required creating upland hayfields and pasture sown with European seed, an improved system of roads, extensive fencing, and the

Cor	heads	horse	hors	oxen	Cows	three 3 year olds	two 2 year olds	1 year olds	swine	Improved Lands		Pasture Lands	Mills
Cornal Wiggin	3	1	1	4	8	4	0	6		50		50	2
Simon Wiggin	2	1	1	2	3	3	3	2	0	30		25	
Andrew Wiggin	3	1	2	2	11	2	4	6	1	50		50	
Noah Barker	2	1	1	0	7	2	2	5	1	45		55	
William Pottle	2	1	1		4	3	6	4		30		15	
Joseph mason	1	1	1		2		1			12		6	
Daniel mason	2	0	0	0	1	0	0	1	0	0			
Bradstreet wiggin	1	1	1	2	2	0	2	2	0	15	0	0	
Joseph mason Jur	1	1	1	0	2	0	2	0	0	9	0	4	
Jeremiah mason	1	1	1	0	1	0	0	0	0	0	0	0	
Nathan Talyr	1	1	1	0	2	0	2	0	0	12		12	
Samual Clarke	4	1	2	0	2	0	0	0	0	12	0	13	1
Moses Thirston	1	1	0	0	3	1	2	5	0	35	0	15	
Samual Lane	2	1	0	0	1	0	0	0	0	3	0	0	
Nicholas wiggin	1	0	2	0	1	0	0	0	0	0	0	0	
Henory wiggin	1	1	0	0	2	0	0	0	0	0	0	0	
Joshua Hill	2	1	1	0	4	2	1	0	0	12		8	
John Hill	1	1	1	2	3	0	2	4	0	16		18	
John Jons	1	1	1	0	2	0	4	0	0	15		16	
Timothy Jons	1	0	0	0	1	0	0	1	0	0	0	0	

extermination of predators such as the wolf.[40] Only through such a far-reaching transformation of the landscape could animal husbandry be made viable in New England.

Samuel purchased his first farm animal before he was twenty-one. "I Bo't a Calf & hired it kept, and it is now a Cow . . . which is of great Service toward my Support, for Milk, Butter & Cheese: I also have a heifer, & eight Sheep."[41] Getting a start in animal husbandry was important, even to a single male with a trade.

In New England's climate, cattle lived outside whenever pasture was available. Tax law suggests that four acres of pasture per cow was considered essential.[42] During the winter, stock required shelter. Until Samuel built his barn in 1743, he at first boarded his cow with other farmers and then, the following winter, kept cows in his new barkhouse. Every summer, hay had to be mowed, hauled to the barn, and stored for winter feed. Grass from wet lowland areas supplied the New England farmer with plentiful hay during the early colonial period, but by the 1740s farmers were creating hayfields out of the uplands to meet the increasing demand. Much of the clearing that took place was not to create land for tillage but to support more cattle.

Samuel's own gradual acquisition of land was in large part intended to support his livestock. As Samuel's farm grew, so did his stock of animals. His livestock numbers appear to fit the pattern of a typical colonial farm. A farm such as the Lanes' probably was comparable to the average in Falmouth, Maine, for 1760: one horse; two oxen; three or four cows; one or two swine; and a flock of nine or ten sheep.[43]

By the 1770s, Samuel had approximately fifteen acres of hay lands and forty acres of pasture in Stratham.[44] As New Hampshire tax law of the time indicates, Samuel's pasture would have been capable of supporting ten cows or steers; the greatest number of bovine animals he actually kept in any year was twelve. Samuel's hayfields produced sufficient hay for these animals, plus a horse or two. On the rare occasion that Samuel noted hay by the ton, his yield was three tons per acre of hayfield. In 1781 he laid away 720 cocks, or 36 tons of hay cut from twelve acres; the following year's yield was slightly less, 691 cocks, or 34 tons of hay.[45]

The barn Samuel built when he first married was modest in size, just thirty-six feet wide and twenty feet deep. It provided several lev-

(*Facing page*) Account of polls and rateable estates in Stratham, 1742. Stratham Town Records. *Courtesy New Hampshire Division of Records Management and Archives.*

The annual town inventory, on which taxes were based, suggests the importance of livestock, land, and mills to the rural community. At the date of this particular inventory, Samuel Lane had just arrived in town. His assets were few compared to those of the Wiggins.

Farm in Canaan, Connecticut; engraving from the *Columbian Magazine, or Monthly Miscellany*, March 1789. *New Hampshire Historical Society.*

A farmer had to have at least four acres of land to adequately maintain each animal he owned. The hay his land yielded was best stored in a barn, but such was not always possible. Samuel Lane was constantly building additions to his barn to hold his livestock's winter feed. Barns in the eighteenth century were most commonly of the so-called English type seen here, with a door in the side rather than at the gable end.

els for hay storage, with a scaffold at the front, a main scaffold over the center aisle, and a scaffold in the northeast corner.[46] Although adequate in the early years, when his farm was small, this barn proved too small as his acreage increased. In 1761 he added to the front of the barn, doubling the structure's size and creating another scaffold. A 1782 addition at the other end mirrored the 1761 structure. Samuel called it his "New Brn," and that year he put hay on his "New Scaffold."

A recent assessment concludes that, at least in Pennsylvania, "the generally small size and poor quality of [American] cattle resulted not from lack of feed but from lack of concern about feed quality and care."[47] The first cattle in New Hampshire, a "coarse Danish cattle," were imported by John Mason in 1633. Little concerted effort was made to improve the cattle through scientific breeding programs until the end of the eighteenth century.[48] Around 1750 an English traveler, James Birket, described the farm animals he saw in New England: "their Cattle are small but Seemingly very strong, having Short thick bodies and Short Limbs."[49] Other commentators, both past and present, have been more critical, finding the local cattle "thin, scrawny, and sickly."[50] The author of *American Husbandry* minced no words in his assessment: "Most of the farmers in this country are, in whatever concerns cattle, the most negligent ignorant set of men in the world. Nor do I know any country in which animals are worse treated. . . . After the hardest day's work, all the nourishment they are like to have is to be turned out into a wood, where the shoots and weeds form the chief of the pasture."[51]

Samuel confirmed the hardships New England cattle sometimes endured. In 1762, after a "most hard Seveer Cold long Winter," he wrote: "Many People having large Stocks of Cattle, & but few of them fit to Kill, presumed to keep them over, on a little Hay, trying to keep them alive by Corn Brouse &c hoping for a Moderate Winter; but the Winter proving verry hard Many Cattle & Horses & Swine & abundance of Sheep & Lambs Died; tho' indeed not So Many as might Justly have been Expected in So Scanty a Season."[52]

"Brousing Cattle in the Woods" was a traditional way to feed cattle over the winter. Samuel tried to avoid such treatment. He wintered them inside even if that required leasing space in another's barn, and he acquired adequate pasture and hayfields to feed them. Yet he appears to have tacitly accepted inferior treatment of farm animals as the norm. His comment that not nearly as many cattle died as "might Justly have been expected" suggests that he too was hardened to the realities of minimal care.

Farmers were acutely aware of the correlation between the amount and type of feed and the work cattle could do. During the drought years of 1761 and 1762, for example, "People were put to Difficulty to get their Plowing done for want of Hay."[53] Those that fed their steers hay over the winter sometimes found themselves short and substituted corn. As a result, Samuel wrote in 1750, " 'tis observ'd that oxen were Never in better Heart to Plow than they are this Spring."[54] Despite this demonstration of its efficacy, however, grain was too expensive a commodity for most New Hampshire farmers to feed their cattle.

Out of necessity, the mere survival of cattle in the harsh New Hampshire climate seems to have been the farmer's overriding concern, diverting attention away from more ambitious goals of improving the breed. In 1749, Samuel wrote of "the Uncommon Difficultys People have been put too for a living themselves" and added "but More especially to keep their Cattle alive." Just to keep animals alive often required special measures. In 1749, Samuel reported, "many go 40, 50, or 60 Miles into the Woods, to Cut Meadows; and Drive th[eir cattle] into the Woods & Brouse them: Some cut leaves off trees & carry into their Barns &c for Cattle to live on in Winter."[55]

The European critics who blamed the American farmer for cattle that "degenerates by degrees here, and becomes smaller" appear to have underestimated the hardships colonial farmers faced.[56] Far from neglecting their animals, Stratham's farmers, as recorded by Samuel, seem to have gone to extraordinary efforts just to keep their animals alive. This life-and-death struggle understandably precluded more sophisticated measures to improve the breed at this time.

Samuel's own concern for his livestock is clearly evident. When a cow named Black calved in April 1790, he noted that she was twenty-five days late; five years later, when she had twin calves, he commented, "she being about 15 year old."[57] Such observations, although rare, point to a personal interest in his herd's welfare. His

BULL, the male of the ox kind. The marks of a good one for propagation, according to Mortimer, are thefe. He fhould have a quick countenance, his forehead large and curled, his eyes black and large, his horns large, ftraight and black, his neck flefhy, his belly long and large, his hair fmooth like velvet, his breaft big, his back ftraight and flat, his buttocks fquare, his thighs round, his legs ftraight, and his joints fhort.

"The marks of a good bull" from *The New-England Farmer*, 1790; from copy owned by Samuel Lane. *New Hampshire Historical Society.*

European observers often criticized American farmers for their lack of attention to animal breeding, not recognizing that the mere survival of the herd was generally of more immediate concern. Samuel kept cryptic notes as to when a particular cow "took bull." And reference books he owned, at least toward the end of his career, described characteristics to look for to improve his stock.

Great Ox Columbus,

Probably the Largest in the World, weighing about **4000** *Pounds.*

THIS extraordinary Animal will be exhibited during four or five days, at *MUNROE'S COFFEE-HOUSE.*

He was bred in Greenland, N. H. and will not be seven years old until next June—and it is the opinion of good judges, that he has not yet arrived at his full size, and may be made to come up to the enormous weight of 5000 Pounds.

"Great Ox Columbus," bred in Greenland; woodcut from the *Providence (R.I.) Patriot and Columbian Phenix*, April 25, 1827. *Courtesy, American Antiquarian Society.*

Animal husbandry in New Hampshire improved so rapidly that this prize-winning ox, bred in neighboring Greenland a couple of decades after Samuel Lane's death, weighed more than four times as much as the "fat ox" he slaughtered in 1765.

breeding records also indicate an interest that went beyond the mere survival of his herd. In 1791 he observed that "tis Said Cows are likelyest to Stand to y^{r} Buling when they have almost done running."[58]

Cattle served several purposes on the colonial farm, not only providing meat and dairy products for the table and for export but also animal power for crop cultivation and other heavy work. Before the late 1750s, when Samuel began to keep steers for work, he hired others to plow for him. As draft animals "oxen were particularly suitable for work among tree stumps and rocks; the single chain running from yoke to load was an ideally simple tackle."[59] Steers became the chief draft animal, as sleighs, carts, and farm implements of the era were too heavy for horses to pull easily over rough terrain. And after a useful life in the yoke, working cattle provided meat for the family as well.

However harshly treated in comparison to those of Europe, New England cattle helped redress the trade imbalance caused by grain imports. Both live animals and meat were exported to the West Indies and other British colonies and later to other states. Samuel's continual references to beef prices confirms the significance of meat as a market commodity. In 1790 he specifically described the export market for beef: "Abundance of Beaf Kill'd and Ship'd off, at a pretty good price, for Money."[60] He also sold cattle on the hoof in Stratham and Portsmouth.

The livestock market helped make the New Hampshire farm viable. According to one observer, "the farmers find great advantage in keeping a large part of their farms for pasturage, as they are thereby enabled to support large herds of cattle and flocks of sheep which much improve their farms." He estimated that nearly 14 percent of the exports from New England in the decade before the Revolution were in the form of livestock.[61] Samuel set aside ten times

10 Oxen, 10 Horses & Provinder

416 barrels Beef. 20 boxes Spermacati Candles, 19 Maple Desks

45 bbls Beef. 10 boxes Spermacati Candles

500 ft Ranging timber. 180 Sparrs. 200 ft Blocks

10 Tubs Beef

Shipments to the West Indies, Piscataqua Customs Records, early 1770s. Copy at the Portsmouth Athenaeum.

Some of the meat, as well as the livestock, that Samuel Lane sold at the Bank may have ended up in the holds of vessels bound for the West Indies. Between 1770 and 1775, New Hampshire merchants shipped from the port not only large quantities of preserved meat packed in barrels and tubs but also five thousand sheep and fifteen hundred oxen.

Bought 4 Carcases of Beef each weighing 498 Pounds apiece at 3d 3/4 a pound what cost the whole?

If 1 lb cost 3 " 3 what will 1992 Cost?

Answer 31-2-6

If 1992 lb cost 31-2-6 What will 1 lb Cost?

3-3. Proof

An arithmetic exercise, from Jabez Lane's student copybook, 1777. *Lane Family Papers, New Hampshire Historical Society.*

The fact that a school lesson of the day included an exercise in figuring the value of beef underscores the importance of this commodity in the marketplace.

as much land to support livestock as he did to grow crops for human consumption. Throughout New England animal husbandry accounted for more land use than all other agriculture combined. "Grazing animals were one of the linchpins that made commercial agriculture possible in New England."[62]

That Samuel considered cattle a market commodity is clear in his writings; he often spoke of his cows as his "beef." In 1745 he noted, "I brot my Beaf home from the wid Jones'," simultaneously crediting her for one month's pasturing of his cows.[63] In his eyes all cattle were destined for the table. His diary contains an annual round of livestock slaughter. Late fall, when the weather was cold enough to help preserve the meat, ushered in "killing time." Samuel usually slaughtered a cow in November or December. When, following the butchering of a heifer weighing 272 pounds on October 23, 1762, Samuel accounted for the "Beaf I parted with," various individuals had purchased from 5 to 67 pounds.

Not all Samuel's beef sales were local.[64] Veal, beef, lamb, mutton, and pork all appear in his Portsmouth accounts. The 149 pounds from the heifer not "parted with" either went to the seacoast or helped feed his family. According to recent estimates, each member of a colonial household required nearly 50 pounds of beef annually.[65] Samuel's ten-member family could have consumed as much as half the beef he raised. His cows usually fell in the 400–450-pound range, much less than dressed steers weigh today. In January 1765 his "fat ox" gave 721 pounds of beef in addition to its hide and tallow, for a total of 886 pounds.[66]

"Milking," from *The Progress of the Dairy: Descriptive of the Making of Butter and Cheese for the Information of Youth*, New York, 1819. *Courtesy Princeton University Library. Sinclair Hamilton Collection. Visual Materials Division. Department of Rare Books and Special Collections. Princeton University Library.*

Samuel Lane's cows bore names like "Brown," "Gentle," and "Flower." He gave each of his daughters a cow, together with a milk pail, as part of her bridal portion. Almost certainly, the Lane girls were responsible for milking the cows on their father's farm.

Cows were important also for the dairy products they provided, both for consumption at home and for trade with others. As early as 1743, Samuel sold 31 pounds of butter and 16¾ pounds of cheese in Portsmouth. In comparison with some other farms in New England, the Lanes' output was modest but fairly typical. At their peak of production in 1782, they marketed 334 pounds of cheese plus 101 pounds of butter. A single large Rhode Island dairy was producing thirteen thousand pounds of cheese annually by midcentury.[67] New Hampshire boasted no operations on that scale.[68]

Milk production in general was low by modern standards. A cow giving four quarts a day was "very good"; one quart was closer to the norm. It took two gallons of milk to make one pound of cheese, one gallon for a pound of butter.[69]

It is clear that the women of the household had the responsibility for milk, butter, and cheese production. Each Lane daughter received a butter churn as a part of her portion. Her responsibilities probably went beyond processing the raw milk to milking cows and tending calves.[70]

In the 1790s, New Hampshire's historian Jeremy Belknap described "the work of a dairy" as "an employment which always falls to [women's] lot, and is an object of their ambition, as well as interest."[71] In Hallowell, Maine, Martha Ballard "milked cows, fed swine, set hens, and more than once trudged 'up the Crik' looking for a wandering calf."[72] However, the boundaries of this work were not always defined by gender; Caleb Jackson Jr. of Rowley, Massachusetts, "milked the cows before sunrise" on a September morning in 1802, though his mother and sister lived in the house at the time.[73]

"Churning," from *The Progress of the Dairy: Descriptive of the Making of Butter and Cheese for the Information of Youth*, New York, 1819. *Courtesy Princeton University Library. Sinclair Hamilton Collection. Visual Materials Division. Department of Rare Books and Special Collections. Princeton University Library.*

Among the tools and equipment for running a household that Samuel Lane provided to each daughter was a butter churn. It took one gallon of milk to make one pound of butter, two gallons for one pound of cheese. The Lanes' dairy production peaked just prior to the youngest daughter's marriage in 1783. The previous year they sold 101 pounds of butter and 334 pounds of cheese.

Samuel never mentioned milking cows himself, nor is there any suggestion of his routinely tending the dairy herd. Evidence suggests that Samuel's daughters worked alongside their mother, milking the cows, naming them, and caring for their calves. Although Samuel owned cows before he married, his first mention of a cow by name, in this case "Brown," came in 1752 when his daughter Mary was eight years old.[74] The names the Lanes gave their cows express either physical characteristics (including Black, Brown, and Whiteback) or personality traits (Gentle, Blossom, and Flower). Samuel's diary entry for April 3, 1789—"Eunice come. Jentle C-l-d"—likely reflects what was by then a long-standing relationship between Lane women and their herd.[75]

Though cattle were important to the farm for many reasons, most of the meat eaten in the colonies was not beef but pork. Pork was easier to preserve and retained its flavor longer after being smoked, pickled, or salted. Samuel revealed the importance of pork to his family's diet in 1741: "I had nothing [no money] left to procure my years Pork when I began to keep House: but ran in Debt to D[eaco]n Robinson for half a Hog to live on."[76] By various estimates, the colonial household consumed 50 to 100 percent more pork than beef.[77]

The Lanes began keeping swine in the spring of 1743, when neighbor Mason sold them a sow and three piglets; that October they slaughtered the sow for the family's winter pork supply. As late as 1748, Samuel still had no adequate hog shelter, and that winter his neighbor, Nathan Hoag, took "a Pig to keep over 51^{lb} at 4½^{d} p[er] lb."[78] This was remedied the next fall when John Leavit spent more than half a day "Making Hogspen."

Other than for their tendency to escape, swine were fairly easy to keep. Though often left to browse the woods in less settled areas to the west, Stratham's hogs were more likely restrained to the barnyard. Their feed consisted of kitchen and dairy waste, and sometimes they were fattened on corn and root crops such as turnips and potatoes.[79]

In lean years, seacoast farmers, like settlers on the frontier, might also resort to forest browse. When drought, followed by a long hard winter, created a corn shortage in February 1762, a rumor that "many Swine have already Died for hunger in the woods" reached Samuel's ears.[80] With lambs, sheep, and horses also dying for want of hay that winter and another drought following in the spring, farmers began to take measures to ensure feed for their hogs.[81] On September 30, Samuel noted that people were gathering acorns, with satisfactory results: "Abundance of good Pork has been fatted this fall by Beech Nuts & Acorns and but little Corn has been wanted for that end, which has Vastly Saved our Corn."[82]

Except for Samuel and Mary's first year of marriage, their own livestock proved sufficient to supply the household with the beef and pork they needed. The Lanes, however, did not as a rule slaughter their animals themselves. John and Moses Thirston, Benjamin Mason, Zebulon Ring, and John Davis are some of those credited

Butcher, from Denis Diderot, *L'Encyclopédie, ou Dictionnaire Raisonné des Sciences, des Arts, et des Métiers*, 1751–1752. *Courtesy, The Winterthur Library: Printed Book and Periodical Collection.*

Samuel Lane hired a number of different men to butcher his "creatures." He did not slaughter them himself. The careful records he kept show that, over the years, his cattle and swine increased steadily in weight.

with "killing." From 1742 through 1769, one or more of these men dressed an average of 408 pounds of beef and 447 pounds of pork annually for Samuel.[83] The weights of slaughtered cattle and swine increased over time. While at first no cow was heavier than 400 pounds, by the 1760s, Samuel's cows regularly weighed more than 400 pounds dressed, the largest being 453 in 1767. Swine too were fatter. Before 1753 hogs ranged between 189 and 303 pounds. After that date, when Samuel purchased his pastureland from Colonel Wiggin, hog weights increased, reaching 412 pounds in 1761. By 1764, Samuel could call a hog weighing 220 pounds "measley." Twenty years earlier that weight had been about average.

When Samuel moved to Stratham, he took with him eight sheep, which he soon sold to help pay his expenses. Before long he bought five more sheep from Joseph Mason and thereafter kept a flock. Again, his lack of pasture and mowing acreage probably restricted the size of his flock. By 1746 he had increased the size of his farm by several acres, but even then he leased pasture for his sheep. "Brot sheep home," he wrote on November 25, 1746, a reference to his flock's grazing on another's land. Lamb and mutton were popular dishes on Portsmouth tables and appear repeatedly in Samuel's accounts with traders there. Samuel's trip to the Bank the day following the slaughter of two lambs on October 20, 1752, was no coincidence.

Sheep were important for wool as well as for meat. The Lane women appear to have helped tend the sheep. There are no clear gender lines, however, dividing the various tasks associated with raising sheep. Shearing and slaughtering sheep was definitely man's

The first Plate of the Woollen Manufacture exhibiting the Art of
(A) Sheep Shearing (B) The Washing (C) The Beating &(D) The Combing of Wool.
A.

"The Art of Sheep Shearing," engraving from the *Universal Magazine*, London, 1749. *Courtesy American Textile History Museum, Lowell, Massachusetts.*

While the women of the family may have helped wash the sheep in preparation for shearing, the job of shearing the sheep belonged to the men. In some years, Samuel Lane hired a man to handle both tasks.

work in the Lane household; washing the sheep prior to shearing may have been done by both male and female. During the seven years between 1747 and 1756 for which records exist, Samuel had his sheep washed and sheared by a hired man in the late spring. From 1757 until 1797 he credited various men in his daybooks with shearing sheep but no longer for washing. From 1797 until 1800, Samuel hired both washing and shearing again.[84]

This pattern relates to the evolution of the Lane family. When Mary Lane was preoccupied with infants and young children during the first two decades of their marriage, Samuel probably hired laborers to wash sheep, lightening her workload. But by 1757 two of their children—thirteen-year-old Mary and eleven-year-old Samuel—were mature enough to handle washing the sheep. By 1797, when Samuel again hired a laborer to wash and shear his sheep, his family had diminished in size.

Evidence from other households indicates that women usually played a major role in a variety of sheep-related responsibilities. Midwife Martha Ballard not only washed fleeces but also assisted in lambing.[85] Samuel's records are largely silent on this matter, perhaps because managing the flock—feeding, grazing, and lambing—indeed lay within the female sphere of operations.

For most years on the Lane farm, there was a horse or two, but their value to farming operations was less significant than that of the other animals. Steers and oxen were the preferred draft animals for breaking up, plowing, and harrowing, as farm implements of the time were heavy and poorly designed. To Samuel, a horse was primarily a means of transportation and of power for operating his tanyard's barkmill. He rarely mentioned horses in connection with his farming work.

Owning a horse was a status symbol in the eighteenth century; the frequent loans of horses reflect the fact that many households owned none.[86] Until his purchase of a horse in April 1743, Samuel depended on others for his transportation. In January and February of that year he used Mr. Ambrose's mare to go to Hampton and Portsmouth several times. In Samuel's recollections about his first horse he betrayed a hint of pride as he described the mare, "the 1st Horse Kind th[a]t ever I owned," even though it had cost him but £12.[87] Over the next two months he bought tack from Cuffe Nokes and "a Saddle & Houzen," a pair of fetters, bridle bits, and a spur, as well as other old bridle bits from Mr. Pottle.[88] Samuel soon discovered, though, that a horse, like a hog, could be as much trouble as it was convenience; during the spring of 1745 he paid Samuel Peavy for "finding my Mare."[89]

During the Lanes' first decade in Stratham, pasturing a horse proved as great a problem as pasturing cattle. In 1745, only a few months after Benjamin Leavit agreed to pasture Samuel's horse and his cows, the two "agreed . . . to take my Horse out of his pasture. he was in only one night after the 13th of Sep. & that night he got into his [Leavit's] Lot." Even after handling the burden of arranging and paying for pasturage, Samuel could discover that his horse had no respect for the landlord's fencing.[90]

Man and woman riding a horse "double," engraving from *One Hundred Years Progress of the United States*, 1878. *New Hampshire Historical Society.*

A family in eighteenth-century New Hampshire was fortunate if it owned a horse. The Lanes usually did. Their horse often carried more than one rider, was frequently lent to neighbors, and provided animal power to run the tannery's bark mill.

Samuel rarely owned more than one horse at a time. Often that horse carried two riders at once. On April 30, 1747, Samuel took Mary to Hampton, noting that they "went Double." He returned to Stratham alone, and when, three days later, he returned to Hampton to bring Mary back home with him, they "come double."[91] Samuel and Mary gave each of their daughters, as part of their marriage portion, a pillion—a cushion to be attached behind a saddle for a second rider.

Samuel occasionally required equine services from others, even at times when he owned a horse of his own. While his mare was pastured at Exeter, he hired Widow Barker's mare to grind bark. He sold his mare to Nathan Hoag on April 1, 1747, and did not replace her until June 29. During those three months he used Ensign Jewet's horse to go to Hampton several times and also to Portsmouth, Kensington, and Boston, as well as to grind bark.

More commonly, Samuel lent his horse to others. In his 1745 daybook is a separate account listing thirteen individuals who hired his horse for a total of thirty-three days. Perhaps as a result of Stratham's church controversy, Daniel Mason used the Lanes' mare to ride to meeting elsewhere fifteen times in 1745. In return, Daniel Mason made fifteen pairs of shoes for Samuel.[92] Leather work helped underwrite other equine expenses as well. On August 23, 1766, Jonathan Wiggin paid for his wife's pumps by providing breeding services: his "Stalyon to [Samuel's] Mare."[93]

A horse was particularly important to Samuel because of his need to travel in his work, whether to the shops of Portsmouth, to his currier in Salisbury, or to Bow and other western townships. Only a horse could provide the speed and flexibility Samuel needed to meet his various commitments as a trader, surveyor, and proprietors' clerk. In the context of his farming and trading commitments his desire for additional land to support horses and other livestock is readily understandable.

Samuel's references to other "livestock" were infrequent, even though one European traveler observed that New Hampshire's residents "have plenty of Poultry as Geese Turkeys, dunghill fowles Ducks &c."[94] He credited Widow Leavit with a pair of geese, two chickens, and six eggs in November 1747, and in 1759 and 1763 he hired butchers to kill geese.[95] Samuel first mentioned bees in 1761. That August he took in twenty-four pounds of honey. Several years

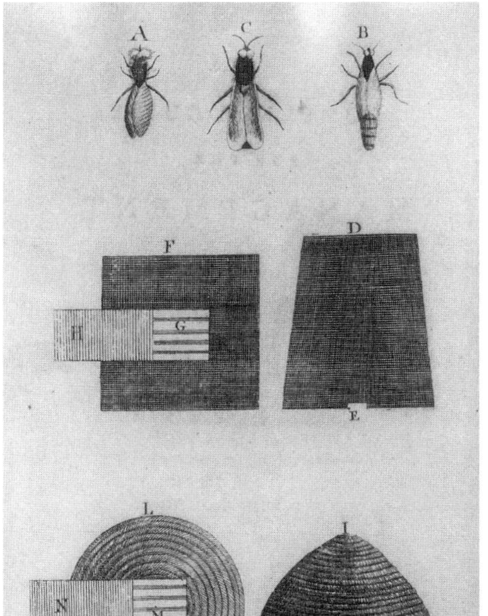

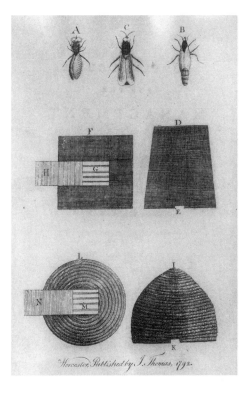

Frontispiece from *A Complete Guide to the Management of Bees*, printed by Isaiah Thomas, Worcester, 1792. *Courtesy, American Antiquarian Society.*

Samuel Lane also kept bees, mentioning them only when he was in danger of losing them through swarming or when he collected an unusual amount of honey. Using simple straw skeps and variants of them for hives, beekeepers had not yet devised means of collecting honey without destroying the bees themselves.

later his production had increased dramatically. On September 10, 1764, he "took Bees, wth 112 lb of Honey."[96]

To maintain growing numbers of grazing animals, land for pasture and mowing was critical. Samuel devoted most of his increased acreage to these uses. And with new lands came greater variety in the hay fields he owned. A contemporary writer described the three types of hay familiar to New Englanders: "Salt-hay is from salt or Spring tide marshes; fresh hay is the natural growth of inland marshes; English or upland hay, is the herbage imported from Europe."[97] Samuel's hay was a combination of all three. His original lots, together with his "swamp," qualified as lowlands. He later bought uplands, including Colonel Wiggin's twenty-two acres, which he turned into a combination of mowing and pasture. The popular grass to plant in these "artificial meadows" was timothy or herd's-grass mixed with clover. Indigenous to the Piscataqua region, herd's-grass was the variety Samuel probably sowed when improving his upland fields.[98] With the purchase of John Piper's farm in 1761, Samuel also acquired several acres of salt marsh on Chestley's Cove. In his detailed accounts of where his hay was cut, he lists thirty-seven separate areas from which he took hay for his creatures. Of those, fifteen refer to lowland areas, nineteen to upland fields, and three to salt marshes. Such variety offered security; even

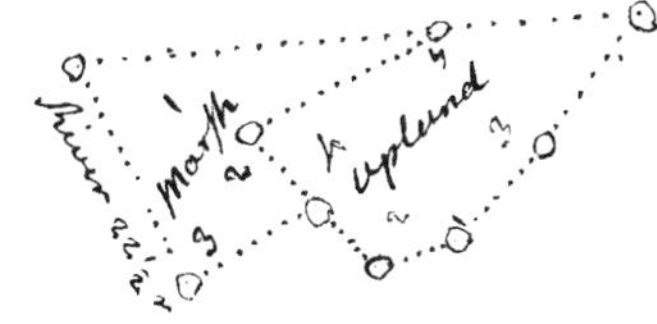

Detail from a survey of "the Estate of Moses Thurston Dec[ease]d," measured December 15, 1763. *Courtesy New Hampshire Division of Records Management and Archives.*

Samuel Lane devoted ten times as much land to maintaining livestock as he did to growing crops for direct human consumption. To feed his animals, he harvested hay from thirty-seven different locations: some salt marsh, some inland swamps or freshwater marshes, and some upland fields.

Haymaking scene, from Louis Liger, *La Nouvelle Maison Rustique, ou Économie Générale de Tous les Biens du Campagne*, Paris, 1755. *Courtesy, The Winterthur Library: Printed Book and Periodical Collection.*

In this French scene a man is mowing hay using a scythe while women rake and turn it over to dry. There is little in the Lane record to indicate that women helped in the field.

in the driest years, his lowlands and salt marsh would produce some hay for his stock.

The Lane hay fields produced as many as forty-three tons of hay in 1784, dropping to as little as fifteen tons in the drought-ridden year of 1761. Most of the hay was English, or fresh, from uplands or freshwater marshes. In "unfruitful" summers such as 1764, nearly half the crop was salt hay. The yield of salt hay was fairly reliable, remaining stable at six to seven tons per year. In a more typical year, salt hay would have constituted a far lower percentage of the total.

By the end of the 1760s, Samuel had acquired land enough to sustain his animals, even in the leanest years. And in the best years, he was able to share not only surplus meat, but also corn and other highly sought after grains with Portsmouth consumers.

Indian Corn is exceeding forward

On a "verry pleesent" September day in 1776, Samuel "carried 30 Bushels Corn to Bank."[99] In and of itself such activity was common enough; by this date agricultural produce regularly flowed seaward from New Hampshire's hinterland. But several circumstances mark this as an important event. The amount, thirty bushels, was quite large, equivalent to an acre's yield. In summarizing that unusual year, Samuel offered a clue as to the significance of his September trip: "This part of the Country has been Supply'd of its own raising; for none co'd be bro't by Water, because of the War."[100]

The hostile British presence in the colonies may have been the motive force, but by 1776, New Hampshire finally was capable of meeting its own needs, in an emergency situation anyway. This represented an important change from the region's earlier dependence on grain imported from the middle colonies. While the political revolution was bringing a dramatic change of government, an even more significant economic transformation had been taking place gradually and almost imperceptibly. The growing commercialization of agriculture was becoming possible only through the combined efforts of farmers like Samuel who, over many years, had been patiently improving land and raising livestock, despite adverse conditions.

In the fields he cultivated, Samuel sowed wheat, rye, barley, oats, peas, turnips, pumpkins, potatoes, cabbages, tobacco, and flax. Certain crops failed to thrive in this northern region; wheat especially fared poorly, and much was imported from the mid-Atlantic region to provide flour for bread.

The cycles of farm work varied little over Samuel's sixty years of husbandry. Weather alone interrupted those patterns of cultivation. Successful farming depended on the weather. Realizing that there was little he could do about the weather itself, Samuel noted unusual circumstances, sometimes with amazement but with little emotion. There was much, however, that humans could do by careful observation of weather and other phenomena to reduce the risk of poor crop yields. Rain, or the lack of it, could affect the timing of spring and fall plowing, and Samuel's records of rainfall helped him consider and explain the condition of the crops in his fields.

With the exception of grasses for mowing, corn was undoubtedly the main crop on New Hampshire's farms, as English traveler James Birket quickly learned when visiting the province around 1750: "their Chiefe grain is Maize or Indian Corn of which they plant a good deal but not Enough for their own Consumption being Obliged to Import large Qn^{tys} from Maryland & Virginia Also from New York & Philadelphia."[101] Corn, being in such short supply, was reserved as much as possible for human consumption, though it was valued as well as a means of fattening livestock for slaughter.

As Samuel's acreage increased, he planted more corn and had less need to buy it at market.[102] In 1753–54 he bought twenty-seven bushels of corn to satisfy the appetite of his growing family. But by

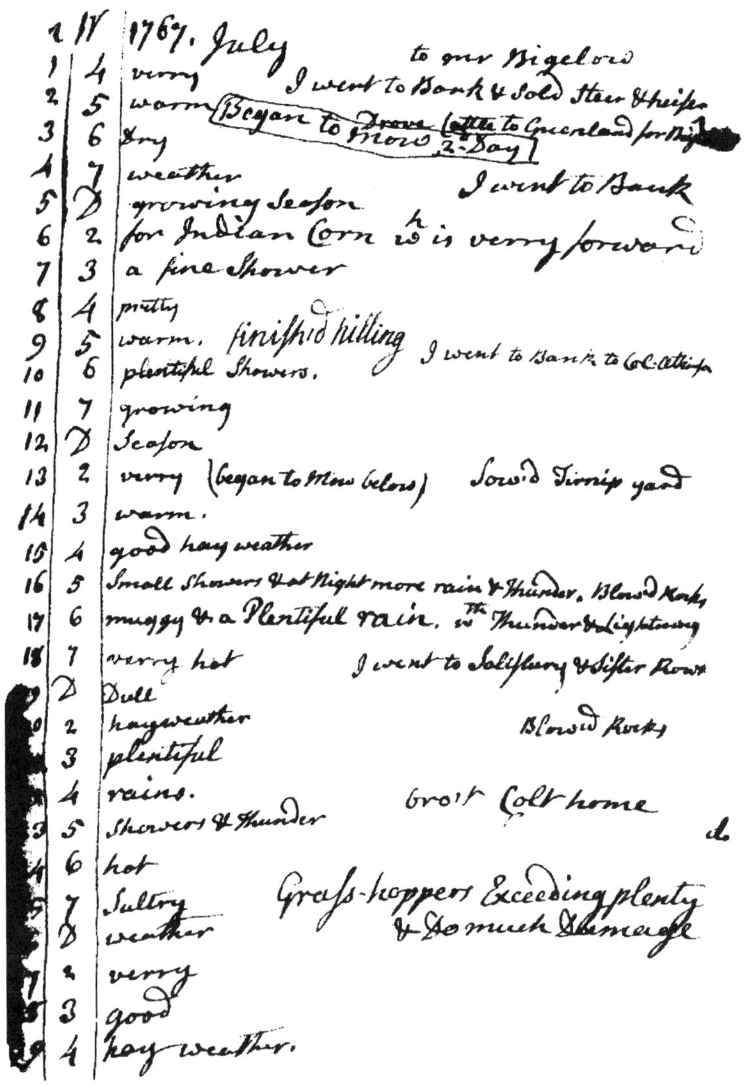
1767. July
1 4 verry — I went to Bank & Sold Steer & heifer to mr Bigelow
2 5 warm
3 6 dry
4 7 weather — I went to Bank
5 D growing Season
6 2 for Indian Corn wch is verry forward
7 3 a fine Shower
8 4 pretty
9 5 warm. finish'd hilling — I went to Bank to Col. Atkinson
10 6 plentiful Showers.
11 7 growing
12 D Season
13 2 verry (began to Mow below) — Sow'd Turnip yard
14 3 warm.
15 4 good hay weather
16 5 Small Showers & at Night more rain & Thunder. Blow'd Rocks
17 6 muggy & a Plentiful rain. wth Thunder & Lightning
18 7 verry hot — I went to Salisbury & Sister Rowe
19 D Dull
20 2 hayweather — Blow'd Rocks
21 3 plentiful
22 4 rains. — Brot Colt home
23 5 Showers & Thunder
24 6 hot
25 7 Sultry — Grass-hoppers Exceeding plenty & Do much Damage
26 D weather
27 2 verry
28 3 good
29 4 hay weather.

Samuel Lane's diary, July 1767. *Lane Family Papers, New Hampshire Historical Society.*

The annual cycle of farm and other work appears, in Samuel Lane's diary, alongside his notes about the weather that so often affected his routine. He recorded the weather at the left of the page beside the date and day of the week, adding notes about special events and progress in his work to the right.

1768 the Lanes' own production more than met their household needs.[103]

Corn was a labor-intensive crop, as its cultivation was condensed into a relatively short growing season. Planted in early May, corn was harvested in mid-October with the advent of killing frosts.[104] In the early years, Samuel planted corn in relatively small patches wherever land was available. In 1750 he planted part of his swamp in corn and at other times planted corn on the other side of the millpond from his house. The fact that the same locations are not repeated annually suggests that Samuel practiced some sort of crop rotation.

Plowing after the fall harvest, or what Samuel called "breaking up," was exceptionally hard work, employing much animal and human power. Breaking up Samuel's new field in 1753 took three days during a spell of "pretty pleasent weather for the Season." On November 19, Samuel's brother Isaiah came from Hampton to help plow. Samuel Neal and young Andrew Wiggin assisted him. The three plowed half a day with William Pottle's plow and two oxen, Neal's steers, and two steers belonging to Andrew Wiggin's father. Presumably, Isaiah Lane stayed and worked the next two days; Andrew Wiggin is credited with "following plow" for both days. On the 20th, John Hill brought his two oxen and two steers to pull Pottle's plow over Samuel's field. On the final day of plowing that year, William Pottle, using his two oxen, his plow, and Samuel Neal's steers, plowed for Samuel.

Depending on the weather, spring plowing took place in April or May, with similar patterns of exchange to arrange for the requisite draft animals, labor, and equipment. Samuel bought his own plow in 1763; he credited a neighboring blacksmith, Nathan Hoag, with plow plates and plow irons weighing twenty-one and one-half pounds.[105] Until then he had always hired the use of a plow. The purchase coincided with Samuel's two oldest sons reaching their middle teens, and from that time on, plowing was another type of labor that Samuel provided to others. Just a little over a month after he bought his plow, he plowed one day for Mr. Adams, charging the minister for his own labor and that of a helper, as well as for the two oxen and the plow.

That year, Samuel "bought" five days of plowing and "sold" three days; for five years, he continued to hire plowing to break up the land in the fall, which required a heavier plow. In 1768 he bought his own "Breaking-up Plow." With two sons then aged twenty and twenty-two, Samuel not only plowed all his own land with family labor alone but also was able to provide five and one-half days plowing to neighboring farmers.[106]

There is a unanimity among observers, past and present, that American farm implements, particularly the plow, were inadequate at best.[107] According to the author of *American Husbandry*, the typical plowshare and moldboards were wooden, and their cutting angle was too blunt to cut into the soil effectively. Even when the moldboard was sheathed with metal, damp soil adhered to it, and it required constant cleaning. Although the plow bottom might be shod with metal, an iron plow cast in a single piece was not made in America until 1797.[108] Because friction was so great, it was often necessary for one man to steer the plow while another stood on the drawbar beam to force the blade deeper. Only one or two acres per day could be plowed with implements so inadequate to the task.[109]

After the land was readied, planting could begin. Samuel, like other colonial farmers, employed the Native American method of planting corn in widely spaced hills. The four seeds traditionally planted in each hill were intended "One for the squirrel, one for the crow, One for the cutworm and one to grow."[110] Traveling clergyman Timothy Dwight explained the reason for hilling corn: "The hill is made, to give a better opportunity for the roots, which, when the stalk is grown to a considerable height, shoot from it several inches above the surface, to insert themselves in the ground with more ease, and less hazard of failure. These roots are called braces; because they appear to be formed for the sole purpose of supporting the stalk."[111]

Weeding the corn was a labor-intensive process, involving three steps. The first, called weeding, was "a simple cutting up of the weeds." Next came "moulding," which created a small hill around the plants "dishing towards the centre." The final step, "hilling," increased the height of the mound.[112]

Samuel followed a regular schedule for cultivating his corn. Planting took place between May 1 and May 23. In a typical year, weeding started at the end of May or early June and was completed by the middle of the month. Moulding began about two weeks later and hilling about two weeks after that.[113] All this work was done by the Lane household, as there is no record of outside labor assisting. Samuel probably planted less than three acres in corn. Where tax inventories list his land use, there are never more than three acres in tillage.

Once harvested, usually in October, the corn required husking to prepare it for storage. Husking appears to have been a task reserved in the Lane household for women and children but did not involve the traditional "frolic." Samuel's only record of this process is in 1750, when he credited Judith Glanvil for one day of husking.[114] The absence of any other references to this task suggests that it was work done by women within the household. The Lanes appear to have viewed husking as an economic necessity, to be handled like any other such task.

Husking bees were not unknown in New Hampshire. On an October Friday, Concord's Timothy Walker "Brot my corn from ye Middle Intervale. At night had a husking."[115] A Kingston husking bee lapsed, moreover, into a scene "of vile lewdness," according to the schoolmaster.[116] Although such social events are considered to have "encouraged hard work and responsibility to the group even as they gave opportunities for sexual experimentation and carousing," there is no evidence that the Lanes ever hosted such a husking.[117] The relegation of this sometimes sociable activity to that of a routine chore may reflect broader economic changes then underway.

Most likely, the Lanes followed the common practice of storing their corn, once husked, in the attic of their dwelling.[118] In 1758, Samuel recorded that "Indian Corn . . . Stunk in our Chambers."[119] In the spring of 1769, Samuel constructed a separate "Corn-House." Such structures were designed to keep rodents away from the grain. That rodents were indeed a nuisance is suggested by Samuel's purchase of a rat trap. By "early in the [nineteenth] century separate corn-cribs had become customary farm buildings to store the ears, though these structures were relatively rare in the eighteenth century."[120]

The number of ears harvested probably varied little from year to year, except as weather and predators affected the crop. The practice of hilling corn, alien to today's farmer, had a pragmatic purpose, directly relating to one of the risks a farmer faced. "A verry great Storm of rain & wind, and Thunder," Samuel observed in July 1751, "hes bent the corn & hurt it verry much." Two weeks later, he marveled at the corn's recovery, possibly aided by the hilling process. "The Indian Corn which was terribly broke & bent down . . . rises up to admiration and turns up Crooked like a Bow." The crop was a disappointment, nevertheless, as many ears had "no kernals on the Cobb a Considerable Distance from the Cud thot to be by reason of the Storm."[121]

Other natural phenomena provided constant threats to the crops. Samuel mentioned drought damaging his crops in twenty of his sixty years of farming. While droughts "Pinch'd the fruits of the Earth pretty much," wet weather also took its toll.[122] The year 1758 turned out to have "a verry Wet Summer," resulting, as Samuel noted, in "Indian Corn being backward & verry green." An early dip in temperature could be devastating. "A verry great frost," on August 29, 1752, "kill'd the corn stalks, So that they immediately turn'd white; also kill'd Beans and almost every green thing: and corn being then in the Milk, it was So Blasted (especially in the out Towns) that there was hardly any Sound corn this year; and people were putt to it for Seed."[123]

Besides climatic perils, predators stalked New Hampshire's fields and orchards. Worms, grasshoppers, mice, and a fungus called "meldew" or rust plagued Samuel's farm. In 1743, a combination of pests and adverse weather conditions produced devastating results:

> in the first of this Summer there Seem'd to be a prospect of a good crop of grass or Hay but it was cut exceeding Short many ways, Some burnt up by the Drought, and abundance in many places was Devoured by an uncommon devouring worm, which worms come in Such innumerable Swarms as that they eat all before them, & were so thick in mowing time that they meerly [nearly?] made people Sick when mowing there grass, which they were oblig'd to cut down with all Speed or else the worms would devour all

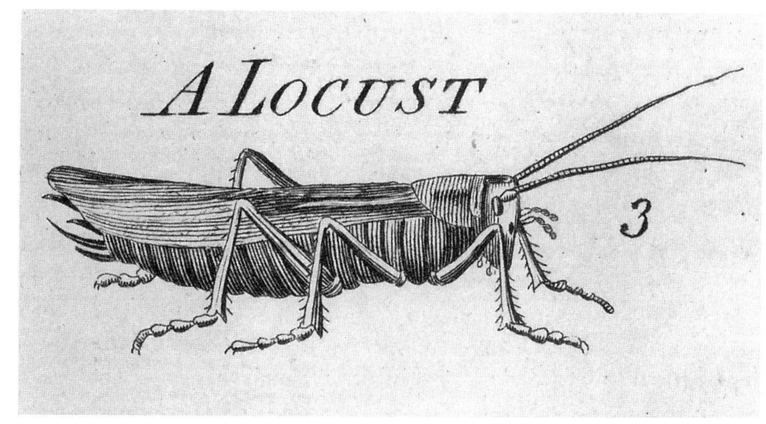

Grasshopper, from George Selby Howard, *The New Royal Cyclopaedia and Encyclopaedia*, London, 1788. *Courtesy, The Winterthur Library: Printed Book and Periodical Collection.*

Drought, premature frosts, and pests were the most common threats to Samuel Lane's corn and grain crops. He recorded "devouring worms" and grasshoppers causing damage during eleven summers. Mice and rats also destroyed their share of his harvest.

their grass. they also eat the corn So that people thot they would devour it all, but the corn come on after the worms left it, So that there was a plentiful crop. the grasshoppers also in other places exceeded the worms & destroy'd abundance of grass & english corn; all which devourers caus'd hay to be exceeding Scarce this Summer.[124]

Such disasters were not uncommon. Samuel's year-end summaries note damage from worms and grasshoppers eleven times, from mildew or rust five times, as well as from mice once. Unfortunately, the farmer had few remedies other than to attempt to beat the predators by harvesting early. In 1788, however, after explaining that "the worms have Eat orchards verry much," Samuel noted that, in an apparent effort to combat the crawling pests, "Some People Tars their Trees."[125] Clearly evident in all Samuel's writings is his concern about the effect such events would have on product availability and market price.

From 1741 to 1800, Samuel assessed his corn yields as follows: exceptional (plentiful, great)—ten years; good (comfortable)—twenty-four years; "midling"—fourteen years; and short (slim, scarce, light)—thirteen years.[126] His record of corn ground at the local gristmill provides a more measurable hint of his yield. Samuel's neighbor, Captain Wiggin ground at least sixty-four and three-quarters bushels of grain for Samuel in 1779. Presumably most was Indian corn; only one-half bushel was designated as rye. The next year, Samuel recorded, "I think Capt Wiggin has ground 58½ Bushels Since we Reckon[ed] & 31½ not posted." Apparently Samuel's arrangement with Wiggin included a direct exchange, perhaps shoeing his family for grinding a certain quantity of grain.[127] The amounts of corn ground decreased after 1783,when three members of Samuel's family married and left home.

A Pennsylvania study estimates that a family of five would have

Winnicut gristmill, Stratham; from the Historic American Building Survey, photographed by L. C. Durette, 1937. *Library of Congress.*

Stratham's picturesque Winnicut gristmill survived surprisingly intact into the twentieth century. Toward the end of his life, Samuel Lane frequently mentioned going to Winnicut mill, though in earlier years the Wiggins had ground most of his corn in their mill adjoining his property.

required thirty bushels of corn annually for its own consumption. Presumably, a New Hampshire family, unaccustomed to the use of wheat because of its scarcity, would have needed even more corn. When Samuel recorded in 1762 that "Corn is not to be Bought this Winter," he added "many People are obliged to Use flower and Bisket for their Common bread."[128]

Indian corn, though the most prominent, was but one of the grains Samuel cultivated. He also planted rye, oats, wheat, and occasionally barley. As the author of *American Husbandry* observed in 1775: "The crops commonly cultivated are, first, maize, which is the grand product of the country, and upon which the inhabitants principally feed. It is not to the exclusion of common wheat, which in a few districts is cultivated with success."[129]

Some blamed New England's climate for the failure of wheat to prosper there. "It is the climate of this province which entirely regulates its agriculture, and . . . render[s] the culture of common wheat not near so advantageous as that of maize."[130] However, Samuel himself associated poor harvests of wheat (which he and others also referred to as English grain) with the presence of the blight known as rust or "meldew." Samuel mentioned this problem as early as 1763, when "a Midling crop of English grain" was "much hurt by mildews or Rust." What later came to be called black-stem rust had plagued New England since the 1660s. The blight contributed to the decline of wheat farming in the region, increasing dependence on the mid-Atlantic colonies for grain. By 1800, "wheat bread had become practically unknown on farmers' tables throughout most of New England."[131]

Although bothersome, black-stem rust did not stop Samuel from planting wheat. He sowed both summer and winter varieties on a regular basis. Stratham was more fortunate than other areas and produced relatively good wheat. Samuel commented on a new variety of wheat introduced in the late 1770s which farmers hoped would resist the rust: "This year [1780] there has been a Remarkable Demand for Siberian Wheat for Seed. And the principle part of it that ever has been Rais'd in these parts before this year, grew in Stratham & Newmarket; and it having a name for yielding great increase Many People came from almost all parts, far and near after it for Seed."[132] Siberian wheat proved no more immune to rust than its predecessor; in 1781 drought and disease combined to "cut off our English grain (Especially Siberian Wheat) verry Much and considerable Wheat So blasted, that it was not Reap'd."[133]

Reaping wheat or other so-called English grains, from Louis Liger, *La Nouvelle Maison Rustique, ou Économie Générale de Tous les Biens du Campagne*, Paris, 1755. *Courtesy, The Winterthur Library: Printed Book and Periodical Collection.*

Samuel Lane regularly planted wheat despite the blight known to threaten it in New England. The men of the household harvested grain with a sickle, standing the stalks in shocks to dry. In 1798 a foreign traveler passing through Essex County at harvesttime remarked that he "did not, at any time, happen to see women doing this work." Julian Ursyn Niemcewicz, *Under Their Vine and Fig Tree: Travels through America in 1797–1799*.

One man with a sickle could harvest an acre of wheat a day. In 1769, Samuel reaped his winter rye on July 28, his summer rye on August 5, his wheat on August 7, and finished his harvest of all English grain (as opposed to American Indian corn) on August 10. Until late fall, after the corn was harvested, the stalks were left to dry in shocks. As outdoor chores slackened for the season, the work of threshing the grain with a flail occupied the central aisle of the barn.

The poor English grain yields may in part be atttributed to the New England farmer's failure to make adequate use of manure. Jeremy Belknap noted "very little use is made of any manure excepting barn dung."[134] Manure shortages, moreover, appear to have restricted cultivation. Allowing livestock to range freely made collecting dung impractical, and one agricultural reformer exclaimed that dung "cannot be had for Love nor Money."[135] Contemporary scientific theory held not so much that manure added nutrients to the soil as that it kept the soil loose, allowing the roots to spread more easily.[136]

Samuel used available dung in cultivation of his crops but never indicated just why he believed it good practice. Even before he owned either cart or steers to pull it, he hired labor and equipment to "hall dung," which suggests that he was conscious of good husbandry practice in this regard.

Another common criticism of colonial practice was the general failure to rotate crops. According to the author of *American Husbandry*, New England farmers "have not a just idea of the importance of throwing their crops into a proper arrangement, so as one may be a preparation for another, and thereby save the barren expense of a mere fallow."[137] Without any specific mention of Samuel's planting plans, it is not clear to what extent and on what basis he rotated his crops. It appears that he did so to some degree: in 1777 he sowed English grain "over the pond" and at Mason's; in 1779, by the barn, at the knoll above, and by the old barn; and in 1781, on Lamprey's knoll and by the old barn.[138]

Stratham's coastal location may have made rotation somewhat less critical than in inland areas. Salt water and tidal silt naturally renewed the salt marshes, and the resulting hay produced a manure of high quality, which was very productive when applied to upland fields.[139]

Orchards supplied another important crop for both household and market. As Belknap explained, "no good husbandman thinks his farm complete without an orchard."[140] The chief product of New England's apple orchards was at that time cider, "the common drink of all . . . inhabitants, rich and poor alike."[141] Samuel did not own a cider press and had others make his cider. In 1763, the year of Samuel's greatest apple production, Jethro Hill made him fifty-three

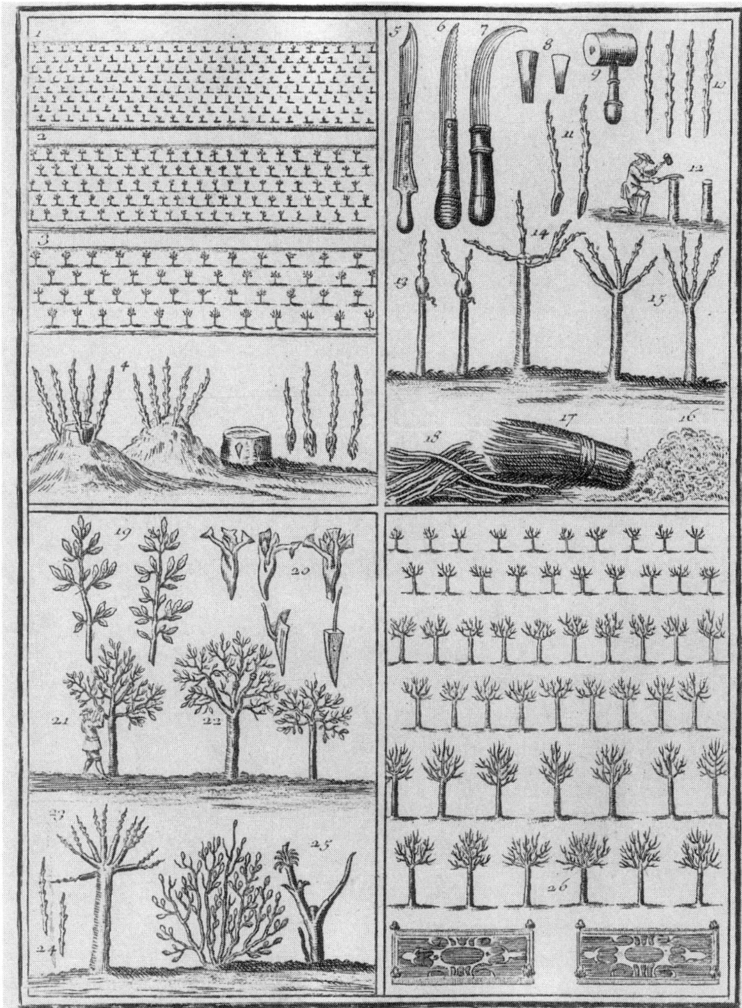

Orchards, engraved plate from Louis Liger, *La Nouvelle Maison Rustique, ou Économie Générale de Tous les Biens du Campagne*, Paris, 1755. *Courtesy, The Winterthur Library: Printed Book and Periodical Collection.*

Samuel Lane continued to expand and diversify his holdings with the purchase of additional property. One of the farms he bought included a flourishing orchard. Following this acquisition, cider appeared increasingly in the record of his Portsmouth trade.

barrels of cider, which Samuel sold in Portsmouth for £5 or £6 a barrel.[142] He carried cider regularly to customers at the Bank, either for consumption there or export. According to one writer in 1775, an orchard, though not usually a major part of the average farm's acreage, was typically "as profitable as any other part of the plantation."[143]

In attempting to manage the many aspects of his farm, Samuel gathered information wherever and whenever possible. He copied a remedy for diarrhea in cattle from a book of Mr. Wiggin's for future reference: "Calves that Scoure, give them Chalk Scraped among milk, pouring it down with a Horn: if this does not Succeed, give them bole armenic in large doses & use the Cold Bath every Morning."[144]

Memoranda like those he wrote at the end of his 1777 diary indicate an interest in experimentation to improve his crops:

> Memd^m^ Some Say all round Seed Sho'^d^ be Sow'^d^ at the full of the Moon
> Memd^m^ Some Say turnip Seed Sow'^d^ in the Increase of the Moon will run too much to tops: and if Sow'^d^ in the wane to root.[145]

Samuel's own experience and observation of those around him was ever his primary teacher in the practice of farming. He no doubt embraced to some degree the old adage that " an ounce of Experience is better than a pound of Science."[146] His fairly extensive library contained only two books related to agriculture, George Cooke's *Complete Farmer* (1770) and Samuel Deane's *The New-England Farmer* (1790).[147] When Samuel first acquired these books, he already boasted three decades of farming experience. But even if the advice they contained had relatively little impact on his farm practice, the very presence of these books in his library is evidence of an attitude accepting of change and improvement. Marginal notes in his copy of *The New-England Farmer* indicate that he read it carefully and considered its recommendations.

Necessity is the Mother of invention —

Saying, written by Samuel Lane in his copy of *The New-England Farmer*, 1790s. *New Hampshire Historical Society.*

When the property of a wealthy landowner just down the road from the Lanes came up for sale in 1772, it was exactly the kind of farm, though on a grander scale, that Samuel over time had been building for himself. The advertisement placed in the *New Hampshire Gazette* featured the property's diversified crop and pasture land.

> TO BE SOLD OR LETT, A Farm lying in Stratham, distant eleven Miles from Portsmouth, and four from Exeter. It contains One Hundred and Fifty

The Wingate house and farm in Stratham, photographed in the late 1800s. From Charles E. L. Wingate, *History of the Wingate Family in England and in America*, 1886. *New Hampshire Historical Society.*

In 1772 the Reverend Paine Wingate from Hampton Falls became Samuel's neighbor. The farm he purchased from the Leavitt family was one of the most prosperous in the vicinity. While serving in Congress, the minister, who became one of Samuel Lane's closest friends, wrote to his wife that he had found in his life "peace, competency and contentment." These were also Samuel Lane's goals.

Acres of Mowing, Tillage and Pasture Land, with several Acres of Salt-Marsh, has a fine Growth of young Wood upon it, an Orchard, and a large Dwelling House and Barn.[148]

Samuel Lane's goal now was to see, during his lifetime, each of his children settled on such a farmstead, with the security it could provide both for himself and for his children's families far into the future.

Son Joshuas Teem Plow'd for me

Samuel Lane's sons were crucial to the realization of his vision for the future, and their labor was necessary to its success. Because land was the foundation of rural prosperity and because male labor worked the land, sons gave their parents hopes for security and comfort in their old age.

Labor was a critical resource in the colonies. Few colonial farms were self-sufficient in labor; in farming communities like Stratham, labor was exchanged on a regular basis. Throughout the agricultural year, neighborly cooperation was vital to running a farm.[149] However much conflict and tension existed within these small communities, collaboration in the form of labor exchanges took place.[150]

In central Massachusetts the Williams family called on neighbors to work off debts by ditching, plowing, mowing hay, and harvesting grain.[151] In similar circumstances, Samuel depended on his own kin and the families around him to work his farm. There is no hint of permanent wage laborers in the Lane record except perhaps for the "old England man" Samuel hired in 1743 to work for him in the

When it can with convenience be ſo ordered, it is an excellent piece of huſbandry, to make a hog-paſture of an orchard. Their dung is allowed to be the very beſt of manure for the trees. They will keep the ground light and looſe; deſtroy inſects that infeſt the trees, and feed heartily on the premature apples that fall, which the farmer is too often tempted to grind up for cyder. And the ſhadow of the trees will be very grateful and comfortable to them in ſummer. An orchard may be prepared with clover, as well as any other ſpot of ground.

Passage from *The New-England Farmer* about the advantages of pasturing hogs in an orchard. *New Hampshire Historical Society.*

The marks Samuel Lane made in the margin of a book about agriculture that he acquired in the 1790s show that, even at a point late in his career, he read and considered the author's advice.

Plowing scene, from Louis Liger, *La Nouvelle Maison Rustique, ou Économie Générale de Tous les Biens du Campagne*, Paris, 1755. *Courtesy, The Winterthur Library: Printed Book and Periodical Collection.*

To make his land productive, Samuel Lane required considerable male help, which at first he hired. As his three sons matured, they helped him with every aspect of farm work. He was also able to lease their labor to neighboring farmers, along with his equipment and animal power (usually oxen rather than horses). A surprising number of farmers at this time did not maintain plows or oxen of their own.

"Now he labours in the Field," from a child's picture book, made for Freelove Wheeler (1752–1831) by William Colwell (1780–1817), Foster, Rhode Island. *Courtesy Rare Book Department, The Free Library of Philadelphia.*

A family considered itself fortunate when sons became old enough to work on the farm.

shoe shop "Some times."[152] Stratham was typical of the New England described by the author of *American Husbandry*, who remarked that day laborers "are not common in the colonies."[153]

As Samuel's farm and family evolved, so did his need for and use of labor. In the early years, when his acreage and family were both small, the farm's labor requirements were modest and could be satisfied by himself, his apprentice, and a relatively small number of neighbors. Before purchasing his own breaking plow in 1768, he always required some specialized labor, as he owned neither the cattle nor equipment to do all the tasks of cultivation on his tillable land. Otherwise, his hiring of nonfamily labor varied, depending on his sons' ages and marital status.

As his sons matured, Samuel hired less outside labor, and eventually his household became a net supplier of agricultural labor to the Stratham market.[154] By the late 1780s, after his sons had married and left his household, Samuel once again began to buy labor. Such a sequence of events was common in the life cycle of a farm family.[155]

"Marriages must abound greatly," wrote the author of *American Husbandry* for the benefit of his English audience, "in a country where a family, instead of being a burden, is an advantage."[156] Such a statement was clearly self-evident to the Stratham farmer. Samuel realized not only that labor lay on his own hearth but also that his use and control of it was temporary. There were precious few years between the time his sons were old enough to be productive and when they began families of their own. In older communities with limited land, it was "an unhappy fact" for many young men that the prospect of settling on a farm in the community of their birth was remote.[157] This circumstance created tension between parents and children, as well as among siblings.[158] However much fathers wanted their sons to begin their own families, such a move would destroy a vital source of labor on their own farms. It was with mixed emotions, therefore, that parents bestowed their blessing on betrothed couples.

Samuel, moreover, never forgot the lessons gained from his own experience growing up in Hampton. When engaged to wed Mary James, he initially looked to settle in their families' community without success. Instead, the young couple found it necessary to go out on their own to settle in another town, fortunately not too far away. Samuel took steps to ensure that his sons would not endure a similar fate. Over time, he conceived an ingenious way to satisfy the competing needs of different generations for land through a cooperative system of ownership and production.

On June 3, 1774, Samuel deeded to each of his two eldest sons a farm in Stratham. There were, however, obligations attached. Young Samuel's agreement mirrored that of his brother Joshua:

Agreement of Samuel Lane Jr. with his father, June 3, 1774. *Lane Family Papers, New Hampshire Historical Society.*

Samuel Lane devised a way in which he and his youngest children could benefit from the labor and help of his oldest sons even after they married and set up households of their own. To each of his oldest sons, he gave a farm, with the understanding that part of its produce every year would come to him for his support.

I promise to my Father Samuel Lane of Stratham that
I will yearly and Seasonably Every year During his Natural
Life Render and Deliver to him or his order the one complete
Half Part of the Neat Produce and income of all that Shall
grow on that forty three acres and one Hundred & forty two rod
of Land which he Baught of John Piper. with the Edifices thereon
which Promices he my Said father has given me a Deed of bearing
Even Date with these Presents and that I will Pay and Deliver
Said Produce when Demanded

Witniss my Hand June the 3rd 1774

Sam Lane Junr

I promise to my Father Samuel Lane of Stratham that I will yearly and Seasonably Every year During his Natural Life Render and Deliver to him on his order the one Compleat half part of the Neat produce & income of all that Shall grow on that twenty Seven Acres of Land which he Bought of George Veazey, with the Edifices thereon which Premises he My Said Father has given me a Deed of bearing even Date with these presents and that I will pay & Deliver Said produce when Demanded.[159]

Even after the Lane boys married and became technically free from the obligations of Samuel's own houshold, he would be maintaining control, through the above agreement, over a portion of their labor. Evidence suggests that Samuel never demanded the due that the agreements guaranteed him.[160] However, his intent was clear. His sons remained obligated to their family in some measure, even as they became household heads themselves.

The record suggests that both generations found the agreement beneficial. Almost a quarter of a century later, Samuel divided a fifty-two-acre woodlot in Newmarket, the "oak land," between his eldest sons. They then agreed to a new obligation with their father that reflected changed needs and family circumstances. Again, the siblings' agreements showed no substantial differences:

I promise to my Father Samuel Lane, that he Shall have the whole use & improvement of all the Land he has given me a Deed of, which he Bought of John Robinson—also one third part of the Salt Hay on that piece of Salt Marsh he has given me a Deed of in Chestlys Cove So Called, to be Delivered in his Barn yearly & every year During his Natural Life—and also that I will procure for him, halled to his Dwelling House, cut, Split up fit for his fire, yearly During Said Term, four Cords of good fire wood; one half of it good hard wood; the other half Hemlock & pine; and more if he wants it—also that he Shall have the Use of that piece of Wood Land in Epping which he has given me by Deed . . . and likewise that 20 acres more or less of wood land in the oak Land so Called, which he has given me a Deed of. Note the incomes if not Demanded in his Life time, is not to be Demanded by any person after his Decease.[161]

The differences between the 1774 and 1798 obligations are significant. After twenty-five years, the encumbrance on the sons' farm production, likely never demanded in any case, was removed, making their freehold status complete. In 1798, Samuel imposed restrictions only on lands apart from his sons' farms. The new conditions reflected Samuel's changing needs as he aged. His reservation of "the whole Use & improvement of" certain lands must be considered the equivalent to old-age insurance. Those lands were available to him, should he need the income. The articles Samuel specifically enumerated point to his own awareness that his age, eighty at the time, was limiting his ability to arrange for basic necessities—firewood, cut and delivered, and hay for his now relatively small number of livestock.

As far as labor was concerned, a cooperative relationship between Samuel and his sons continued despite their now married state. His second son, Joshua, married Hannah Tilton in 1769 when he was twenty-one years old. The couple spent their first year of married life in a new house Samuel had built on the Piper farm he had bought in 1761. This arrangement was temporary, as that farm was destined for his eldest son. Samuel needed, in the meantime, to find property for Joshua. Just one month after Joshua's wedding, his father placed the following advertisement: "WANTED a small Settlement convenient for a Tanners Trade of about 40 or 50 Acres of good Land: for which Cash will be given (if it suits) by Samuel Lane of Stratham."[162]

WANTED a ſmall Settlement convenient for a Tanners Trade, of about 40 or 50 Acres of good Land for which Caſh will be given (if it ſuits) by Samuel Lane of Stratham.

Advertisement placed by Samuel Lane for a farm for his son Joshua, *New Hampshire Gazette*, December 29, 1769. *New Hampshire Historical Society.*

At a time when most young people found it necessary to move to inland towns to obtain land, Samuel Lane managed to establish his sons on farms nearby.

Before long, son Joshua moved to George Veasey's farm on Rocky Lane, which his father purchased for him in 1770. This farm of twenty-seven acres adjoined another that Samuel bought the following year and was within two miles of Samuel's own farm. Such a location promoted the continued cooperation of father and son. The Veasey house was in some disrepair; Samuel replaced the sills and undertook other improvements to provide his son's family a good dwelling. The couple moved in on November 1, 1770, and that same month Samuel began an account "of Some things done for Son Joshua."[163] It included putting two windows in the house and supplying fencing materials, nails for the house and barn, and rocks and bricks for the foundation and chimney.

Father and son made a concerted effort to improve the property in 1771. To help plow Joshua's fields in April, Samuel provided six cattle and their feed. On May 16, he "went to View Joshua's House," and one week later they "hew'd Timber for Joshuas Leen to."[164] In mid-June they tore down the chimney, fixed the house foundation, and began to rebuild the chimney. On July 1, Samuel wrote: "Calley Avery Merril & my Self . . . began to frame Joshua's Leanto."

After the structure was finished, Samuel hired James Merril to paint the entire house. In late August, he "Ston'^{d} Joshuas Celler & Dary &c." Exactly two months later, work on the shop chimney be-

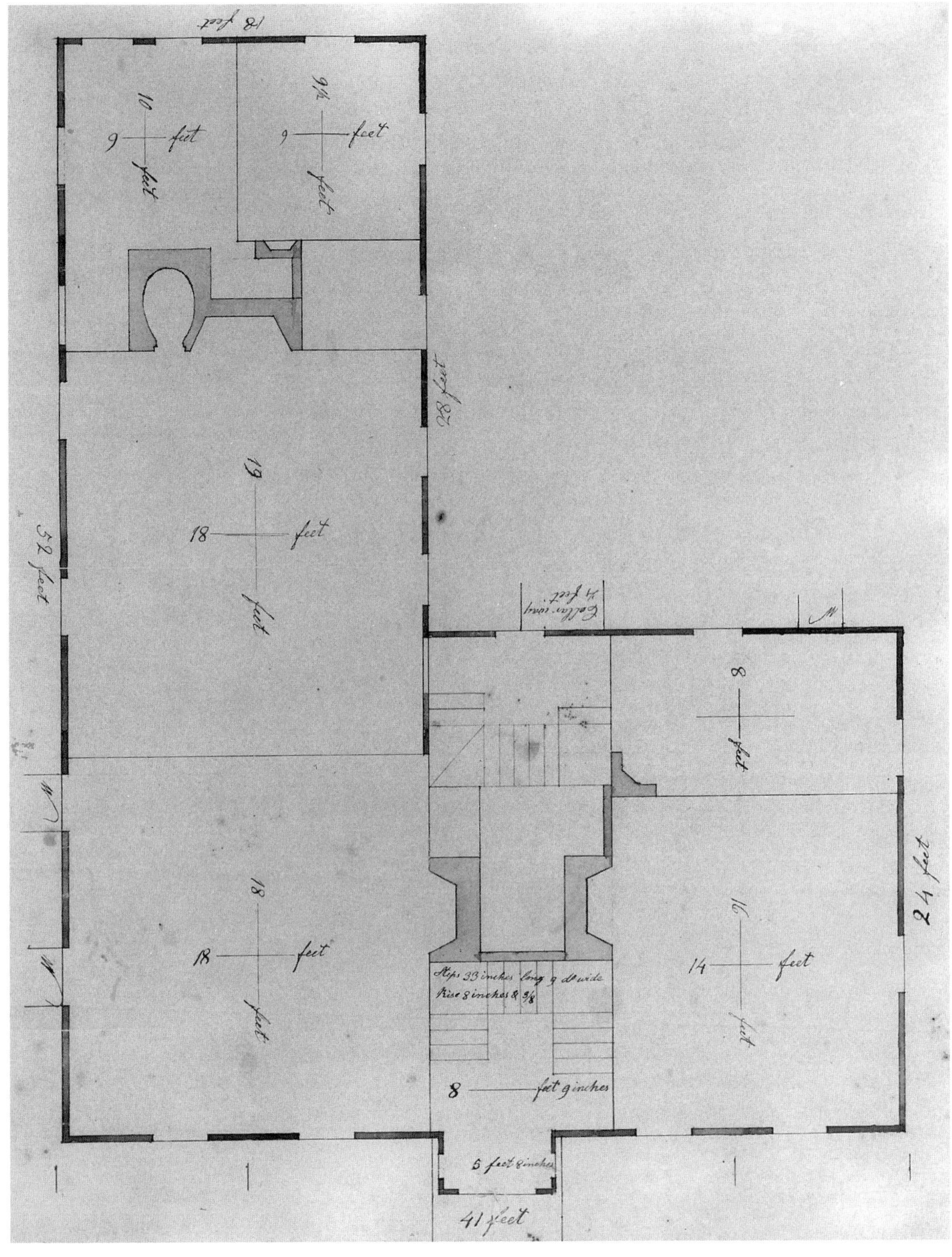

House plan, dating from the 1700s, in Lane family papers. *New Hampshire Historical Society.*

Samuel Lane built a new house for his eldest son, Samuel, and spent considerable time and effort improving the farm and farmhouse he purchased for Joshua.

gan. Finally on November 25, 1771, Samuel finished his work for Joshua that year, and tallying up his expenses he found they totaled £52.19.0 lawful money or £1,059 old tenor, including materials, labor, food, and drink.

The project for 1772 was Joshua's dairy. In June, Samuel hauled more rocks to Joshua's farm for the foundation and began work on June 24. The last remark concerning his work for Joshua came in July when they "finish'd Joshuas Sinkroom." Samuel also provided a cheese press for the dairy.[165]

Although Samuel kept a careful account of the work he did for Joshua, he never collected from his son for any of the work. At the same time, he kept a general account with Joshua; debits included one pound of powder, one-half bushel wheat, one gallon molasses, the labor of Ben and his oxen for "1 long Day getting in Stalks" and, last but not least, sole leather. Joshua's credits were one day of planting and making a pair of boots and shoes. As time passed, Samuel appears to have forgiven and even stopped recording his son's debts that had accrued in the course of their exchanges with each other.

Woodcut of house from *New Hampshire Gazette*, November 23, 1772. *New Hampshire Historical Society.*

The credits in Samuel's 1790 daybook show farmwork by Joshua, his sons, and his steers, as well as making two pairs of shoes. By 1792, Joshua's account was mostly fiction; at the bottom Samuel left a memorandum, "I think not to Demand this Acco[t] of Son Joshua." So that his executor would not miss the point he added, "I would not have this account Demanded of Son Joshua unless I demand it in my Life time."[166] In 1792, Joshua, the head of his own household for over twenty years, had entered a reciprocal relationship with his father in which each relied on the other for help, just as if they were members of the same household; neither felt the necessity to reckon their account with the other.

Diary entries for Joshua's work—carrying cider, beef, and hay to Portsmouth; plowing; hauling dung; and other miscellaneous work—are common enough to suggest that collaboration between father and son continued on a regular basis. Notes and exchanges of goods were a different matter. Until 1792, Samuel appears to have collected on loans made to his sons. When Samuel ordered six tall clocks from Kensington's Jeremiah Fellows on October 27, 1783, Joshua paid his father in installments for his clock. On December 4 he paid 40 shillings "toward his Clock." The clock arrived on December 9, and Samuel paid Fellows $28. That same day, Joshua paid his father 20 shillings, and on February 21, 1784, 66 shillings. Joshua's cash payments were the equivalent of $21; he paid the balance with the use of his steers.[167]

Joshua and his father had one other agreement, documented only in 1772. Samuel bought the Robinson Farm to the west of Joshua's on Rocky Lane in 1771, and Joshua farmed it "to the halves" the following year. He returned to his father income derived from rye, oats, corn, hay, flax, cider, cabbages, and pasturing steers, to the value of £11.17.0. It is not clear how long this arrangement continued.

Samuel treated his eldest son similarly. Samuel Junior's marriage to Hannah Cate on October 25, 1770, enabled Samuel to finalize his plans for settling his sons. When the younger Joshua had married the year before, the only option Samuel had was to offer him temporarily the new house he had built specifically for his oldest son. He then rushed to find another place for Joshua before his eldest son's nuptials. Samuel succeeded in finding property for Joshua and moved him to the Veasey farm just one week before his oldest brother married. The former Piper farm then became available for young Samuel and his bride.

Samuel was concerned as well that there be no misunderstanding among his sons about the future of his own homestead. In 1770, Jabez, his youngest son, was only ten years old and lame; that circumstance, as well as Samuel's continued need to support his own family, was no doubt an important factor in his decision to reserve his home farm for Jabez. He first made sure that neither older son would have to worry about acquiring land on which to live and farm, nor did they have to wait for their father to retire from farming and divide his land before establishing their families. Samuel's intent was becoming clear. When, in 1774, Samuel gave his two oldest sons the deeds to their farms, he had just decided to marry for a second time. If not apparent before, it must have been obvious then that Samuel Lane intended his own farm for Jabez.

Make my lame leg as long

Samuel was remarkably evenhanded in passing on property to his children.[168] He did, however, make subtle distinctions in the transfers of realty to his two oldest sons. Samuel Junior received the larger, forty-three-acre farm, with a new dwelling house; Joshua's farm contained twenty-seven acres and a refurbished farmhouse. Each son paid his father a modest £5 for his farm. Samuel favored his eldest son and namesake in other ways. On June 3, 1774, when Samuel transferred the farm's deed to Samuel Junior, he also passed title to twenty-four acres of land at Stratham's Great Hill and about two acres of salt marsh at Chestley's Cove. There was no symbolic purchase of these additional lands by his son; the father transferred them "for & in consideration of the Love goodwill & affection which I have & do bear towards my beloved Son."[169] That year,

The Prodigal Son
Printed by J. Brown, Phila. (He receives his Patrimony.)
W.P. Sculp 1795

"The Prodigal Son (He Receives His Patrimony)," line engraving, printed by J. Brown, Philadelphia, 1795. *Courtesy The Library Company of Philadelphia.*

For a while, Lane's youngest son, Jabez, feared that he might be in danger of losing out on his inheritance. In the end, Samuel, then over eighty, signed a deed for his own farm to Jabez, along with an agreement comparable to the others to ensure his own future support.

Samuel had transferred to his namesake a total of sixty-nine acres of Stratham land.

On the same day, he gave Joshua a deed to his farm, again in exchange for £5 and a reservation of half the income. But that was the extent of his transfer to Joshua until ten years later. In January 1784, Samuel gave Joshua the thirty-two-acre farm abutting his to the west, two acres of salt marsh in Chestley's Cove in Stratham, and a five-acre parcel in Epping. It took Samuel ten years to balance to any degree the legacies of his two eldest sons.

However, in the intervening years he had made another gift to his son Samuel—all the rights to his lands in Bow, which by now consisted of one original right, seven twenty-acre lots, and several other parcels. These lands remained speculative in nature, and their value was questionable.

Although these gifts of realty to his two oldest sons appear remarkably equivalent, Samuel was acting according to a pattern found elsewhere as well in eighteenth-century New England, that "property holders made fine discriminations among their heirs."[170] To a certain extent, Samuel seems to have favored his eldest son. Not only did Samuel Junior receive more acreage in Stratham, albeit a modest amount, but also the quality of those lands and their value was greater. The Piper farm lay on the main highway between Exeter and Portsmouth and contained more of the valuable lowlands for pasture and hay fields than did the Veasey Farm on Rocky Lane. The value of Joshua's land was four-fifths that of his oldest brother.

The improvements Samuel made to the properties magnified this discrepancy. Samuel's house was new and considerably more valuable than the renovated dwelling passed on to the younger Joshua.[171] Actually, it is surprising that the difference between the shares of the two brothers was not larger. Samuel was, more than most people, aware of traditional inheritance patterns. The estates he was involved with as legal advisor and surveyor often involved double shares passed on to eldest sons. Samuel's eldest received a bonus but not a full double share.

Also, the gift of Bow lands to Samuel Junior is significant, at least in its symbolism. As proprietors' clerk for Bow, Samuel had invested much of his life in the success of that venture. The proprietors—by the 1780s essentially Walter Bryent and Samuel Lane—continued to press their claims in the courts. Having his namesake assume an interest in Bow undoubtedly had emotional implications for Samuel. Although the power and value of the propriety was much diminished by 1780, Samuel perhaps found comfort in having his eldest son maintain the connection to those lands.

As Samuel's own life demonstrated, household needs changed over time.[172] He planned well, anticipating the material needs of his children as they married and had children of their own. At the important point of transition from single to married state, Samuel had given each son or daughter a significant "portion" of his estate when he felt that it could best be used.

Silhouette of Jabez Lane, by William King, c. 1805. *New Hampshire Historical Society.*

Jabez, the youngest of the eight Lane children, had suffered a lame leg from the age of six. His career as a farmer and shoemaker followed a remarkably similar path to that of his father. Samuel Lane also experienced a knee problem when young.

It is misleading to compare Samuel's gifts to his sons and daughters on an individual basis. Samuel was considering the welfare not of individual sons or daughters but of their families as economic units. He sought to maintain rough equivalency among those families. Samuel anticipated that his daughters' spouses would contribute the real estate necessary to support a stable household. Each daughter took from Samuel's own household domestic goods to furnish the home provided by her husband. On the other hand, his sons brought land and dwellings to their unions; there is little mention of any household goods courtesy of their father. The property he gave his sons was worth considerably more in monetary terms than his daughters' portions; at the same time, however, the real estate was encumbered. Considered as families rather than as individuals, his children emerged from their weddings on a fairly equal footing; each child had a home, in most cases a farm, and the domestic requisites to set up a productive household.

Most families preferred to have their children comfortably settled in their own town, but land scarcities in older towns precluded many from attaining that ideal. Four of the five local families whose sons married Lane daughters found themselves unable to provide land enough for their sons to remain in the community. On the other hand, Samuel had managed to settle two sons on substantial Stratham farms and was laying plans for settling the third.

SAMUEL FOSTER,
Shoe Maker in Portſmouth,
HEREBY informs the Public, That he has now removed to this Town, and taken the Shop lately improved by Mr. *John Edwards*, adjoining Mr. *Benjamin Slades*, in Queen Street Where he Makes, *Mens Shoes* of all Sorts, as neat and Cheap as any Shoe Maker in Town, *Womens* Silk, Cloth, Calamanco and Leather Shoes, as neat and Strong as ever was Made or brought from the famous Shoe Town of Lynn. —— Children's Shoes of all Sorts. —— And all Perſons who favour him with their Cuſtom may depend on being faithfully and punctually ſerved.

Advertisement of Portsmouth shoemaker, Samuel Foster, *New Hampshire Gazette*, June 24, 1768. *New Hampshire Historical Society.*

Shoemaking as an occupation had changed considerably since Samuel Lane's apprenticeship years. Ready-made shoes from Lynn, Massachusetts, were beginning to compete with those of local make. To expand the family's production into fabric as well as leather footwear, Samuel Lane sent eighteen-year-old Jabez for further training with Samuel Foster, a Portsmouth shoemaker most likely from Lynn.

Samuel's youngest son, Jabez, presented a dilemma. Born in 1760, Jabez was "naturally of a weakly constitution, and lame in one knee from the age of about 6 years, so as to be obliged, at times, to use a crutch, and generally walk[ed] with a cane."[173] Jabez described himself as a "cripple."[174] Samuel first mentioned his son's handicap in February 1766: "Jabez [was] taken with his Knee Pain."[175] Perhaps seeing parallels with his own childhood lameness and resulting Latin schooling, Samuel followed his father's strategy. Though Jabez was preparing for college, the Revolution intervened in his case, and Jabez adopted instead his father's trade.[176] For five weeks during the winter of 1778, Jabez worked with a Portsmouth shoemaker, Samuel Foster, in whose shop he "learn'd to make Cloth Shoes." Samuel reported further that eighteen-year-old Jabez, "Does Considerable at that and other light work."[177]

The craft of shoemaking, by the second half of the eighteenth century, was entering a period of transition. A market was developing for retail as opposed to custom-made shoes, and Lynn, Massachusetts, was becoming an important shoemaking center. In 1796, Samuel noted that "in the Oracle [news] Paper . . . , the shoes annually Export[ed] from Lynn, amount to near, three Hundred Thousand pair."[178] Jabez's training with Samuel Foster may have been in part inspired by this growing competition, for Foster advertised his shoes "as neat and Strong as ever was Made or brought from the famous Shoe Town of Lynn."[179] In the 1770s at least one shoemaker trained in Lynn was producing fabric shoes in Exeter as well.[180]

Jabez continued to make leather shoes as well as cloth ones, and worked regularly in his father's tanyard. In 1781 and 1782, together father and son tanned thirty-two and one-half hides and fifty calf-

Leather purse, embossed "Unity" on interior and "Liberty" on exterior, bearing ink inscription "Jabez Lane of Stratham his pocketbook." *Courtesy William W. Lane.*

In spite of his handicap, Jabez Lane worked, together with his father, in the tanyard that eventually would become his. Though no proof exists that the Lanes embossed leather, they almost certainly provided the material from which this pocketbook was constructed.

skins. By 1785, Samuel's output had dropped to six hides and eleven calfskins, while Jabez tanned nine hides and twenty-five calfskins on his own account.[181] Though considered a "cripple," Jabez was capable of many forms of work. He plowed, hoed the rye, went on trading trips to Portsmouth, and took hides to the curriers. By the summer of 1800, when Samuel was nearly eighty, he wrote, "Son Jabez has undertook to get my Hay; & most of my other work."[182]

When Jabez's mother died in 1769, he was only eight years old. Within two years of her death, both of his older brothers married and settled with their own families, leaving Jabez the only boy with four older sisters. Before too long his widowed father began trying to rectify his unmarried state. Samuel paid visits to a series of eligible widows. In 1774 he began to court in earnest Newmarket's Rachel Colcord, recently widowed at the age of forty-seven. On February 22 of that year he went to her house for some boards and enjoyed a "Pipe & Sydr" while there. A scant two months later, on April 20, he proposed. Rachel responded that she would "think on it" but surrendered "1 K-ss." Over the next two months she gave

"Now he seeks a Partner for Life," from a child's picture book, made for Freelove Wheeler (1752–1831) by William Colwell (1780–1817), Foster, Rhode Island. *Courtesy Rare Book Department, The Free Library of Philadelphia.*

About five years after his wife Mary's death, Samuel Lane determined to marry again. After paying visits to a number of eligible widows, he identified forty-seven-year-old Rachel Colcord of neighboring Newmarket as a likely prospect. Samuel proved a persistent suitor. On one of his many visits he took her "8 Choklates," and shortly after she accepted his proposal.

Samuel no definite answer, at one point informing him that another gentleman was courting her also. Undeterred, Samuel made several more visits, took her to visit Stratham, and gave her "8 Choklates." Finally, she rewarded his persistence; on May 30, Rachel Colcord accepted his proposal and later told him she was very pleased and surprised that any man would have gained her hand so soon after her first husband's death. They married in June, and she came to live in Stratham that September.[183]

Rachel and Gideon Colcord had six sons and one daughter. It seems likely that two of her children moved with her to Stratham, Eunice (age seven) and Benjamin (age nine). Job, age fourteen at the time, was apprenticed to a trade; his three older brothers, Gideon, Nathaniel, and Josiah, probably remained in Newmarket at the Colcord homestead. Although Josiah was to serve out his time with his mother until age twenty-one, as specified by Gideon Colcord in his will, there is no evidence that he lived in Stratham before he

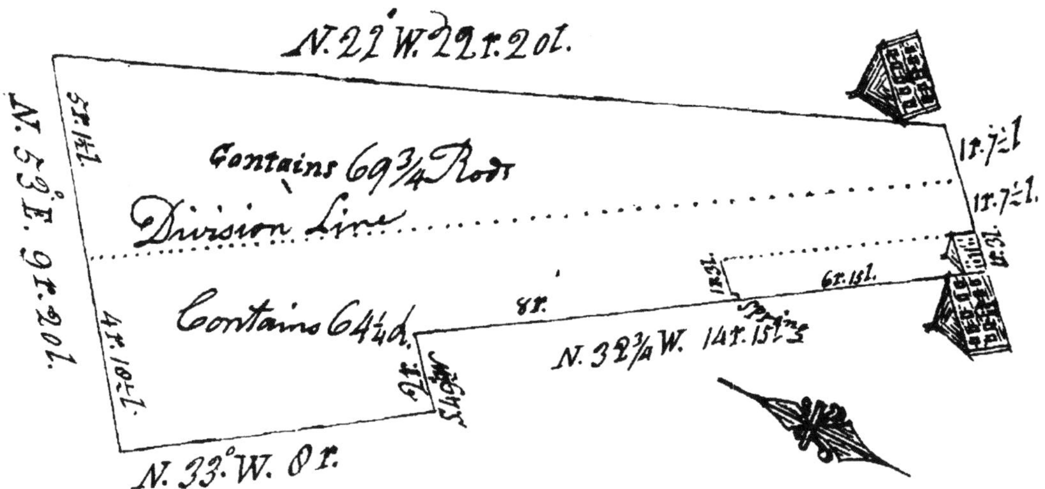

"Plan of a piece of land in Newmarket," in a part of town that later became Newfields, recording a lot division between J. Colcord and H. Burly; April 1796. *Courtesy New Hampshire Division of Records Management and Archives.*

Through his second marriage—in 1774 to Rachel Colcord—Samuel Lane became closely tied to the Colcord family of Newmarket. In 1783 the link between the two families grew even stronger when Samuel's son Jabez married Rachel's daughter Eunice. Jabez and Eunice set up housekeeping in a second dwelling then standing on their father's farm.

reached his majority in 1776. His mother may have had him serve his remaining time in Newmarket where she retained one-half interest in the real estate during her life.

When Rachel married Samuel, she controlled considerable property, which would revert to her upon his death. Her first husband, Gideon, bequeathed her "one Half of my Real Estate Dureing her Life . . . Also I give her the whole of my Household Goods Dureing her Widdowhood and the one half in case She Should marry again and the one half of my Live Stock."[184] Gideon was more liberal than most husbands, granting Rachel use of his real estate irrespective of her marital status. Many husbands specified that that privilege would terminate if their wives remarried.

The only Colcord children Samuel mentioned consistently during this period were Benjamin and Eunice. Even so, upon Samuel's marriage to Rachel, his household nearly doubled in size overnight. The combination of the two families seems to have been embraced by parents and children alike. Eunice, the only daughter in the Colcord family, entered the Lane household at an exciting time; within the next few years two stepsisters, Susanna and Martha Lane, both married. Jabez acquired a male companion in Benjamin, something he had lost with the marriages of his two brothers.

Benjamin eventually apprenticed with his stepfather, Samuel. As far as the records show, Samuel treated his stepson as he did any apprentice.[185] Throughout the 1780s, Ben appears regularly in Samuel's accounts performing agricultural labor for others. There is no indication as to whether Ben learned the trades of tanning and cordwaining as well. He left Samuel's service in 1787; that April, Jeremiah Norris made "Bens freedom Suit."[186]

With the Colcord marriage also came the first and only mention of a slave in the Lane household. Gideon Colcord included among his bequests to his widow "my Negro gairl for Ever (called Dinah)."[187] In the spring of 1783, Samuel noted "Jabez, Eunice, Benja, and Dinah had the measles," thereby confirming the slave's continued presence in the household.[188]

Samuel exhibited a personal interest in his extended family, noting significant events such as visits, illness, and deaths but did not record births, as was his custom with his own family. His interest extended to trading with his stepson Gideon Colcord and lending several of the Colcord boys money. In addition, Samuel helped the new members of his family in other ways. Until at least 1783, he made shoes for the Colcords; Jabez made their shoes the following year.

The two families found themselves even more closely linked in 1783 when Jabez and Eunice announced their intention to marry. Eunice was sixteen and Jabez twenty-three at the time.

Samuel always treated Jabez's legacy a little differently from that of the young man's two older brothers. This distinction stemmed from three likely causes: that Jabez was his youngest son, that he married his stepsister, and that he was lame. In the first case, Samuel appears to have compensated for Jabez's youth by adopting the practice of ultimogeniture, or passing the family property to the youngest rather than the oldest son. This type of inheritance favored nearly all interested parties. Samuel could retain his farm until he was ready to retire, while his oldest sons could establish their own families without waiting for a promised family farm.[189] Samuel found means to settle each older son on a farm of his own while continuing to rely on his own farm to support himself and his younger children and stepchildren.

When Jabez and Eunice decided to marry, Samuel and Rachel still lived on the family farm. They decided to offer Jabez and Eunice the farmhouse that Samuel had acquired with neighbor Mason's farm in 1777. It was an ideal, if temporary, solution to their problem. The house was on the property Samuel had designated for Jabez and only one hundred rods east of his own house; Jabez could work alongside his father on the farm, in the shop, and at the tannery, which was to become his. At the same time, he and Eunice could enjoy their own dwelling on the same property.

In the months before the two were married, Jabez set about fixing up the house: reshingling the roof, clapboarding the walls, repairing and whitewashing the chimneys, and adding and repairing windows. Unlike the repair of his two brothers' houses, the account for this work is in Jabez's own account book, not that of Samuel. The total, £9.8.0, includes twenty days of Jabez's own labor, £3 worth, but it is not clear who paid the bill, Jabez or his father.[190]

The couple moved into their new home on October 20, eighteen days after their wedding. Jabez's new status as household head did not alter the cooperative work relationship between father and son. Jabez continued his work in the various Lane enterprises as he had before. In outward appearance the union seems to have followed the pattern established for Samuel's other children, with the husband bringing real property and the wife personal property to the relationship. Eunice brought one-half her parents' household goods to her marriage. Her father's will also had directed that she be paid £5 "at the age of Eighteen years or at marriage Day." At his death in 1773, Gideon Colcord's household goods were appraised at £32.13.8. It appears that Eunice would have brought to her marriage several beds and bedding, table linens, a couple of desks or chests of drawers, chairs, tables, fireplace utensils, kitchen and dining ware, and a spinning wheel.[191] However, their value, about £16.6.10, was only about one-quarter of the value of the household goods each of Samuel's daughters received.

As Eunice was his stepdaughter and had been a member of his household for nine years, Samuel decided to give the couple a portion of household goods to complement the things Eunice received from her father's estate. Preparing for this extraordinary move, Samuel first made a list "of Some things left in my House after Sarah had taken hers which belong'd to my first Wife." On October 20, 1783, the day Jabez and Eunice moved to their new home, Samuel made a list, primarily containing textiles, headed, "I gave Son Jabez out of the above things as follows." The first item on the list was "1 feather Bed that was his Mothers."[192] Samuel's roles with respect to sons and daughters converged with the marriage of Jabez and Eunice, prompting him to provide the young couple with both personal and real property to ensure their success.

Jabez's situation was different for still a third reason; his weak constitution and lameness may have led Samuel to regard his youngest as less competent to deal with worldly matters. In the case of the older brothers, Samuel gave them the deeds to their farms within a few years of their marriages. But although he made out a deed to Jabez for his ninety-three-acre farm, together with other Stratham lands, the year following his son's marriage, Samuel kept possession of this property, with assurances that it ultimately would pass to his youngest son.

Jabez had fallen into an ambiguous status; he was neither a freeholder nor a dependent in his father's household. He kept his own accounts and carried on his shoe business independent of his father, but his tannery work was sometimes indistinguishable from Samuel's. And their farming appears to have been a cooperative venture also. After 1783, Samuel's diary mentions Jabez plowing, carrying hides to the currier, and trading in Portsmouth for him. There was some division of the lands on the farm between the households of father and son, and Samuel often noted work he performed for Jabez. They kept their livestock separate; Samuel noted specifically when Jabez's cattle went to the Bank.[193]

The seemingly cooperative and harmonious relationship between father and son evident in the accounts masked a certain amount of tension and anxiety on Jabez's part over his situation. The 1784 deed to his Stratham farm was not recorded until January 23, 1800. Such delays were not unusual in the transfer of property between family members, but in a December 1799 letter to his father, Jabez voiced concern. Addressing his "honoured father, Deacon Samuel Lane," Jabez wrote:

> Before I entered the stage of action, I was led by your own declaration to Suppose, I should have some solid foundation to rest upon, for the support of my family, or else in my state of incapacity for hard labour, I should not have made the Experiment, until I had, by some means or other, acquired property, or perhaps not at all.—after I had asked your consent in Marrying, and likewise asked you to give me some real Estate, which you declined saying it was as Safe in your hands as mine, I laid aside for a number of months my plan of entering into a family state,—I mentioned to one of my Brothers, my determination, which was not to marry, 'till I had some real Estate I could call my own,—he said that was the way you did by him at first, but in a little while after, gave him a Deed without any more asking; and you would do the same by me in a little while, he tho't I need not be concern'd about it . . . but when year after year roll'd away and it was not done, I felt by degrees, more and more uneasy.[194]

Thus, the Lanes were not free after all from the intergenerational tension that so many colonial families harbored. It appears that Jabez had been able to lay aside his uneasiness and quietly accept his predicament until the disparity between his own and his brothers' situations widened, with the additional lands Samuel gave them in 1798. Jabez could contain his unhappiness no longer: "my disappointment and tryal was as great as it was possible for me to bear."

Jabez's letter had two purposes, to express his long-repressed sentiments and to persuade Samuel to pass him title to the property. His arguments apparently struck a respondent chord in Samuel, who knew firsthand the trials of a young couple with little property and who had seen similar situations among his friends and neighbors in Stratham. Jabez pointed out the advantages his brothers enjoyed in holding title to their property, particularly the income that had accrued to them. In addition, brothers Samuel and Joshua had sold some of the land and passed some of it on to their own children, options unavailable to the youngest son. Jabez was in his prime: "I am now in the fortieth year of my Age [and] find my Self Surrounded by a large, and consequently an expensive family." He further observed that his "Brothers have arrived at that period in life when their families are decreasing, they are now Small in comparison with mine."[195] He then asked plaintively, "when in the name of common sense, will it be necessary for me to have property, if the present is not the time."[196]

Jabez sought to reassure his father that a transfer was in everyone's best interest. He outlined the various ways in which his father's intent might be thwarted, either by chance or malice, if left in the hands of others after his death. As for Samuel's support, Jabez promised his father, "you might ease yourself of that care, which must be a burden at your time of life as I Should be willing, to carry on the whole place, and render you, in conjunction with my Brothers, as much produce of every kind, as you Should want to Expend."[197]

Samuel's advanced age and sense of mortality certainly shaped his reaction to Jabez's letter. When he was only sixty-eight years old,

"Grown old, he retires from Business," from a child's picture book, made for Freelove Wheeler (1752–1831) by William Colwell (1780–1817), Foster, Rhode Island. *Courtesy Rare Book Department, The Free Library of Philadelphia.*

Though Samuel Lane never officially retired, his business activities gradually tapered off. On April 27, 1791, he noted, "I Measur'd (Assist'd by Grandson James Lane) Josiah Thirstons Land: which is the last I ever Expect to Measure." During the last two years of his life, having established all three sons on farms of their own, Lane owned no real estate at all.

during a visit to family in Sanbornton, he predicted that visit was "perhaps the last time."[198] In 1790 he described his strength as failing, and in 1794, a litany of complaints began, including pains in his feet and legs, deafness, shaking fits, and vomiting. His declining health, as well as his own sentiments concerning the disposition of his estate, undoubtedly combined to make Jabez's arguments compelling.

Jabez continued his plea: "You used to say you intended to make my lame leg as long as the other, (to use your expression) and my Eldest Brother told me a number of years ago, that he told you, he was willing you should give me, as much as you did him & Br Josu both (on Account of my being lame)."[199] Samuel may have been waiting for his son to broach the subject, for, on January 23, 1800, Jabez entered in his journal, "I went Exeter put Deeds on record."[200]

The deed Samuel executed in 1800 was the one drafted in 1784, three months after Jabez and Eunice's marriage. It essentially followed the scheme outlined in the letter. Jabez received 103 Stratham acres, 93 of which constituted the home farm. Although Jabez's brothers were obliged to pay their father £5 in return for their farms, his was an outright gift.[201] Compared to Joshua's sixty-one acres and Samuel Junior's sixty-eight and one-half acres, Jabez was indeed compensated for his lameness. And more land was to follow. In 1802, Samuel gave him a fifty-acre lot in Pittsfield, and three years after that, seventeen acres of "oak land" in Newmarket. Jabez gladly signed the obligation "to my honoured father Samuel Lane Esqr that he shall have the whole use and improvement of all the Land he has given me by Deed."[202] Samuel's youngest entered the new century with a peace of mind he had not enjoyed since his marriage to Eunice in 1783.

By 1805 then, Samuel Lane had disposed of the bulk of his estate. Each daughter was married and had left his household with a valuable selection of domestic goods and skills with which to establish a home. Samuel had transferred all his property to his sons, reserving enough income from their land to live out his last days in comfort. During the last two years of his life, Samuel owned no real estate at all. Just as his daughters produced textiles for their portions, his sons too contributed to their portions by working alongside their father, cultivating and improving the lands that were to become theirs.

Father Died 7 oClock evening

Samuel Lane's last diary entry, written in December 1801, was typically factual, "pretty cold." By then his failing health had severely

Dining Room of Dr. Whitridge's, Tiverton, [Rhode Island] as It Was in the Winter 1814–1815, watercolor by Joseph Shoemaker Russell, c. 1850. *Courtesy Old Dartmouth Historical Society, New Bedford Whaling Museum.*

For the last six years of his life, Samuel Lane was deaf and nearly blind. He spent his final years confined to his house. His children shared in his care.

limited his activity, and most of his diary entries detailed either weather observations or family events. After Samuel turned seventy, ailments began to take increasing prominence in his daily life. On February 20, 1794, he wrote, "I was taken with a Rheumatic Pain in my Right foot; which held about 4 Months. then went into my left foot, & held about a Month." His foot problems were recurrent; in 1802 he noted, "My great toes began to be Sore as Usual & held about a Week." In 1796 he referred to himself as "verry Deaf."[203] Dizziness, sickness, and vomiting accompanied his last years, and although he noted them in various writings, it was without remorse, bitterness, or anger. As always, his religion helped him accept what he could not change.

Secure in the knowledge that he had prepared his sons and daughters to succeed him, Samuel laid his pen down for the last time on his eighty-fifth birthday. As he had done every year, perhaps each time thinking it might be his last, he recorded, "I enter'd the 86th year of my Age."[204] Now not only deaf, but also nearly blind, he could write no more. Three years later, his grandson, Edmund Lane, visited Samuel for the last time. Entering the room where his grandfather now lived, Edmund remembered seeing Samuel "sitting in his easy chair upright his hands lying beside him his eyes open but being blind he did not see me & deaf did not hear me . . . his beard unshaven for a week or more, and his white hair hanging loosely over his head."[205]

Samuel was roombound for his last years, but the seeds he had sown were at work within his family. Jabez's papers are neither as extensive nor as complete as Samuel's, but the parallels to those of his father are striking. Among the son's records is a "Catalogue of Books ownd by Jabez Lane," as well as an "Account of the Things I give my Daughter Martha Mathes Towards her Portion out of my

Estate."[206] Jabez's sense of family continuity mirrored that of his father, though subtle differences appear as well.

Samuel had been content to support his family by the work of his hands. His main assets were in his farm and tanyard. Outside investment took familiar forms—land and loans of money, mostly to friends and neighbors. Although other outlets for capital existed around him, especially mills and stocks of merchant goods, he remained conservative.

Jabez, though likewise a skilled craftsman and a large landowner, availed himself of commercial opportunities his father had avoided. On November 20, 1781, Jabez "Sent a Silver Dollar to bilboa by Jer Colcord, as a Venture." Perhaps he had second thoughts about this speculation; he spread his risk on March 9, 1782, by selling one-quarter of the "venture" to his sister Sarah. Their return was equivocal. In June he wrote, "we Received 4 y^{ds} & above ½ of gause. he [Jeremiah Colcord] had half for his Trouble. remains for us 2 y^{ds} and ¼ & Better." That return was inducement enough to try again, but the second venture was less salutary. In August 1782, "sent half a Dollar to Sea By Jer Colcord," Jabez noted in his daybook and later added "which I Lost."[207] Another sign of Jabez's changing outlook was his half interest in a sawmill purchased in 1797. His father speculated too but in the more traditional vehicles of land and an occasional lottery ticket.[208]

The different outlooks of father and son are clearly apparent in Jabez's actions immediately following his father's death. On Christmas day in 1806, Jabez wrote in his journal, "Father taken worse."[209] Four days later, Samuel died quietly in his sleep.

Within a month of his father's death, Jabez began to cut timber for a new house frame. Although Samuel's house had served his family well, Jabez had more ambitious designs for a dwelling. Despite the continued presence in the old house of Samuel's widow, Rachel, preparations for the new house continued unabated; Jabez took down the well house and moved the shop. Just three months after Samuel's death, Jabez took his stepmother back to her residence in Newmarket for good; four days later he began to take down the chimney of the house she had lived in for thirty-three years. By the end of that year, he wrote: "This year I took down the House that was my fathers and built a new House which I moved into Oct 20th having lived in the old House [neighbor Mason's house] very Comfortably 24 years, In all which Time there was no breach made in our family, the Lord prepare us for what is before us."[210]

Comfort, "competence," and security, underpinnings of Samuel's world, were not quite adequate for Jabez. Clearly, his religious outlook and dependence on the divine will echoed that of his father, but that alone was not enough for complete satisfaction in his post-

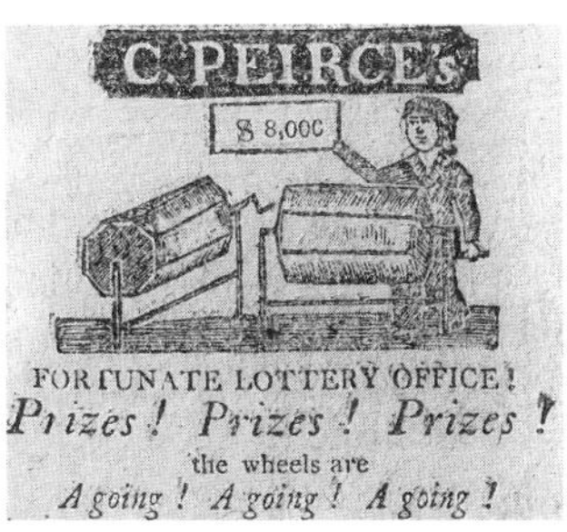

Advertisement with a woodcut of a lottery machine, Peirce's Lottery Office, Portsmouth; in *Portmouth Oracle*, 1806. *New Hampshire Historical Society.*

Samuel Lane did not disdain entering a lottery now and then to support a worthy local cause. While Lane's generation worked and yearned for competency and security for themselves and their families, the subsequent generation invested differently in their future and welcomed a greater degree of risk.

colonial world. Jabez's ambitions were colored by the growing commercial environment around him.

Jabez lived only three years in his new house, succumbing to illness himself in 1810. Even in death his notion of security differed from that of his father's generation. Jabez left a substantial estate of over $8,000, including his Stratham property, a farm in Lee, and personal goods. The inclusion of $500 in Exeter Bank stock sets his world apart from that of his father. Jabez intended that the income from the stock would support Eunice for seven years after his decease.[211] Such a financial vehicle was never employed by Samuel; his security rested in land and in individuals. Jabez was part of the new economic and financial climate, which would spur economic growth during the nineteenth century. Stocks, though available to Samuel in his later years, did not promise him the security he needed to live out his last years, as there can be little doubt he did, in peace and comfort.

Afterword: Settling in the World

Before dawn on Thanksgiving Day, November 21, 1793, Samuel Lane lay awake "recollecting the Many Mercies and good things" for which he was thankful. After rising, he wrote out a list of those things.[1] The list was long, for in his seventy-five years, Samuel had led a satisfying and successful life by almost any standard of the day. From his windows he could look out over his shops and barn to fields beyond, and from his doorway watch the traffic pass on the main road from Portsmouth to Exeter. He could note the time of sunrise by his watch or listen for the chime of the clock in the great room. A certain excitement animated his reflections; this chilly Thursday held the promise of going to meeting and hosting a family gathering.

On that morning, Samuel gave thanks not only for his life, health, Bible, and minister but also for physical comforts and luxuries such as "wearing clothes," "Bed & Beding," "Lamp Oyl & Candles,"and "good and Useful Books." These he valued not so much for their own sake as for helping him and those around him lead meaningful and productive lives. Samuel thanked God for his "Clock and Watch to measure my passing time by Day and by Night." He saw no contradiction between his spiritual needs and "'the necessary business of life." Even money glorified life by giving him the ability "to bye other Necessaries and to pay my Debts & Taxes &c."

Samuel was grateful for everything his world held. Beginning as a landless shoemaker, he was now a prosperous farmer with large land holdings on Stratham's main thoroughfare. Although in some

Photograph showing the site of Samuel Lane's farm, the house that Jabez Lane built there the year after his father's death, and the Lane shoeshop, as they appeared around 1938–1940. *Courtesy Priscilla Lane Moore Tapley.*

The family farm that Jabez Lane inherited from his father would remain in the Lane family for 150 years after Samuel Lane's death.

years many around him suffered shortages, his diligence and planning precluded such hardships from attending his family. In addition, at a time when land scarcities obliged neighbors' sons to settle in remote places, Samuel settled each son on a substantial farm near his own in Stratham. He thereby ensured both their future and his own security, as old age approached.

Samuel was exceptional in his time for keeping his own farm intact and at the same time passing on an appropriate inheritance to each of his children. This was a goal that had eluded many across New England during the eighteenth century. Over more than eighty years of often repetitive, painstaking, and sometimes strenuous labor, New Hampshire's Samuel Lane slowly but surely succeeded in settling first himself and then his family in the world. Though he may never have realized it, Samuel's legacy to his children involved not only the means to continue life as he knew it but also the resources to succeed in the changing atmosphere of a new century.

Notes

The New Hampshire Historical Society (here cited as NHHS) and the New Hampshire Division of Records Management and Archives (the "State Archives," here cited as NHSA) together hold the Samuel Lane manuscript material on which this book is based.

To avoid confusion caused by Old Style/New Style dates, text dates have been simplified to conform to the Gregorian calendar. However, for the months January through March, the text may cite a Gregorian calendar date while the source given in the Notes may carry a Julian calendar date (for instance, a March 1741 text date whose source is the 1740 Day Book).

Samuel Lane included general comments in his diary at the beginning and conclusion of each year. The reader will find these referenced as a "preface" or "summary."

Introduction

1. Samuel Lane, Thanksgiving list, November 21, 1793, Lane Family Papers, New Hampshire Historical Society.

2. Lane Family Papers, 1727–1899, New Hampshire Historical Society. This collection (4.5 linear feet) consists primarily of the papers of Samuel Lane but also includes those of other generations of his family. Hereafter cited as Lane Papers.

3. *The Diary of Matthew Patten of Bedford, N.H. from 1754 to 1788* (Concord, N.H.: Rumford Printing Co., 1903; reprint, Camden, Maine: Picton Press, 1993), and Abner Sanger, *Very Poor and of a Lo Make: The Journal of Abner Sanger*, ed. Lois K. Stabler (Portsmouth, N.H.: Peter E. Randall for the Historical Society of Cheshire County, 1986). The original manuscript diaries of Matthew Patten are also in the New Hampshire Historical Society collection; those of Abner Sanger are at the Historical Society of Cheshire County.

4. [Reverend James Miltimore], "Extract from a Sermon preach'd at Stratham, Jan. 11th 1807, Being the Sabbath after the Interment of Deacon Samuel Lane," Lane Papers.

5. Ibid., and also another manuscript, in the same handwriting, headed "No.2," Lane Papers.

6. Ebenezer Lane, "Some Remarks and Reminiscences of the Lane Family," July 31, 1841, p. 4, Lane Papers.

7. A shoe, made by Samuel Lane's brother Ebenezer for his daughter Huldah, is preserved in the New Hampshire Historical Society museum collection. See illustration on p. 39.

8. Glenn A. Knoblock, "From Jonathan Hartshorne to Jeremiah Lane: Fifty Years of Gravestone Carving in Coastal New Hampshire," *Markers: Annual Journal of the Association for Gravestone Studies* 13 (1996): 74–111.

9. Esther Stevens Fraser, "Pioneer Furniture from Hampton, New

Hampshire," *Antiques* (April 1930): 312–16; Brock Jobe, ed., *Portsmouth Furniture: Masterworks from the New Hampshire Seacoast* (Boston: Society for the Preservation of New England Antiquities, 1993), pp. 92–93. The attribution of a group of furniture to Samuel's uncle is based on a chest he signed at the age of twenty-one. Young craftsmen, just out of apprenticeship, were those most likely to sign their work. There is a possibility that some of this furniture was made by the as-yet-unidentified master of joiner Samuel Lane.

10. *Johnson's Wonder-working Providence, 1628–1651*, ed. J. Franklin Jameson (London, 1654; reprint, New York: Charles Scribner's Sons, 1910), p. 188.

11. "Maverick's Description of New England," communicated by Henry F. Waters, *New-England Historical and Genealogical Register* 39 (January 1885): 35.

12. Rev. George Whitefield, quoted in George Francis Dow, comp., *Two Centuries of Essex County Travel: A Collection of Narratives and Observations Made by Travelers, 1605–1799* (Topsfield, Mass.: Topsfield Historical Society, 1921), p. 72.

13. James Birket, *Some Cursory Remarks Made by James Birket in His Voyage to North America, 1750–1751* (New Haven, Conn.: Yale University Press, 1916), p. 13.

14. John Farmer and Jacob B. Moore, *A Gazetteer of the State of New-Hampshire* (Concord, N.H.: Jacob B. Moore, 1823), p. 148.

15. David T. Courtwright, "New England Families in Historical Perspective," in *Families and Children: The Dublin Seminar for New England Folklife Annual Proceedings, 1985*, ed. Peter Benes (Boston: Boston University, 1987), pp. 11–23.

16. "Census of 1773, Taken by Order of His Excellency John Wentworth, Governor," in *New Hampshire State and Provincial Papers*, 10: 623–29.

17. Alexander Ormond Boulton, "New England's Slave's Quarters," *Journal of Regional Cultures* 3 (fall/winter 1983): 57–74.

18. *New Hampshire Gazette*, August 2, 1771 (John Hickey advertisement).

19. Alexander Hamilton, *Hamilton's Itinerarium, Being a Narrative of a Journey from Annapolis, Maryland through . . . New Hampshire from May to September, 1744* (St. Louis: Privately printed, 1907), p. 153.

20. Kenneth Scott, "Colonial Innkeepers of New Hampshire," *Historical New Hampshire* 19 (spring 1964): 22, citing selectmen's recommendation.

21. The southern portion of Newmarket, adjoining Stratham, became Newfields in 1895.

22. James Hill Fitts, *History of Newfields*, ed. N. F. Carter (Concord, N.H.: Rumford Press, 1912), p. 170, quoting petition of 1746.

23. For references to this road, see the charter of Stratham, March 20, 1716, quoted in D. Hamilton Hurd, *History of Rockingham and Strafford Counties* (Philadelphia: J. W. Lewis & Co., 1882), p. 542, and Fitts, *History of Newfields*, p. 180, citing bridge lottery authorization of 1768.

24. Several early accounts document travelers passing along this route on their way from the coast to the Merrimack Valley and beyond. See also R. M. Scammon, "Down the King's Great Highway: A Sketch of Stratham," *Granite Monthly* 26 (March 1899): 140.

25. Luigi Castiglioni, *Viaggio: Travels in the United States of North America, 1785–87* (Milan: Marelli, 1790; reprint, Syracuse, N.Y.: Syracuse University Press, 1983), p. 56; Timothy Dwight, *Travels in New England and New York*, 4 vols. (Cambridge, Mass.: Belknap Press of Harvard University Press, 1969), 1:303; and Birket, *Some Cursory Remarks*, p. 4.

26. Birket, *Some Cursory Remarks*, p. 4, and *The Diary of William*

Bentley, 4 vols. (Salem, Mass.: Essex Institute, 1907), 2:390. Note that in the latter account the name Stratham was accidentally omitted until near the end of the description.

27. Marquis de Chastellux, *Travels in North America in the Years 1780, 1781, and 1782* (Chapel Hill: University of North Carolina Press for the Institute of Early American History and Culture, 1963), p. 484, and *Diary of William Bentley*, 2:388.

28. Eliphalet and Phinehas Merrill, *A Gazetteer of the State of New-Hampshire* (Exeter, N.H.: C. Norris & Co., 1817), p. 197.

29. Fitts, *History of Newfields*, chap. 11. Samuel Lane included the opening of this bridge in a list at the end of his journal, as among the most important happenings during his lifetime.

30. Jeremy Belknap, *Belknap's New Hampshire: An Account of the State in 1792: A Facsimile Edition of Volume III of The History of New Hampshire*, ed. G. T. Lord (Hampton, N.H.: Peter E. Randall, 1973), p. 251.

31. Birket, *Some Cursory Remarks*, p. 6.

32. *The Diaries of George Washington* (Boston: Houghton Mifflin Co. for the Mount Vernon Ladies' Association of the Union, 1925), 4:44.

33. For background on the development of ports, see Benjamin W. Labaree, "The Seaport as Entrepôt," *The Log of Mystic Seaport* 29 (July 1977): 34-41.

34. James L. Garvin, "That Little World Portsmouth," in Jobe, *Portsmouth Furniture* (see n. 9), p. 15.

35. Piscataqua Customs Records, copy at Portsmouth (N.H.) Athenaeum.

36. Donna-Belle Garvin and James L. Garvin, *On the Road North of Boston: New Hampshire Taverns and Turnpikes* (Concord: New Hampshire Historical Society, 1988), pp. 89–91.

37. Birket, *Some Cursory Remarks*, p. 9.

38. Castiglioni, *Viaggio*, p. 55.

39. Samuel Lane, Diary, April 10, 1765; Day Book, 1760, 1764. Lane Papers (hereafter cited as Diary or Day Book). King and Queen streets were changed to Congress and State streets at the time of the Revolution.

40. Robert Rogers, *A Concise Account of North America* (London: Author, 1765), p. 51.

41. James L. Garvin, "The Old New Hampshire State House," *Historical New Hampshire* 46 (winter 1991): 202–28, and Garvin and Garvin, *On the Road North of Boston*, p. 132, quoting New Hampshire Province Treasury Records, 1753–57, New Hampshire Division of Records Management and Archives (hereafter cited as NHSA).

42. Birket, *Some Cursory Remarks*, p. 2.

43. Silvio A. Bedini, *Early American Scientific Instruments and Their Makers* (Washington, D.C.: Museum of History and Technology, 1964), pp. 85–92.

44. William Appleton advertised in the *New Hampshire Gazette*, beginning in 1765.

45. William Hart, account books, 1757–96, New Hampshire Historical Society.

46. Dwight, *Travels*, 1:316.

47. Birket, *Some Cursory Remarks*, p. 4.

48. Washington, *Diaries*, 4:46.

49. *New Hampshire Gazette*, May 11, 1770.

50. Diary, June 16, 1753, and May 17, 1762.

51. Castiglioni, *Viaggio*, p. 56.

52. Washington, *Diaries*, 4:46.

53. Dwight, *Travels*, 1:302.

54. Chastellux, *Travels in North America*, p. 488.

55. See Charles E. L. Wingate, ed., *Life and Letters of Paine Wingate:*

One of the Fathers of the Nation, 2 vols. (Medford, Mass: Privately printed, 1930).

56. John F. LaBranche and Rita F. Conant, *In Female Worth and Elegance: Sampler and Needlework Students and Teachers in Portsmouth, New Hampshire, 1741–1840* (Portsmouth, N.H.: Portsmouth Marine Society, 1996), pp. 35–38.

57. Petition, Stratham, January 15, 1776, Lane Papers.

58. Association Test, Stratham, NHSA.

59. Annie Wiggin Scammon, "Historical Sketch of the Town of Stratham," *Exeter News-Letter*, September 1, 1916.

60. Diary, 1749, 1752, 1753, 1762.

61. *New Hampshire Gazette*, June 20, 1766.

62. Diary, January 14, 1763.

63. Francisco de Miranda, *The New Democracy in America: Travels of Francisco de Miranda in the United States, 1783–84* (Norman: University of Oklahoma Press, 1963), p. 180.

64. Diary, February 26, 1751.

65. Ibid., February 21, 1748, and January 18, 1780.

66. The twelve feet of snow that Samuel Lane recorded in 1747–48 exceeded the more recent record-setting snows of 1995–96, which probably totaled about nine to ten feet of snow. Communication from Gregory A. Zielinski, research associate professor, Climate Change Research Center, University of New Hampshire, March 8, 1999.

67. Courtwright, "New England Families," p. 17, and J. Worth Estes and David M. Goodman, *The Changing Humors of Portsmouth: The Medical Biography of an American Town, 1623–1983* (Boston: Francis A. Countway Library of Medicine, 1986), p. 5.

68. Diary, 1762, summary.

69. Ibid., October 2, 1761.

70. Miltimore, "Extract from a Sermon," Lane Papers.

71. Samuel Lane, "An Account of the Books I own; Numbered as follows, March 5, 1762," Lane Papers. Some of the books Samuel Lane owned are now in the New Hampshire Historical Society library collection.

72. Miltimore, "Extract from a Sermon," Lane Papers.

73. Ebenezer Lane, "Some Remarks," p. 6, Lane Papers.

74. R. M. Scammon, "Down the King's Great Highway," p. 157.

75. Ibid., p. 143.

76. Warren Brown, *History of Hampton Falls, N.H.*, vol. 2 (Concord, N.H.: Rumford Press, 1918), p. 20.

77. Agreement for music lessons, Stratham, April 8, 1782, Stratham town records, NHSA.

78. Diary, August 22, 1782.

79. Ebenezer Lane, "Some Remarks," p. 6, Lane Papers.

80. Belknap, *Belknap's New Hampshire*, p. 251.

1. *Mastering a Trade*

1. Samuel Lane, Diary, April 5 and June 2, 1781; Jabez Lane, "A Tanyard Journal," 1781, Lane Papers, New Hampshire Historical Society (hereafter cited as Lane Papers).

2. Edwin Tunis, *Colonial Craftsmen and the Beginnings of American Industry* (Cleveland, Ohio: World Publishing Co., 1965), p. 32.

3. Samuel Lane, "The Years of the Life of Samuel Lane . . ." [a manuscript chart], Lane Papers.

4. Joshua Lane, Journal, Lane Papers.

5. Eccles. 11:10.

6. Karin Calvert, *Children in the House: The Material Culture of Early*

Childhood, 1600–1900 (Boston: Northeastern University Press, 1992), pp. 51–52, 60, 73.

7. John C. Miller, *The First Frontier: Life in Colonial America* (New York: Dell Publishing Co., 1966), pp. 210–11. Note the difference by 1790, cited in Calvert, *Children in the House*: "The first seven years of life are a period of greater importance in the business of education, than is generally imagined" (p. 61).

8. John P. Demos, *A Little Commonwealth: Family Life in Plymouth Colony* (New York: Oxford University Press, 1970), p. 139.

9. Joseph Dow, *History of the Town of Hampton, New Hampshire: From Its Settlement in 1638, to the Autumn of 1892* (Salem, Mass.: Salem Press, 1893; reprint, Hampton, N.H.: Peter E. Randall, 1977), p. 473.

10. "Years of the Life," Lane Papers.

11. Ibid.

12. Robert Bruce Mullin, ed., *Moneygripe's Apprentice: The Personal Narrative of Samuel Seabury III* (New Haven, Conn.: Yale University Press, 1989), p. 59.

13. William H. Mulligan Jr., "The Transmission of Skill in the Shoe Industry: Family to Factory Training in Lynn, Massachusetts," in *The Craftsman in Early America*, ed. Ian M. G. Quimby (Winterthur, Del.: The Henry Francis duPont Winterthur Museum, 1984), p. 243.

14. Edgar M. Hoover Jr., *Location Theory and the Shoe and Leather Industries*, Harvard Economic Studies, vol. 55 (Cambridge, Mass.: Harvard University Press, 1937), p. 159.

15. At Lynn, Massachusetts, the center of New England shoe production during the late eighteenth and nineteenth centuries, "the following tools and appliances were regarded as essential: A lap-stone, Hammer, stirrup, whet-board, pincers, nippers,—sometimes—shoulder-stick (one or more), long stick, pettibois, toe-stick, fender, bead, scraper, knives of different descriptions, such as skiver, paring-off knife, heel-knife, etc., awl, bristles, tacks, wax, a piece of sponge, pastehorn, bottles for blacking, gum—and acid in later times—chalk, dogfish skin . . . stitch-rag, grease, channel-opener—usually called an open-channel—and apron." David N. Johnson, *Sketches of Lynn or the Changes of Fifty Years* (Lynn, Mass.: Thos. P. Nichols, 1880), p. 31.

16. Joshua Lane, Will, December 16, 1760, Lane Papers.

17. William Cronon, *Changes in the Land: Indians, Colonists, and the Ecology of New England* (New York: Hill and Wang, 1983), p. 140; and Howard Russell, *A Long Deep Furrow: Three Centuries of Farming in New England* (Hanover, N.H.: University Press of New England, 1976), p. 161; Percy Wells Bidwell and John I. Falconer, *History of Agriculture in the Northern United States, 1620–1860* (Washington, D.C.: Carnegie Institution of Washington, 1925; reprint, New York: Peter Smith, 1941), pp. 136–37.

18. R. A. Salaman, *Dictionary of Leather-Working Tools, c. 1700–1950, and the Tools of Allied Trades* (New York: Macmillan, 1986), p. 19; *A New and Complete Dictionary of Arts and Sciences* (London: W. Owen, at Homer's Head, 1764), p. 295.

19. Samuel Lane, Day Book, 1737, Lane Papers (hereafter cited as Day Book).

20. Ibid., 1751.

21. D. A. Saguto, "The 'Mysterie' of a Cordwainer," *Chronicle of the Early American Industries Association*, vol. 34, no. 1 (1981), p. 2.

22. Ebenezer Lane, "Some Remarks and Reminiscences of the Lane Family," July 31, 1841, Lane Papers.

23. *The Diary of Matthew Patten of Bedford, N.H. from 1754 to 1788* (Concord, N.H.: Rumford Printing Co., 1903; reprint, Camden, Maine: Picton Press, 1993), pp. 132–34.

24. Day Book, 1745, 1757.

25. Hoover, *Location Theory*, p. 159.

26. Blanche Evans Hazard, *The Organization of the Boot and Shoe Industry in Massachusetts before 1875* (Cambridge, Mass.: Harvard University Press, 1921), p. 8.

27. Thomas J. Schlereth, "Artisans and Craftsmen: A Historical Perspective," in *The Craftsman in Early America*, ed. Ian M. G. Quimby (Winterthur, Del.: The Henry Francis duPont Winterthur Museum, 1984), p. 38.

28. William Rorabaugh, *The Craft Apprentice: From Franklin to the Machine Age in America* (New York: Oxford University Press, 1986), p. 6.

29. Alfred F. Young, "George Robert Twelves Hewes (1742–1840): A Boston Shoemaker and the Memory of the American Revolution," *William and Mary Quarterly*, 3rd ser., vol. 38 (October 1981): 570–71.

30. Ibid., p. 571.

31. Donna-Belle Garvin, Survey of Craftsmen in the Piscataqua Area (unpublished); New Hampshire Provincial Probate Court, New Hampshire Division of Records Management and Archives (hereafter cited as Provincial Probate Records, NHSA); Bruce C. Daniels, "Defining Economic Classes in Colonial New Hampshire," *Historical New Hampshire* 28 (spring 1973): 59–60. Daniels defined five economic classes: wealthy (91–100 percentile), prosperous (71–90), middle (31–70), lower (11–30), and poor (0–10). The average estate value dropped to £2,573.3.0 after accounting for claims on the estates. Three of seventeen Piscataqua area shoemakers who died between 1754 and 1770 were insolvent at the time of their deaths.

32. Records of Hampton (Old Parish), December 1731 and January 1732, cited in [Jacob Chapman] and James H. Fitts, *William Lane of Boston, Mass., 1648, Including the Records of Edmund J. Lane and James P. Lane* (Exeter, N.H.: News-Letter Press, 1891), p. 10; Joshua Lane, Will, December 16, 1760, Lane Papers.

33. Dow, *History of Hampton*, pp. 396, 565, 573.

34. Provincial Probate Records, NHSA, docket no. 3326; Daniels, "Defining Economic Classes," pp. 60–61. In the period 1761–70 prosperous estates were valued between £9,930 and £18,904, middle estates between £1,705 and £9,929.

35. See Daniel Vickers, "Working the Fields in a Developing Economy: Essex County, Massachusetts, 1630–1675," and Laurel Thatcher Ulrich, "Martha Ballard and Her Girls: Women's Work in Eighteenth-Century Maine," in *Work and Labor in Early America*, ed. Stephen Innes (Chapel Hill: University of North Carolina Press for the Institute of Early American History and Culture, 1988). See Laurel Thatcher Ulrich, *A Midwife's Tale: The Life of Martha Ballard, Based on Her Diary, 1785–1812* (New York: Alfred A. Knopf, 1990). Ulrich minutely details the interrelationship between family labor and changing needs through the family's life cycle. The experience of a Rowley, Massachusetts, family is one example. See Daniel Vickers, "Competency and Competition: Economic Culture in Early America," *William and Mary Quarterly*, 3rd ser., 47 (January 1990): 7.

36. Rorabaugh, *The Craft Apprentice*, p. 6.

37. Ibid., p. vii.

38. Robert Francis Seybolt, *Apprenticeship and Apprenticeship Education in Colonial New England and New York* (New York: Teachers College, Columbia University, 1917; reprint ed., New York: Arno Press and the *New York Times*, 1969), p. 45.

39. "Apprenticeship: Career Education Colonial Style," *Journal of Research and Development in Education* 8 (summer 1975): 22, 25.

40. "Years of the Life," Lane Papers.

41. Samuel Lane, Diary, April 20, 1754, Lane Papers (hereafter cited as Diary).

42. "Years of the Life," Lane Papers.

43. Day Book, 1736.
44. Ibid., 1737.
45. Jackson Turner Main, "Standards of Living and the Life Cycle in Colonial Connecticut," *Journal of Economic History* 43 (March 1983): 103. Main specifically states that boys were the primary source of labor and neglects the contribution of daughters to overall household production.
46. Day Book, 1736, 1737.
47. Chapman and Fitts, *William Lane of Boston*, pp. 17–20.
48. Ian M. G. Quimby, "Introduction: Some Observations on the Craftsman in Early America," in *The Craftsman in Early America* (Winterthur, Del.: The Henry Francis duPont Winterthur Museum, 1984), p. 5.
49. Samuel Lane, Tanning Record, 1734–39, Lane Papers; Day Book, 1737.
50. Day Book, 1736; "Years of the Life."
51. Samuel Lane, *A Journal for the Years 1739–1803 by Samuel Lane of Stratham, New Hampshire* (Concord: New Hampshire Historical Society, 1937), pp. 1–2 (hereafter cited as *Journal*).
52. Ibid., p. 2.
53. J. Leander Bishop, *A History of American Manufactures from 1608 to 1860*, vol. 1 (Philadelphia: Edward Young & Co., 1868; reprint, New York: Johnson Reprint Corporation, 1967), p. 453.
54. Lane, Tanning Record.
55. David Macbride, "Instructions to Tanners," *Philosophical Transactions of the Royal Society of London*, vol. 68 (1778), and "Method of Tanning Oxen-hides," in *A New and Complete Dictionary of the Arts and Sciences; Comprehending All the Branches of Useful Knowledge*, vol. 3, cited by Peter C. Welsh, *Tanning in the United States to 1850: A Brief History*, United States National Museum Bulletin 242 (Washington, D.C.: Smithsonian Institution, 1964), p. 24.
56. Day Book, 1737.
57. Lane, Tanning Record.
58. Garvin, "Survey of Craftsmen." She lists 57 tanners and 113 cordwainers. Of the seven tanners with inventories, one was insolvent; all owned real estate. Provincial Probate Records, NHSA.
59. Day Book, 1751; Bishop, *History of American Manufactures*, p. 444. Lane later purchased poplar for his own use.
60. Day Book, 1736, 1737.
61. Ibid.
62. Philip D. Morgan, "Task and Gang Systems: The Organization of Labor on New World Plantations," in *Work and Labor in Early America*, Innes, p. 190.
63. Day Book, 1736.
64. Ibid., 1737.
65. Ibid., 1739.
66. *Journal*, p. 24.
67. Ibid., pp. 24–25.
68. Mullin, *Moneygripe's Apprentice*, p. 97.
69. Rorabaugh, *The Craft Apprentice*, p. 8.
70. *Journal*, p. 23.
71. Chapman and Fitts, *William Lane of Boston*, p. 211.
72. See Toby L. Ditz, "Ownership and Obligation: Inheritance and Patriarchal Households in Connecticut, 1750–1820," *William and Mary Quarterly*, 3rd ser., 47 (April 1990): 238.
73. Day Book, 1736, 1739.
74. *Journal*, pp. 23–24.
75. Day Book, 1739.
76. Ibid., 1737, 1739; *Journal*, p. 2.
77. Sarah Simpson and Penelope Kenny, convicted for murdering an in-

fant, were the first executions New Hampshire carried out. "Piscataqua" and "the Bank" were both common early names for Portsmouth.

78. Day Book, 1739.

79. Ibid.

80. *Journal*, p. 26; Day Book, 1739. Thomas Rand's credit in 1739 included "pastureing my heifer a Spell."

81. Dow, *History of Hampton*, 1:396, 2:762; "Years of the Life."

82. Diary, February 7, 1740.

83. *Journal*, p. 24; Diary, 1740.

84. *Journal*, p. 25.

85. Ibid., p. 24.

86. Ibid., p. 25.

87. Rolla Milton Tryon, *Household Manufactures in the United States, 1640–1860: A Study in Industrial History* (Chicago: University of Chicago Press, 1917), p. 197.

88. Bishop, *History of American Manufactures*, pp. 445–46.

89. Ibid., p. 424.

90. Edward Johnson, *Wonder-Working Providence*, cited by Welsh, *Tanning in the United States*, p. 5.

91. Carl Bridenbaugh, *The Colonial Craftsman* (New York: New York University Press, 1950), p. 38.

92. *Journal*, pp. 25, 27; contracts, March 2 and July 7, 1741, Lane Papers.

93. *Journal*, p. 26.

94. Ibid.

95. Ibid.

96. Contract, March 2, 1740/41, Lane Papers.

97. *Journal*, p. 29.

98. Diary, 1741.

99. Ibid.; *Journal*, pp. 27–28.

100. *Journal*, p. 28.

101. Diary, 1741.

102. Contract, October 20, 1741, Lane Papers.

103. Contract, November 5, 1741, Lane Papers.

104. Diary, 1741. Note that both Samuel's grandfather, William Lane, and his brother Jeremiah were tailors.

105. *Journal*, p. 2.

106. Ibid., pp. 28–29.

107. Diary, 1741, summary.

108. *Journal*, p. 28.

109. Ibid.

110. Ibid., p. 30.

111. Diary, 1744.

112. Ibid., 1742; Day Book, 1747.

113. Day Book, 1783.

114. Diary, June 12 and June 30, 1747.

115. Day Book, 1743–1750.

116. Diary, 1743–1747.

117. *Journal*, p. 30; Day Book, 1743.

118. *Journal*, p. 30.

119. Diary, 1743, 1744.

120. Day Book, 1750.

121. *Journal*, p. 29.

122. Ibid., p. 37.

123. Johnson, *Sketches of Lynn*, p. 23.

124. *Journal*, p. 29; Day Book, 1743.

125. Diary, 1743.

126. *Journal*, p. 31.

127. Diary, 1742, 1743.
128. Abraham, born October 27, 1728, was the son of Samuel's mother's sister, Huldah (Robie) Perkins.
129. Diary, 1743.
130. Diary, 1744; indenture, June 10, 1777, Lane Papers.
131. Contract, December 29, 1746, Lane Papers.
132. New Hampshire Provincial Deeds, 42:307, 27:401, 29:541, NHSA.
133. Diary, 1745.
134. Ibid., 1744, 1745.
135. Ibid., 1749.
136. Day Book, 1750.
137. Ibid., 1746–1749.
138. Tunis, *Colonial Craftsmen*, p. 16.
139. Rorabaugh, *The Craft Apprentice*, p. 6; bond, May 15, 1755, Lane Papers; Diary, 1754, 1755; Day Book, 1755.
140. Indenture, June 10, 1777, Lane Papers.
141. Day Book, 1745.
142. Contract, September 26, 1751, Lane Papers.
143. Day Book, 1747, 1748.
144. Ibid., 1747.
145. Ibid., 1752.
146. Hoover, *Location Theory*, p. 160.
147. Indenture, June 10, 1777, Lane Papers; Diary, 1751.
148. Day Book, 1752. He dug only a partial cellar under the house in 1741.
149. Ibid., 1750, 1754.
150. Main, "Standards of Living," p. 107.

2. *Shaping Community*

1. Samuel Lane, "A Memorandum of a Number of Gentlemen of Character," Lane Family Papers, New Hampshire Historical Society (hereafter cited as Lane Papers).
2. Joseph Dow, *History of the Town of Hampton, New Hampshire: From Its Settlement in 1638, to the Autumn of 1892* (Salem, Mass.: Salem Press, 1893; reprint, Hampton, N.H.: Peter E. Randall, 1977), 2:901.
3. Samuel Lane, Diary, April 20, 1754, Lane Papers (hereafter cited as Diary).
4. John Love, *Geodaesia: or the Art of Surveying, and Measuring Land Made Easy* (New York: Samuel Campbell, 1793).
5. Richard M. Candee, "Land Surveys of William and John Godsoe of Kittery, Maine, 1689–1769," in *New England Prospect: Maps, Place Names, and the Historical Landscape: The Dublin Seminar for New England Folklife Annual Proceedings, 1980*, ed. Peter Benes (Boston: Boston University, 1982), p. 10.
6. Ibid., p. 11.
7. A. W. Richardson, *English Land Measuring to 1800: Instruments and Practices* (Cambridge, Mass.: Society for the History of Technology and M.I.T. Press, 1966), p. 129.
8. Samuel Lane, "An Account of the Books I own," Lane Papers.
9. *A New and Complete Dictionary of Arts and Sciences*, 4 vols. (London: W. Owen, at Homer's Head, 1764), 4:3121.
10. Richardson, *English Land Measuring*, p. 128.
11. Diary, January 15, 1746.
12. This compass is in the collection of the New Hampshire Historical Society.
13. *Boston Gazette*, June 18, 1745, cited by George Francis Dow, *The*

Arts and Crafts in New England, 1704–1775 (Topsfield, Mass.: Wayside Press, 1927; reprint, New York: Da Capo Press, 1967), p. 271.

14. Samuel Lane, Day Book, 1749, Lane Papers (hereafter cited as Day Book).

15. Ebenezer Lane, "Some Remarks and Reminiscences of the Lane Family," July 31, 1841, p. 11, Lane Papers. The maker was Thomas Greenough Sr. See Charles E. Smart, *The Makers of Surveying Instruments in America since 1700* (Troy, N.Y.: Regal Art Press, 1962), p. 57.

16. Samuel sent three pairs of pumps on both September 1 and 25, and another two pairs on October 30; all were valued at £12.16.0 Boston money. The compass cost £12.10.0. He passed the Greenough instrument on to his son Samuel, who gave it to his son Ebenezer. Day Book, 1754; Diary, October 24, 1754.

17. Love, *Geodaesia*, p. 93.

18. Charles E. Clark, *The Eastern Frontier: The Settlement of Northern New England, 1610–1763* (New York: Alfred A. Knopf, 1970), p. 185. The problem introduced by swag in surveys is also discussed by Donald A. Wilson, "The Early Grants and Charters in New Hampshire," in "Proceedings of the Seminar on the History of New Hampshire Relating to Surveying" (Merrimack Valley College and New Hampshire Land Surveyors Association, 1979), p. 40.

19. David A. Bundy, *100 Acres More or Less: The History of the Land and People of Bow, New Hampshire* (Canaan, N.H.: Phoenix Publishing, 1975), p. 22; Bow Town Records, New Hampshire Division of Records Management and Archives (hereafter cited as NHSA).

20. Love, *Geodaesia*, p. 59.

21. Ibid., p. 60.

22. Clark, *Eastern Frontier*, p. 186.

23. Diary, March 31, 1750.

24. Samuel Lane, Account Book, Lane Papers, p. 142 (hereafter cited as Account Book); Day Book, 1760.

25. The rod also was called a perche or pole; Samuel used the term *rod* only.

26. Love's *Geodaesia* contains "A Table of Square Measure" on p. 52 (illustrated here on p. 52), which contains the following units: inch, link, foot, yard, pace, perch, chain, acre, and mile.

27. Candee, "Land Surveys," pp. 39–40.

28. Love, *Geodaesia*, p. 66; Samuel Lane, Field Book, Stratham Town Records, Lane Plans, NHSA. On the cover of Lane's "pokitbook" is written, "if I it Loose and you it find I pray return it with a willing mind." Other field notes on single sheets of paper exist, but this is the only extant book.

29. Love, *Geodaesia*, p. 66.

30. The documents relating to this survey are in the Stratham Town Records and in the New Hampshire *Provincial Deeds* 33:257, NHSA.

31. Diary, January 4 and January 6, 1747.

32. Provincial Deeds, 33:257–58, NHSA.

33. Love, *Geodaesia*, pp. 123, 125, 128, 130. Richard Candee's article on the Godsoes ("Land Surveys") explains the several methods employed during the seventeenth and eighteenth centuries.

34. Samuel took "the oath of Surveyor of Land" in 1743. Diary, February 26, 1743.

35. G. F. Dow, *Arts and Crafts in New England*, p. 257.

36. Day Book, 1737.

37. Writing included deeds, bonds, leases, advertisements, wills, or any other documents of a public nature.

38. Day Book, 1753, 1755.

39. Ibid., 1745, 1757.

40. Ibid., 1755–1757, 1761.

41. The "Register of New-Hampshire for 1768" lists only eight "Practising Attorneys." *Collections of the New Hampshire Historical Society* 1 (1824): 280.

42. Day Book, 1764; Diary, Febuary 19, 1765.

43. Day Book, 1755.

44. In the probate records contained in vols. 33–39 of the *New Hampshire State and Provincial Papers* (40 vols. [Concord: State of New Hampshire, 1867–1943]), Samuel's name appears in conjunction with twenty-nine estates from 1745 until 1772.

45. *Acts and Laws of New Hampshire, 1680–1726*, The Colony Laws of North America Series, ed. John D. Cushing (Wilmington, Del.: Michael Glazier, 1978), pp. 34, 102–3.

46. Stratham Town Records, Lane Plans, NHSA.

47. Rockingham County Probate, no. 4070; *New Hampshire Gazette*, December 3, 1773.

48. Rockingham County Probate, no. 4070.

49. *Acts and Laws of New Hampshire*, p. 103.

50. The two other committeemen who signed the return of the widow's dower were John Taylor and Thomas Moore Jr.

51. Stratham Town Records, NHSA; Diary, 1774.

52. Rockingham County Probate, no. 4070.

53. Stratham Town Records, Lane Plans, NHSA.

54. Ibid.; Diary, 1775.

55. Diary, 1775.

56. See *The Diary of Matthew Patten of Bedford, N.H.* (Concord, N.H.: Rumford Printing Co., 1903). Patten served a similar role in the Merrimack Valley.

57. George Whitefield, *A Continuation of the Reverend Mr. Whitefield's Journal, From a few Days after his Return to Georgia to his Arrival at Falmouth, on the 11th of March 1741: The Seventh Journal* (London: W. Strahan, 1741), pp. 33–34.

58. Ibid.

59. Clark, *Eastern Frontier*, p. 280.

60. Jere R. Daniell, *Colonial New Hampshire: A History* (Millwood, N.Y.: KTO Press, 1981), p. 183.

61. Edward M. Cook Jr., *The Fathers of the Towns: Leadership and Community Structure in Eighteenth-Century New England* (Baltimore: Johns Hopkins University Press, 1976), p. 22.

62. Ibid., p. 141.

63. Ibid., p. 40.

64. Daniell, *Colonial New Hampshire*, p. 181.

65. Diary, March 26, 1744.

66. Stratham Town Record Books, 1:95, 97, NHSA.

67. Ibid., 1:98, 100.

68. Sydney E. Ahlstrom, *A Religious History of the American People* (New Haven, Conn.: Yale University Press, 1972), p. 286.

69. The Portsmouth minister, the Rev. Mr. Shurtleff, "reported '*a general Out-cry*' at a meeting held on Friday, November 27, 1741, and the widespread belief among a crowd that evening 'That CHRIST *was coming to Judgment*' when they saw reflections from a chimney fire in several windowpanes." *The Christian History . . . For the Year 1743* (Boston, 1744), pp. 384–85, cited by Clark, *Eastern Frontier*, p. 280 n.

70. Cited by Daniell, *Colonial New Hampshire*, p. 180.

71. James P. Lane, *Lane Families of the Massachusetts Bay Colony* (Norton, Mass.: Privately printed, 1886), p. 55. Samuel's signature appears with thirty-five others.

72. Diary, preface, 1741.

73. Ibid., preface, 1743.

74. Ibid., preface, 1744.

75. Committee "to agree with a minister" to Rev. Mr. Henry Rust, September 4, 1744, in *Sinkler et al. v. Leavit*, New Hampshire Provincial Court Records, no. 25518, NHSA.

76. Diary, September 30, 1744.

77. Provincial Court Records, no. 25518, NHSA.

78. James Duncan Phillips, *Salem in the Eighteenth Century* (Cambridge, Mass.: Riverside Press, 1937), p. 166.

79. *Journal*, p. 31.

80. Diary, 1745.

81. Stratham Town Records, 1:112–14, NHSA.

82. John Langdon Sibley and Clifford K. Shipton, *Biographical Sketches of Those Who Attended Harvard College*, 17 vols. (Boston: Massachusetts Historical Society, 1873–1975), 11:112; *Journal*, p. 32.

83. Sibley and Shipton, *Biographical Sketches*, 5:374. With the exception of their youngest child, Jabez, born in 1760, Samuel and Mary took the rest of their children to be baptized at Hampton, where there was no question about the legitimacy of the sacrament.

84. Stratham Church Records in Stratham Town Records, NHSA (hereafter cited as Stratham Church Records).

85. The findings here support Zuckerman's thesis that a system of "accommodative consensus" evolved in eighteenth-century towns. Michael Zuckerman, *Peaceable Kingdoms: New England Towns in the Eighteenth Century* (New York: Alfred A. Knopf, 1970), p. 8.

86. Stratham Church Records.

87. The old meetinghouse measured 48 by 36 feet; the new one was 63 by 45 feet.

88. The other committee members were Thomas Wiggin, Stephen Bordman, Joseph Hoit, Daniel Clark, John Taylor, and Simon Wiggin.

89. *New Hampshire State and Provincial Papers*, 9:781.

90. Stratham Church Records. The rationale behind this solution was that the site not be "detrimental to any of S^{d} Inhabitants, by extending the Distance of their Travel to Meeting." Matthew Patten described a similar problem in Bedford and wrote on September 9, 1755: "spent the forenoon in falling on a Method for an accommodation to the town about setting the Meeting house and at last drew a paper to Set it at Noah Thayers." *Diary of Matthew Patten*, p. 20.

91. Stratham Church Records.

92. Alice Morse Earle, *The Sabbath in Puritan New England* (New York: Charles Scribner's Sons, 1896), pp. 45–46.

93. Stratham Church Records.

94. Ibid. Pew ownership was not without its risks. Owners were responsible for funding the meetinghouse, and should construction expenses have outstripped the available funds, each pew owner ("undertaker" in Samuel's vocabulary) was to make up the deficit in proportion to the value of the pew. Any surplus would be returned in a similar manner.

95. Stratham Church Records; Stratham Town Records, 1:160.

96. Stratham Church Records.

97. Ibid. Supplies for two raisings elsewhere included "two or three barrels of licker" and "20 Gallons of Rhumb and 20 pounds of Sugar to go with the Rhumb." Ola Elizabeth Winslow, *Meetinghouse Hill 1630–1783* (New York: Macmillan Co., 1952; reprint, New York: W. W. Norton & Co., 1972), p. 63.

98. For the story of another raising in which Ephraim Barker was involved, see Charles E. Clark, *The Meetinghouse Tragedy* (Hanover, N.H.: University Press of New England, 1998).

99. Stratham Church Records.

100. Ibid.
101. Ibid.
102. *Acts and Laws of New Hampshire*, p. 135.
103. Stratham Town Records, 7:83–84, NHSA.
104. Josiah Henry Benton, *Warning Out in New England, 1656–1817* (Boston: W. B. Clarke Co., 1911), p. 91.
105. Ibid., pp. 95–96.
106. Stratham Town Records, 7:90, NHSA.
107. Provincial Court Records, no. 7246, NHSA.
108. Stratham Town Records, 2:121, 124, NHSA.
109. *New Hampshire Gazette*, March 19, 1773.
110. Day Book, 1762.
111. Diary 1751, 1752; Stratham Town Records, NHSA.
112. Stratham Town Records, 2:141–42, NHSA.
113. Memorandum to the town of time and travel, May–November 1775, Lane Papers.
114. Day Book, 1744.
115. Diary, April 26, 1758.
116. Ibid. 1748, Summary.
117. Ibid., April 16, 1747. "The enemy appeared early in the Spring of 1747, and in the course of the Summer made frequent attacks." Chandler E. Potter, *The Military History of the State of New Hampshire: 1623–1861* (Baltimore: Genealogical Publishing Co., 1972), p. 99. Samuel noted the presence of "troublesome" Indians in 1746 also.
118. Joseph B. Walker, ed., "Diaries of the Rev. Timothy Walker," in *Collections of the New Hampshire Historical Society* 9 (1889): 124.
119. *New Hampshire State and Provincial Papers*, 29:177, cited in William Henry Fry, *New Hampshire as a Royal Province*, Studies in History, Economics and Public Law, vol. 29, no. 2 (New York: Columbia University, 1908), p. 241.
120. The commission, appointed April 9, 1736, consisted of "George Clark, Francis Harrison, Cadwalder Colden, Abraham Van Horn, Philip Levingston, John Hamilton, John Wells, John Reading, Cornelius Van Horne, William Provost, William Skene, William Sherriffe, Henry Cope, Erasmus James Phillips, Otto Hamilton, Samuel Vernon, John Gardiner, John Potter, Ezekial Warner & George Cornel, or any five or more of you." All were officials from other provinces. *New Hampshire State and Provincial Papers*, 19:274.
121. Diary, September 1, 1737.
122. Fry, *New Hampshire as a Royal Province*, p. 262.
123. Ibid., p. 263.
124. Cited by James L. Garvin, "The Range Township in Eighteenth-Century New Hampshire," in *The New England Prospect* (see n. 5), p. 65.
125. Diary, November 25, 1748.
126. Day Book, 1748. Matthew Patten bought food in Penacook on a trip to the same area in 1763, twenty and one-half pounds of pork and one-half bushel of ground corn. *Diary of Matthew Patten*, p. 126.
127. *Diary of Matthew Patten*, pp. 121–22.
128. Bow Town Records, NHSA.
129. Diary, June 13, 1750; Commission, June 15, 1750, Lane Papers. The surveyor was Joseph Blanchard.
130. *New Hampshire State and Provincial Papers*, 6:14.
131. *Diary of Matthew Patten*, p. 126.
132. Ebenezer Lane, "Some Remarks," p. 11, Lane Papers.
133. Samuel also agreed on January 11, 1749/50 to survey Township Number Six, present-day Henniker, for a group that contained many Stratham residents. Spring arrived early that year, and he never got to Hen-

niker as the ice broke up and his party could not cross the rivers. Agreement, January 11, 1749/50, Lane Papers; *Journal*, p. 34.

134. The nature of proprietorship changed from the seventeenth to the eighteenth century in that nearly all the seventeenth-century proprietors were residents. The towns and proprietorships were virtually one and the same. In the eighteenth century, nonresident proprietors were the majority in most town grants.

135. Roy Hidemichi Akagi, *The Town Proprietors of the New England Colonies* (Philadelphia: University of Pennsylvania, 1924), p. 177.

136. In 1777, Samuel purchased lottery tickets himself. Account Book, p. 236.

137. Clark, *Eastern Frontier*, p. 170.

138. Douglas Edward Leach, *The Northern Colonial Frontier, 1607–1763* (New York: Holt, Rinehart, and Winston, 1966), p. 172.

139. Ezra Stiles, "Itineraries," *Ezra Stiles Papers* (New Haven, Conn.: Yale University Library, 1976, microform).

140. Akagi, *Town Proprietors*, p. 3.

141. Shaw Livermore, *Early American Land Companies* (New York: Commonwealth Fund, 1939), p. 30.

142. Akagi, *Town Proprietors*, pp. 74, 75.

143. *New Hampshire State and Provincial Papers*, 18:470.

144. Clark, *Eastern Frontier*, p. 182.

145. Well-connected Bow proprietors included Massachusetts governor Shute, Mark Hunking (New Hampshire council president), George Jaffrey (New Hampshire treasurer), Richard Waldron (New Hampshire secretary), four members of the Governor's Council, numerous members of the New Hampshire General Court, as well as Wentworth relatives.

146. *Journal*, p. 33.

147. Account Book.

148. Robert B. Todd, "Patterns on the Land: The Origins of New Hampshire Townships and Their Original Lotting," in "Proceedings of the Seminar on the History of New Hampshire Relating to Land Surveying," p. 63.

149. Harrison Colby, "History of Bow," in *History of Merrimack and Belknap Counties, New Hampshire*, ed. D. Hamilton Hurd (Philadelphia: J. W. Lewis & Co., 1885), pp. 264–65.

150. Ibid., p. 265.

151. Rev. N. F. Carter, *History of Pembroke, N.H., 1730–1895* (Concord, N.H.: Republican Press Association, 1895), pp. 18–19.

152. Colby, "History of Bow," p. 265.

153. Bow Town Records, NHSA.

154. "Newmarket Scrapbook" (compiled from the *Newmarket Advertiser*), p. 23, NHHS.

155. The surveying party consisted of Walter Bryant, surveyor; Jonathan Fifield; Josiah Wiggin; Reuben Hill; Francis Follet; Samuel Leavit Jr.; John Clark; and Samuel Lane.

156. Moses Foster moved to Suncook prior to 1743 and "commanded the garrison in the fort." Presumably, the fort doubled as his residence. It was on the east side of the Merrimack in the southwest corner of Suncook. Carter, *History of Pembroke*, 1:396, 405; 2:98.

157. Bow Town Records, NHSA; Diary, 1748.

158. John E. Flynn, *Beyond the Blew-Hills* (Stoughton, Mass.: Stoughton Historical Society, 1976), cited in Candee, "Land Surveys," pp. 11–12.

159. Bow Town Records, NHSA.

160. Ibid.

161. Diary, June 27, 1749.

162. Bow Proprietors Records, p. 63, NHSA.

163. Diary, August 8, 1749; Bow Town Records, NHSA.

164. *New Hampshire State and Provincial Records*, 9:63.

165. Provincial Court Record, no. 22667, NHSA.

166. *Bow v. Mann*, Provincial Court Record, no. 23326; *Bow v. Merrill*, Provincial Court Record, no. 23325, NHSA.

167. Ibid., no. 23325.

168. *Bow v. Merrill*, Provincial Court Record, no. 22602, NHSA.

169. J. B. Walker, "The Controversy between the Proprietors of Bow and Those of Penny Cook, 1727–1789," *Proceedings of the New Hampshire Historical Society* 3 (June 1895–June 1899), pp. 273–74.

170. Walker, "Controversy," p. 280.

171. Akagi, *Town Proprietors*, p. 64.

172. Day Book, 1755.

173. Ibid.

174. Ibid., 1757. This work stemmed from another trespass suit pressed by Bow in 1753 against Benjamin Rolfe, David Foster, and Joseph Hall. True to their strategy, the value of the suit was £300. Provincial Court Record, no. 23324, NHSA.

175. A copy of the Bow Proprietors' Records, by Samuel Lane, March 17, 1756, in Provincial Court Records, no. 22602 (*Bow v. Merrill*), NHSA.

176. Bundy, *100 Acres*, p. 34. For example, the charges for Samuel's first surveying trip to Bow came to £196.

177. *New Hampshire State and Provincial Papers*, 9:67–68. Charles Clark wrote: "Instead of capitalizing on their holdings, proprietors often invested heavily in surveys, fortifications, and public works such as roads and bridges without any compensating gain, at least for many years" (*Eastern Frontier*, p. 172). Actions of the Bow Proprietors support this general contention.

178. Bow Town Records, p. 101, NHSA.

179. Day Book, 1758.

180. Account Book, p. 1.

181. Bow Town Records, p. 134, NHSA.

182. Account Book, p. 4.

183. *New Hampshire State and Provincial Records*, 9:62–63.

184. Ibid., 9:72.

185. Bow Town Records, NHSA.

186. Day Book, 1759, 1760.

187. The 1755 suit against Merrill (Provincial Court Record, no. 18847, NHSA) was valued at £200, well under the £300 limit at which suits could be appealed to England. The 1759 action claimed Rolfe, Carter, Simons, and Evans were trespassing on 1,000 acres (no. 17051). Additional suits were brought by Bow or its agents against Ebenezer Virgin (no. 16908) in 1760 and against Henry Lovejoy (no. 6158), Jeremiah Kimball (no. 6160), Abraham Kimball (no. 6169), Green French (no. 6179), and John Chadwick (no. 6181), all in 1761. See also Provincial Court Record, no. 17051, NHSA.

188. Diary, 1760; Day Book, 1760.

189. Provincial Court Record no. 17051, NHSA; Diary, 1761; Day Book, 1761.

190. Francis Ayers to Daniel Peirce, December 24, 1762, Bow Town Records, NHSA.

191. Akagi, *Town Proprietors*, pp. 173–74.

192. Bow Town Records, NHSA.

193. Ibid.

194. Account Book; Effingham Town Records 1:73, 75, 83, 85, 99, 105, 109, 119 (on microfilm, New Hampshire State Library).

3. *Exchanging Commodities*

1. Samuel Lane, Diary, May 5, 1759, Lane Papers (hereafter cited as Diary).
2. Ibid.
3. W. T. Baxter, *The House of Hancock: Business in Boston, 1724–1775* (Cambridge, Mass.: Harvard University Press, 1945), pp. 216–17.
4. Samuel Lane, Day Book, 1743, Lane Papers (hereafter cited as Day Book).
5. Ibid., 1748.
6. Jeremy Belknap, *Belknap's New Hampshire: An Account of the State in 1792: A Facsimile Edition of Volume III of The History of New Hampshire*, ed. G. T. Lord (Hampton, N.H.: Peter E. Randall, 1973), p. 159.
7. Port of Piscataqua Customs Records, copy at Portsmouth Athenaeum. Shipments of spermaceti candles, listed by the 25-pound box, and of train oil, by the 31.5-pound barrel, tallied by Donna-Belle Garvin, 1999. For the importance of whale oil as a commodity in the eighteenth century, see Richard C. Kugler, "The Whale Oil Trade, 1750–1775," *Seafaring in Colonial Massachusetts* (Boston: Colonial Society of Massachusetts, 1980), pp. 153–75.
8. "List of the vessels which have cleared outwards at the Port of Piscataqua in New England between the 24th of June 1752 and the 29th day of September following . . . ," reproduced in Charles E. Clark and Charles W. Eastman Jr., comps., *The Portsmouth Project: An Exercise in Inductive Historical Scholarship Designed for Beginning College Courses and for Secondary Schools* (Somersworth: New Hampshire Publishing Co., 1974), p. 16.
9. Export records copied by Samuel Lane from *The American Museum* into his copy of *The New-England Farmer*, now in the New Hampshire Historical Society library.
10. Day Book, 1760.
11. Ibid., 1763.
12. Gregory Nobles, "The Rise of Merchants in Rural Market Towns: A Case Study of Eighteenth-Century Northampton, Massachusetts," *Journal of Social History* 24 (fall 1990): 8.
13. Day Book, 1755.
14. Ibid., 1754.
15. Ibid., 1743–45.
16. Ibid., 1756.
17. Ibid.
18. Ibid., 1745.
19. Diary, April 28, 1753.
20. Day Book, 1759.
21. Ibid.
22. Out of a total revenue of £1,956.2.0, £1,186.3.0 came from tanning or shoemaking work. Day Book, 1768.
23. Christopher Clark, "Household Economy, Market Exchange and the Rise of Capitalism in the Connecticut Valley, 1800–1860," *Journal of Social History* 13 (winter 1979): 174.
24. Joan M. Jensen, *Loosening the Bonds: Mid-Atlantic Farm Women, 1750–1850* (New Haven, Conn.: Yale University Press, 1986), noted a similar phenomenon with butter produced by farm women: "Butter making enabled large numbers of rural people to participate in the early nineteenth-century American capitalist economy through the purchase of manufactured goods . . . their increased income allowed them to buy more consumer goods" (p. 93).
25. Day Book, 1759.
26. Laurel Thatcher Ulrich, "Wheels, Looms, and the Gender Division

of Labor in Eighteenth-Century New England," *William and Mary Quarterly* 55 (January 1998): 3–38.

27. Alice Morse Earle, *Home Life in Colonial Days* (New York: Macmillan Co., 1898), pp. 234–38.

28. Peter Kalm, *Peter Kalm's Travels in North America*, ed. Adolph B. Benson (New York: Wilson-Erickson, 1937), 1:335.

29. Earle, *Home Life*, p. 235.

30. Laurel Thatcher Ulrich, *A Midwife's Tale: The Life of Martha Ballard, Based on Her Diary, 1785–1812* (New York: Alfred A. Knopf, 1990), pp. 29, 38.

31. Day Book, 1762; Diary, May 1, 1769.

32. James T. Lemon, *The Best Poor Man's Country: A Geographical Study of Early Southeastern Pennsylvania* (Baltimore: Johns Hopkins University Press, 1972), p. 158.

33. Samuel's daybooks show flaxseed sown as ranging from one-quarter to more than one and one-half bushels. Nathaniel Bouton's *The History of Concord* (Concord, N.H.: Benning W. Sanborn, 1856), p. 527, puts the seeding rate at one and one-half to three bushels per acre. James Lemon cites the Barnard diary, showing one acre sown with one bushel of seed (*Best Poor Man's Country*, p. 267).

34. Diary, April 19, April 23, May 3, May 21, May 22, 1777.

35. Ibid., April 5, April 13, 1773.

36. Ibid., May 17, 1794; June 1, 1770; June 6–8, 1793.

37. Day Book, 1764, 1766.

38. Ulrich, *Midwife's Tale*, p. 38.

39. Day Book, 1766. In southern Canada, Kalm noted that the flax was harvested for some time before they "spread it on fields, meadows, and pastures, in order to bleach it." It being early September when he made that observation, Kalm might have been observing the rotting or retting process, not bleaching, which was usually done at a later stage. (*Peter Kalm's Travels*, 2:493.)

40. Bouton, *History of Concord*, p. 527.

41. Samuel Lane, Account Book, p. 206, Lane Papers (hereafter cited as Account Book).

42. Day Book, 1763, 1764.

43. Bouton, *History of Concord*, p. 527.

44. Virginia Parslow, "From Flax Seed to Yarn," *Handweaver and Craftsman* 3 (spring 1952), p. 31.

45. Day Book, 1757.

46. Ulrich, *Midwife's Tale*, p. 103.

47. Day Book, 1744.

48. Based on Samuel's own records from 1772 to 1800, 77 sheep produced 222 pounds of wool, or an average of 2.88 pounds of wool per shorn sheep.

49. Day Book, 1747.

50. Ibid., 1762.

51. In June 1767, Anne Veasey was paid 40 shillings a week for spinning; she spun 46 skeins in just over 15 days work. In 1778, Samuel accounted for Sarah Mason's spinning 33 days but made no note of the quantity of yarn produced. Day Book, 1767, 1778.

52. Ibid., 1753.

53. Ibid., 1761.

54. *New Hampshire Gazette*, March 20, 1761.

55. Lemon, *Best Poor Man's Country*, p. 155.

56. This loom appears in Jabez Lane's 1810 inventory, "Loom 6 doll[ar]s Reeds & Harness 6 doll[ar]s . . . Gears to Loom 1.50 cts." Rockingham County Probate, no. 8256 OS.

57. Day Book, 1761.

58. Other weavers earned more than Unis Kelly. Zebulon Ring and Joseph Mason Jr. earned sixpence New Tenor per yard or 10 shillings Old Tenor. Laurel Ulrich finds that differential rates of pay usually reflected the complexity of the weave.

59. Samuel Lane, *A Journal for the Years 1739–1803 by Samuel Lane of Stratham, New Hampshire* (Concord: New Hampshire Historical Society, 1937), p. 41. Hereafter cited as *Journal.*

60. Day Book, 1768.

61. *Journal*, p. 41; Diary, May 14, 1770.

62. Diary, February 1, 1772.

63. Ibid., January 28, 1797.

64. Ibid., November 21, 1759.

65. For transcriptions of all five lists, as well as a detailed analysis, see Jane C. Nylander, "Provision for Daughters: The Accounts of Samuel Lane," in *House and Home: The Dublin Seminar for New England Folklife Annual Proceedings, 1988*, ed. Peter Benes (Boston: Boston University, 1990), pp. 11–27.

66. Day Book, 1762.

67. *New Hampshire Gazette*, October 2, 1761.

68. Elizabeth A. Perkins, "The Consumer Frontier: Household Consumption in Early Kentucky," *Journal of American History* 78 (September 1991): 502.

69. The declining proportion of bedding to the entire portion is obvious: Suse Lane's 1773 portion contained £698 worth of bedding, 52.4% of the total; Martha's 1776 portion had £634 worth, or 48.1% of the whole; Bathsheba's 1777 portion had £554 worth, 44.7% of the total. Lane Papers.

70. See chap. 4, "Frosty Mornings and Stinging Fingers: The Effects of Winter," in Jane C. Nylander, *Our Own Snug Fireside: Images of the New England Home, 1760–1860* (New York: Alfred A. Knopf, 1993).

71. Day Book, 1762.

72. Ibid., 1748.

73. In 1758 the Lanes sold 12 pounds of butter and 20¾ pounds of cheese; the latter was offset by a 5½-pound cheese purchase.

74. Diary, September 1761.

75. Day Books, 1761, 1762.

76. Ibid., 1782.

77. Ibid.

78. The conclusions here support the findings elsewhere of Joan M. Jensen, who writes, "During the century from 1750 to 1850, then, the dairy work of both women and men changed significantly. From a peripheral part of farm work, dairying moved to a central place on many farms of southeastern Pennsylvania and northern Delaware" (*Loosening the Bonds*, p. 113).

79. Returns to Portsmouth shops recorded in his daybooks include a handkerchief in both 1755 and 1758; chintz in 1760, 1764, and 1766; taffeta in 1764; and galloon in 1771. All but the last occurred while Mary was still alive.

80. Diary, October 27 and December 9, 1783; February 24 and June 23, 1784; January 6, 1785.

81. Samuel's own clock is likely the one included in Jabez Lane's inventory. Rockingham County Probate, no. 8256 OS.

82. Those books were "a Bible Parsons 7 Discourses Bunyons Sighs From Hell Earls Sacramental Exercises Erskines Gospel Sonnets." Later he added "Watt's World to Come Wright on being Born Again." "An Account of the Books I Own," March 5, 1762, Lane Papers.

83. Henry Rust's first wife, Anna Waldron, was the daughter of an influential New Hampshire family. She died in 1733, and he married again,

two years later, a widow named "Marthew." Little more is known about her. John Langdon Sibley and Clifford K. Shipton, *Biographical Sketches of Those Who Attended Harvard College*, 17 vols. (Boston: Massachusetts Historical Society, 1873–1975), 5:372.

84. Diary, 1754, back cover. Between 1754 and 1766, Samuel remarked about that year's schooling with Madam Rust at the end of the year on the back cover of his diary.

85. Linda K. Kerber, *Women of the Republic: Intellect and Ideology in Revolutionary America* (New York: W. W. Norton & Co., 1986), p. 203.

86. Bernard Bailyn, cited in *The Encyclopedia of Education*, Lee C. Deighton, ed. (New York: MacMillan Co. & Free Press, 1971).

87. Cited by John C. Miller, *The First Frontier: Life in Colonial America* (New York: Delacourte Press, 1966), p. 207.

88. *Journal*, p. 32.

89. Diary, 1765, summary. Edwin J. Perkins (*The Economy of Colonial America* [New York: Columbia University Press, 1988]) found that "the supply of specie was not deficient in the North American economies," noting that the supply of money increased with the rise in prices (p. 164). Lane's comments suggest that the fluctuation in money's value was often a greater culprit than the supply itself, although scarcity too was a problem, as he noted in 1763 and 1765.

90. *New Hampshire Gazette*, August 2, 1765; July 25, 1766.

91. Day Book, 1745.

92. Samuel Justis McKinley, "The Economic History of Portsmouth, N.H. from its First Settlement to 1830, Including a Study of Price Movements There, 1723–1770 and 1804–1830" (Ph.D. diss., Harvard University, 1931), p. 342.

93. Day Book, 1755.

94. The ratio of value of Old Tenor to Lawful Money was 20:1. The sum of £2,675 New Hampshire Lawful Money was equivalent to £100 sterling. John J. McCusker and Russell R. Menard, *The Economy of British America, 1607–1789* (Chapel Hill: University of North Carolina Press, 1985), p. 136.

95. Day Book, 1766.

96. Baxter, *House of Hancock*, p. 117. James T. Lemon and Harrington note similar practices arising from the shortage of cash in Pennsylvania and New York (Lemon, *Best Poor Man's Country*, p. 28; Virginia D. Harrington, *The New York Merchant on the Eve of the Revolution* [New York: Columbia University Press, 1935; reprint, Gloucester, Mass.: Peter Smith, 1964], p. 103).

97. Day Book, 1752, 1760, 1768.

98. Baxter, *House of Hancock*, p. 18. Harrington, *New York Merchant*, found the same phenomenon, few cash transactions, among New York merchants.

99. Margaret E. Martin, *Merchants and Trade of the Connecticut River Valley, 1750–1820* (Northampton, Mass.: Smith College, 1939), p. 158.

100. Day Book, 1760.

101. Ibid., 1756.

102. Ibid., 1758.

103. Ibid., 1761.

104. Martin, *Merchants and Trade*, p. 179.

105. Ibid., p. 176.

106. Ibid.

107. Diary, 1786, 1787, summaries.

108. Both the Exeter selectmen and Penhallow offered rewards for information. *New Hampshire Gazette*, September 21, 1786.

109. Charles H. Bell, *History of the Town of Exeter, New Hampshire* (Exeter, N.H.: 1888), pp. 96–98.

110. *Journal*, p. 55.
111. Diary, 1787.
112. Day Book, 1787.
113. Ibid., 1787, 1795.
114. Weare Drake to Samuel Lane, February 11, 1793, Lane Papers.
115. T. H. Breen (*Tobacco Culture: The Mentality of the Great Planters on the Eve of the Revolution* [Princeton, N.J.: Princeton University Press, 1985]) contends that "credit is a form of communication and throughout the world, societies discuss debt in highly moral terms" (pp. 29–30).
116. Written on a flyleaf in Lane's copy of *The Modern Gazetteer*, NHHS.
117. *Journal*, pp. 32–33.

4. *Building Continuity*

1. Bettye Hobbs Pruitt, "Self-Sufficiency and the Agricultural Economy of Eighteenth-Century Massachusetts," *William and Mary Quarterly*, 3rd ser., 41 (July 1984): 338, 355, 364.
2. Ibid. The idea of rural self-sufficiency has become known among historians as "the agrarian myth."
3. Daniel Vickers, "Competency and Competition: Economic Culture in Early America," *William and Mary Quarterly*, 3rd ser., 47 (January 1990): 3–29.
4. *The Confession of Faith: The Larger and Shorter Catechisms* (Glasgow: n.p., 1763), NHHS.
5. Samuel Lane, Diary, 1762, Summary, Lane Papers (hereafter cited as Diary).
6. Samuel Lane, Day Book, 1762, Lane Papers (hereafter cited as Day Book).
7. Ibid., 1754.
8. Lane Account Book, Lane Papers (hereafter cited as Account Book).
9. New Hampshire Provincial Deeds, 60:318; 40:401–3, 405–7, New Hampshire Division of Records Management and Archives (hereafter cited as NHSA).
10. Diary, Day Book, 1743.
11. Samuel wrote in his journal: "May 1743. I Bought 2½ Acres of Land of John Purmort & Neighbour Mason, Called my Swamp and hired Some Money to help pay for it of Saml Neal." *A Journal for the Years 1739–1803 by Samuel Lane of Stratham, New Hampshire* (Concord: New Hampshire Historical Society, 1937), p. 30. Hereafter cited as *Journal.*
12. *American Husbandry*, ed. Harry J. Carman (London: J. Bew, 1775; reprint, New York: Columbia University Press, 1939), p. 42.
13. Day Book, 1745.
14. Ibid.
15. Ibid.
16. Samuel Lane, undated memorandum, Lane Papers.
17. The account of Samuel's attempt to purchase this land is contained in a four-page memorandum. Also included in the Lane Papers is a deed written in Samuel's hand conveying ten acres to him from Andrew Wiggin, dated January 8, 1746/47. The stated price was £56.5.0 Lawful Money, equivalent to £225 Old Tenor. This was the agreement between the two that was never consummated.
18. Rockingham County Deeds, 110:520, NHSA; Diary, November 18 and 21, 1778; January 28, 1779.
19. The £166 Lawful Money that John Crocket paid for twelve acres in Stratham nearly equalled the £195 that his three brothers-in-law together paid for their farms in Northwood and Sanbornton.

20. Rockingham County Deeds: Clark-Clark, 179:280; Norris-Clark, 108:224; Chandler-Clark, 115:166; Hoit-Thompson, 110:443–44; NHSA.

21. Day Book, 1752.

22. See Howard Russell, *A Long Deep Furrow: Three Centuries of Farming in New England* (Hanover, N.H.: University Press of New England, 1976), pp. 185–91, for a discussion of the types of fences and methods of their construction.

23. Agreement, Leavit-Lane, May 17, 1757, Lane Papers. There is a similar agreement between Lane and Andrew Wiggin III dated April 7, 1760.

24. Committee decision, April 18, 1766, Lane Papers.

25. Diary, April 20, 1753.

26. Samuel's figures included "reckoning in Provisions," undoubtedly including drink. Over the same period, Samuel purchased 7¾ gallons of rum in Greenland and Portsmouth, presumably for the laborers.

27. Day Book, 1753.

28. Ibid., 1754.

29. See Diary, February 15, 17, 18, and 19; March 3 and 8, 1777.

30. Day Book, 1760.

31. Edwin J. Perkins, *The Economy of Colonial America* (New York: Columbia University Press, 1988), p. 59.

32. Hugh D. McLellan, *History of Gorham, Maine* (Portland, Maine: Smith & Sale, 1903), p. 454.

33. See Paul G. E. Clemens and Lucy Simler, "Rural Labor and the Farm Household in Chester County, Pennsylvania, 1750–1820," in Stephen Innes, ed., *Work and Labor in Early America* (Chapel Hill: University of North Carolina Press, 1988), pp. 112, 117.

34. *American Husbandry*, pp. 48, 53.

35. Stratham Town Records, vols. 1–4, NHSA.

36. *New Hampshire Laws*, 3:215.

37. Day Book, 1756.

38. Diary, October 13 and November 8, 1763; writ, Young to Lane, October 19, 1763, Lane Papers; *New Hampshire Laws*, 3:215–17.

39. In 1732, Stratham claimed 117 horses, 146 oxen, 648 cattle, and 53 swine. Jay Mack Holbrook, *New Hampshire 1732 Census* (Oxford, Mass.: Holbrook Research Institute, 1981), pp. 12–13.

40. William Cronon, *Changes in the Land: Indians, Colonists, and the Ecology of New England* (New York: Hill and Wang, 1983), p. 128.

41. *Journal*, p. 26.

42. Maurice H. Robinson, *A History of Taxation in New Hampshire* (New York: Macmillan Co. for the American Economic Association, 1902), p. 36.

43. Percy Wells Bidwell and John I. Falconer, *History of Agriculture in the Northern United States, 1620–1860* (Washington, D.C.: Carnegie Institution of Washington, 1925; reprint, New York: Peter Smith, 1941), pp. 105–6.

44. In 1773 he claimed 15 acres of mowing land; the next inventory, 1778, the same amount of land appeared as mowing. There is no note of pastureland in 1773; but he listed 40 acres in 1778, which decreased to 30 acres in 1779 and remained at that number through 1785. Day Book, 1772, 1778–1785.

45. Day Book, 1781, 1782.

46. See Day Book, 1760, "where I lay my hay."

47. James T. Lemon, *The Best Poor Man's Country: A Geographical Study of Early Southeastern Pennsylvania* (Baltimore: Johns Hopkins University Press, 1972), p. 163.

48. Joseph B. Walker, "The Farm of the First Minister: An Address," in *The House and Farm of the First Minister of Concord, N.H., 1726–1906*

(Concord, N.H.: n.p., 1906), p. 19; Lemon, *Best Poor Man's Country*, p. 160.

49. James Birket, *Some Cursory Remarks Made by James Birket in His Voyage to North America, 1750–1751* (New Haven, Conn.: Yale University Press, 1916), p. 13.

50. Walter Ebeling, *The Fruited Plain: The Story of American Agriculture* (Berkeley and Los Angeles: University of California Press, 1979), p. 71.

51. *American Husbandry*, p. 59

52. Diary, 1762.

53. Ibid.

54. Ibid., April 1750, summary. Thomas Anburey agreed: "Indian Corn is certainly the heartiest and most strengthening food for cattle and poultry, and gives their meat firmness and excellent flavor." Cited in Russell, *Long Deep Furrow*, p. 135.

55. Diary, 1749; *Journal*, pp. 68–69.

56. Peter Kalm, *Travels into North America (1748–51)*, 3 vols. (London and Warrington, 1770–71), 1:102, cited in Bidwell and Falconer, *History of Agriculture*, p. 107.

57. Diary, April 17, 1790; March 2, 1795.

58. Ibid., 1791.

59. Ebeling, *Fruited Plain*, p. 71.

60. *Journal*, p. 95.

61. *American Husbandry*, pp. 42, 44.

62. Cronon, *Changes in the Land*, p. 139.

63. Diary, November 23, 1745; Day Book, 1746.

64. Day Book, 1762.

65. Carole Shammas, "How Self-sufficient was Early America?" *The Journal of Interdisciplinary History* 13 (autumn 1782): 252n; Lemon estimated that of the average 450 pounds of dressed beef, the Pennsylvania household would consume 250 pounds and sell 200 pounds (*Best Poor Man's Country*, p. 163).

66. Diary, November 19 and December 16, 1763; November 27, 1765. This is comparable to the dressed weight of Timothy Walker's cattle, 400–500 dressed pounds. Bidwell and Falconer, *History of Agriculture*, p. 108.

67. Russell, *Long Deep Furrow*, pp. 160–61.

68. Job Colcord told Samuel in 1797 that "Noah Robinson of Wakefield had bro't down 45 Hundred to Butter this year." That probably was the output of many farms in the area. Diary, 1797.

69. Lemon, *Best Poor Man's Country*, p. 163.

70. Russell, *Long Deep Furrow*, p. 315.

71. Jeremy Belknap, *Belknap's New Hampshire: An Account of the State in 1792: A Facsimile Edition of Volume III of the History of New Hampshire*, ed. G. T. Lord (Hampton, N.H.: Peter E. Randall, 1973), p. 178.

72. Laurel Thatcher Ulrich, "Martha Ballard and Her Girls: Women's Work in Eighteenth-Century Maine," in Stephen Innes, ed., *Work and Labor in Early America* (Chapel Hill: University of North Carolina Press for the Institute of Early American History and Culture, 1988), p. 75.

73. Vickers, "Competency," pp. 4, 11.

74. On December 31, 1745, he wrote "young cow calved," but on April 5, 1752, "Brown C-lv'd."

75. Diary, April 3, 1789.

76. *Journal*, p. 28.

77. Shammas, "How Self-sufficient was Early America?" p. 252n; Lemon, *Best Poor Man's Country*, p. 166.

78. Day Book, 1748.

79. Bidwell and Falconer, *History of Agriculture*, p. 111; Kevin M. Sweeney, "Gentlemen Farmers and Inland Merchants: The Williams Family

and Commercial Agriculture in Pre-Revolutionary Western Massachusetts," in *The Farm: Dublin Seminar for New England Folklife Annual Proceedings, 1986*, ed. Peter Benes (Boston: Boston University, 1988), p. 64.

80. Diary, February 1762.

81. One man brought five horsehides to Samuel during the hard winter of 1762.

82. Diary, November 1762.

83. Day Book, 1742–69. The beef average is calculated without data from 1762 and 1765, because these years appear to be aberrations. In 1762 he had 918 pounds of beef; in 1765, 1,774. Using those years raises the average to 497 pounds annually. In 1762 he probably slaughtered more cattle because of feed shortages; in 1765 he slaughtered a yoke of oxen although there was no shortage of either beef or hides that year.

84. Day Books, 1747–1800.

85. Laurel Thatcher Ulrich, *A Midwife's Tale: The Life of Martha Ballard, Based on Her Diary, 1785–1812* (New York: Alfred A. Knopf, 1990), p. 264.

86. In 1732, Stratham had 134 household heads and 117 horses; some households had more than one horse. In the 1742 tax inventory 23 households were listed; 9 had no horses, 11 had one horse, and 3 had two horses. Jay Mack Holbrook, *New Hampshire 1732 Census* (Oxford, Mass.: Holbrook Research Institute, 1981), pp. 13, 16; Stratham Town Records, NHSA.

87. *Journal*, p. 30.

88. Day Book, 1743.

89. Ibid., 1744.

90. Ibid., 1745.

91. Ibid., 1747. In his *History of Concord* (Concord, N.H.: Benning W. Sanborn, 1856), Bouton described "rode double—that is, the wife with her husband, seated on a pillion behind him" (p. 528).

92. Day Book, 1745.

93. Ibid., 1766.

94. Birket, *Some Cursory Remarks*, p. 13.

95. Day Book, 1747; Diary, June 26 and July 27, 1759; September 23, 1763.

96. Diary, August 25, 1761; September 10, 1764.

97. William Douglass, *A Summary, Historical and Political, of the First Planting, Progressive Improvements, and Present State of the British Settlements in North-America*, 2 vols. (Boston: Rogers and Fowle, 1749), 2:209.

98. "I had a peck of Herdsgrass Seed," Diary, 1794. See also Samuel Deane, *The New-England Farmer* (Worcester, Mass.: Isaiah Thomas, 1790), p. 285.

99. Diary, September 25, 1776.

100. Ibid., October 11, 1776, and 1776 summary.

101. Birket, *Some Cursory Remarks*, p. 10.

102. Colonials distinguished Indian corn or maize (a variety unknown in England at the time) from English corn, a term denoting four European cereals: wheat, oats, rye, and barley. Here I use corn to refer to the American variety, maize.

103. Day Book, 1754, 1768.

104. Joseph B. Walker, "Indian Corn and Its Culture: A Lecture . . . Before the N.H. State Agricultural Society, Delivered at Manchester, Dec., 1868," in *A Collection of Addresses and Papers Prepared for Various Occasions by Joseph B. Walker of Concord, N.H.*, 5 vols. (1852–1909), 1:128.

105. Day Book, 1763.

106. Ibid., 1763, 1768.

107. See *American Husbandry*, p. 81; Jared Eliot, *Essays upon Field Husbandry in New England* (Boston, 1760); Bidwell and Falconer, *History of Agriculture*, pp. 87, 123–24; Russell, *Deep Long Furrow*, pp. 183–84.

108. Joseph B. Walker, "Plowing, 1873," in *A Collection of Addresses and Papers Prepared for Various Occasions by Joseph B. Walker*, 1:248.

109. Bidwell and Falconer, *History of Agriculture*, pp. 123–24; Walker, "The Farm," p. 18.

110. Ebeling, *Fruited Plain*, p. 61.

111. Timothy Dwight, *Travels* (1821 ed.), 1:108, cited by Bidwell and Falconer, *History of Agriculture*, p. 90.

112. Joseph B. Walker, ed., "Diaries of the Rev. Timothy Walker," in *Collections of the New Hampshire Historical Society*, 9:159n.

113. Thomas C. Thompson estimated that Matthew Patten plowed one-half to two days, planted nearly one day, and reaped three to five days; those estimates include all Patten's crops. Thomas C. Thompson, "The Life Course and Labor of a Colonial Farmer," *Historical New Hampshire* 40 (fall/winter 1985): 149.

114. Day Book, 1750.

115. Walker, "Diaries," p. 166.

116. George Francis Dow, *Everyday Life in the Massachusetts Bay Colony* (New York: Benjamin Bloom, 1935), pp. 117–18; Alice Morse Earle also describes a husking in *Home Life in Colonial Days* (New York: Macmillan Co., 1898), p. 136.

117. Ulrich, *Midwife's Tale*, pp. 146, 147.

118. Nylander, *Snug Fireside*, pp. 207–8; Earle, *Home Life*, p. 139.

119. Diary, 1758, summary.

120. Russell, *Long Deep Furrow*, p. 367.

121. Diary, July 29–31, August 12–14, August 22, 1751.

122. *Journal*, p. 85.

123. Diary, 1752, 1758.

124. Ibid., 1743.

125. *Journal*, p. 92.

126. Compiled from year-end summaries in the *Journal* and the diaries.

127. Day Book, 1780–89.

128. *Journal*, p. 72.

129. *American Husbandry*, p. 37.

130. Ibid., pp. 34–35.

131. Bidwell and Falconer, *History of Agriculture*, p. 93.

132. *Journal*, p. 85. Timothy Walker's diary mentions Siberian wheat in 1780 ("Diaries," p. 185).

133. Diary, 1781.

134. Belknap, *Belknap's New Hampshire*, 3:102; see also Sweeney, "Gentlemen Farmers," p. 63.

135. *American Husbandry*, p. 58; Eliot, *Essays upon Field Husbandry*, 1:17.

136. Christopher Grasso, "The Experimental Philosophy of Farming: Jared Eliot and the Cultivation of Connecticut," *William and Mary Quarterly*, 3rd ser., 50 (July 1993): 507.

137. *American Husbandry*, p. 39.

138. Diary, 1777, 1779, 1781.

139. Russell, *Long Deep Furrow*, p. 239.

140. Belknap, *Belknap's New Hampshire*, 3:103.

141. Cited in Bidwell and Falconer, *History of Agriculture*, p. 99.

142. Diary, October 29, 1763; and 1763, summary. The price was the same in the interior. Timothy Walker noted, "Lot Colby paid me £24-10-00 in full for 4 barrels of cider." "Diaries," p. 146.

143. *American Husbandry*, p. 42.

144. Manuscript note in Samuel Lane's copy of *The New-England Farmer*, NHHS.

145. Diary, 1777.

146. Eliot, *Essays upon Field Husbandry*, 1:15.

147. George Cooke's work is no. 138 on Lane's list of books; Samuel Deane's is no. 200 and was purchased by Samuel on December 6, 1790.

148. *New Hampshire Gazette*, March 20, 1772.

149. For cooperation among Maine farm families during the nineteenth century, see Thomas C. Hubka, "Farm Family Mutuality: The Mid-Nineteenth-Century Maine Farm Neighborhood," in *The Farm* (see note 79), pp. 13–23.

150. For familial and community tensions, see Vickers, "Competency," pp. 20–28.

151. Sweeney, "Gentlemen Farmers," p. 65.

152. "Years of the Life," 1743, Lane Papers.

153. *American Husbandry*, p. 54.

154. In 1752 the value of work he hired was £21.12.0 Old Tenor; in 1760, £204.9.0; and in 1768, £66.12.0.

155. See Ulrich, *Midwife's Tale.*

156. *American Husbandry*, p. 53.

157. Robert A. Gross, *The Minutemen and Their World* (New York: Hill and Wang, 1976), pp. 83–84.

158. Ibid., p. 89; see also Vickers, "Competency," esp. p. 23.

159. Joshua Lane and Samuel Lane Jr., Obligations, June 3, 1774, Lane Papers.

160. Jabez Lane to Samuel Lane, December 1799, Lane Papers.

161. Joshua Lane and Samuel Lane Jr., Obligations, June 25, 1798, Lane Papers.

162. *New Hampshire Gazette*, December 29, 1769.

163. Day Book, 1769–72.

164. Diary, May 16 and 22, 1771.

165. Ibid., July 4, 1772; Day Book, 1769–72.

166. Account Book, p. 209.

167. Diary, October 27, December 4 and 9, 1783; Day Book, 1783.

168. Samuel later added a note at the bottom of Mary Crocket's 1762 portion that attests to his preoccupation with evenhandedness: "Marys Weding Gound was Chence Cost 60£ Since then I gave her a Stuff gound to make it as good as a Silk one." Lane Papers.

169. Rockingham County Deeds, 150:102, NHSA.

170. Toby L. Ditz, "Ownership and Obligation: Inheritance and Patriarchal Households in Connecticut, 1750–1820," *William and Mary Quarterly*, 3rd ser., 47 (April 1990): 247.

171. On October 10, 1771, Samuel tallied up the work done on Joshua's house: "this fall & Summer I did abundance of work on Joshua's House, to the Vallue of about 1000£ Cost with Stuff old Ten^{r}." *Journal*, p. 42.

172. Jackson Turner Main, "Standards of Living and the Life Cycle in Colonial Connecticut," *Journal of Economic History* 43 (March 1983): 159. See also Ulrich, *Midwife's Tale*, chap. 2.

173. Edmund J. Lane, "A Genealogy and Brief History of the Lane Family in New Hampshire," unpublished manuscript, 1839, p. 43.

174. Day Book, 1791.

175. Diary, Febuary 12, 1766.

176. Jacob Chapman and James H. Fitts, *William Lane of Boston, Mass., 1648, Including the Records of Edmund J. and James P. Lane* (Exeter, N.H.: News-letter Press, 1891), p. 32.

177. *Journal*, p. 48; Jabez produced 127 pairs of cloth shoes in 1782. Jabez Lane, Day Book, 1782, Lane Papers.

178. Diary, 1796.

179. *New Hampshire Gazette*, June 24, 1768.

180. Benjamin Johnson advertisement, *New Hampshire Gazette*, May 29, 1772.

181. *Journal*, pp. 52–53, 55; Jabez Lane, Tanyard Journal, Lane Papers.

182. Diary, May 3, 1784; April 10, 1787; September 22, 1789; Day Book, 1785; John Stockbridge Jr. Account, Lane Papers; *Journal*, p. 61.

183. Diary, 1774. He remarked of Rachel, "She was Born [at Cape Ann] June 29 1726 old Stile & her Birth Day comes on July 10 N Stile. my Wife is 7 years 9 M^o^ & 7 Days younger th[a]n I," *Journal*, p. 44. See also Doane B. Colcord, *Colcord Genealogy* (Coudersport, Pa.: Mahlon J. Colcord, 1908), p. 50.

184. Gideon Colcord's estate was valued at £8,430.1.8 Old Tenor. As a widow, Rachel's share in the estate was worth £4,452; married to Samuel it was worth only slightly less, £4,071.15.0. Rockingham County Probate, no. 4041 OS, NHSA.

185. Benjamin Colcord's indenture to his stepfather may have started prior to May 1778. Samuel's daybooks between 1772 and 1778 are missing; however, Ben was thirteen at the time and at the age for his apprenticeship to begin.

186. Day Book, 1787.

187. Rockingham County Probate, no. 4041 OS, NHSA.

188. *Journal*, p. 54.

189. See Philip J. Greven Jr., *Four Generations: Population, Land, and Family in Colonial Andover, Massachusetts* (Ithaca, N.Y.: Cornell University Press, 1970). Greven discusses this in chap. 8.

190. Jabez Lane, Day Book, 1783, Lane Papers.

191. Rockingham County Probate, no. 4041 OS, NHSA.

192. Day Book, 1783.

193. See Diary June 17, 1780; November 18, 1793; Day Book, 1787.

194. Jabez Lane to Samuel Lane, December 1799, Lane Papers.

195. By 1799, Eunice and Jabez had five children; the oldest was fifteen and the youngest, five.

196. Jabez Lane to Samuel Lane, December 1799, Lane Papers.

197. Ibid.

198. *Journal*, p. 54. It was not. His last trip there was in 1791.

199. Jabez Lane to Samuel Lane, December 1799, Lane Papers.

200. Jabez Lane, Journal, January 23, 1800, Lane Papers.

201. Rockingham County Deeds, 152:459, NHSA.

202. Jabez Lane, Obligation, January 14, 1800, Lane Papers.

203. "Years of the Life," Lane Papers; *Journal*, p. 61.

204. *Journal*, p. 61.

205. Edmund J. Lane, Recollections of his Grandfather, October 28, 1883, Lane Papers.

206. Jabez Lane papers, Lane Papers.

207. Jabez Lane, Day Book, Lane Papers.

208. Account Book, p. 236.

209. Jabez Lane, Journal, December 25, 1806, Lane Papers.

210. Ibid., January 22, March 24 and 25, April 2 and 6, 1807.

211. Rockingham County Probate, no. 8256 OS, NHSA.

Afterword

1. Samuel Lane, Thanksgiving List, November 21, 1793, Lane Papers.

Index

Page numbers in *italics* indicate an *image* or accompanying caption; page numbers in **bold** indicate a reproduction of a printed or manuscript **document**.